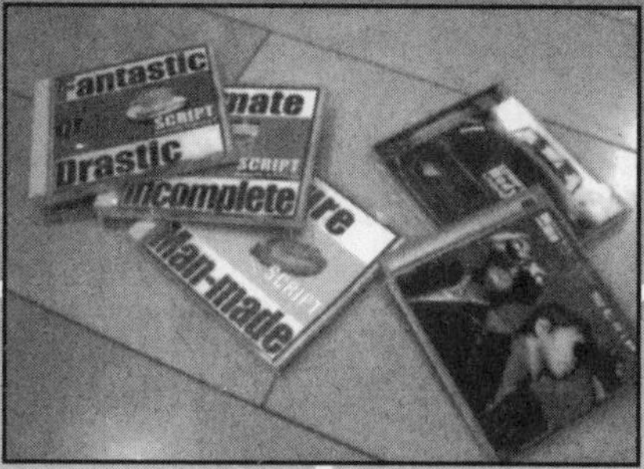
Fantastic
SCRIPT
Drastic
Man-made

These are the CDs I listen to when I'm driving or working. SCRIPT will be singing the theme song for *The Prince of Tennis* movie!! I'm so happy I'm at a loss for words. I'd like to thank the members of SCRIPT for accepting the task, and the movie production staff.

- Takeshi Konomi, 2005

About Takeshi Konomi

Takeshi Konomi exploded onto the manga scene with the incredible **THE PRINCE OF TENNIS**. His refined art style and sleek character designs proved popular with **Weekly Shonen Jump** readers, and **THE PRINCE OF TENNIS** became the number one sports manga in Japan almost overnight. Its cast of fascinating male tennis players attracted legions of female readers even though it was originally intended to be a boys' comic. The manga continues to be a success in Japan and has inspired a hit anime series, as well as several video games and mountains of merchandise.

THE PRINCE OF TENNIS
VOL. 27
The SHONEN JUMP Manga Edition

STORY AND ART BY
TAKESHI KONOMI

Translation/Joe Yamazaki
Consultant/Michelle Pangilinan
Touch-up Art & Lettering/Vanessa Satone
Design/Sam Elzway
Editor/Leyla Aker

Editor in Chief, Books/Alvin Lu
Editor in Chief, Magazines/Marc Weidenbaum
VP of Publishing Licensing/Rika Inouye
VP of Sales/Gonzalo Ferreyra
Sr. VP of Marketing/Liza Coppola
Publisher/Hyoe Narita

Printed in the U.S.A.

Published by VIZ Media, LLC
P.O. Box 77010
San Francisco, CA 94107

SHONEN JUMP Manga Edition
10 9 8 7 6 5 4 3 2 1
First printing, September 2008

PARENTAL ADVISORY
THE PRINCE OF TENNIS
is rated A and is suitable
for readers of all ages.
ratings.viz.com

THE WORLD'S
MOST POPULAR MANGA

SHONEN JUMP Manga

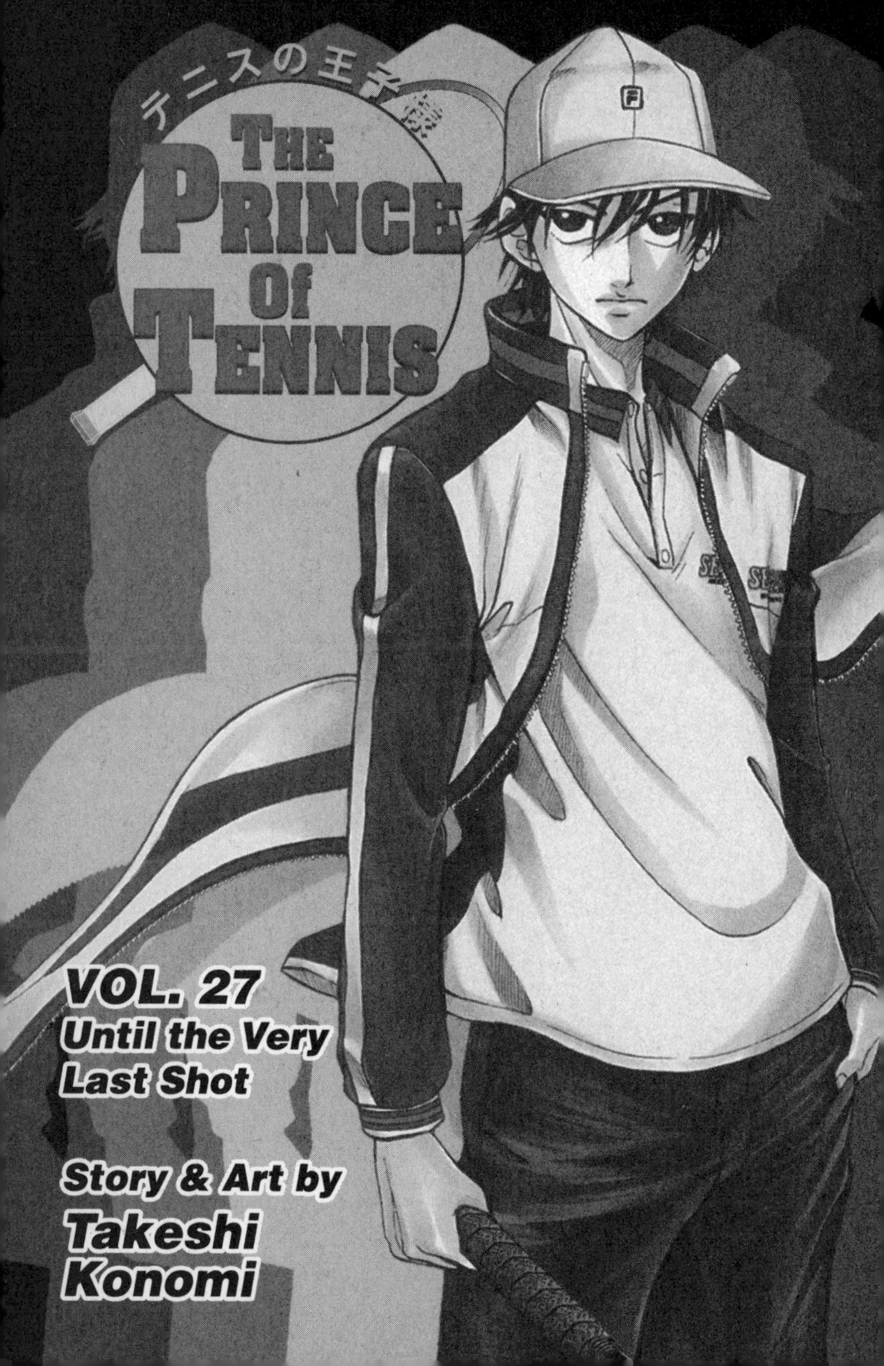
テニスの王子様

The Prince of Tennis

VOL. 27
Until the Very Last Shot

Story & Art by
Takeshi Konomi

ENNIS CLUB

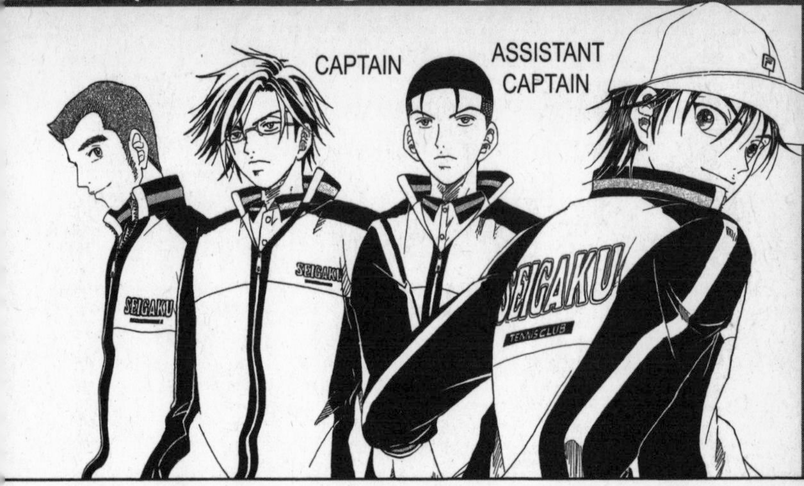
CAPTAIN
ASSISTANT CAPTAIN

● TAKASHI KAWAMURA ● KUNIMITSU TEZUKA ● SHUICHIRO OISHI ● RYOMA ECHIZEN ●

STORY &

Seishun Academy student Ryoma Echizen is a tennis prodigy, with wins in four consecutive U.S. Junior Tennis Tournaments under his belt. He became a starter as a 7th grader and led his team to the District Preliminaries! Despite a few mishaps, Seishun won the District Prelims and the City Tournament, and even earned a ticket to the Kanto Tournament. The team comes away victorious from its first-round matches against Hyotei, but Kunimitsu injures his shoulder and goes to Kyushu for treatment. Despite losing captain Kunimitsu and assistant captain Shuichiro to injury, Seishun defeats Midoriyama and Rokkaku, not only reaching the finals of the tournament but also earning a slot at the Nationals!

Their Kanto Tournament finals opponent is the number-one ranked champion, Rikkai. Seishun loses both doubles matches, but Sadaharu and Shusuke both win their singles matches. With Seishun and Rikkai tied at two games each, the championship match between Ryoma and Genichiro begins! Ryoma holds his own but is struggling against Genichiro's "Furin Kazan" shot...

HARACTERS

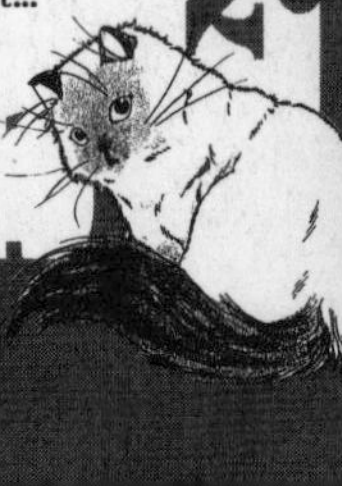

SEIGAKU T

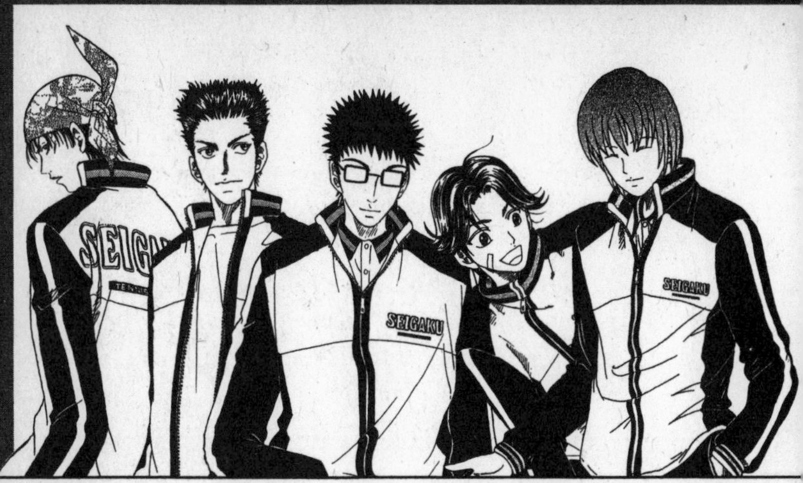

● KAORU KAIDO ● TAKESHI MOMOSHIRO ● SADAHARU INUI ● EIJI KIKUMARU ● SHUSUKE FUJI ●

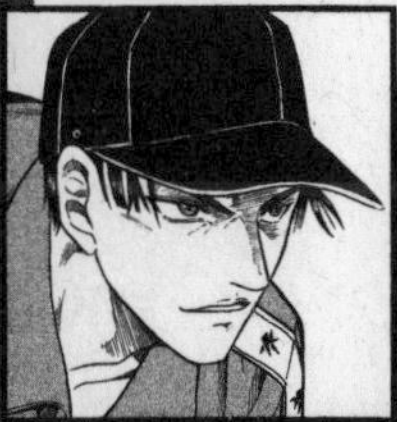

RIKKAI

GENICHIRO SANADA

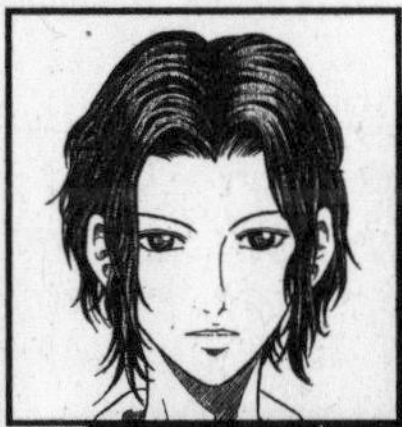

RIKKAI

SEIICHI YUKIMURA

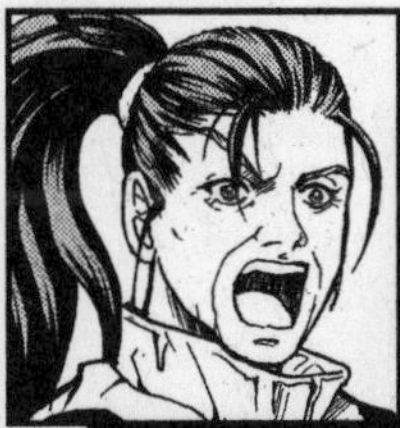

SEISHUN ACADEMY TENNIS COACH

SUMIRE RYUZAKI

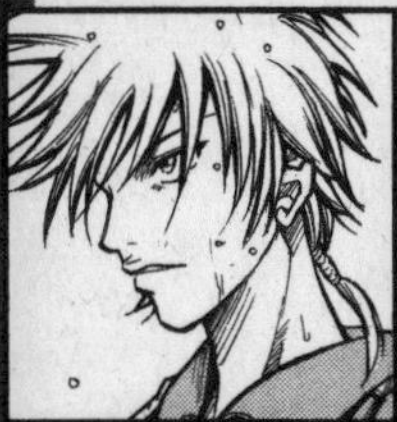

RIKKAI

MASAHARU NIO

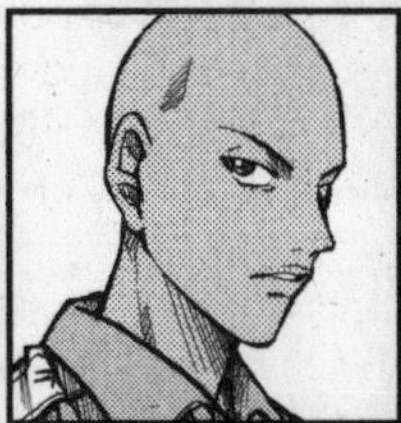

RIKKAI

JACKAL KUWAHARA

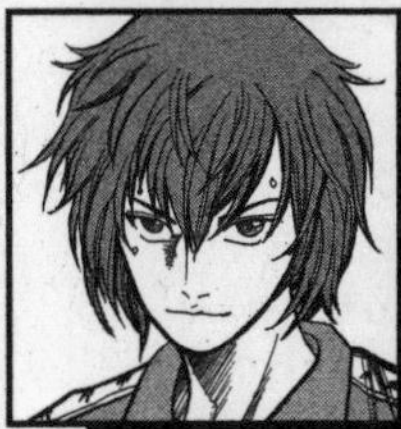

RIKKAI

BUNTA MARUI

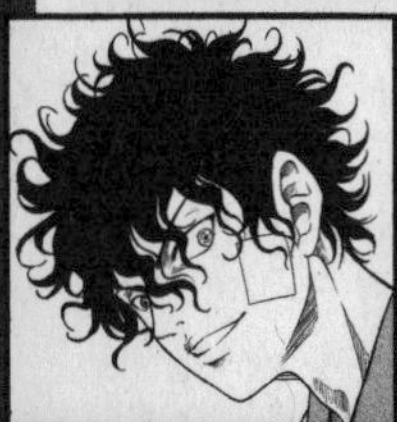

RIKKAI

AKAYA KIRIHARA

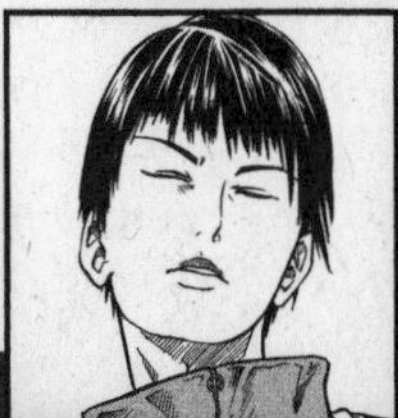

RIKKAI

RENJI YANAGI

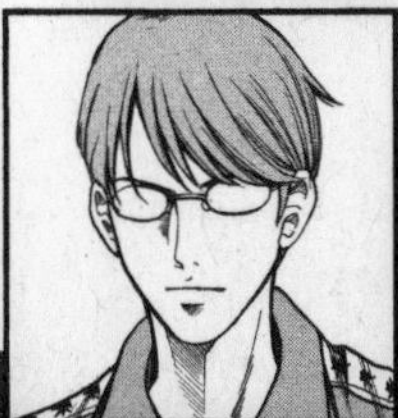

RIKKAI

HIROSHI YAGYU

CONTENTS Vol. 27
Until the Very Last Shot

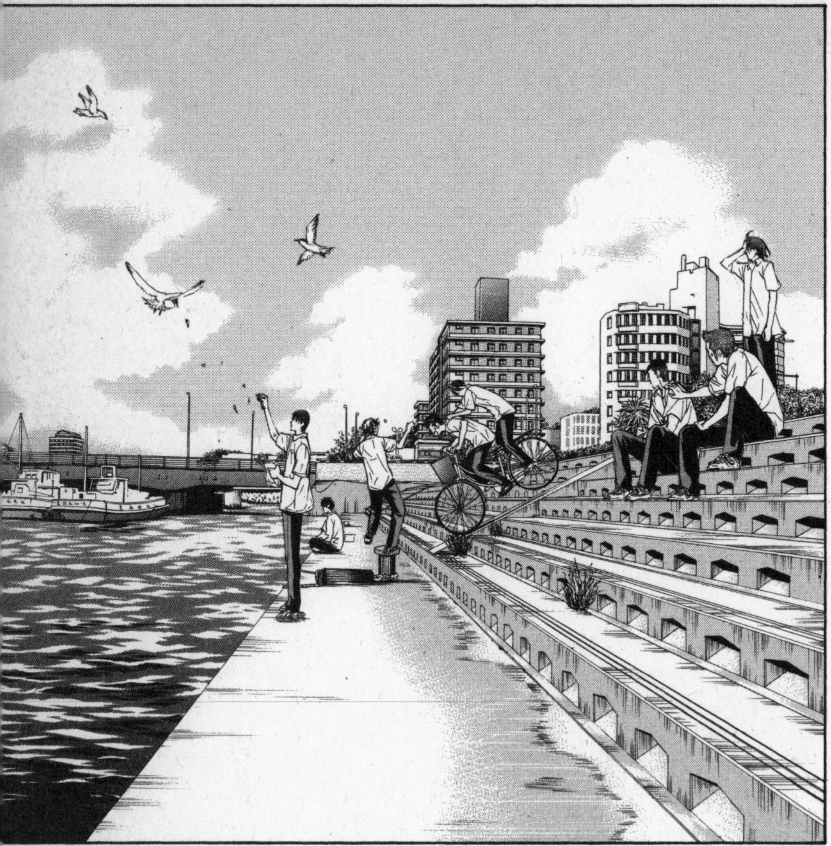

GENIUS 229: UNTIL THE VERY LAST SHOT

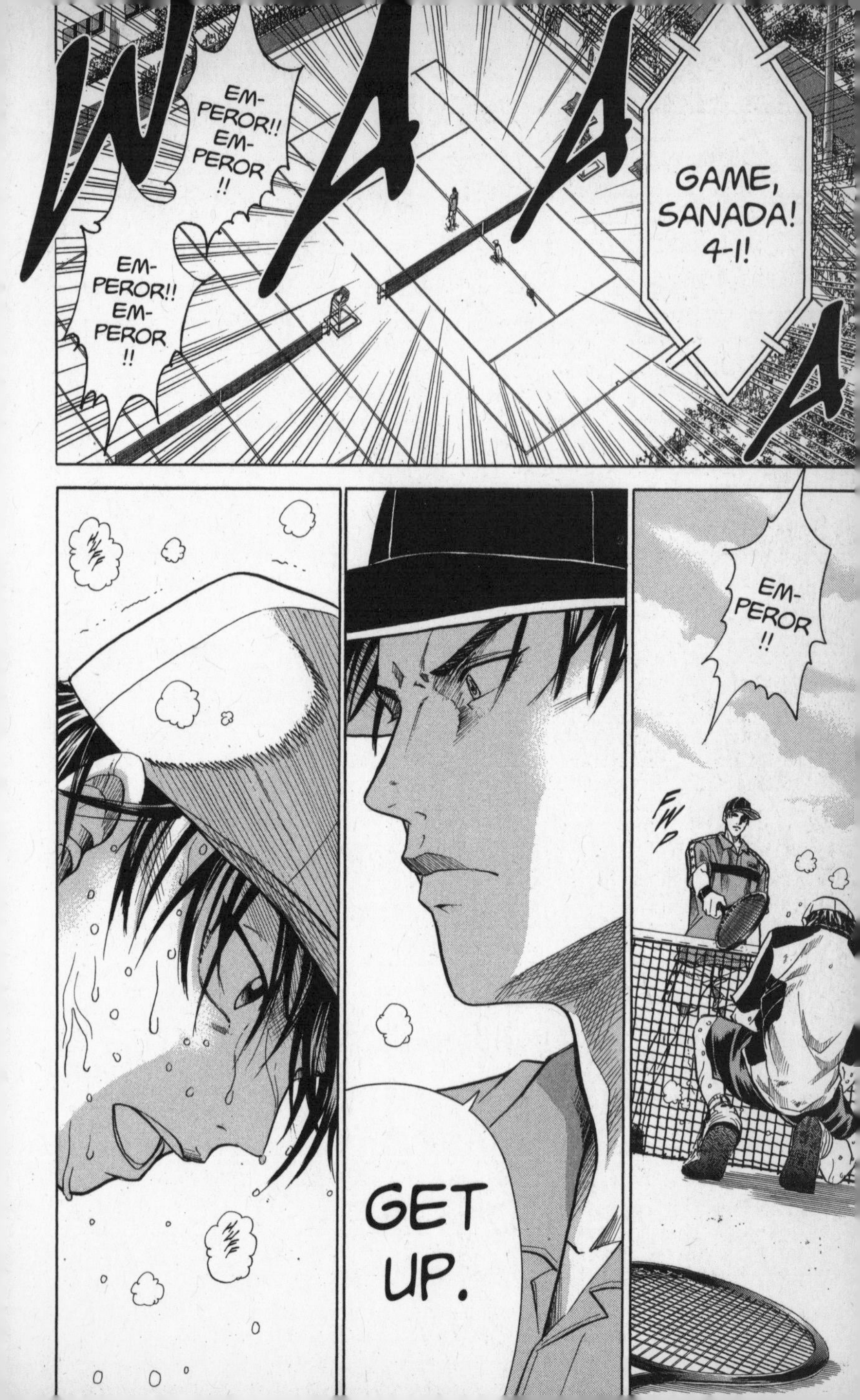
GAME, SANADA! 4-1!
EMPEROR!! EMPEROR!!
EMPEROR!! EMPEROR!!
WAAAA
EMPEROR!!
FWP
GET UP.

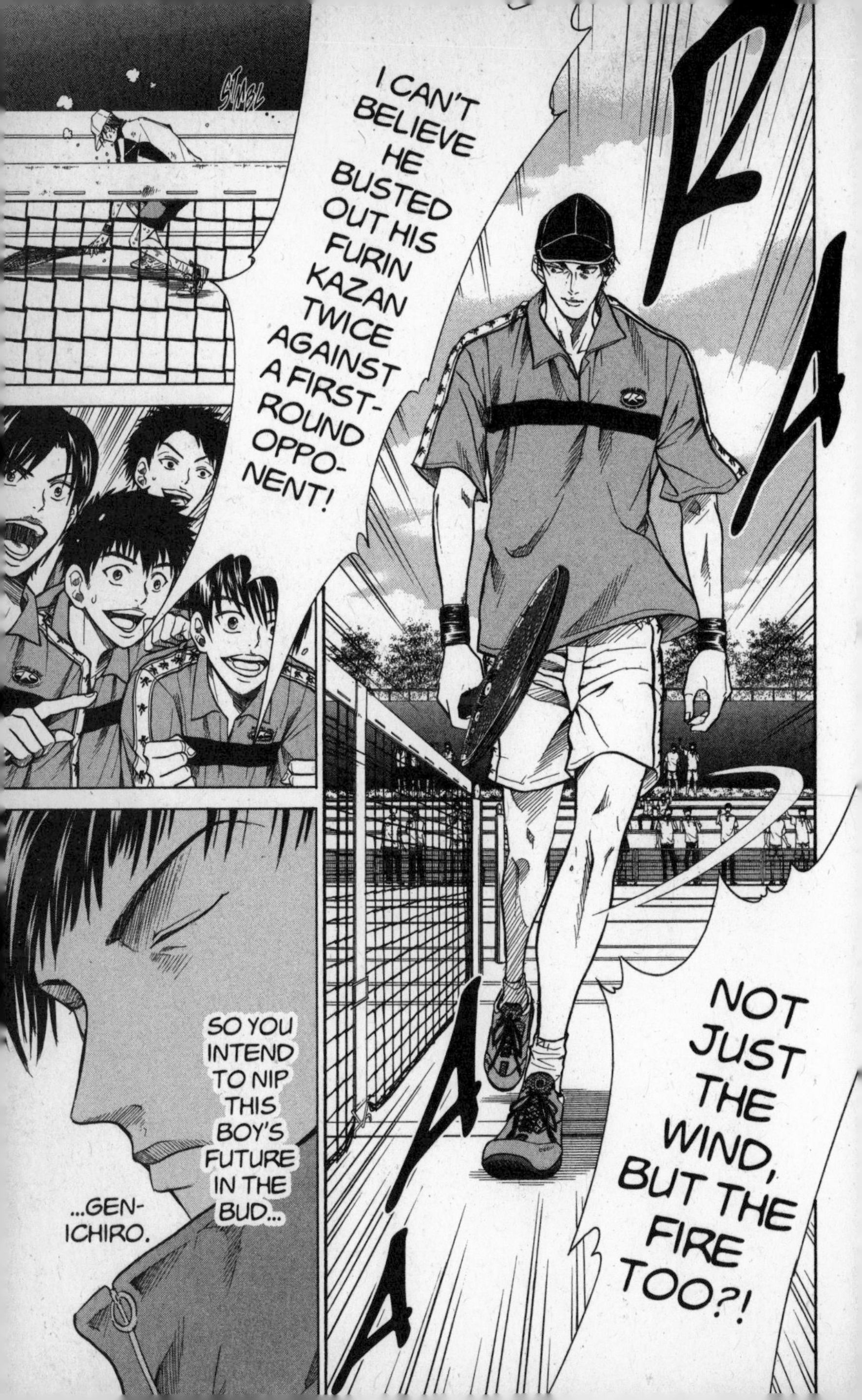
I CAN'T BELIEVE HE BUSTED OUT HIS FURIN KAZAN TWICE AGAINST A FIRST-ROUND OPPONENT!
NOT JUST THE WIND, BUT THE FIRE TOO?!
STMBL
SO YOU INTEND TO NIP THIS BOY'S FUTURE IN THE BUD...
...GEN-ICHIRO.

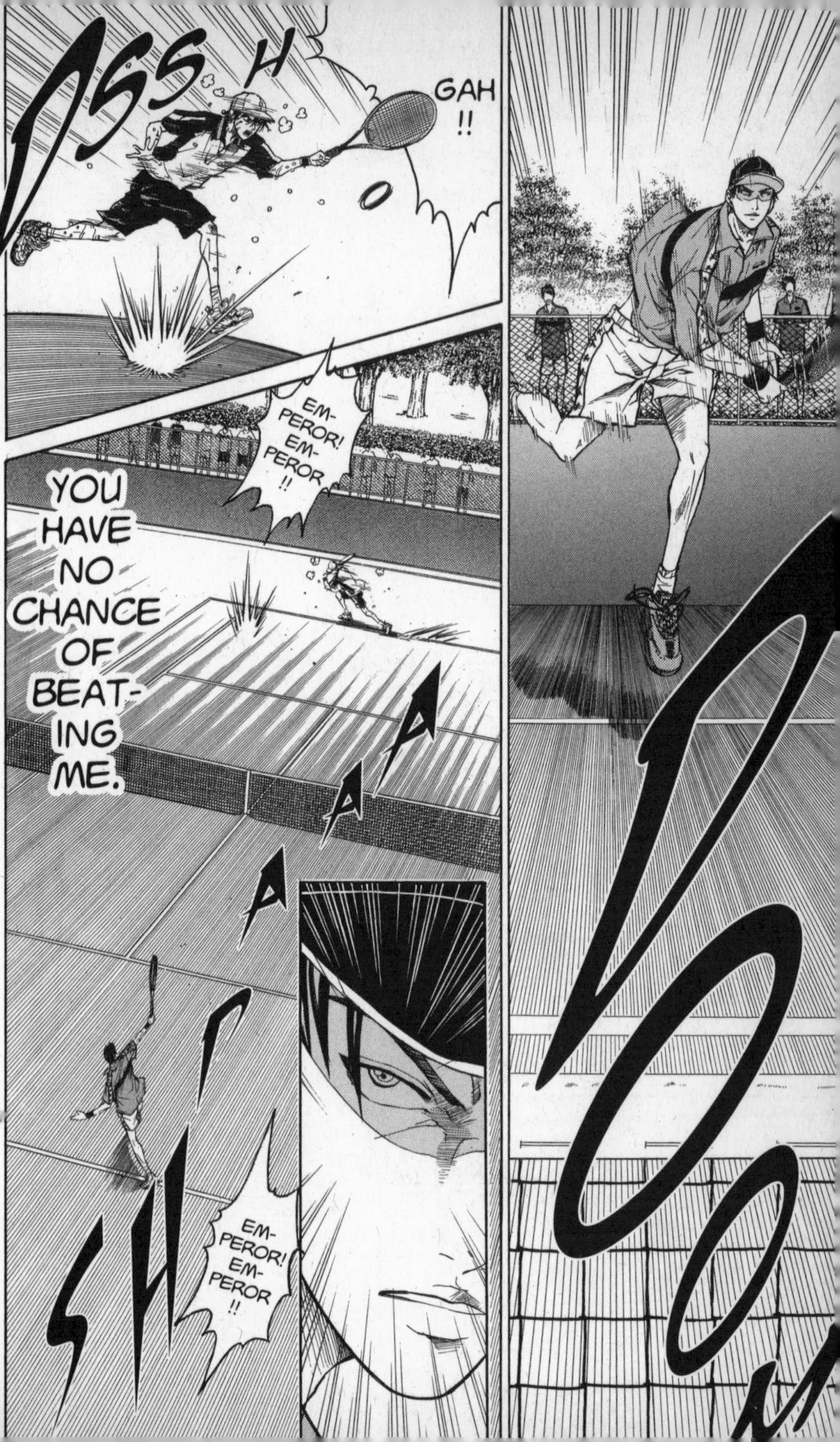
DSSH
GAH !!
EM-PEROR! EM-PEROR !!
YOU HAVE NO CHANCE OF BEATING ME.
EM-PEROR! EM-PEROR !!

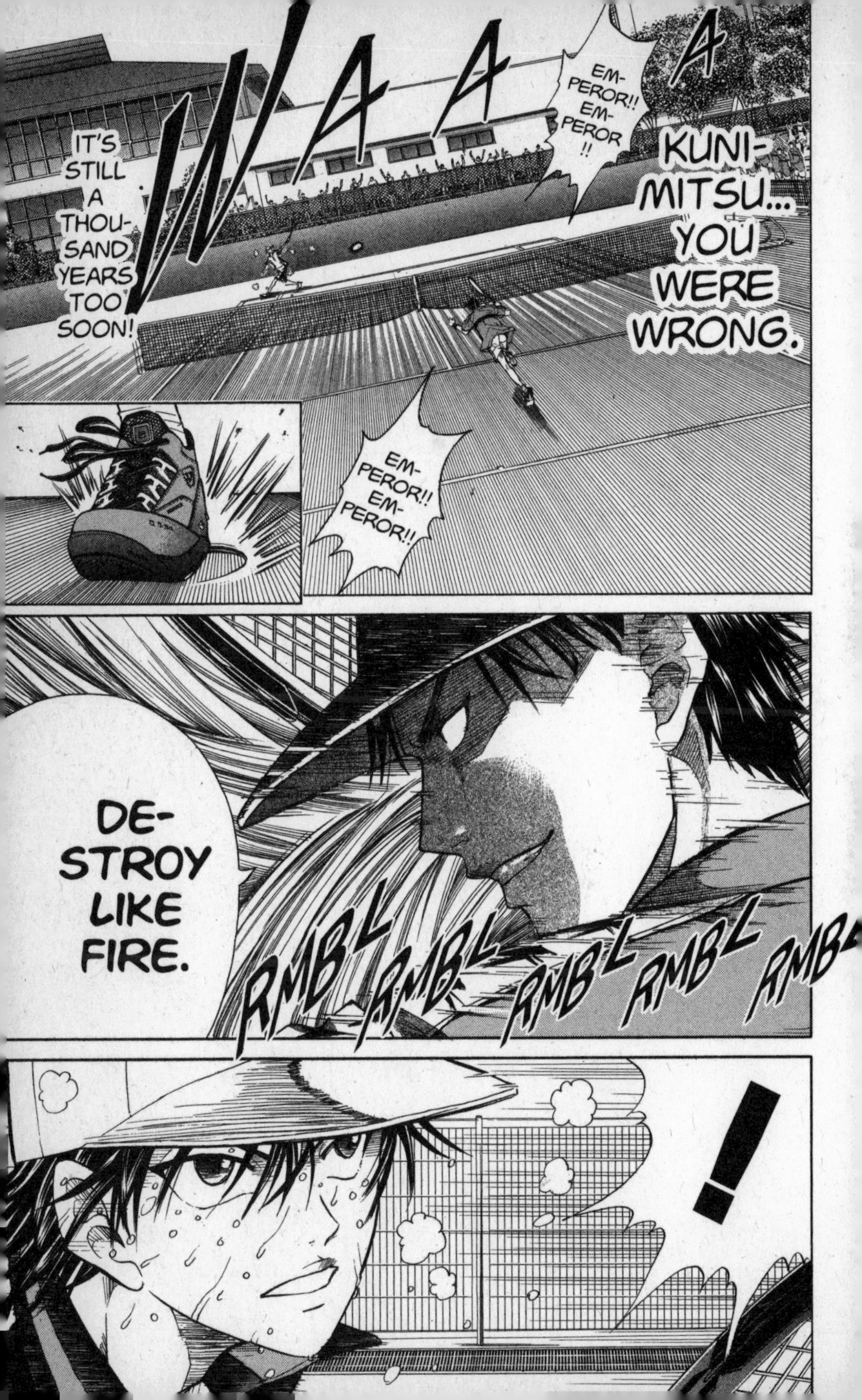

WAAAA
EM-PEROR!! EM-PEROR!!
KUNI-MITSU... YOU WERE WRONG.
IT'S STILL A THOU-SAND YEARS TOO SOON!
EM-PEROR!! EM-PEROR!!
DE-STROY LIKE FIRE.
RMBL RMBL RMBL RMBL RMBL
!

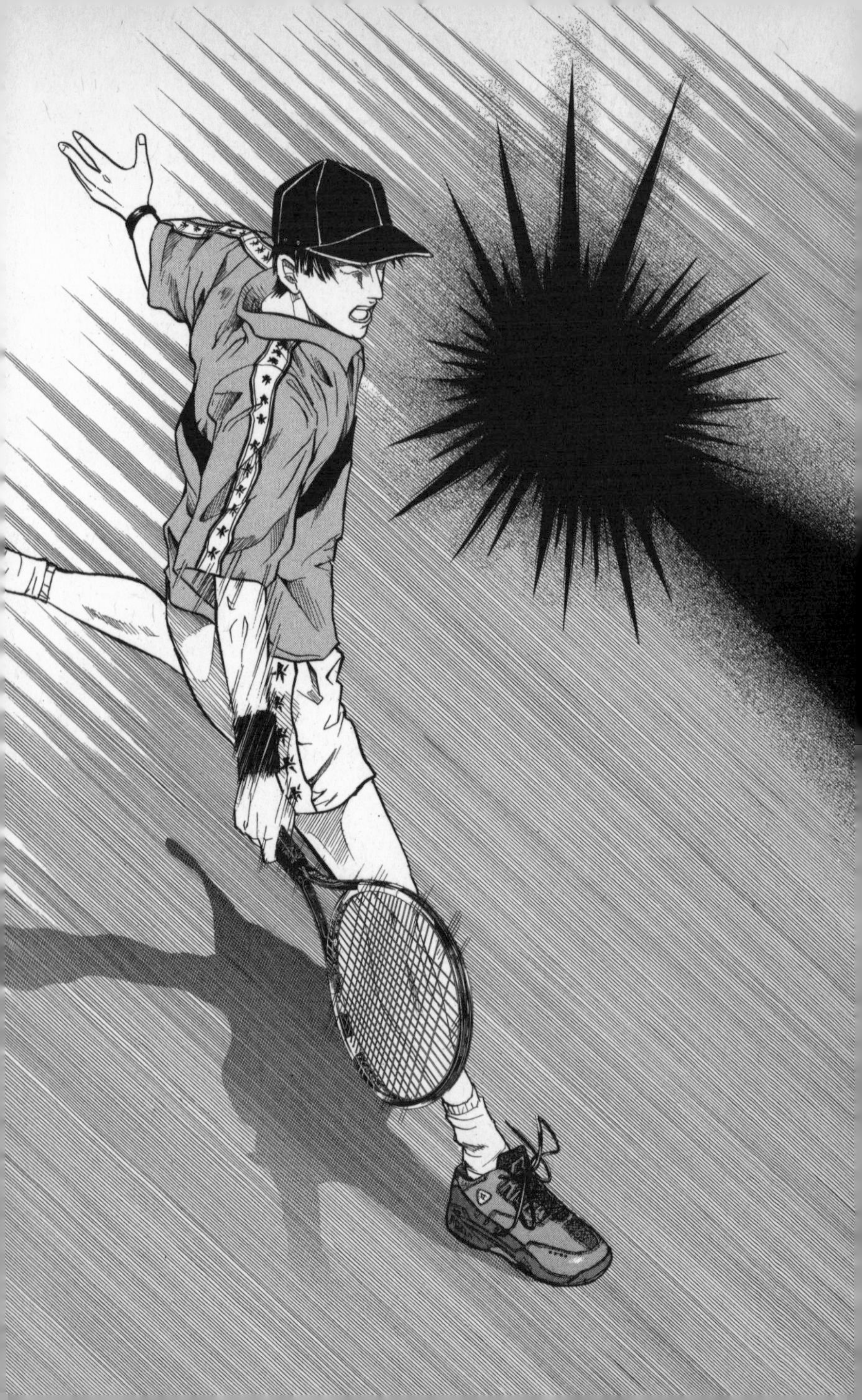

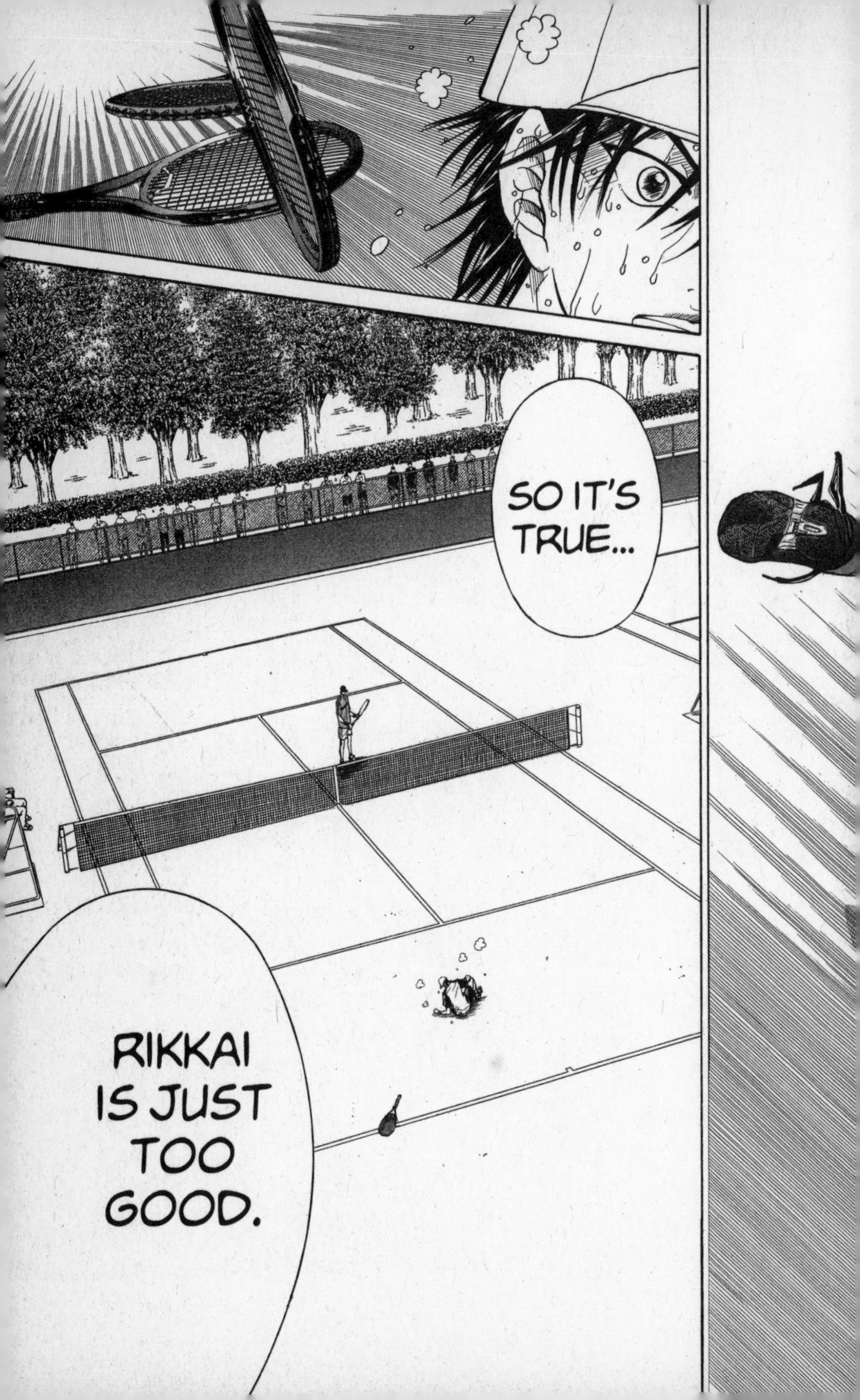
SO IT'S TRUE...
RIKKAI IS JUST TOO GOOD.

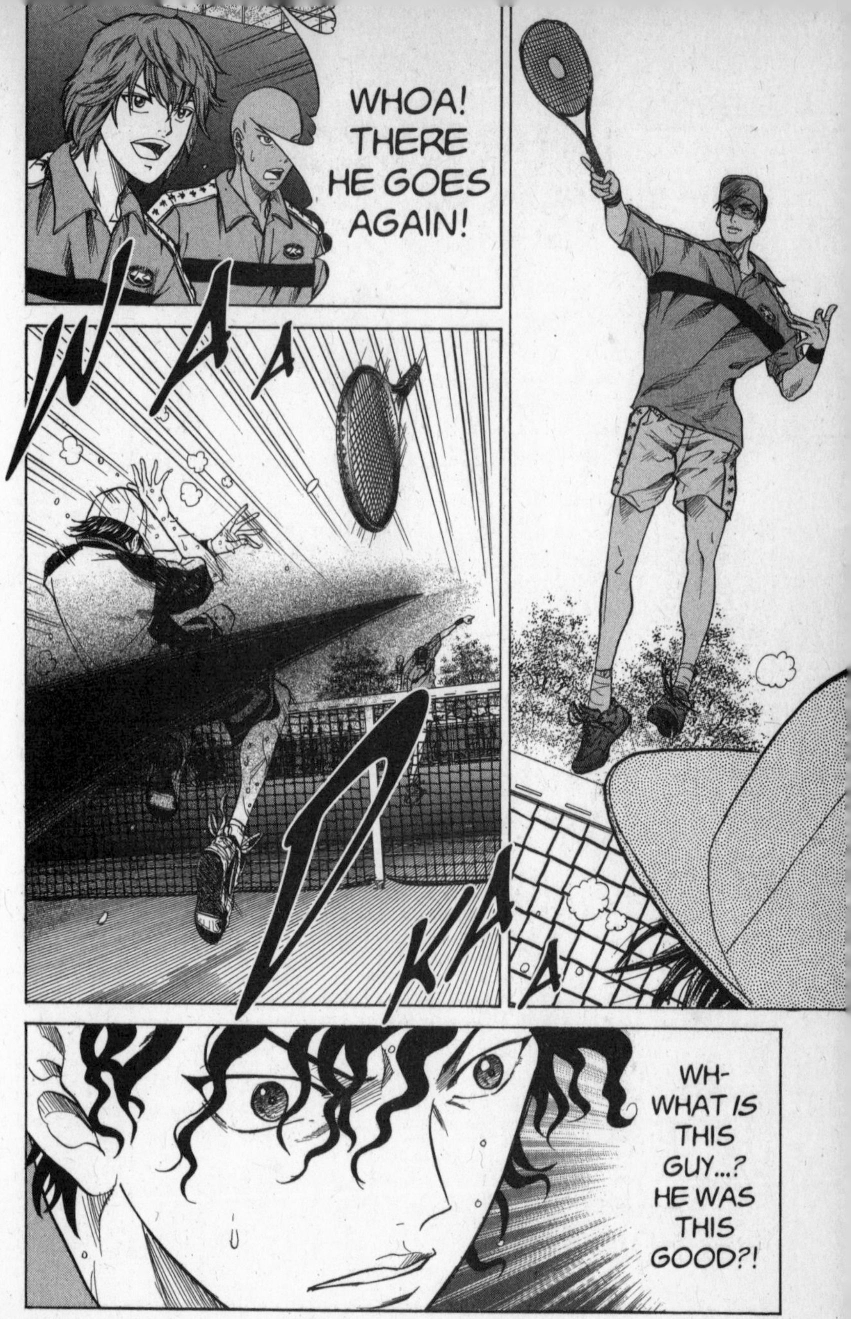
WHOA! THERE HE GOES AGAIN!
WAA
DKAA
WH- WHAT IS THIS GUY...? HE WAS THIS GOOD?!

READ THIS WAY

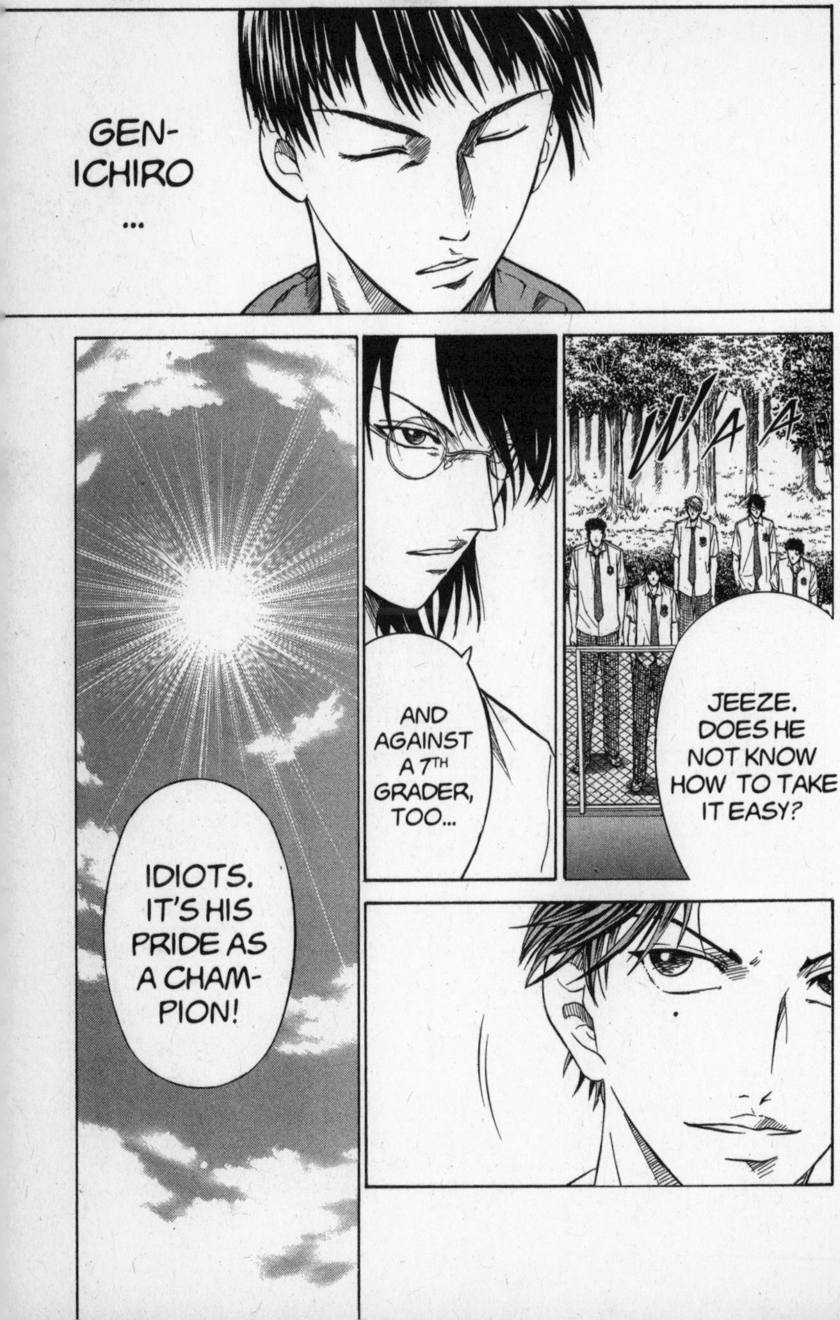
GEN-
ICHIRO
...
WAA
JEEZE. DOES HE NOT KNOW HOW TO TAKE IT EASY?
AND AGAINST A 7TH GRADER, TOO...
IDIOTS. IT'S HIS PRIDE AS A CHAM-PION!

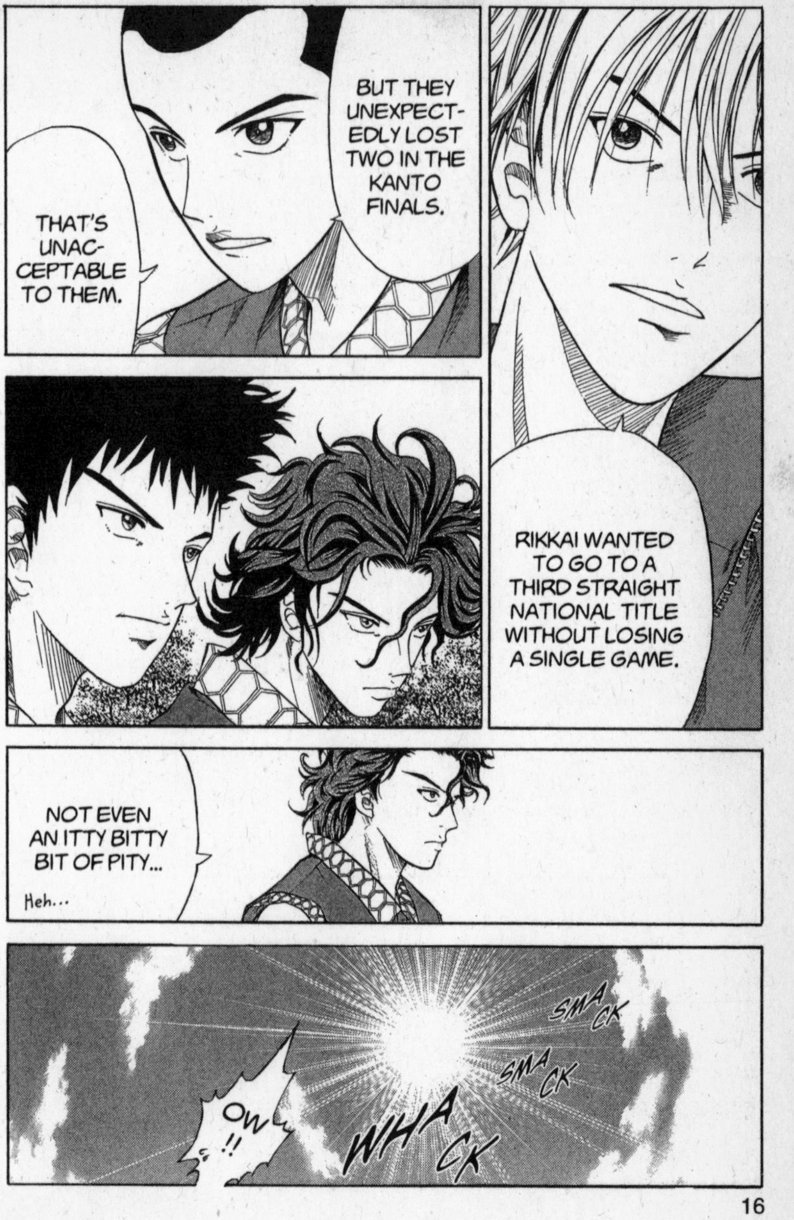
RIKKAI WANTED TO GO TO A THIRD STRAIGHT NATIONAL TITLE WITHOUT LOSING A SINGLE GAME.
BUT THEY UNEXPECT-EDLY LOST TWO IN THE KANTO FINALS.
THAT'S UNAC-CEPTABLE TO THEM.
NOT EVEN AN ITTY BITTY BIT OF PITY...
Heh...
SMACK
SMACK
WHACK
OW!!

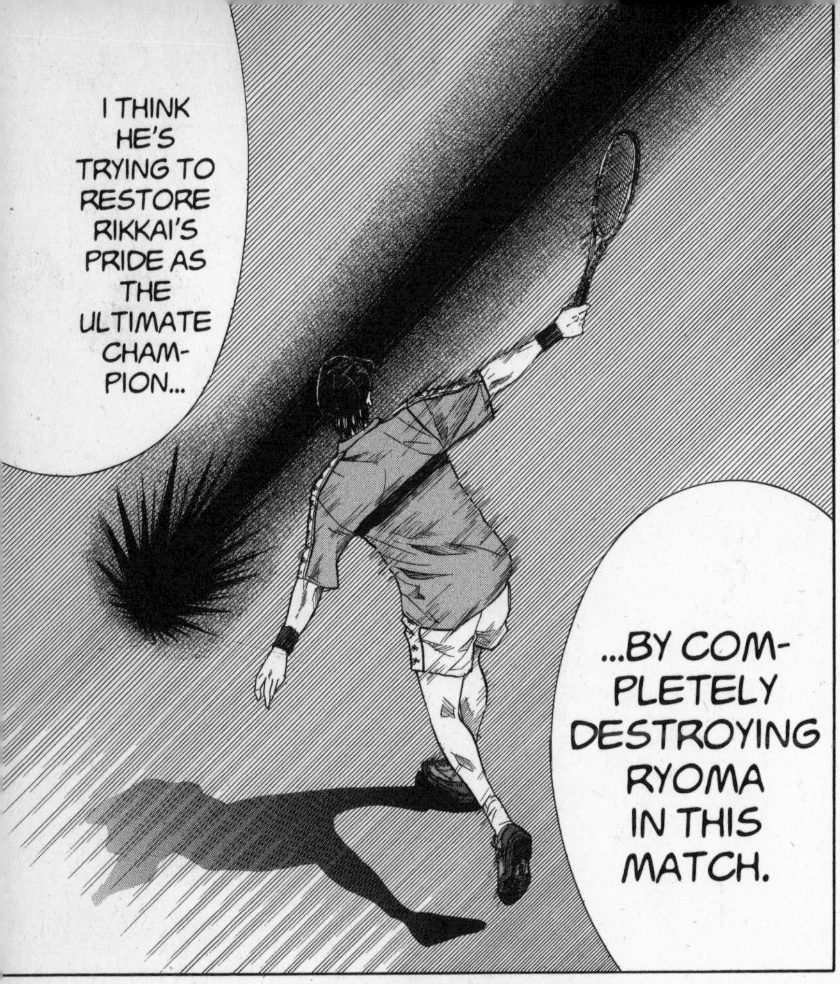
I THINK HE'S TRYING TO RESTORE RIKKAI'S PRIDE AS THE ULTIMATE CHAMPION...
...BY COMPLETELY DESTROYING RYOMA IN THIS MATCH.

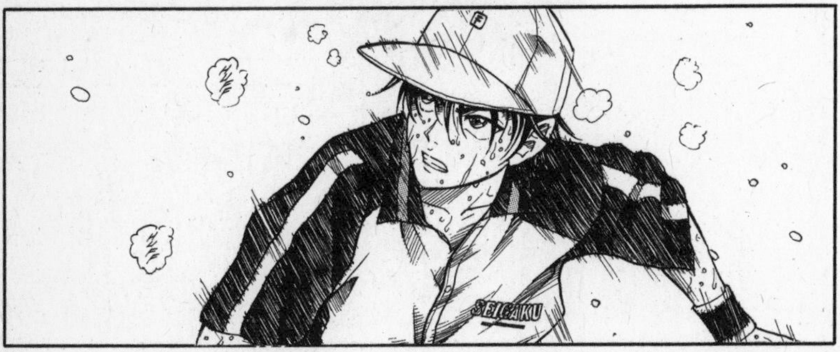
SEIGAKU

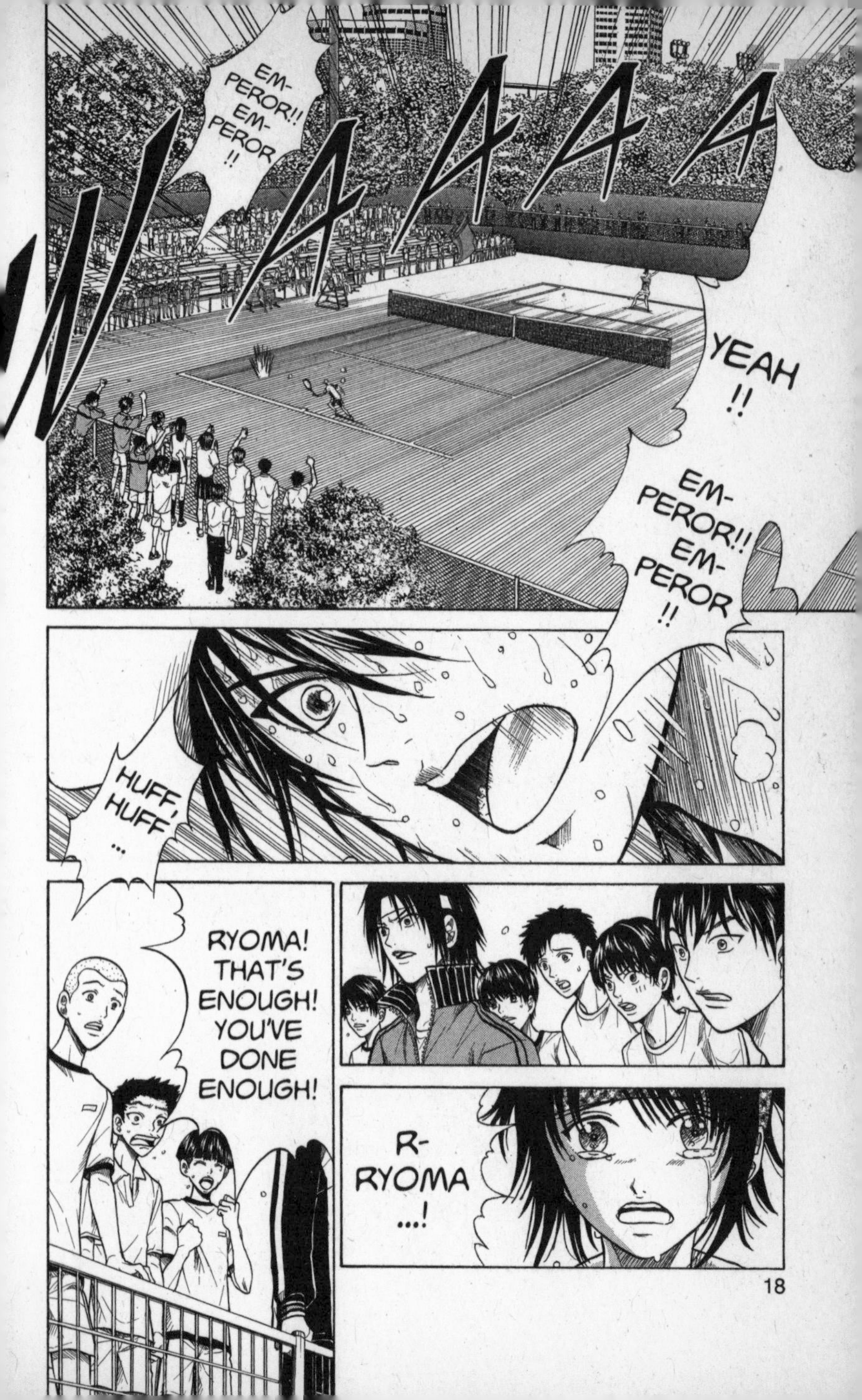
W A A A A A
EM-PEROR!! EM-PEROR!!
YEAH!!
EM-PEROR!! EM-PEROR!!
HUFF, HUFF...
R-RYOMA...!
RYOMA! THAT'S ENOUGH! YOU'VE DONE ENOUGH!

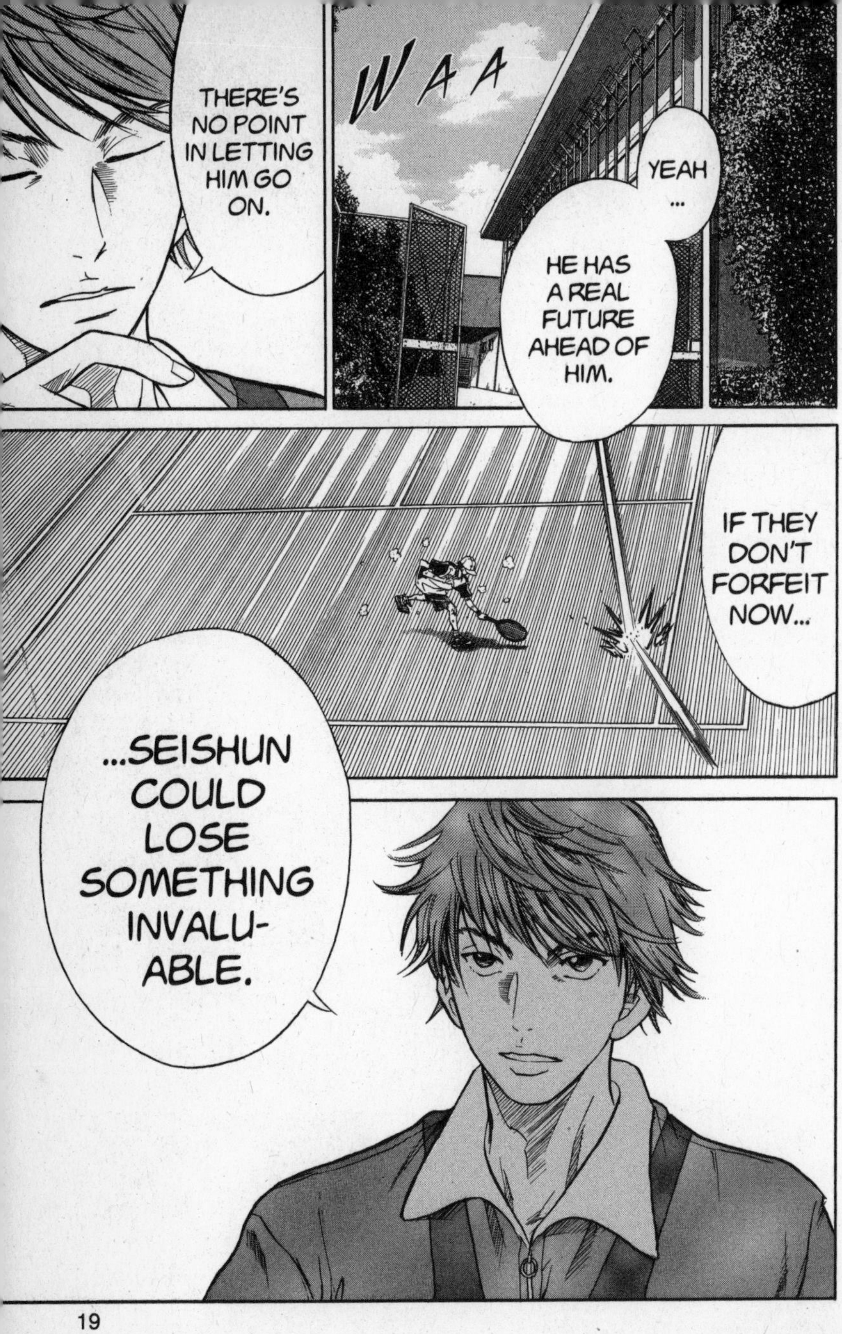
WAA
YEAH ...
HE HAS A REAL FUTURE AHEAD OF HIM.
THERE'S NO POINT IN LETTING HIM GO ON.
IF THEY DON'T FORFEIT NOW...
...SEISHUN COULD LOSE SOMETHING INVALU-ABLE.

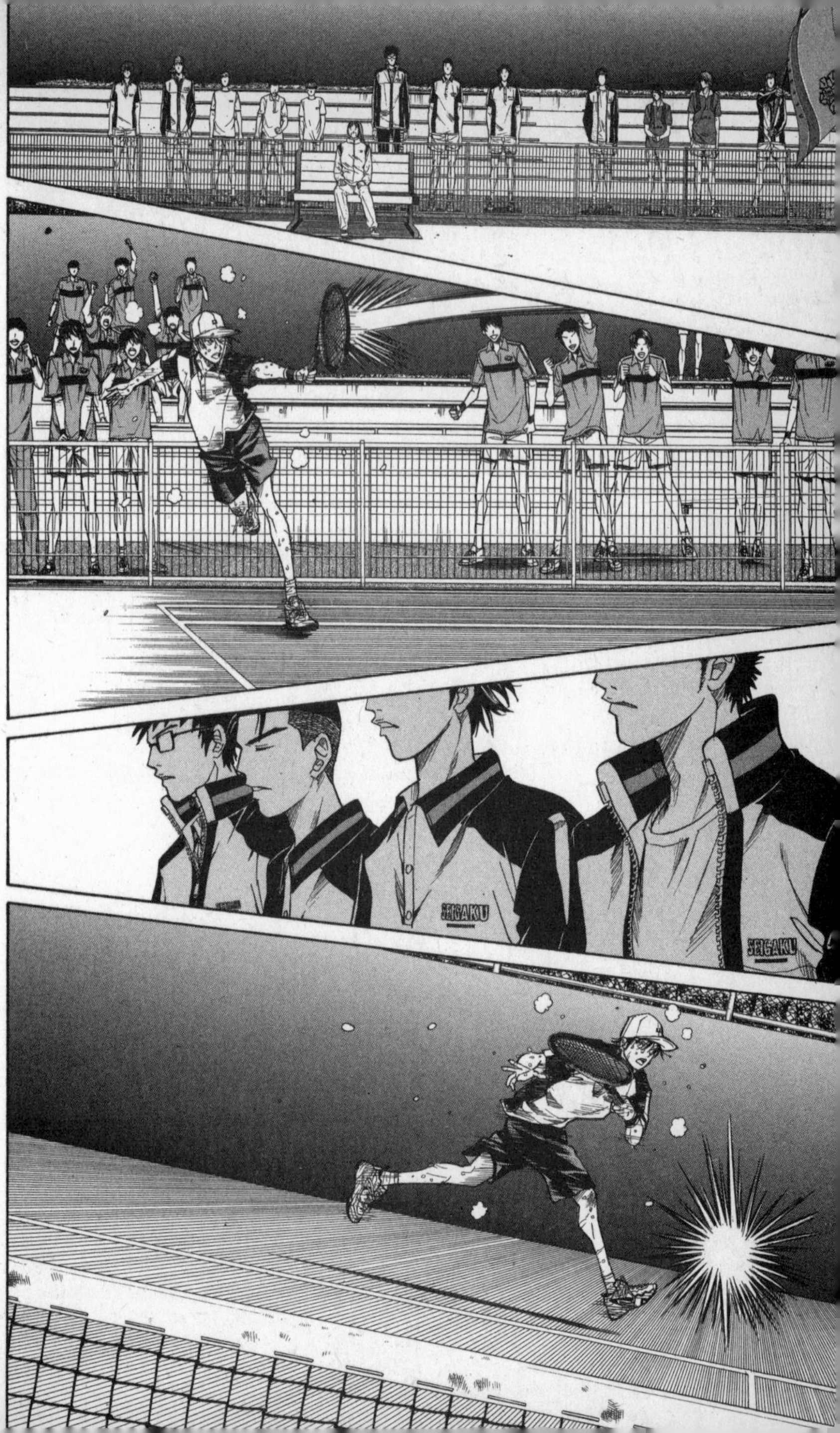
SEIGAKU
SEIGAKU

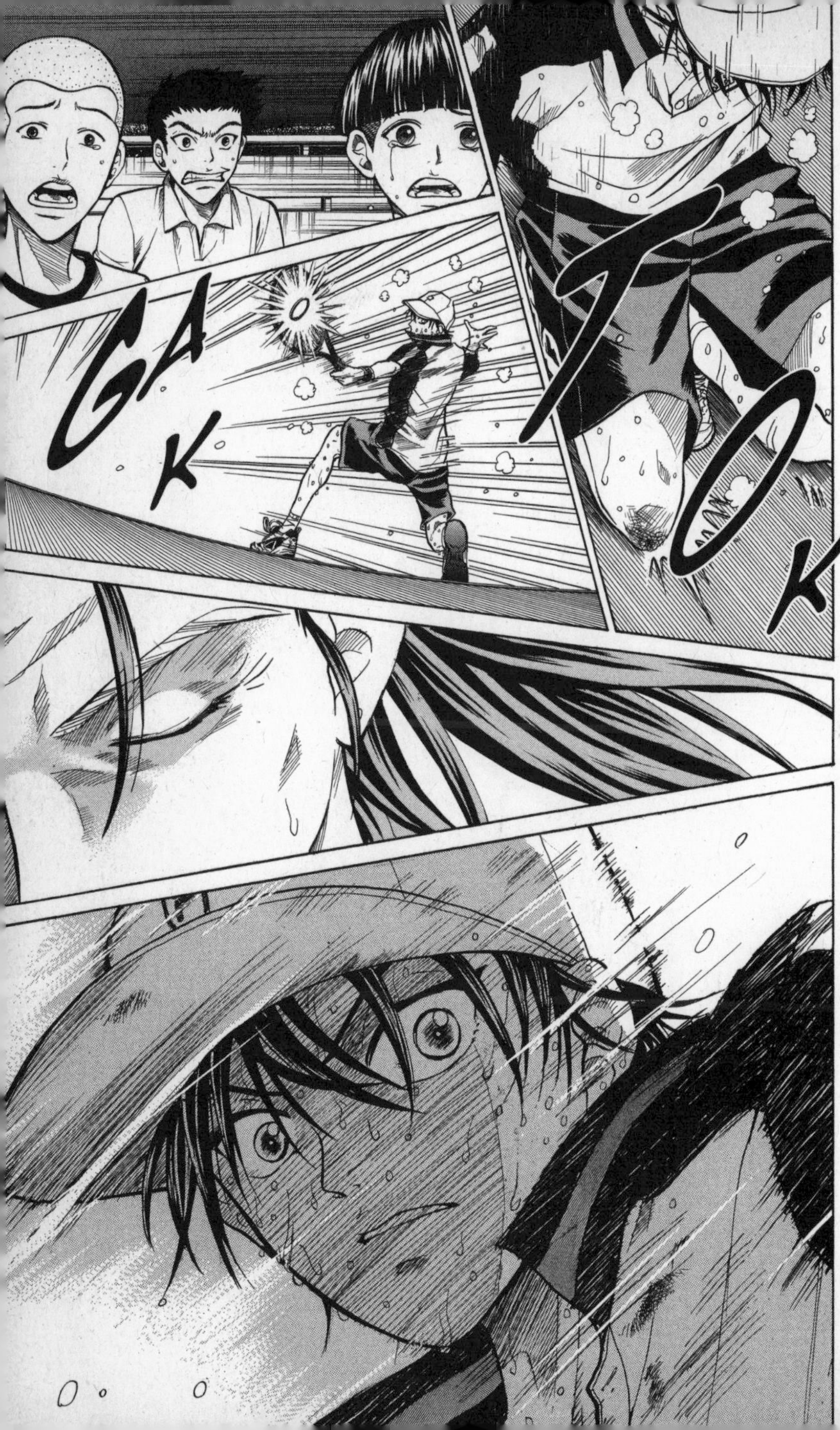
TOK
GAK

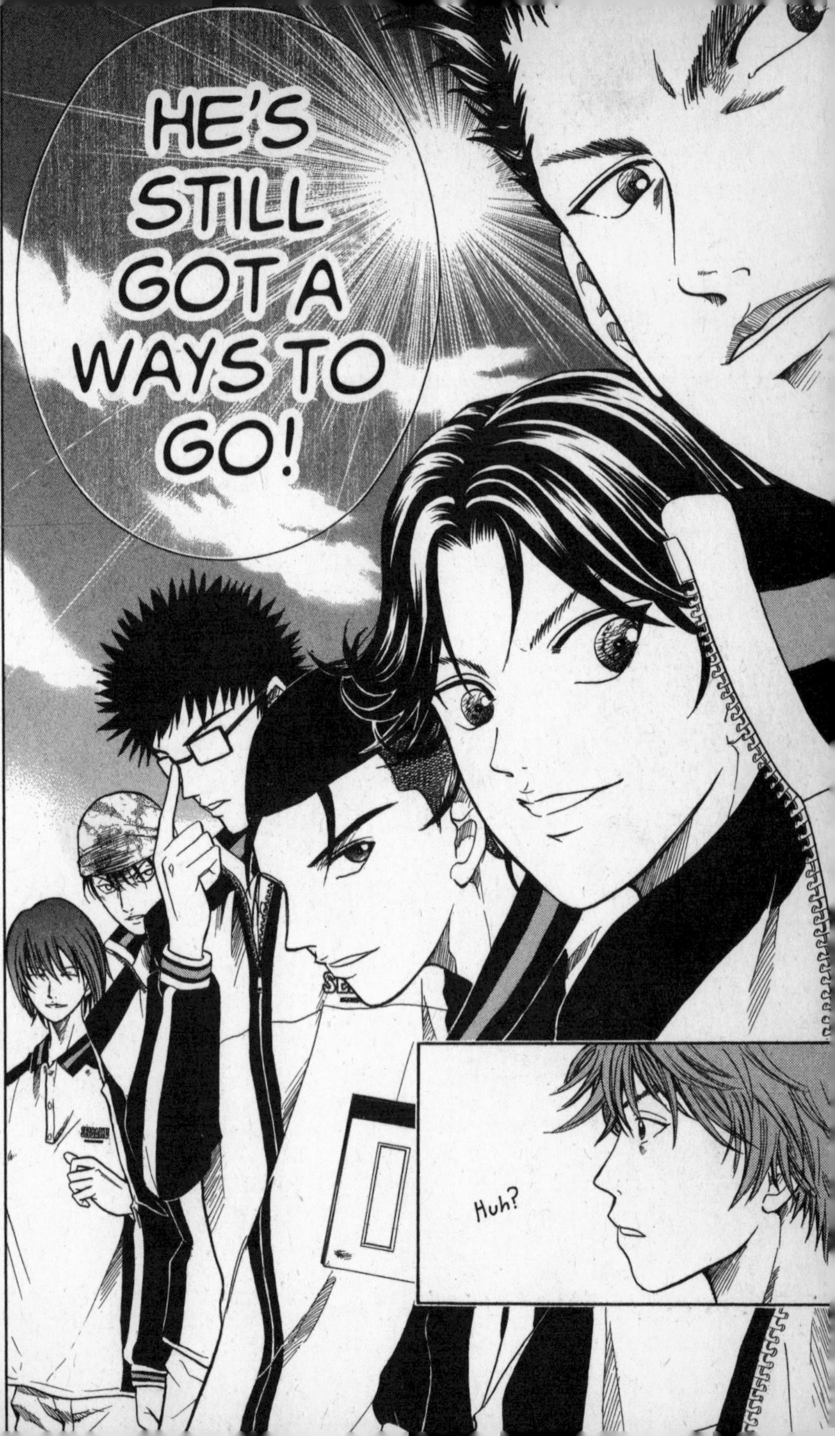
HE'S STILL GOT A WAYS TO GO!
Huh?

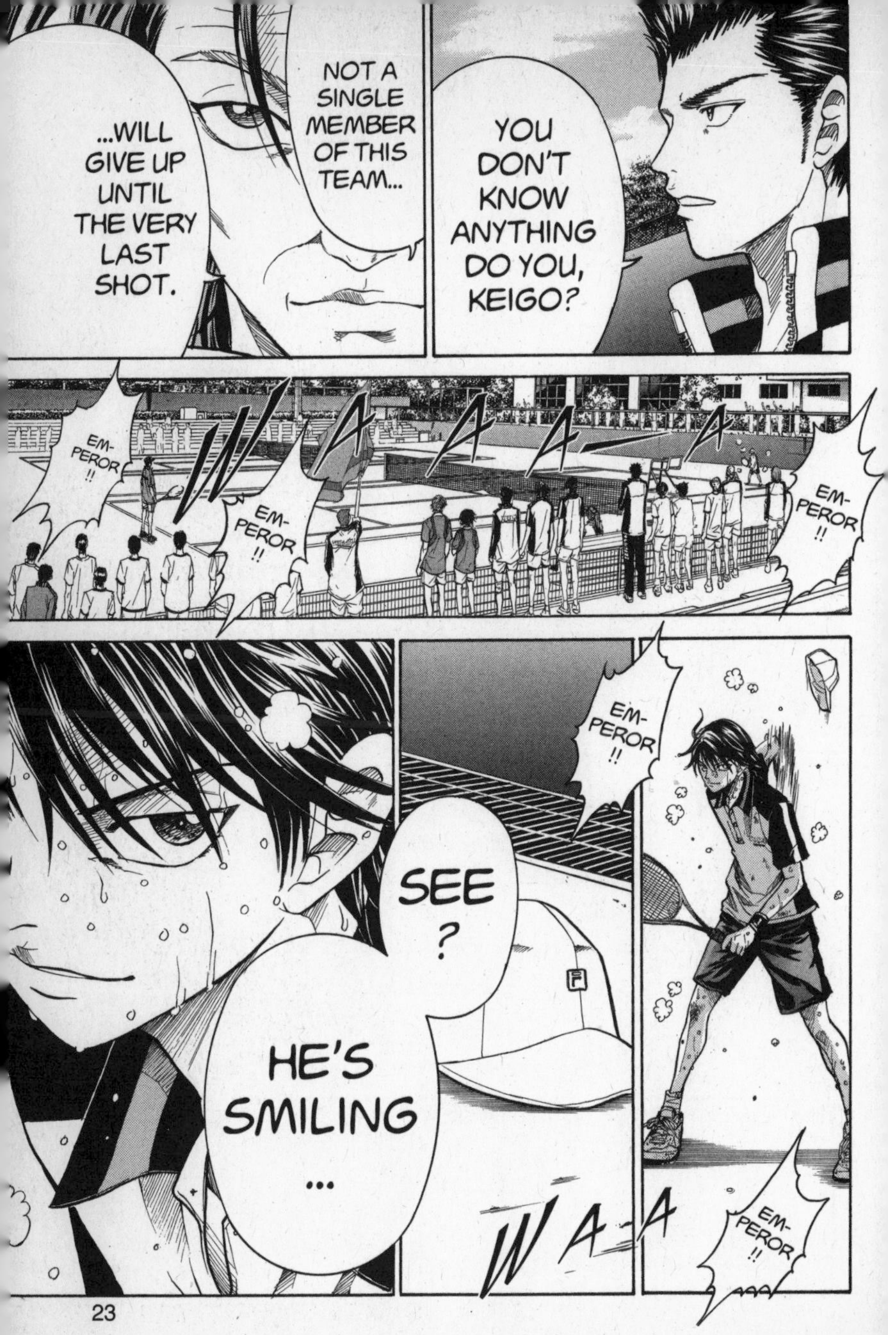
YOU DON'T KNOW ANYTHING DO YOU, KEIGO?
NOT A SINGLE MEMBER OF THIS TEAM...
...WILL GIVE UP UNTIL THE VERY LAST SHOT.
EM-PEROR!!
WAAA-A
EM-PEROR!!
EM-PEROR!!
EM-PEROR!!
EM-PEROR!!
EM-PEROR!!
WA-A
SEE?
HE'S SMILING...

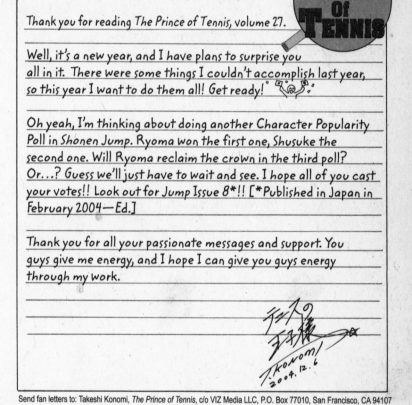

Thank you for reading *The Prince of Tennis*, volume 27.

Well, it's a new year, and I have plans to surprise you all in it. There were some things I couldn't accomplish last year, so this year I want to do them all! Get ready!

Oh yeah, I'm thinking about doing another Character Popularity Poll in *Shonen Jump*. Ryoma won the first one, Shusuke the second one. Will Ryoma reclaim the crown in the third poll? Or...? Guess we'll just have to wait and see. I hope all of you cast your votes!! Look out for *Jump* Issue 8*!! [*Published in Japan in February 2004—Ed.]

Thank you for all your passionate messages and support. You guys give me energy, and I hope I can give you guys energy through my work.

T.Konomi
2004. 12. 6

Send fan letters to: Takeshi Konomi, *The Prince of Tennis*, c/o VIZ Media LLC, P.O. Box 77010, San Francisco, CA 94107

GENIUS 230: SEISHUN'S PILLAR OF STRENGTH

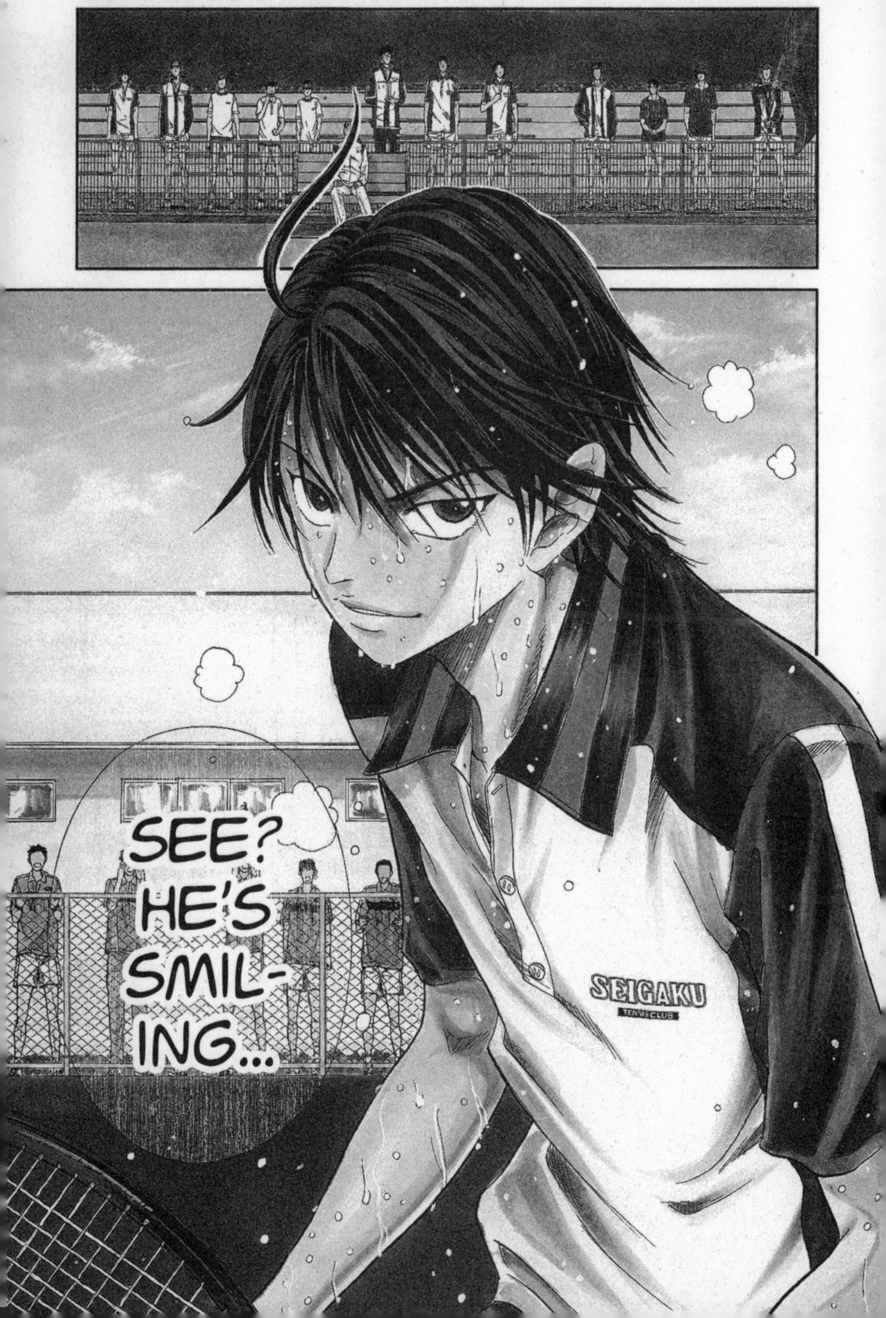
SEE? HE'S SMIL-ING...
SEIGAKU

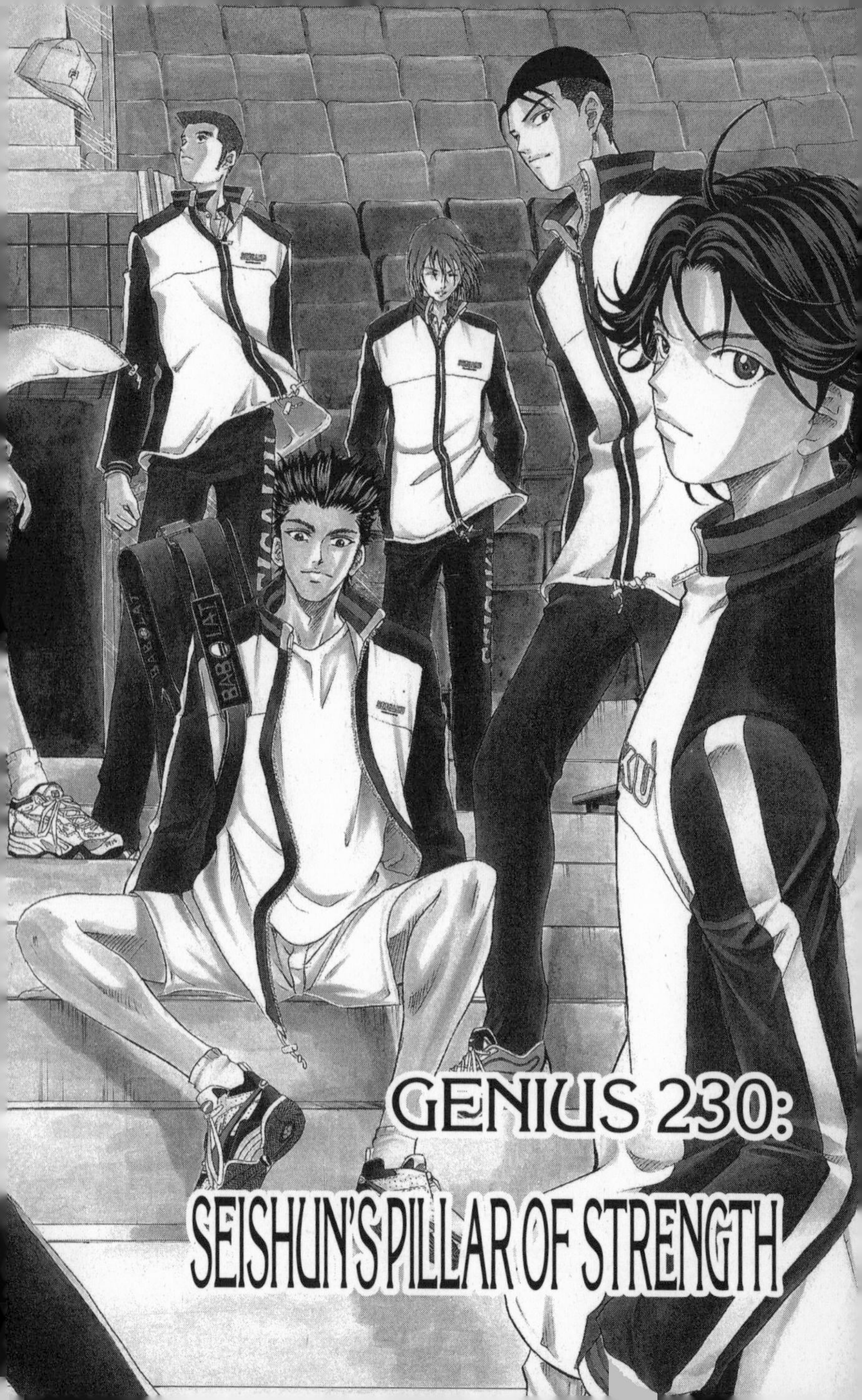
GENIUS 230:
SEISHUN'S PILLAR OF STRENGTH

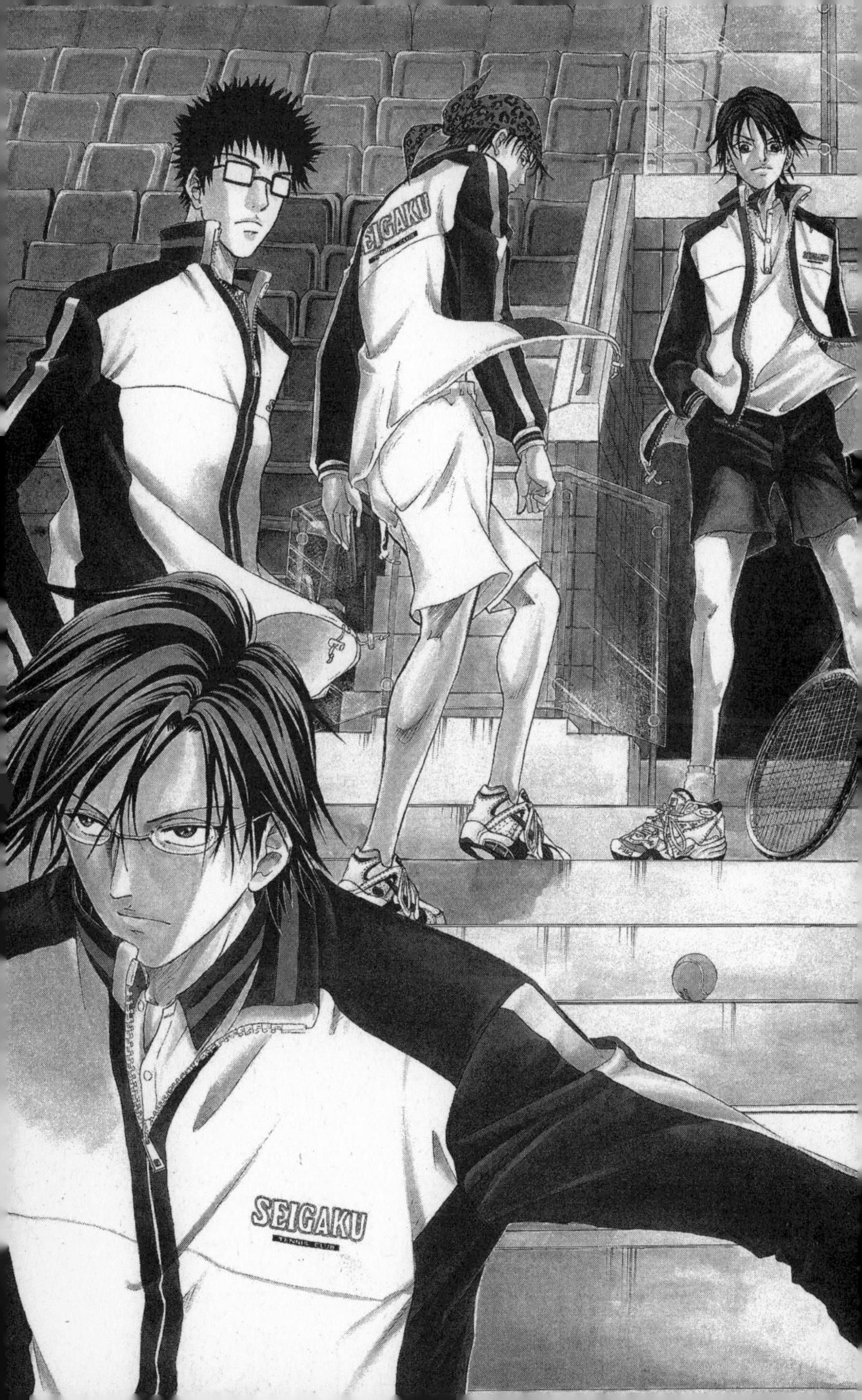
SEIGAKU
TENNIS CLUB
SEIGAKU
TENNIS CLUB

テニスの王子様

THE PRINCE OF TENNIS

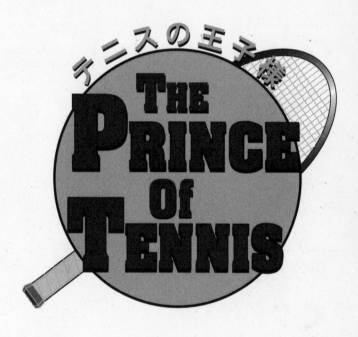

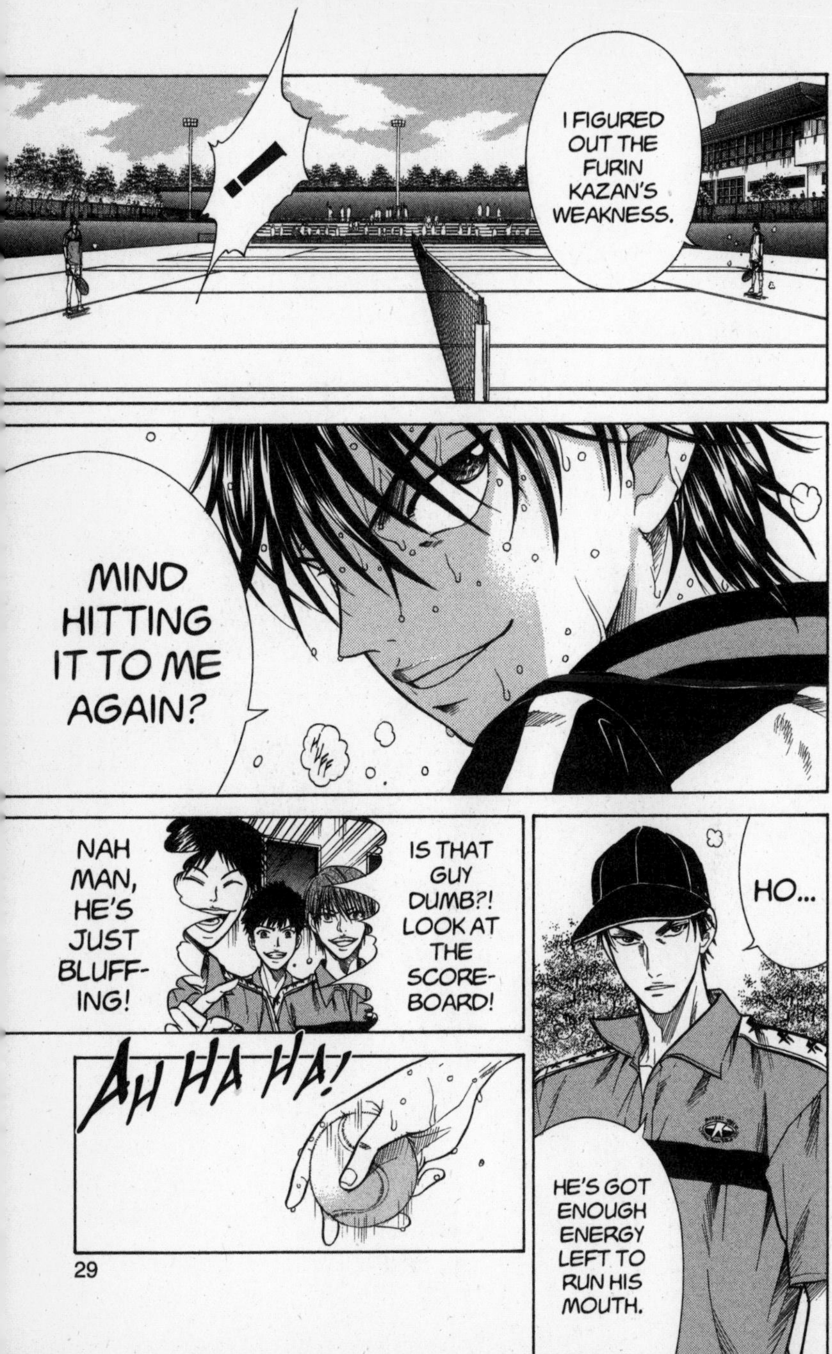
I FIGURED OUT THE FURIN KAZAN'S WEAKNESS.
!
MIND HITTING IT TO ME AGAIN?
HO...
HE'S GOT ENOUGH ENERGY LEFT TO RUN HIS MOUTH.
IS THAT GUY DUMB?! LOOK AT THE SCORE-BOARD!
NAH MAN, HE'S JUST BLUFF-ING!
AH HA HA!

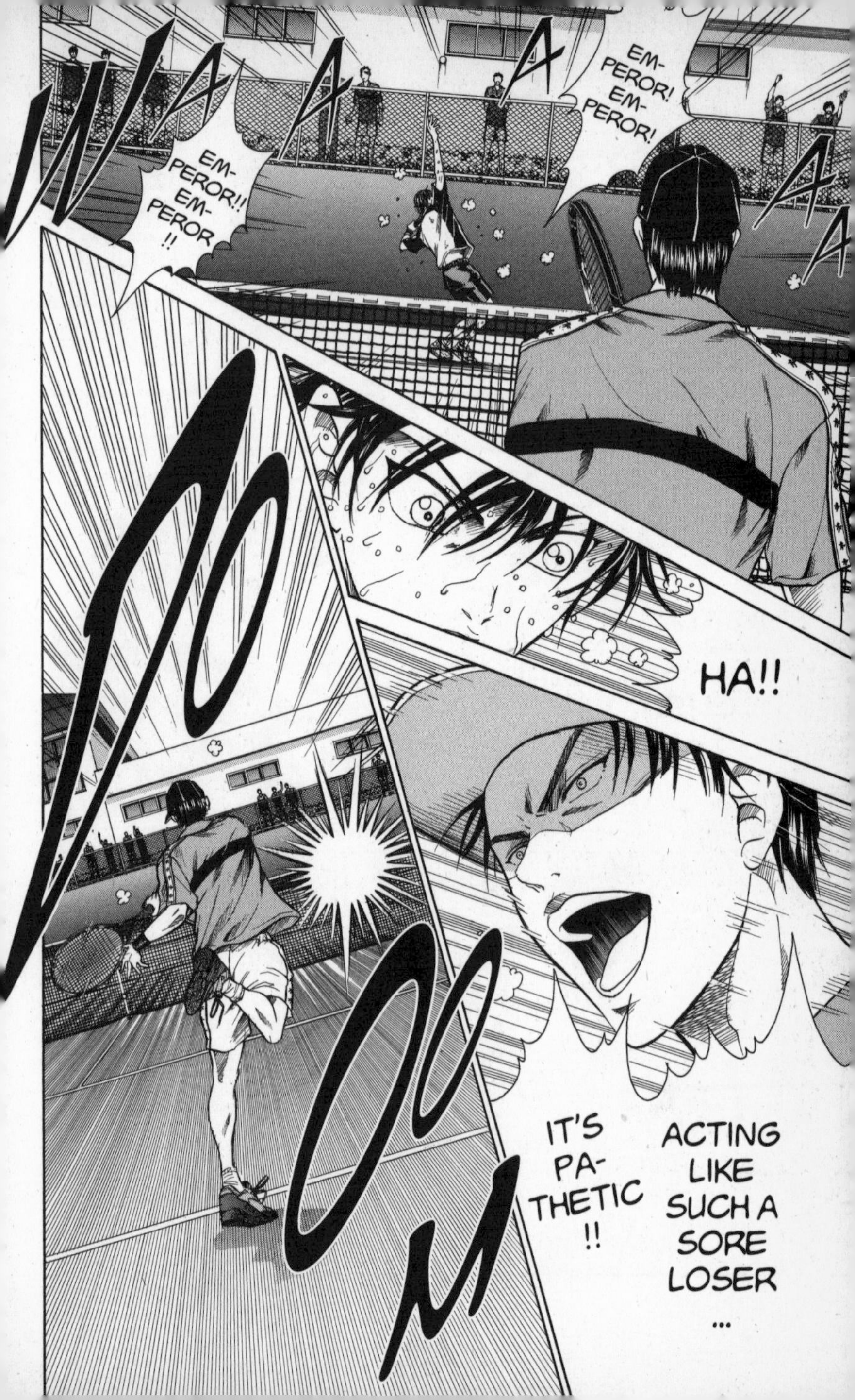
EM-PEROR! EM-PEROR!
EM-PEROR!! EM-PEROR!!
WAAA
AAA
HA!!
ACTING LIKE SUCH A SORE LOSER ...
IT'S PA-THETIC!!

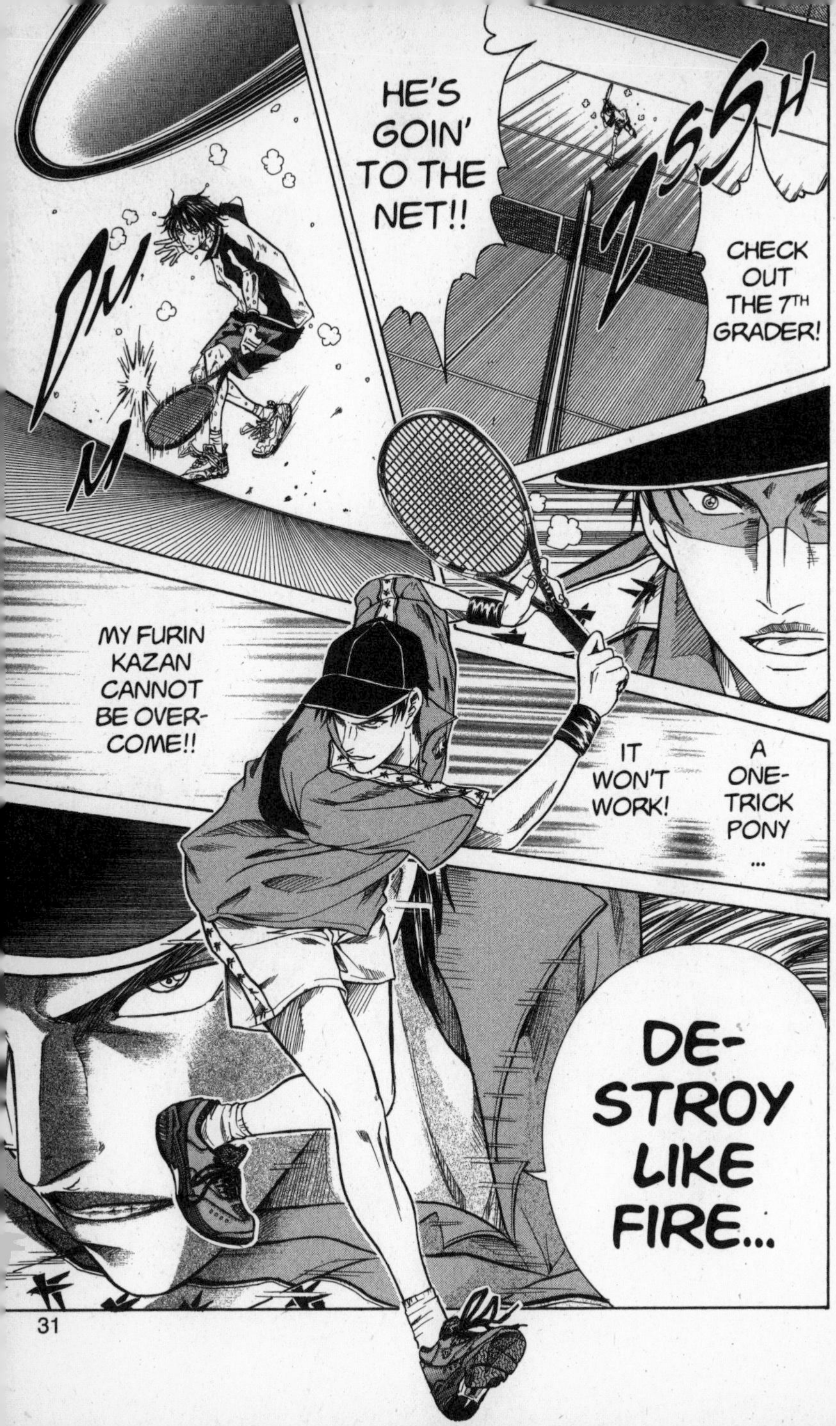

HE'S GOIN' TO THE NET!!
ZSSH
CHECK OUT THE 7TH GRADER!
A ONE-TRICK PONY...
IT WON'T WORK!
MY FURIN KAZAN CANNOT BE OVER-COME!!
DE-STROY LIKE FIRE...

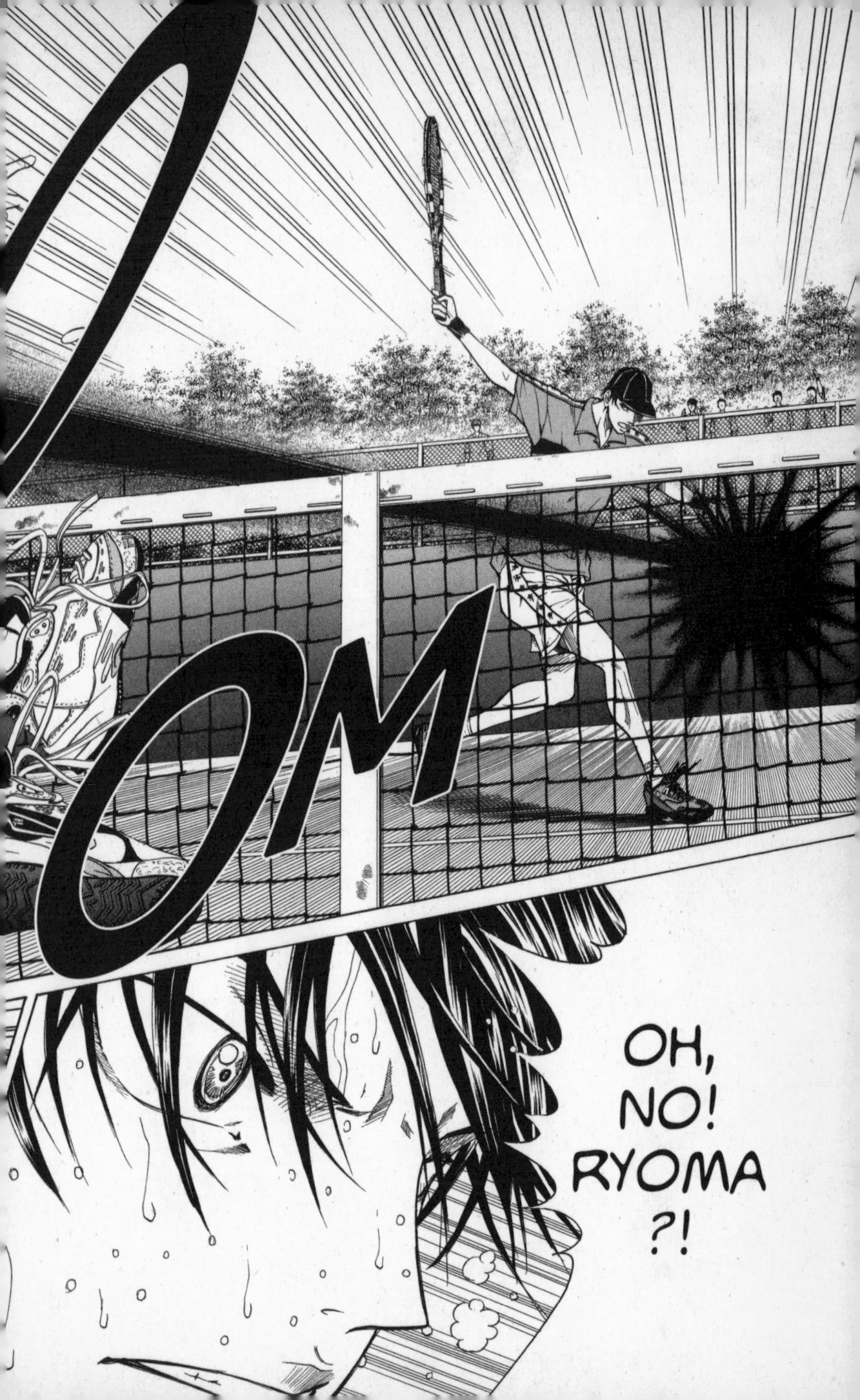
OM
OH, NO! RYOMA ?!

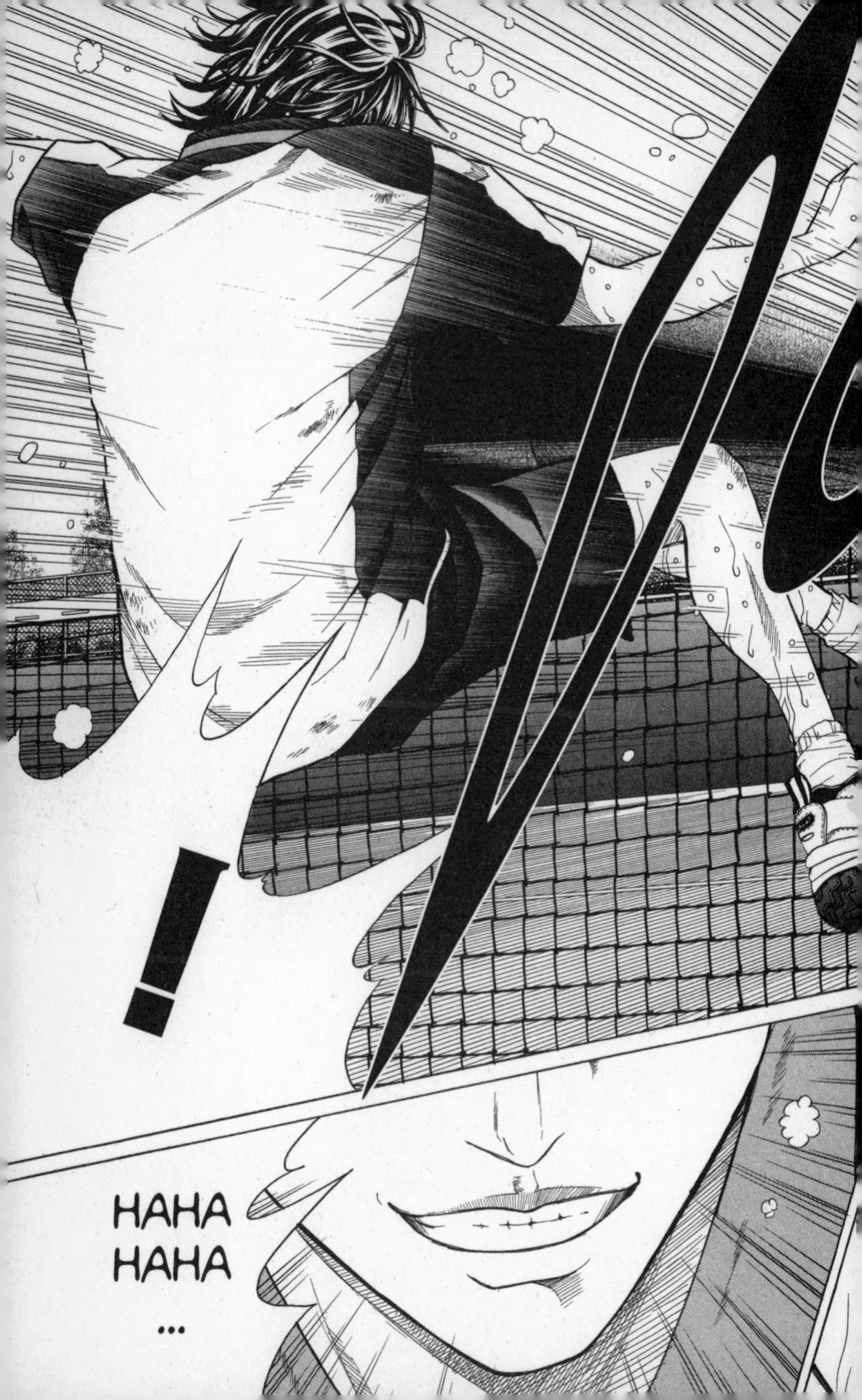
!
HAHA
HAHA
...

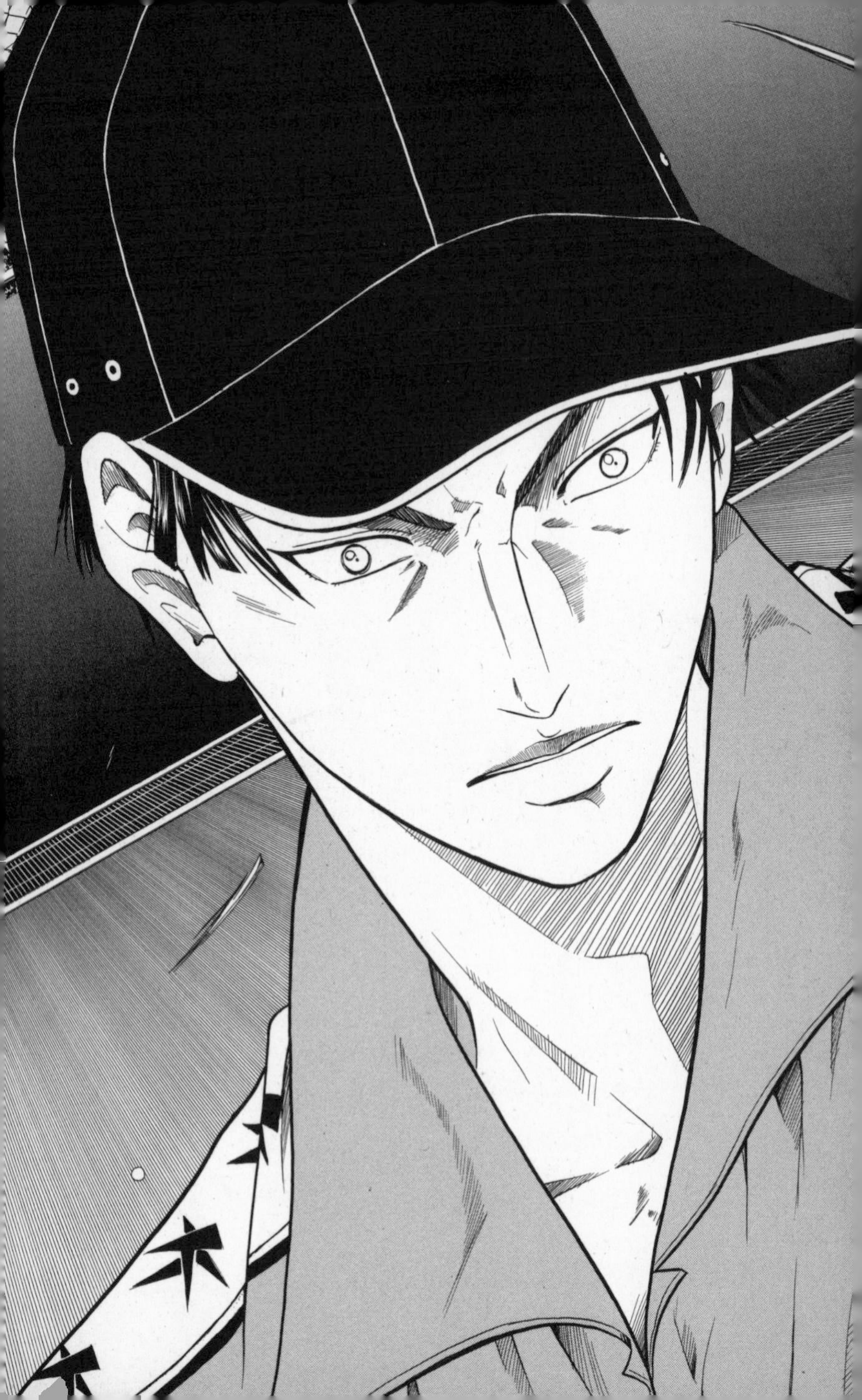

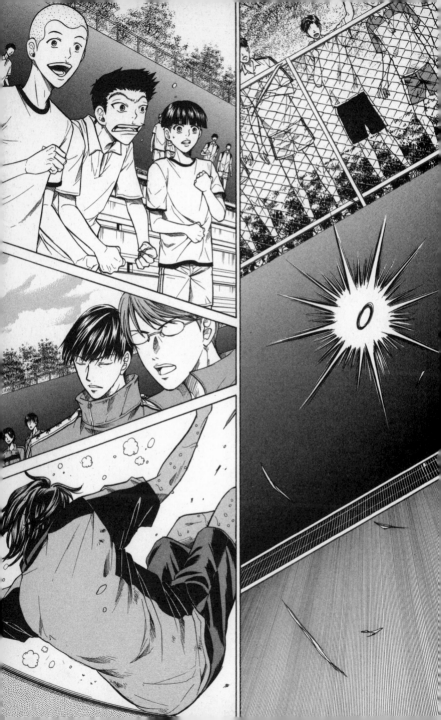

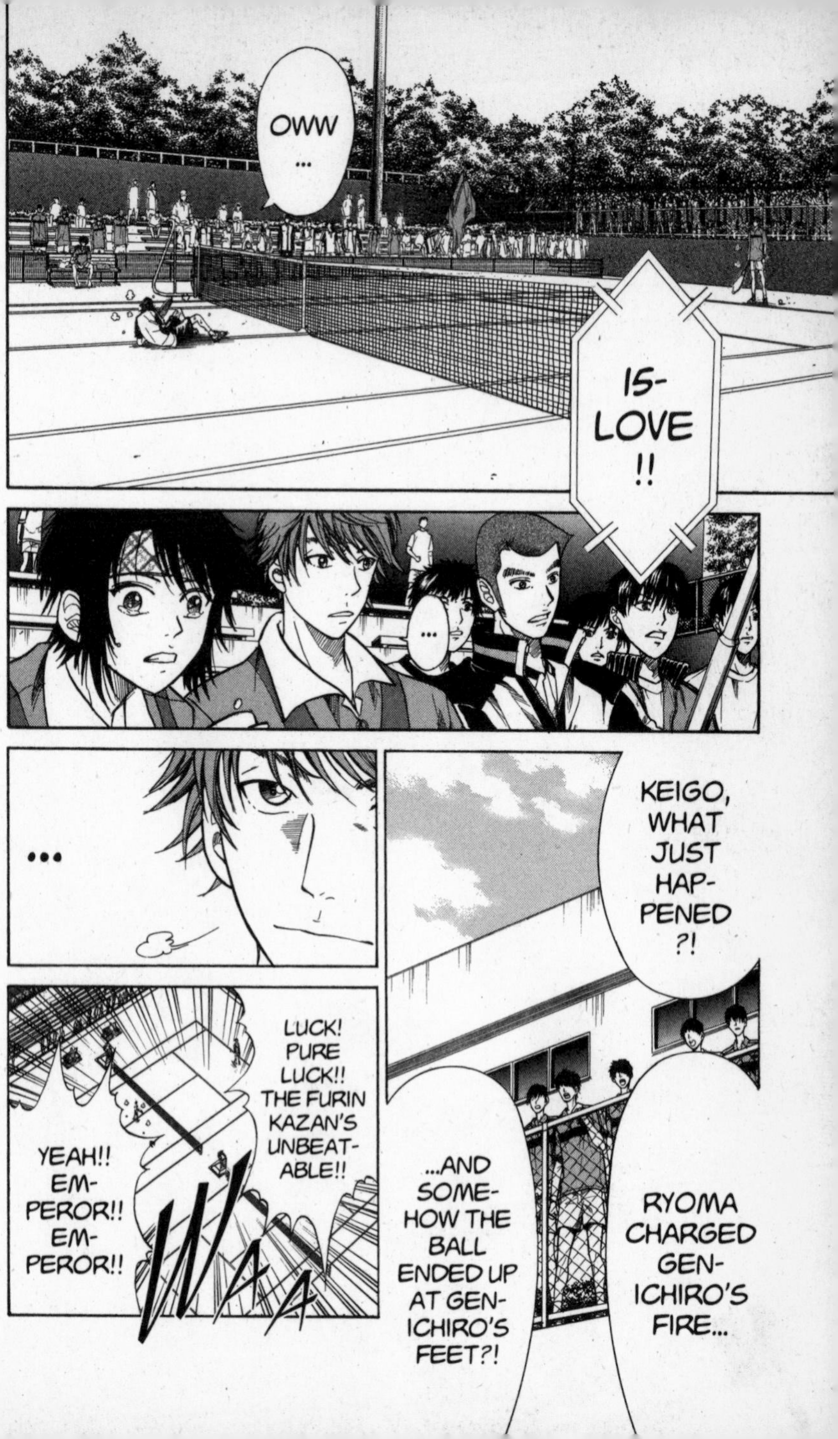
OWW...
15-LOVE!!
...
KEIGO, WHAT JUST HAP-PENED?!
RYOMA CHARGED GEN-ICHIRO'S FIRE...
...AND SOME-HOW THE BALL ENDED UP AT GEN-ICHIRO'S FEET?!
...
LUCK! PURE LUCK!! THE FURIN KAZAN'S UNBEAT-ABLE!!
YEAH!! EM-PEROR!! EM-PEROR!!
WAA

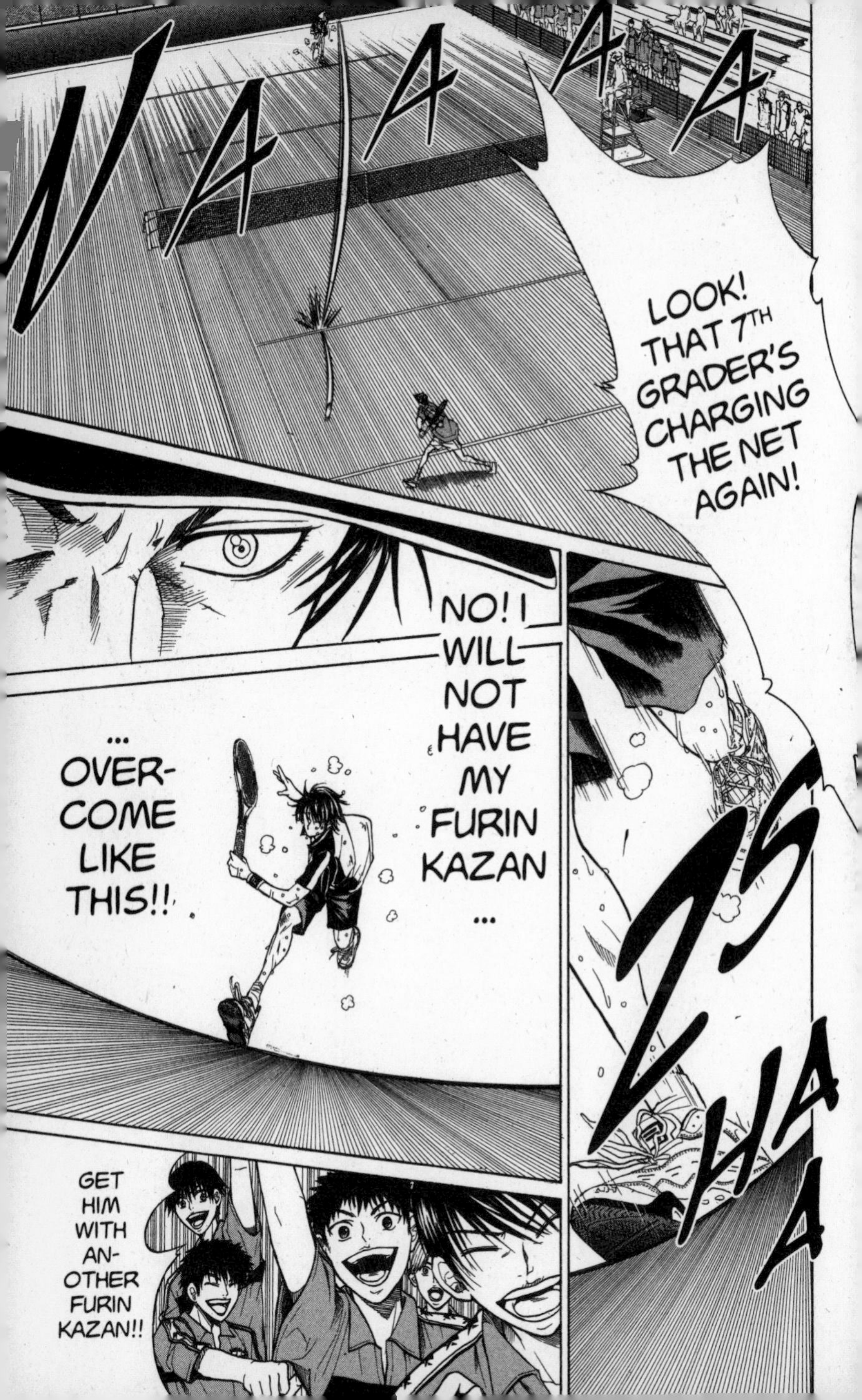
NAAAA
LOOK! THAT 7TH GRADER'S CHARGING THE NET AGAIN!
ZSHAA
NO!! I WILL NOT HAVE MY FURIN KAZAN ...
... OVER-COME LIKE THIS!!
GET HIM WITH AN-OTHER FURIN KAZAN!!

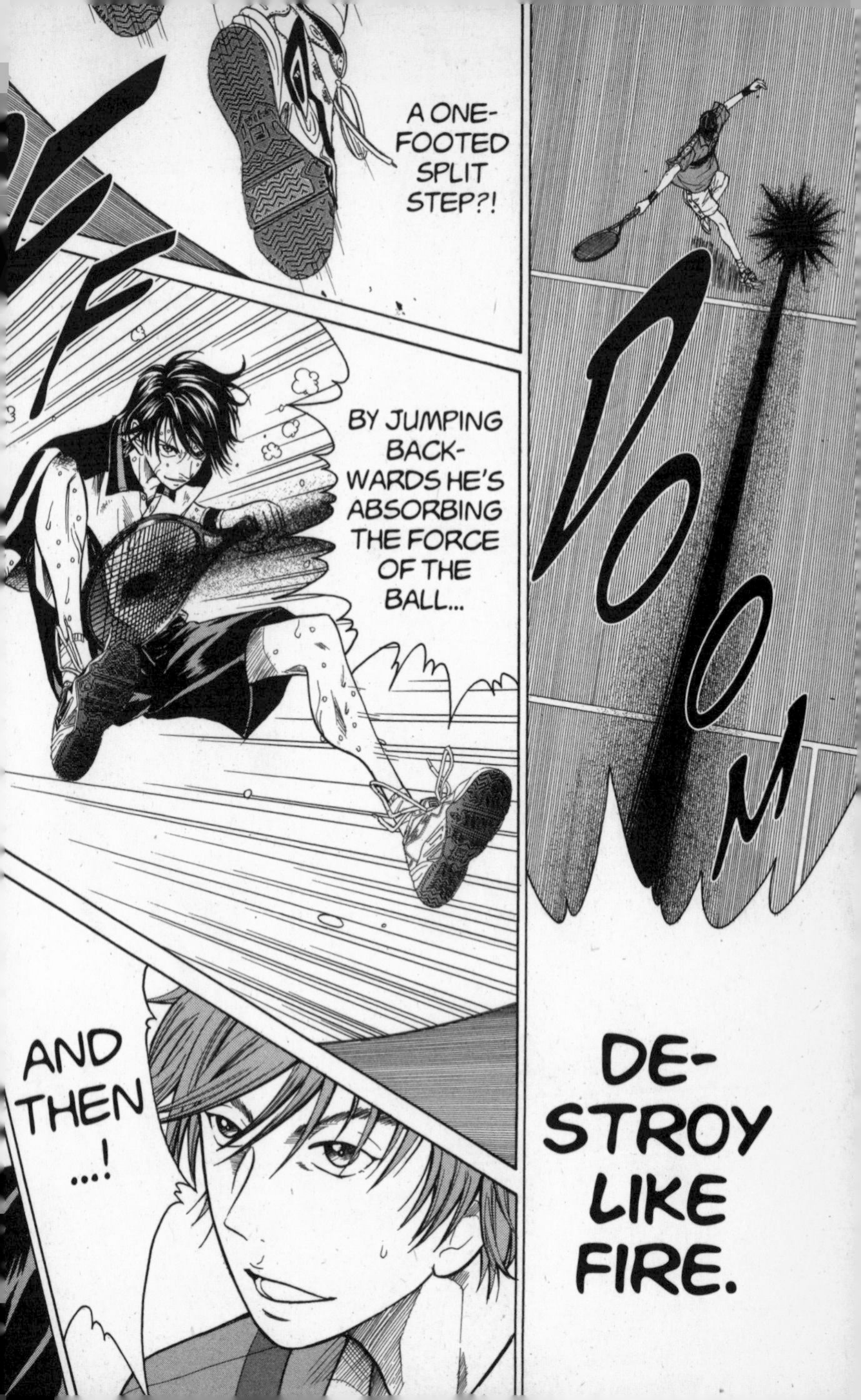
DOOOM
DE-STROY LIKE FIRE.
A ONE-FOOTED SPLIT STEP?!
BY JUMPING BACKWARDS HE'S ABSORBING THE FORCE OF THE BALL...
AND THEN ...!

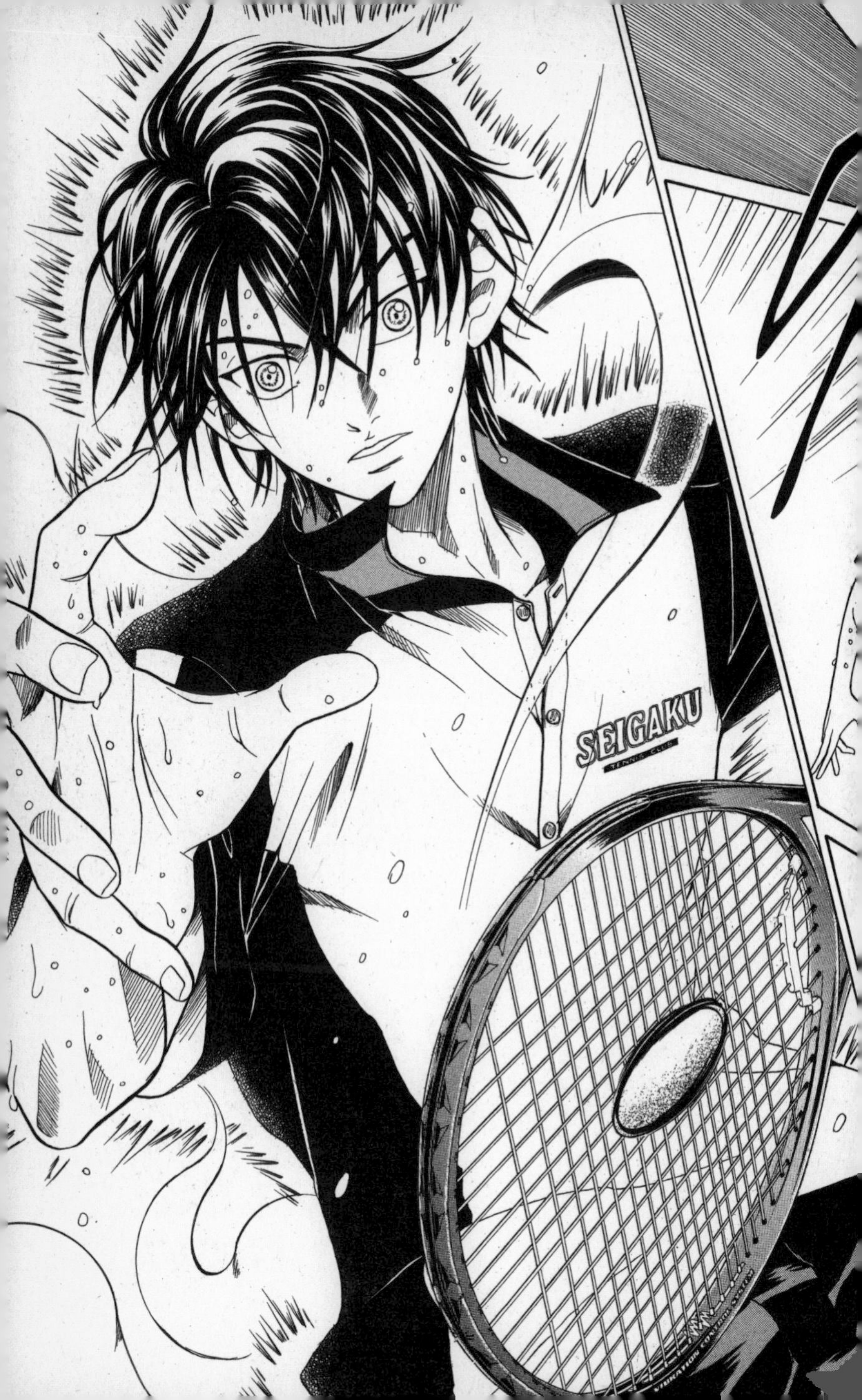
SEIGAKU
TENNIS CLUB

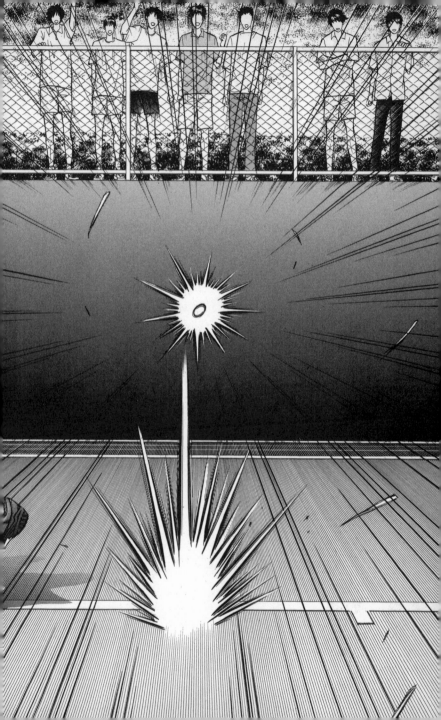

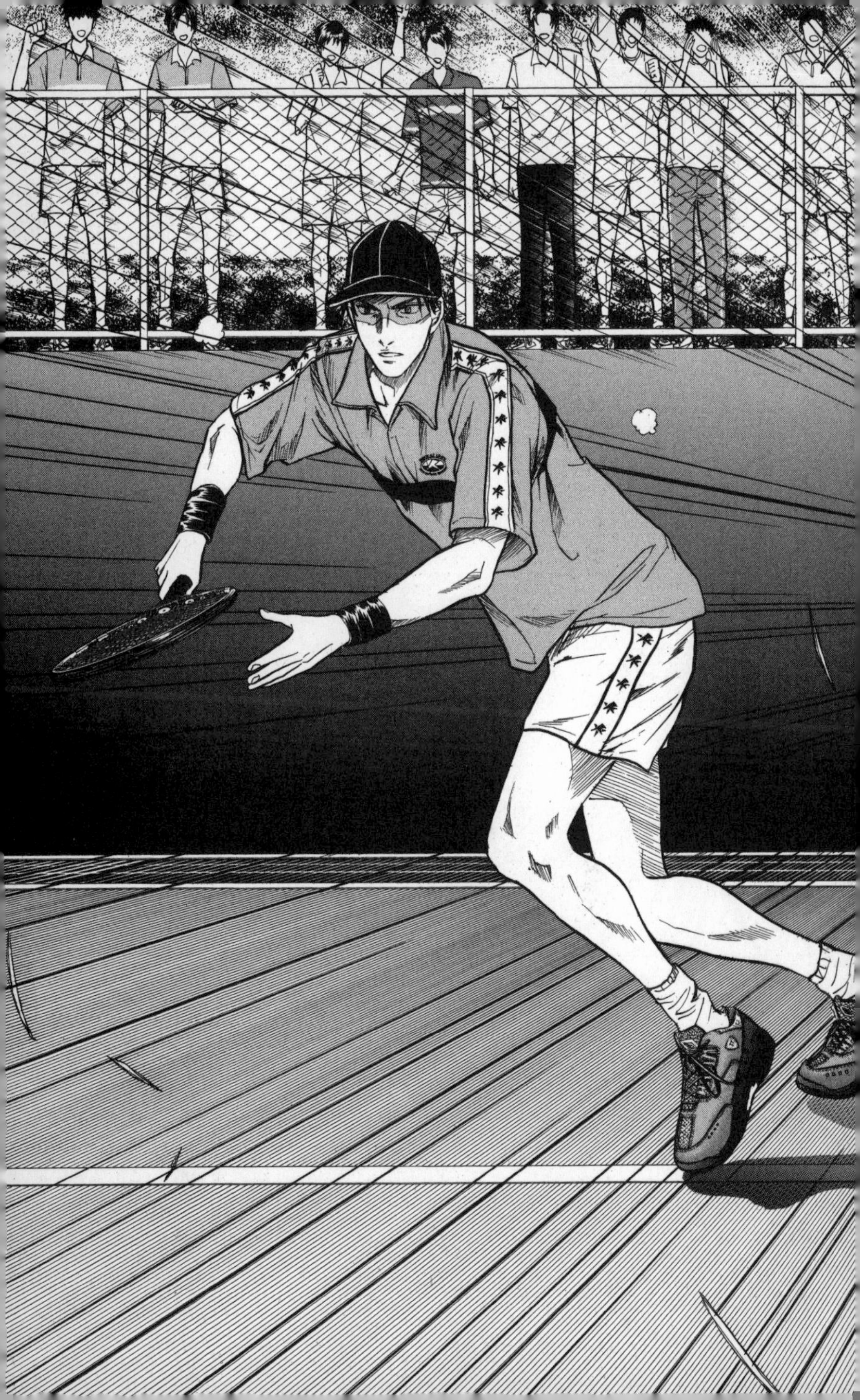

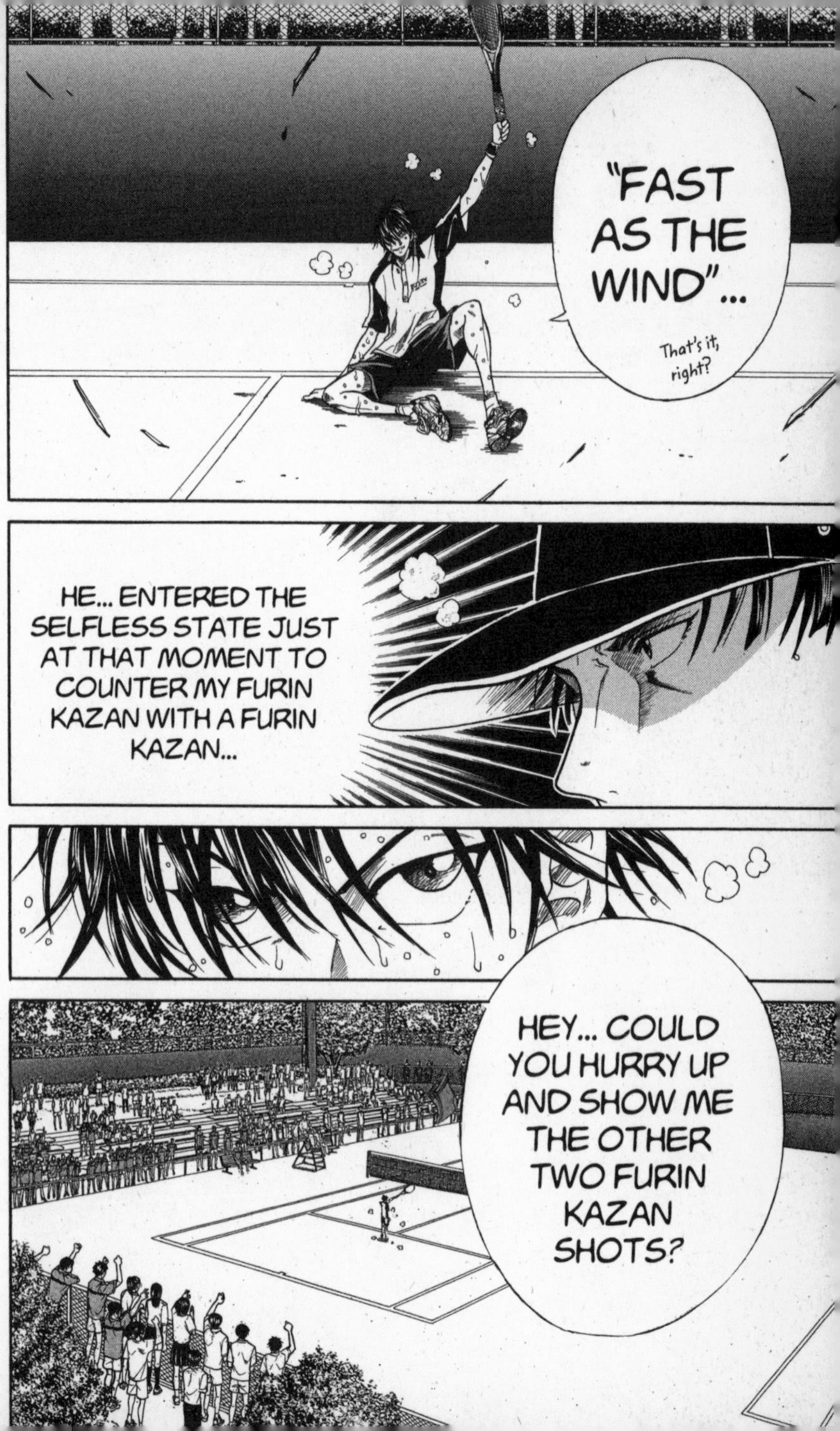
"FAST AS THE WIND"...
That's it, right?
HE... ENTERED THE SELFLESS STATE JUST AT THAT MOMENT TO COUNTER MY FURIN KAZAN WITH A FURIN KAZAN...
HEY... COULD YOU HURRY UP AND SHOW ME THE OTHER TWO FURIN KAZAN SHOTS?

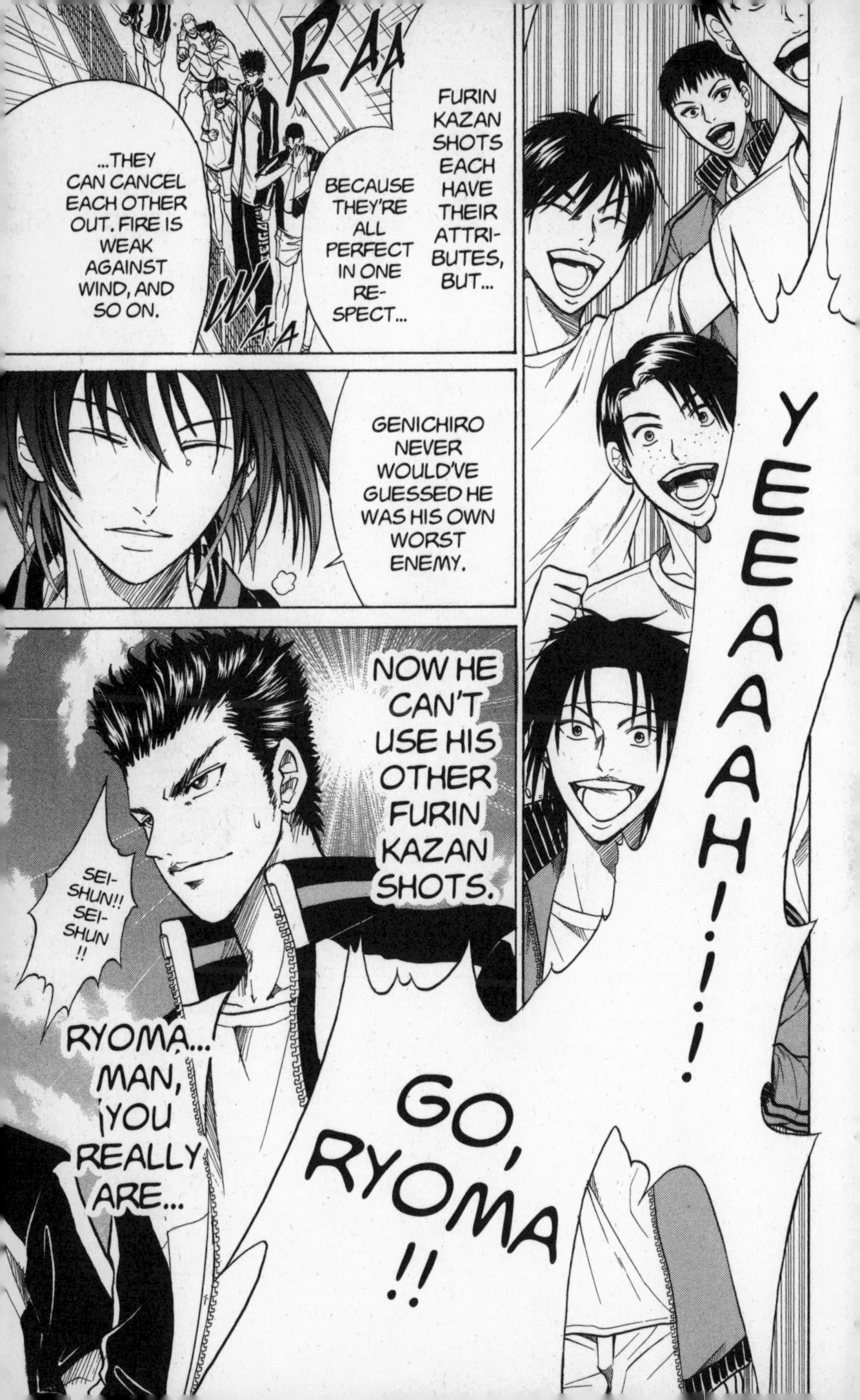
YEEAAAH!!!!
GO, RYOMA!!
FURIN KAZAN SHOTS EACH HAVE THEIR ATTRIBUTES, BUT...
BECAUSE THEY'RE ALL PERFECT IN ONE RESPECT...
...THEY CAN CANCEL EACH OTHER OUT. FIRE IS WEAK AGAINST WIND, AND SO ON.
RAA
WAA
GENICHIRO NEVER WOULD'VE GUESSED HE WAS HIS OWN WORST ENEMY.
NOW HE CAN'T USE HIS OTHER FURIN KAZAN SHOTS.
SEI-SHUN!! SEI-SHUN!!
RYOMA... MAN, YOU REALLY ARE...

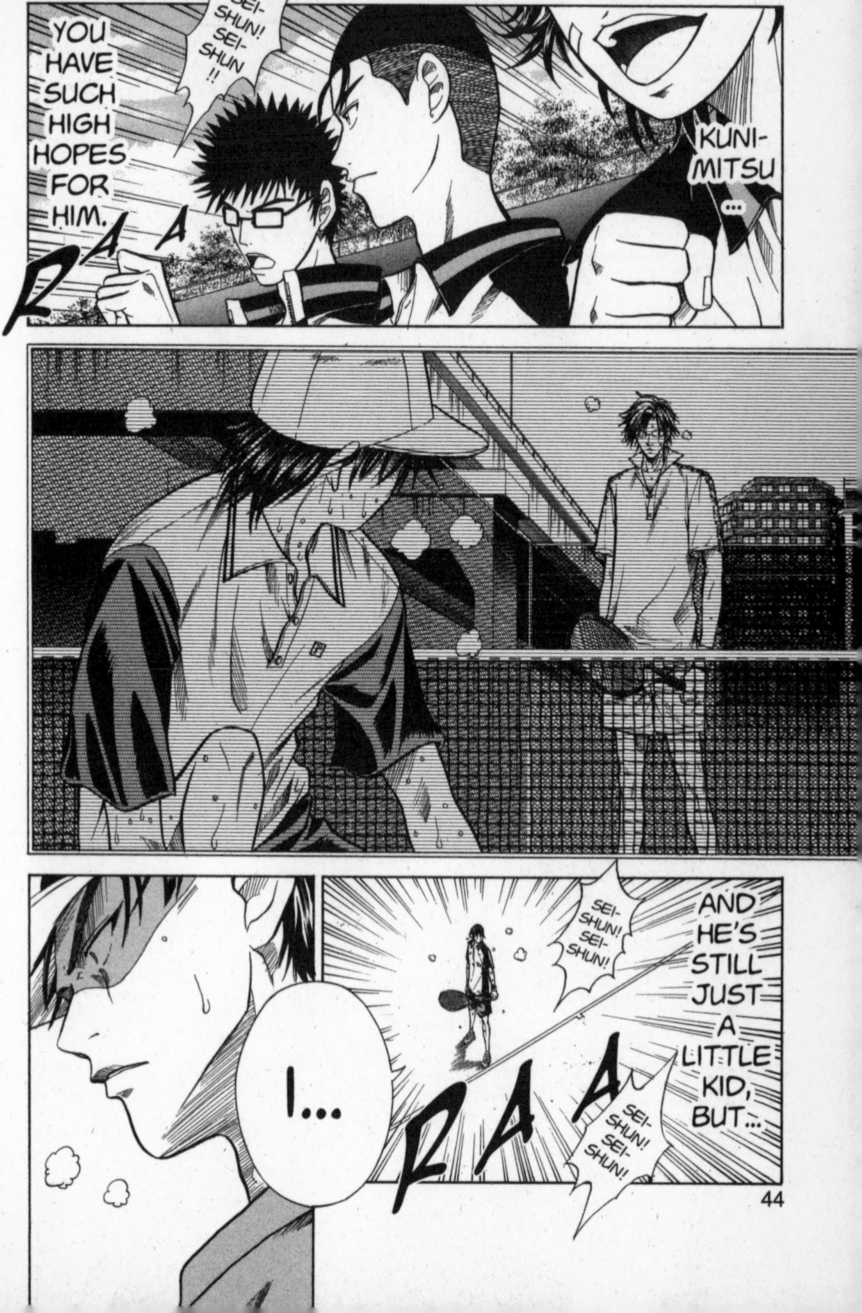
KUNIMITSU...
SEI-SHUN! SEI-SHUN!!
YOU HAVE SUCH HIGH HOPES FOR HIM.
RAA
AND HE'S STILL JUST A LITTLE KID, BUT...
SEI-SHUN! SEI-SHUN!
SEI-SHUN! SEI-SHUN!
RAA
I...

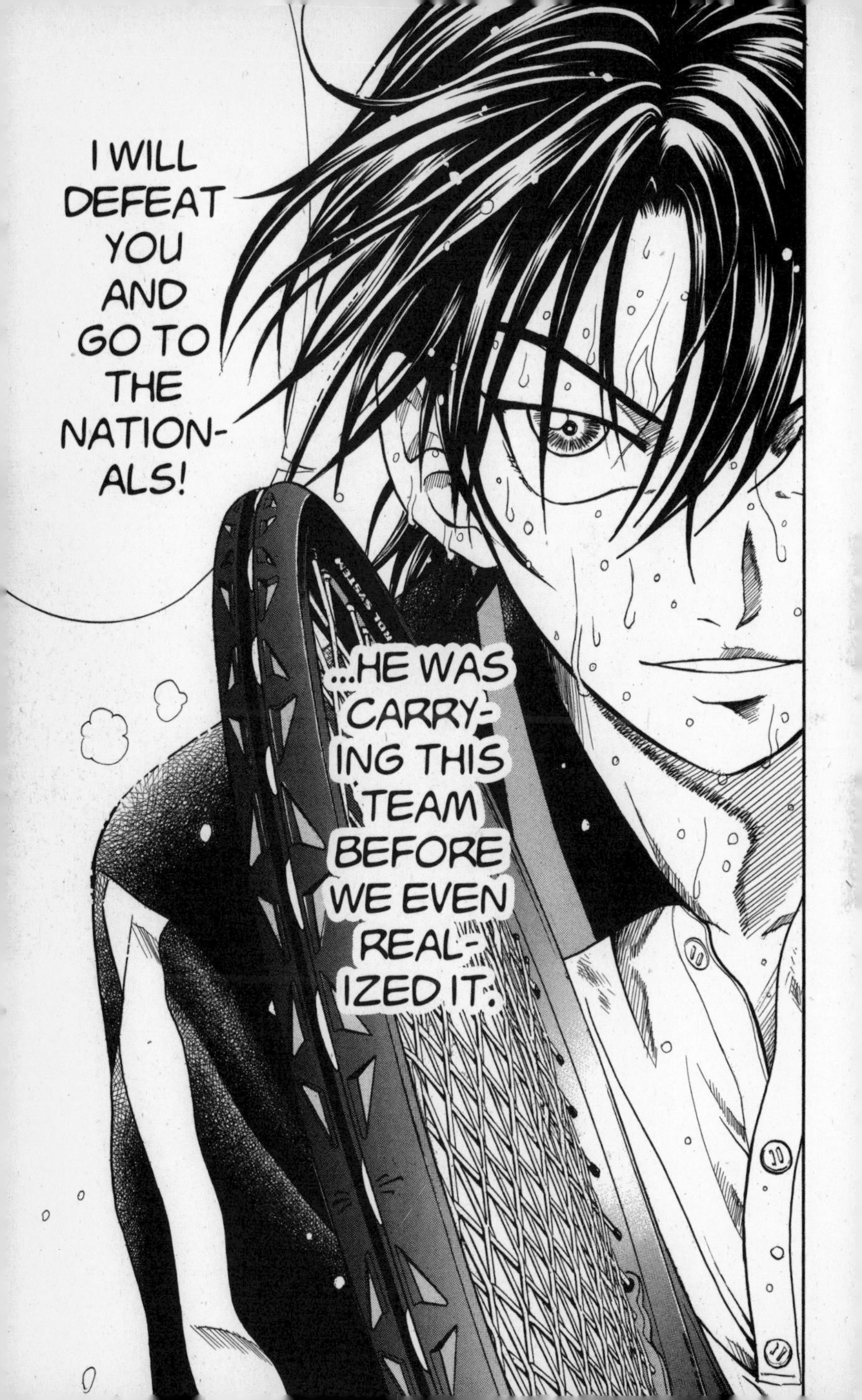
I WILL DEFEAT YOU AND GO TO THE NATIONALS!
...HE WAS CARRYING THIS TEAM BEFORE WE EVEN REALIZED IT.

テニスの王子様

THE PRINCE OF TENNIS

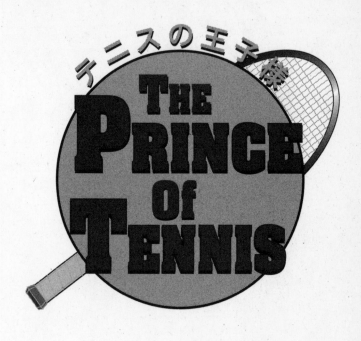

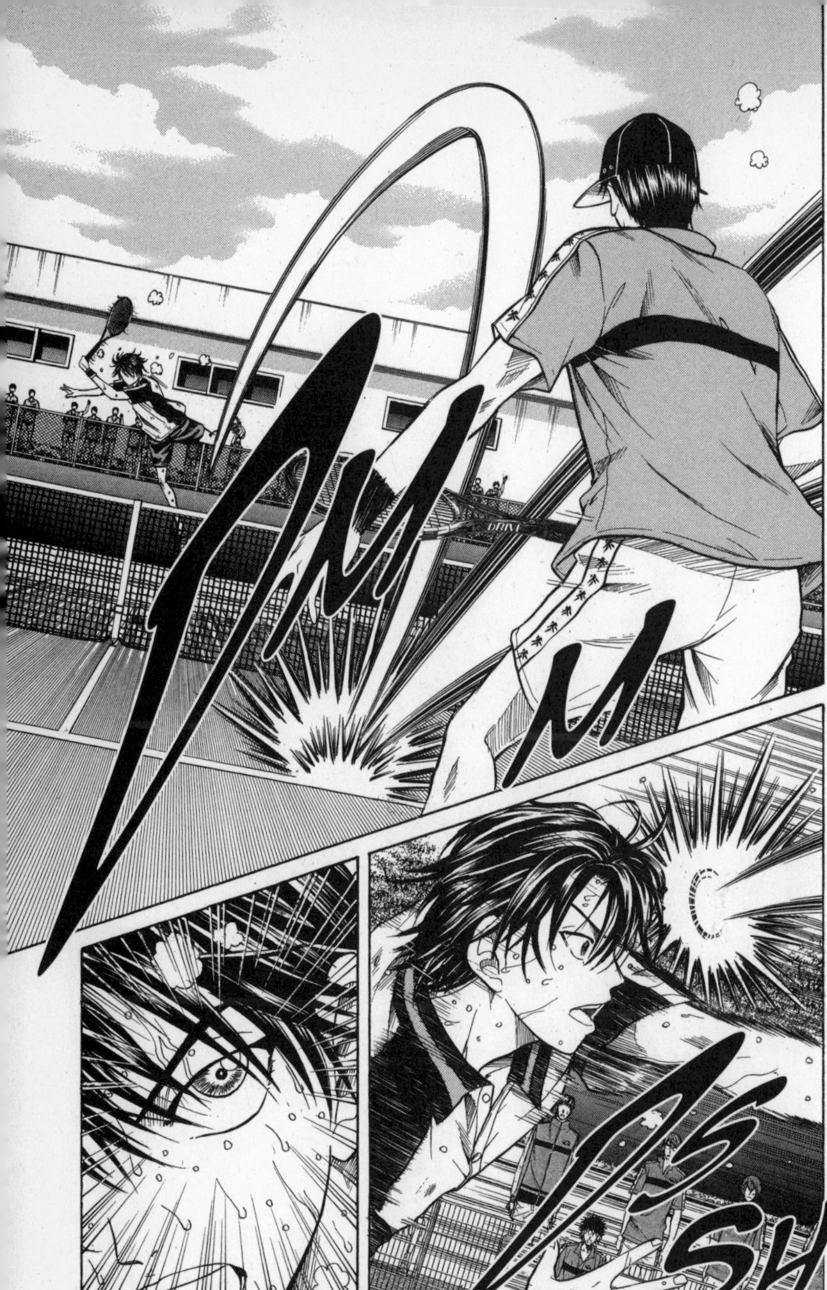

GENIUS 231: MAVERICK

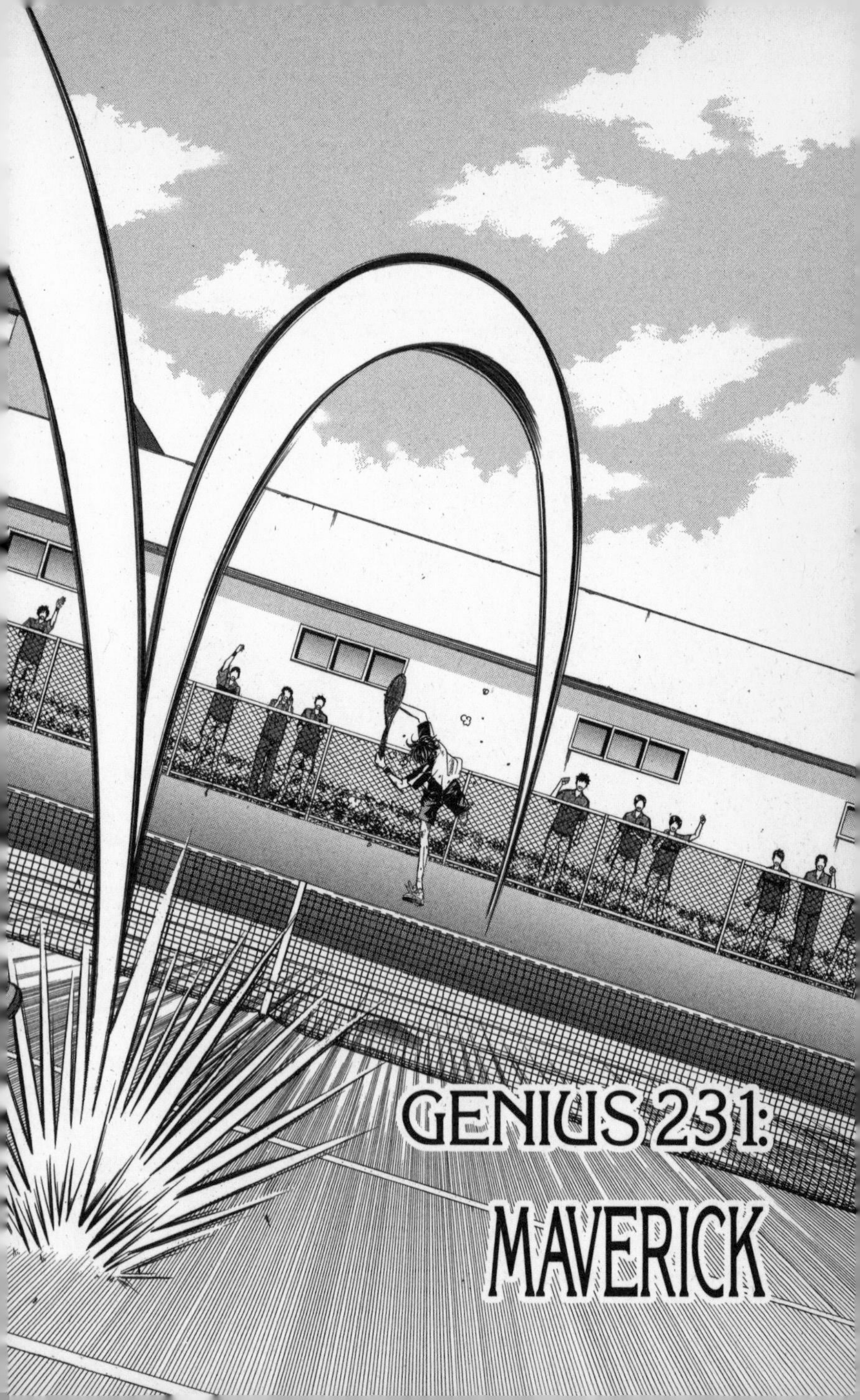
GENIUS 231:
MAVERICK

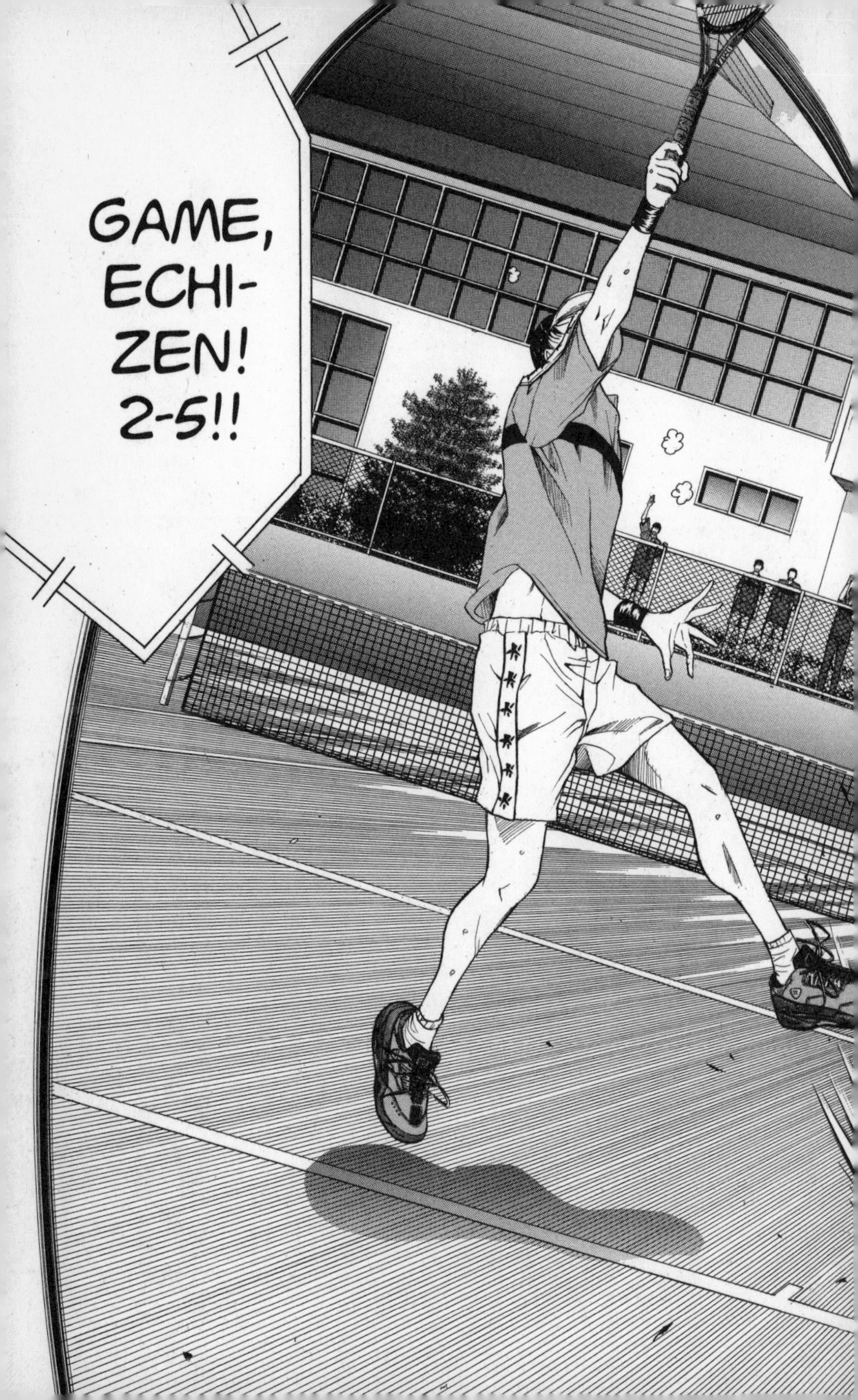
GAME, ECHI- ZEN! 2-5!!

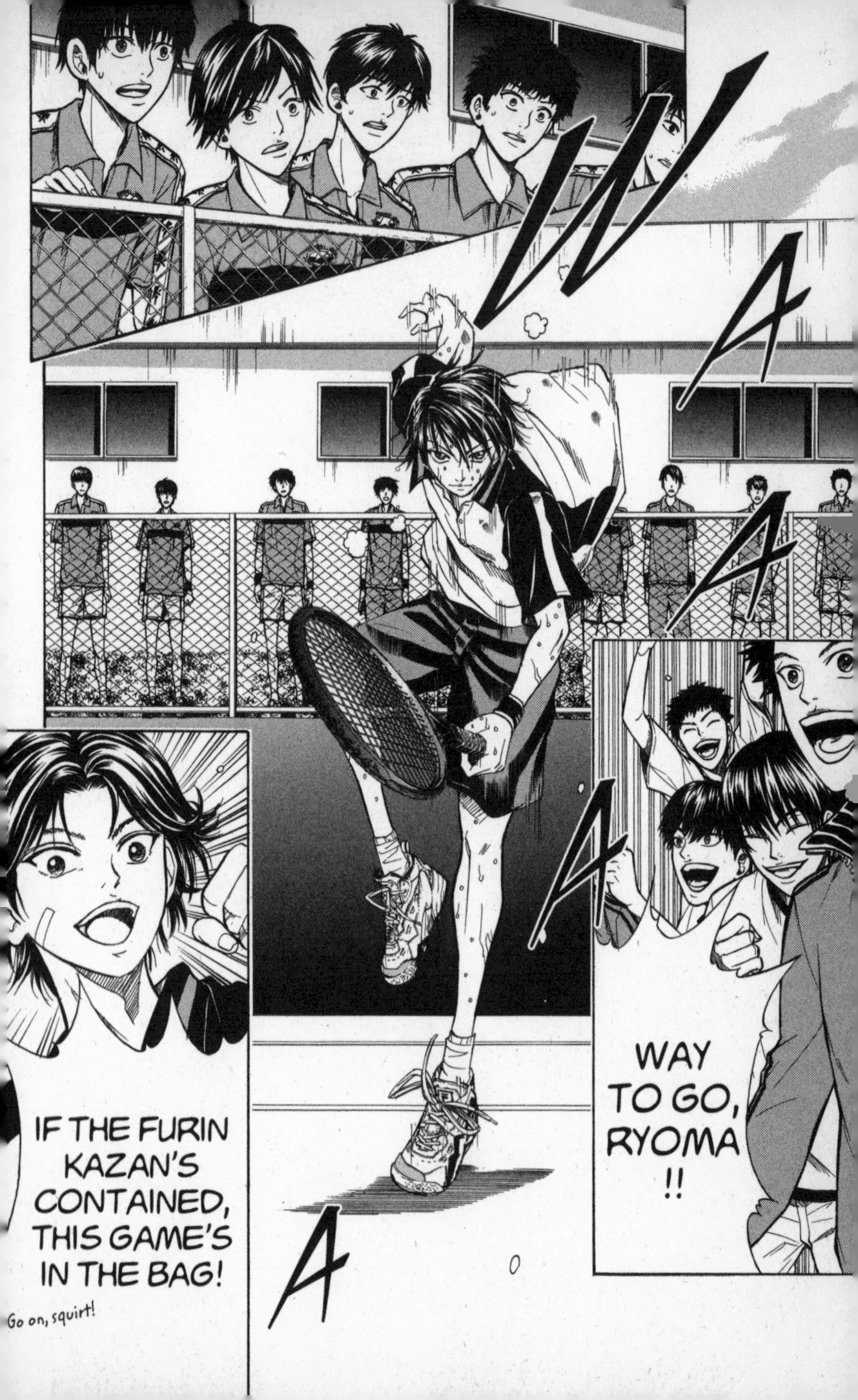
WAAAA
WAY TO GO, RYOMA!!
IF THE FURIN KAZAN'S CONTAINED, THIS GAME'S IN THE BAG!
Go on, squirt!

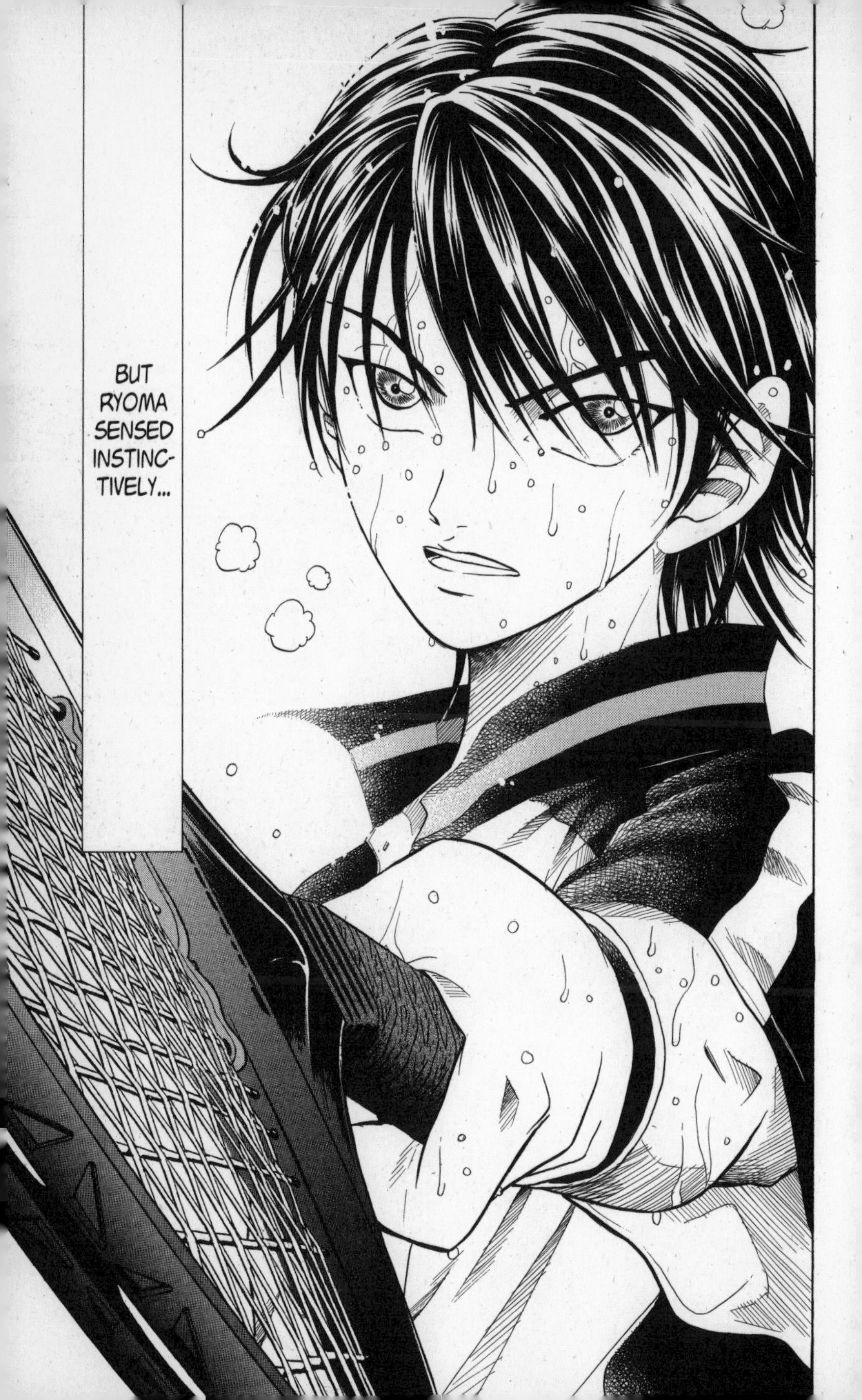
BUT RYOMA SENSED INSTINCTIVELY...

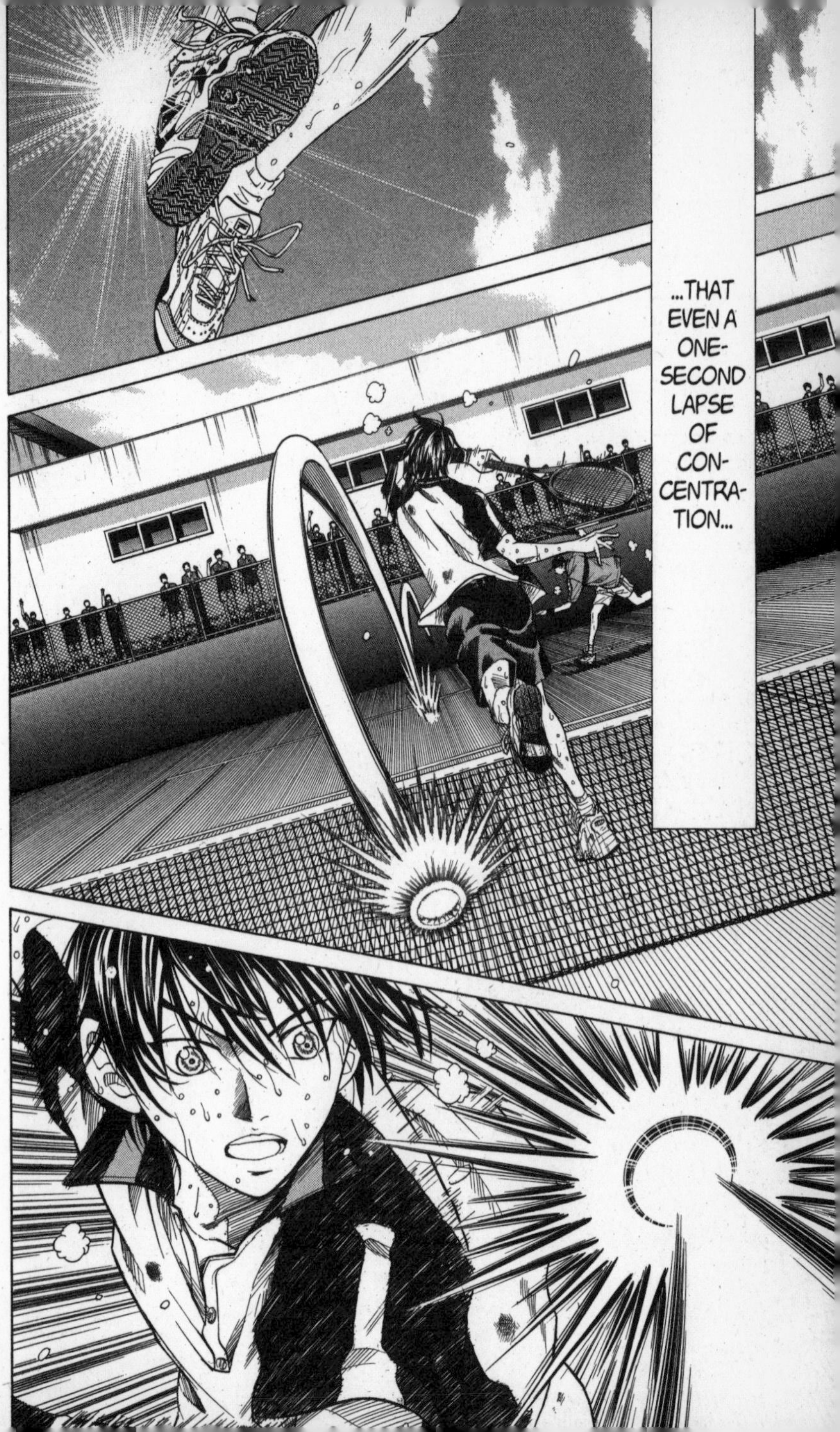
...THAT EVEN A ONE-SECOND LAPSE OF CON-CENTRA-TION...

READ THIS WAY

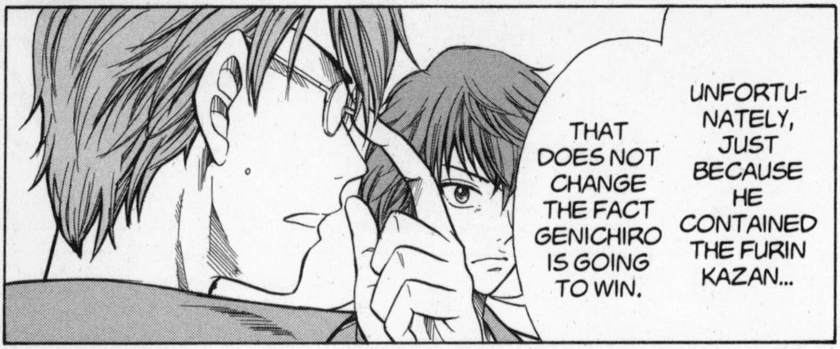
UNFORTU-NATELY, JUST BECAUSE HE CONTAINED THE FURIN KAZAN...
THAT DOES NOT CHANGE THE FACT GENICHIRO IS GOING TO WIN.

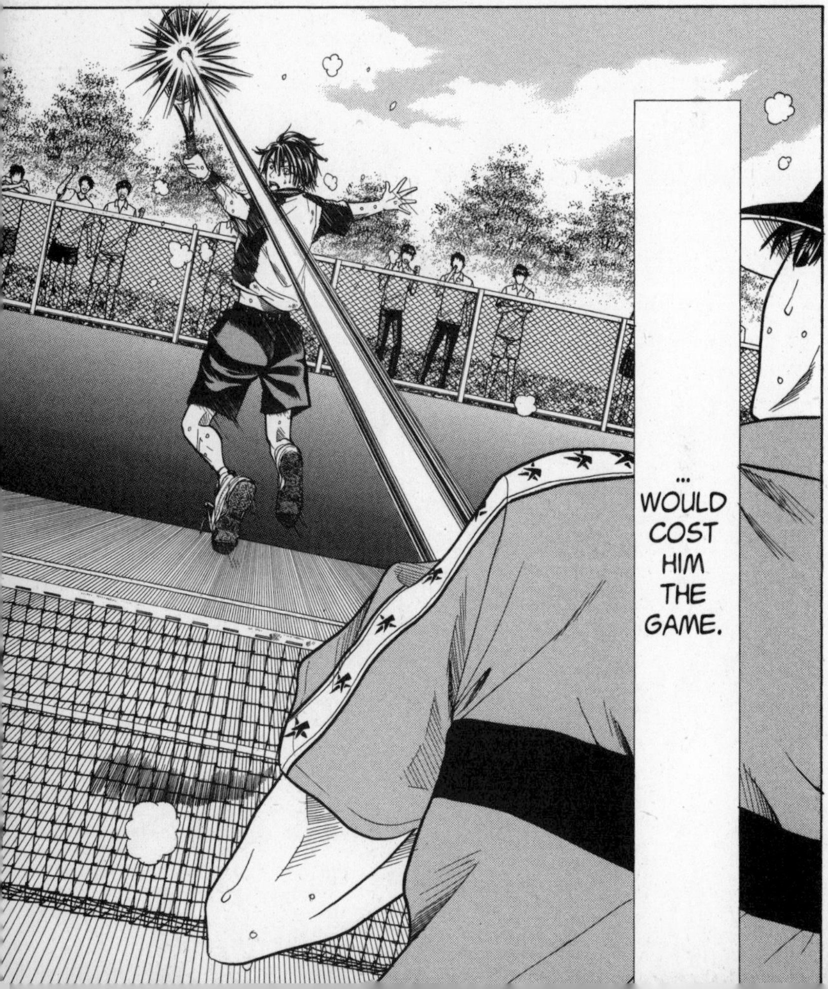
... WOULD COST HIM THE GAME.

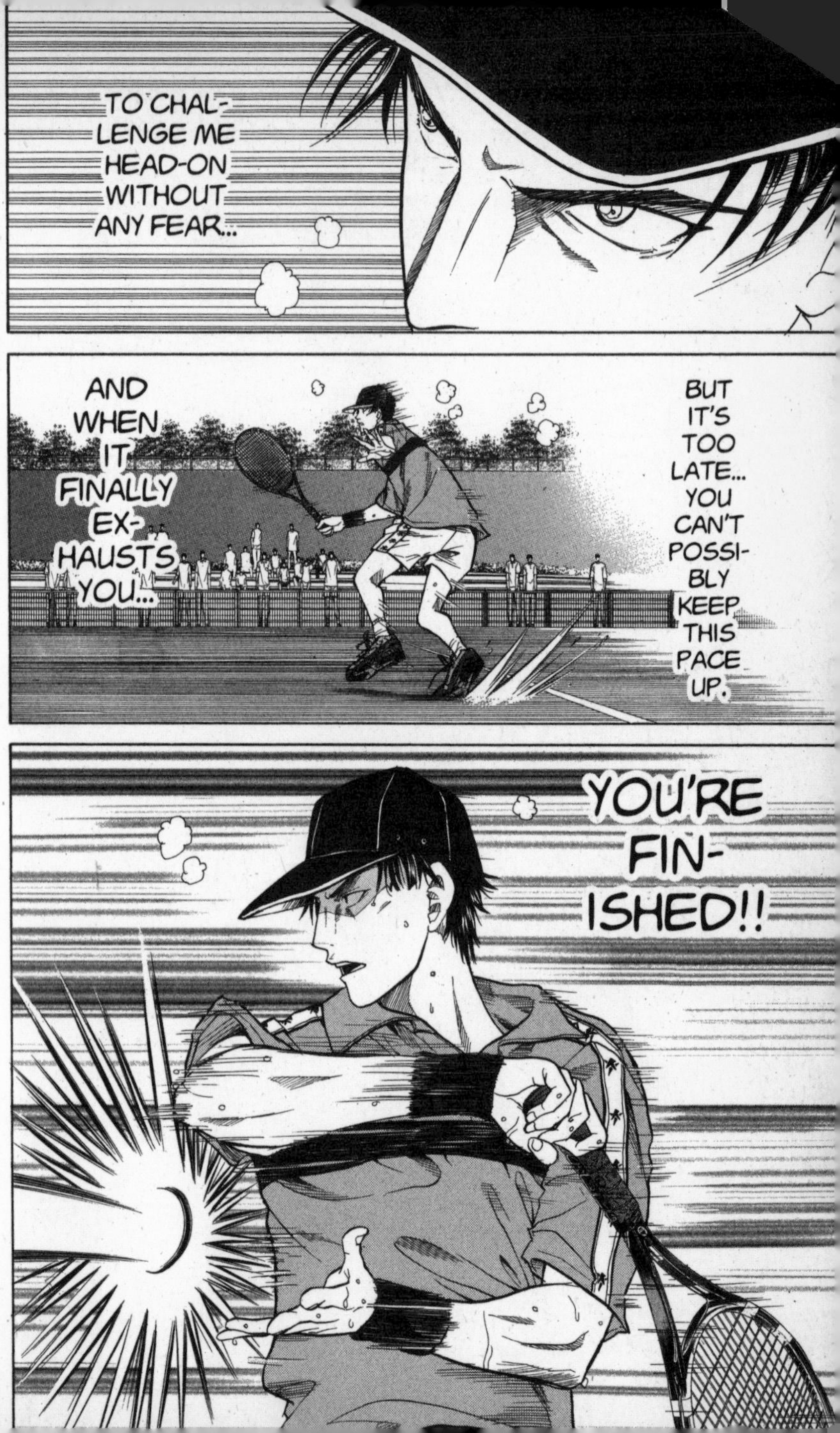
TO CHAL-LENGE ME HEAD-ON WITHOUT ANY FEAR...
BUT IT'S TOO LATE... YOU CAN'T POSSIBLY KEEP THIS PACE UP.
AND WHEN IT FINALLY EX-HAUSTS YOU...
YOU'RE FIN-ISHED!!

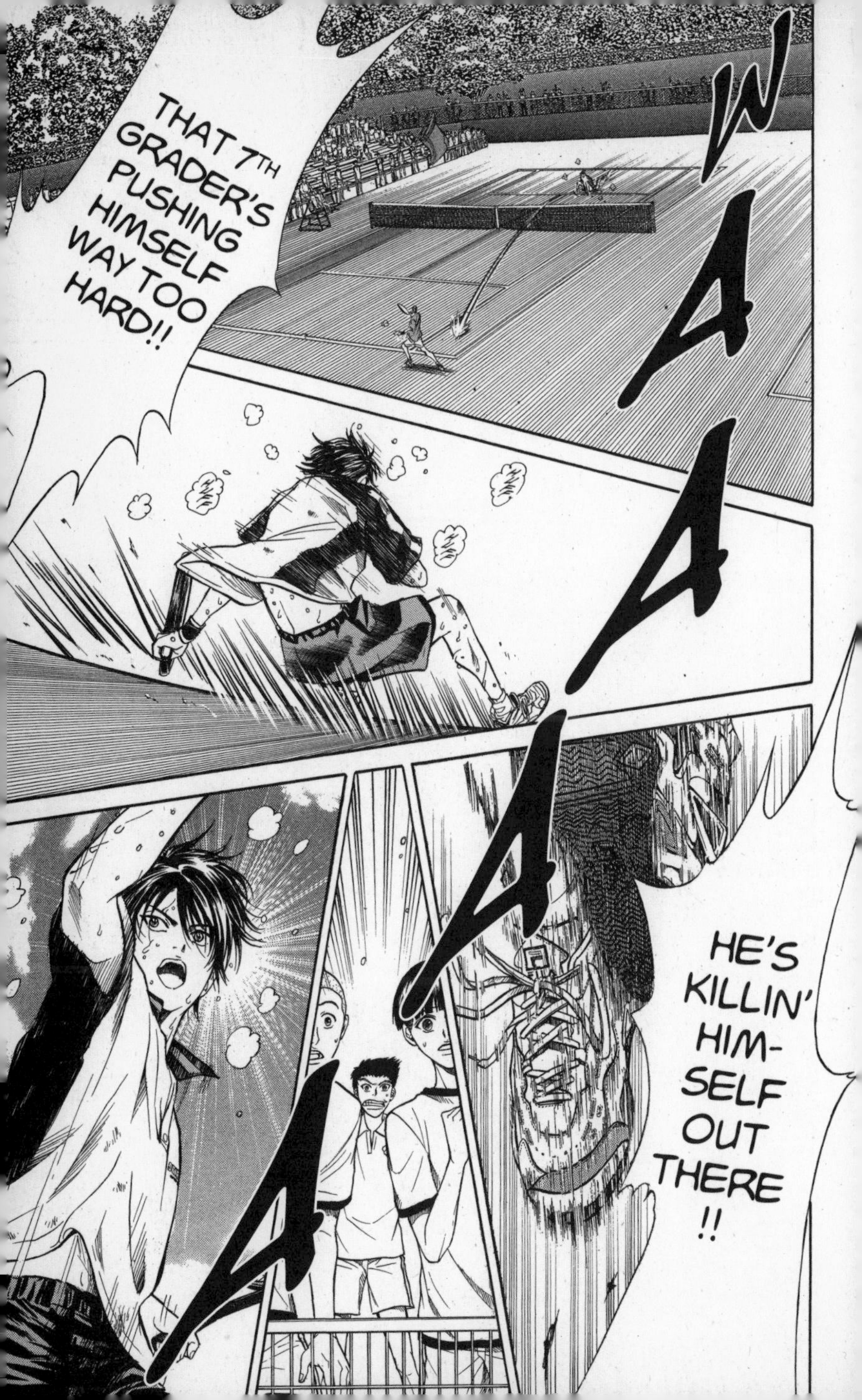
THAT 7TH GRADER'S PUSHING HIMSELF WAY TOO HARD!!
HE'S KILLIN' HIM-SELF OUT THERE!!

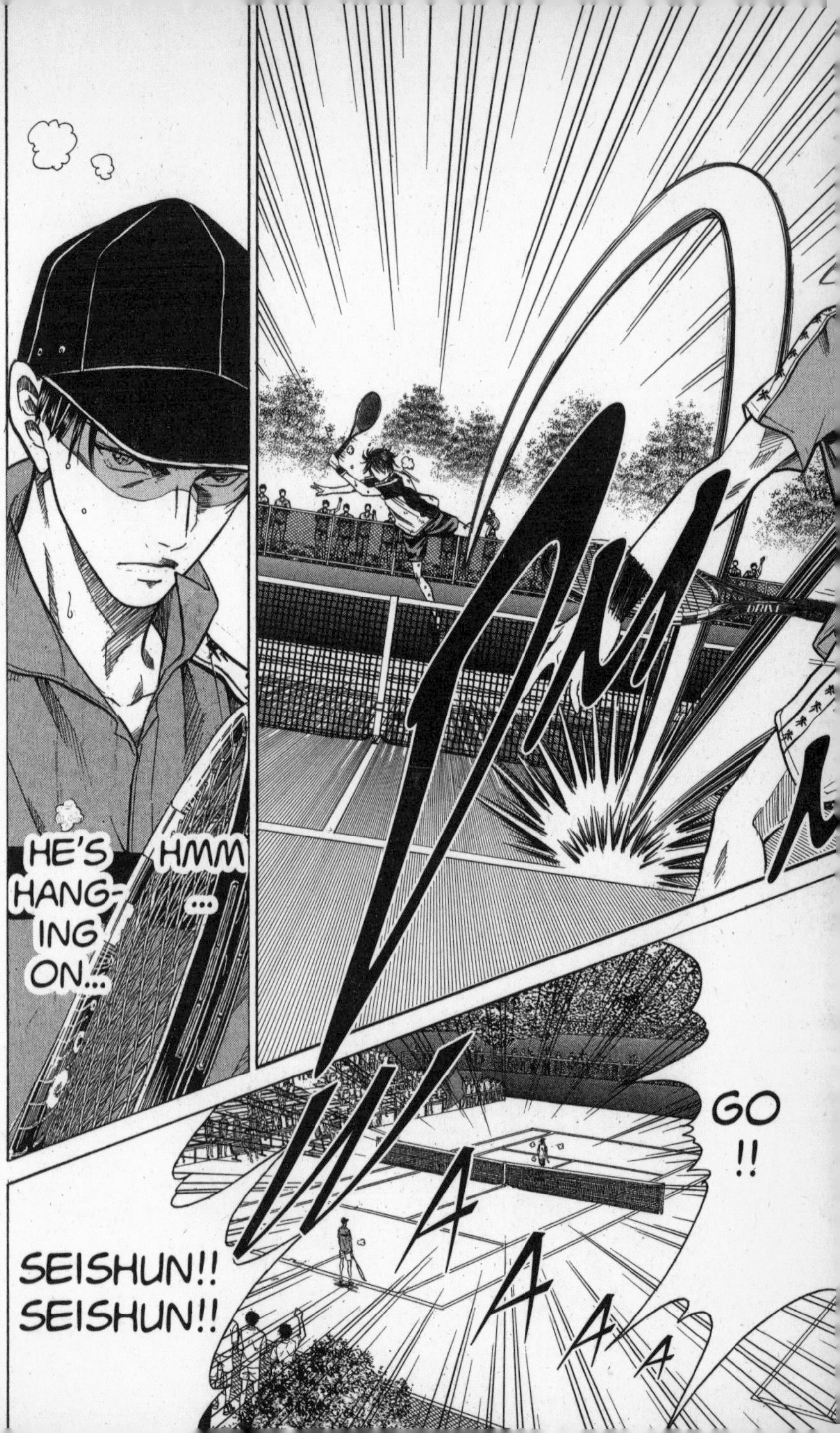
HMM ...
HE'S HANGING ON...
GO !!
SEISHUN!! SEISHUN!!

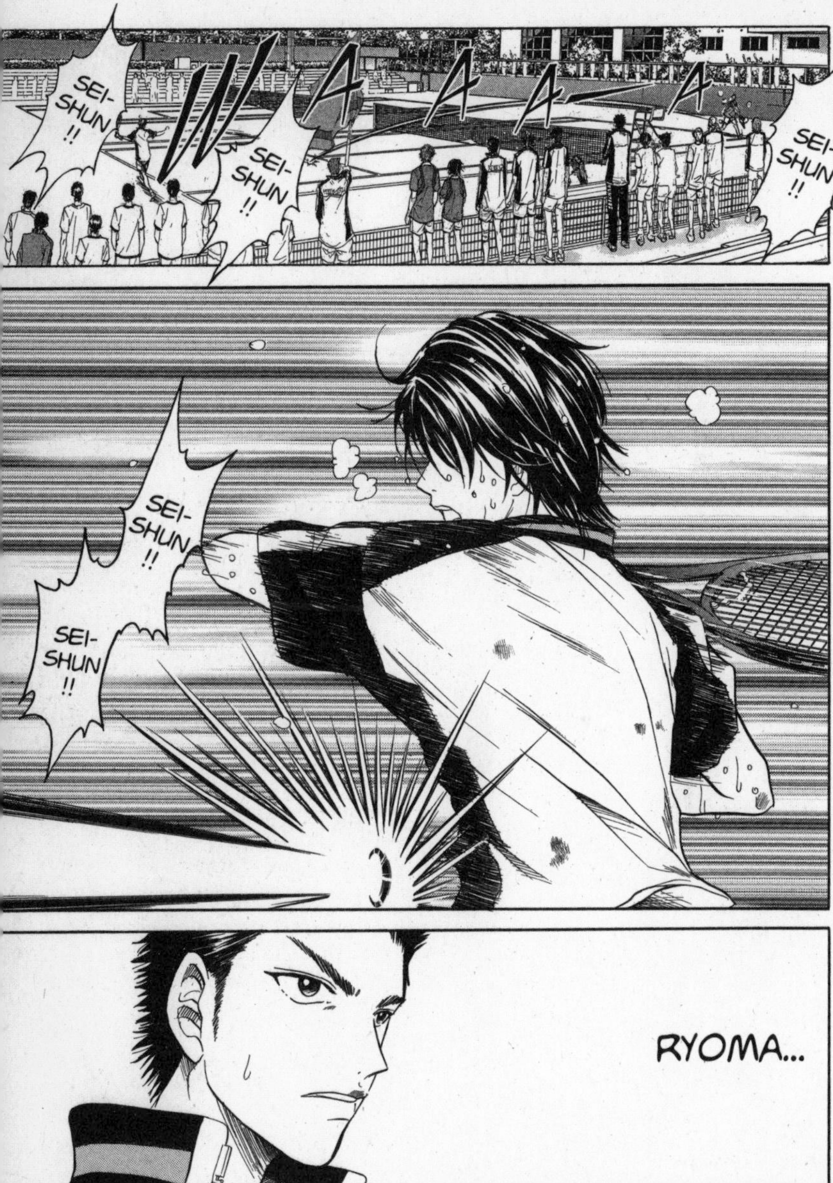
SEI-SHUN !!
WAAA-A
SEI-SHUN !!
SEI-SHUN !!
SEI-SHUN !!
SEI-SHUN !!
RYOMA...

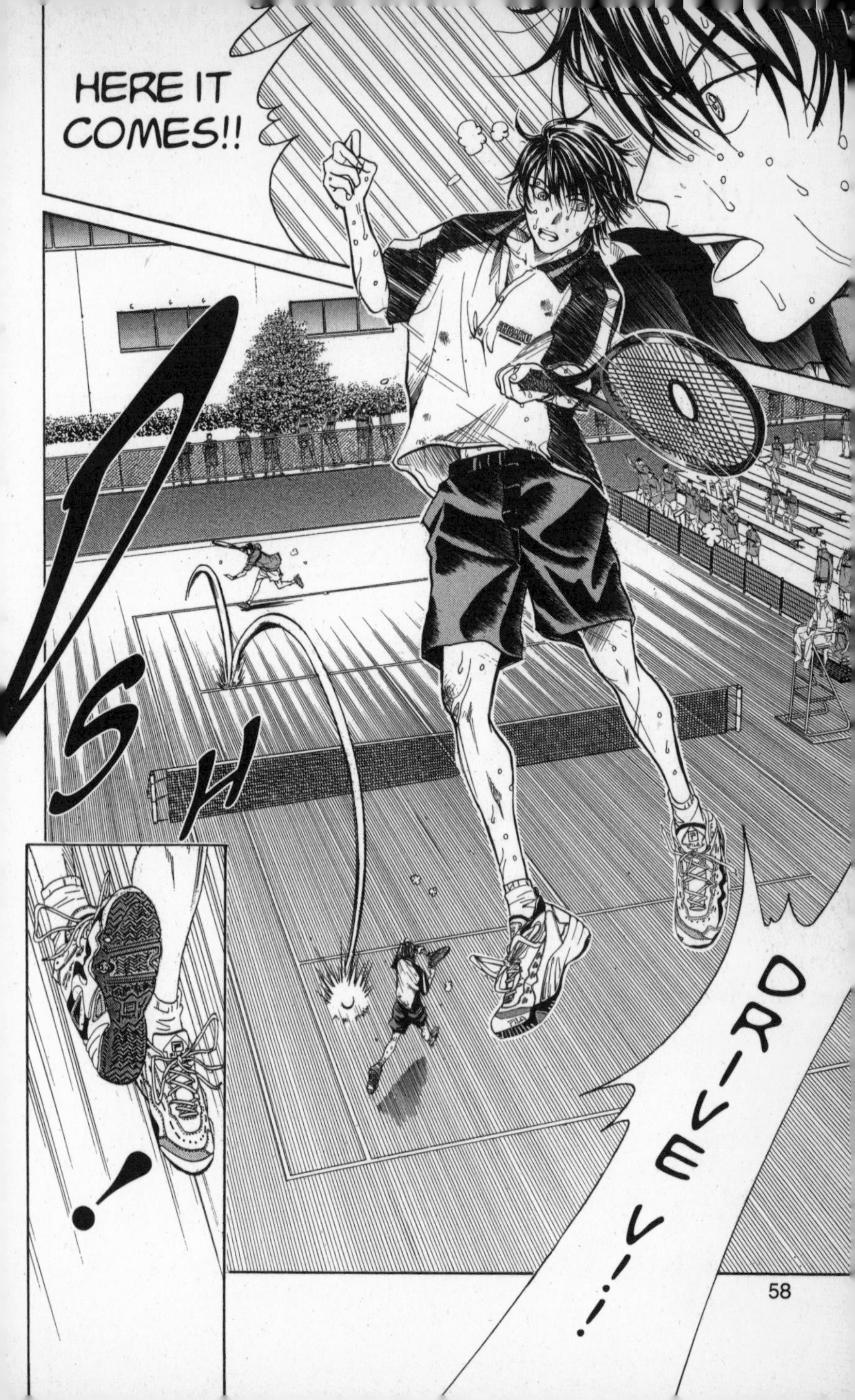
HERE IT COMES!!
VSH
!
DRIVE V!!

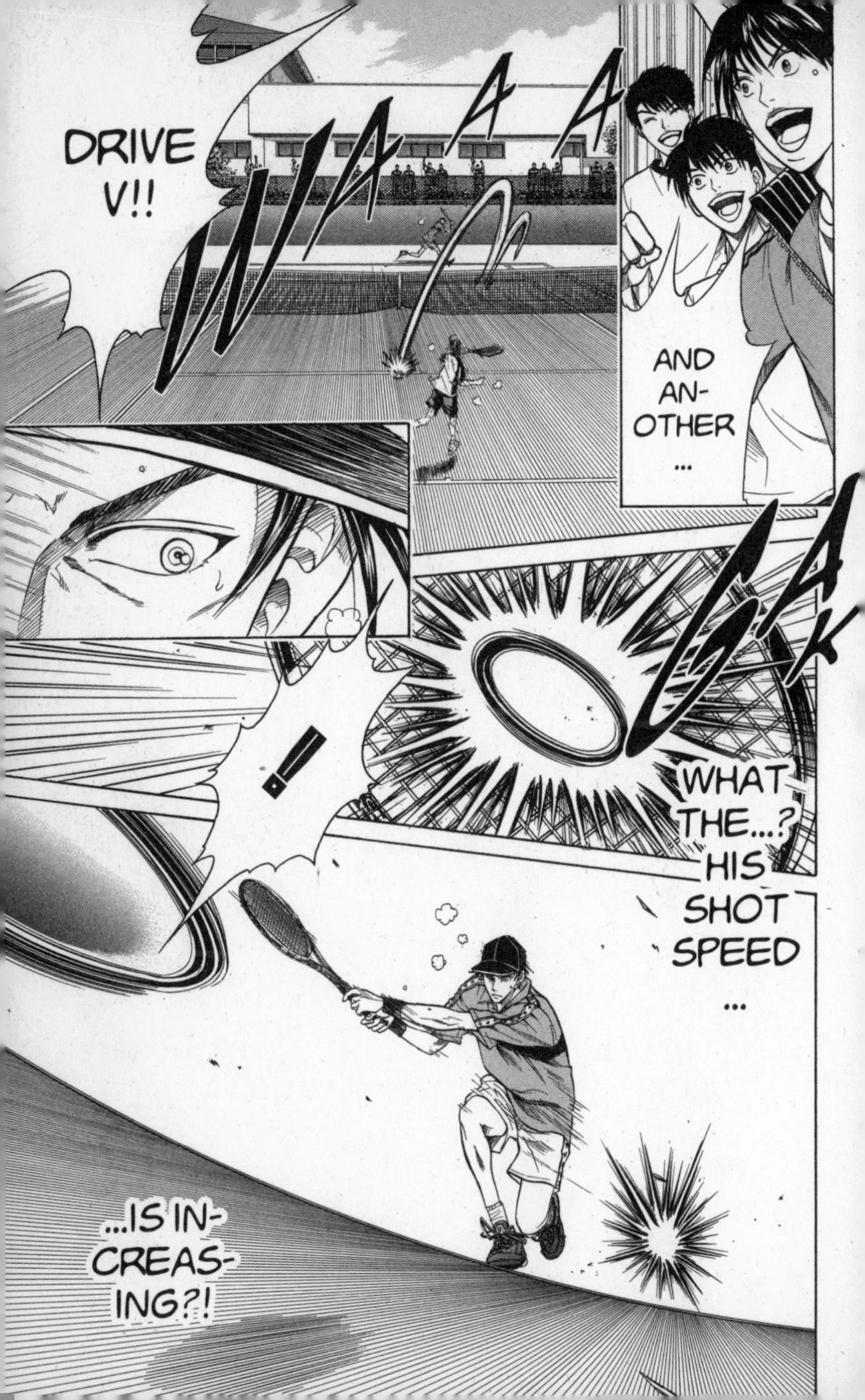
AND AN-OTHER ...
WAAAAN
DRIVE V!!
GAK
!
WHAT THE...? HIS SHOT SPEED ...
...IS IN-CREAS-ING?!

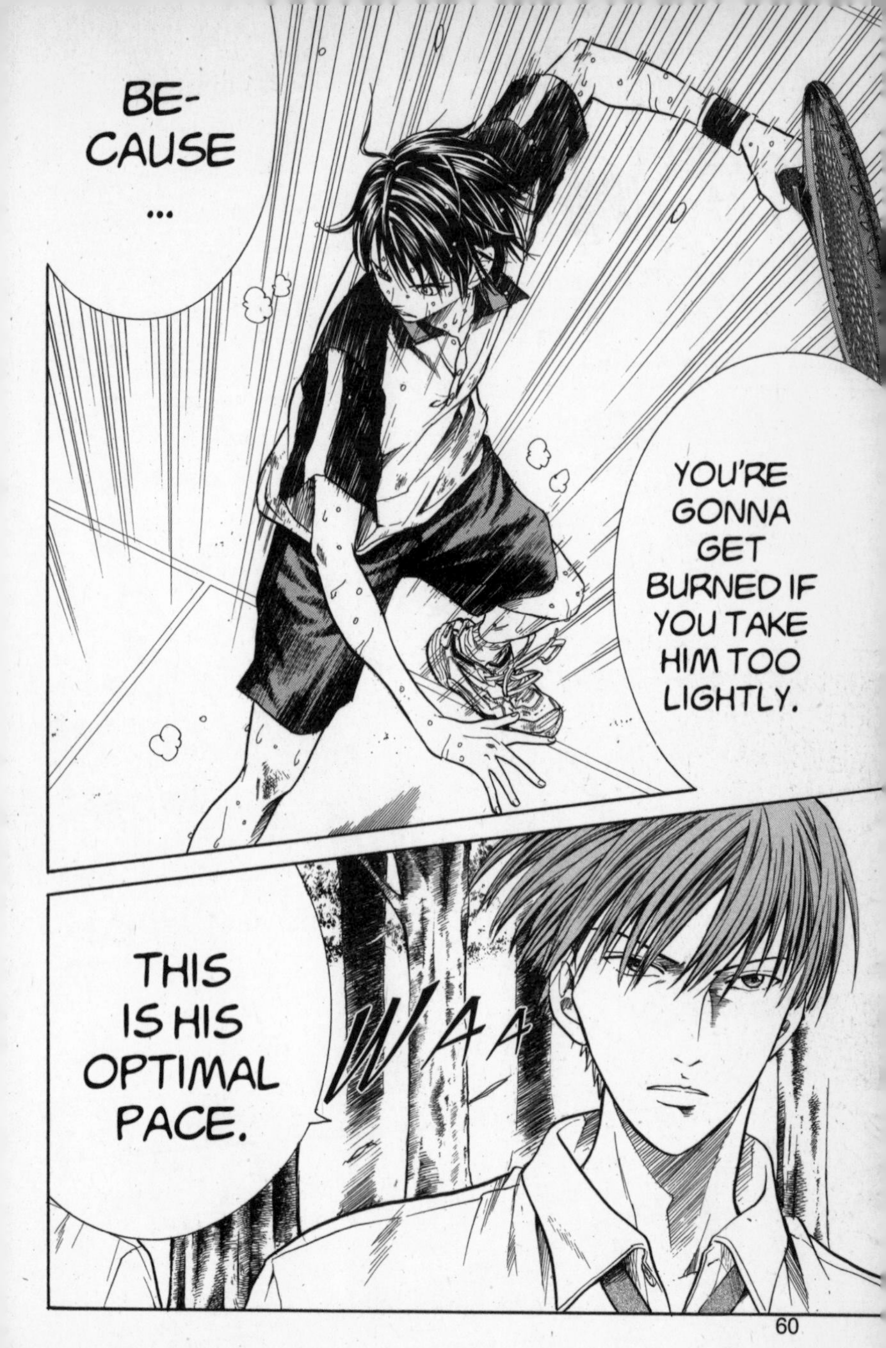
BE-CAUSE ...
YOU'RE GONNA GET BURNED IF YOU TAKE HIM TOO LIGHTLY.
WAA
THIS IS HIS OPTIMAL PACE.

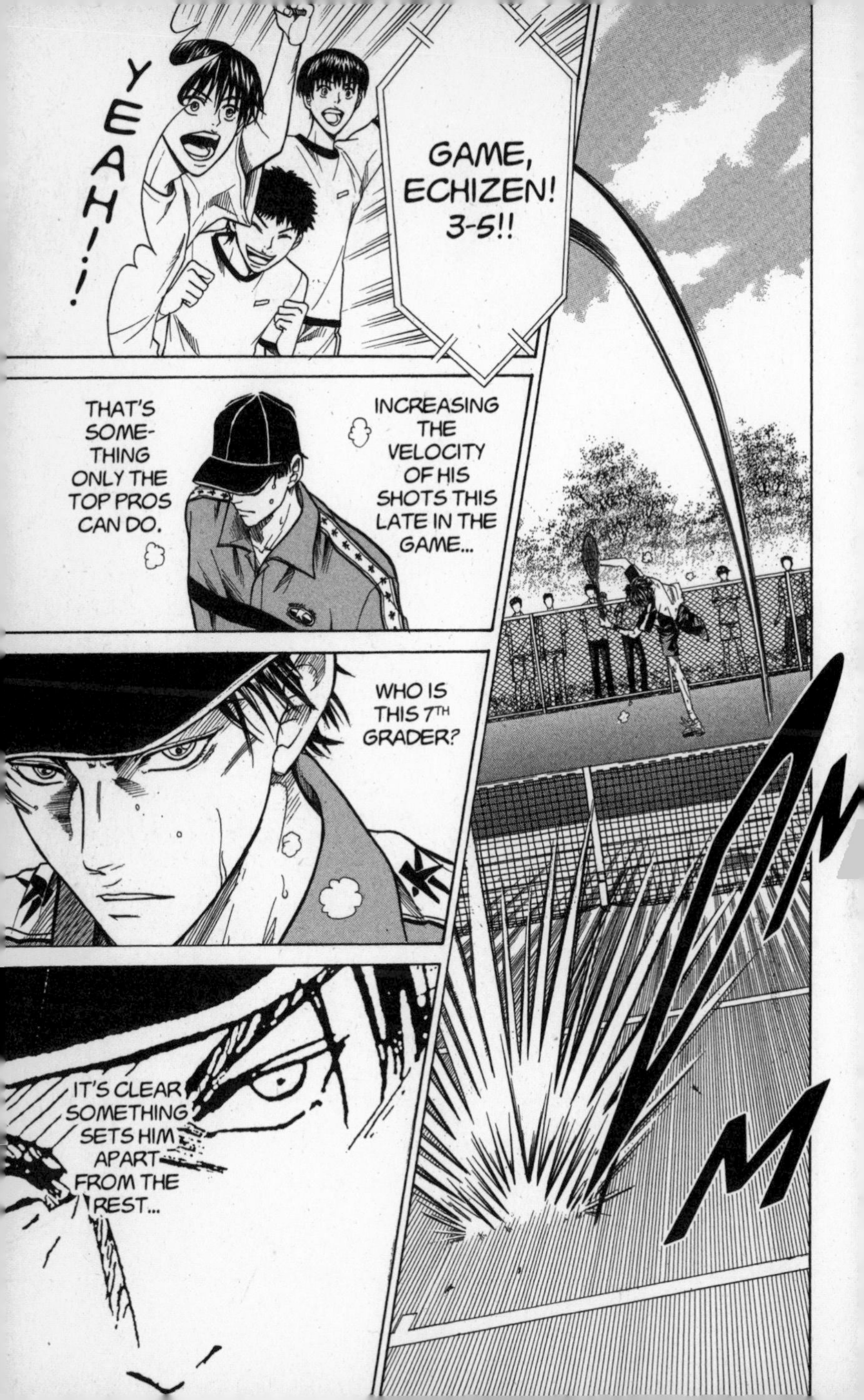
GAME, ECHIZEN! 3-5!!
YEAH!!!
INCREASING THE VELOCITY OF HIS SHOTS THIS LATE IN THE GAME...
THAT'S SOME-THING ONLY THE TOP PROS CAN DO.
WHO IS THIS 7TH GRADER?
IT'S CLEAR SOMETHING SETS HIM APART FROM THE REST...

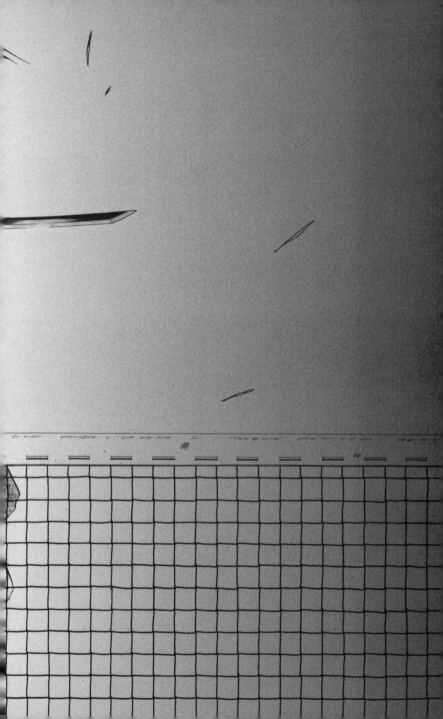

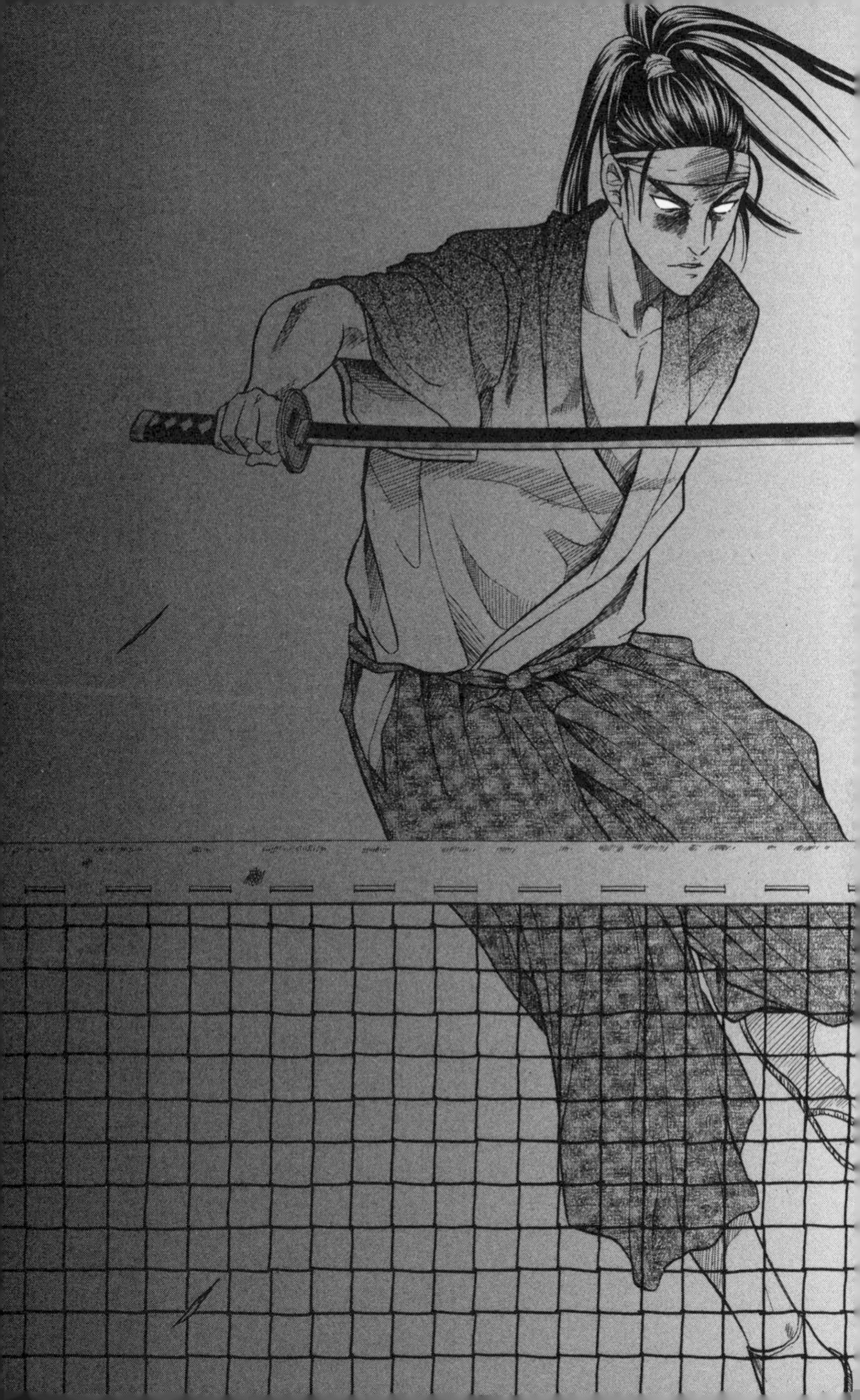

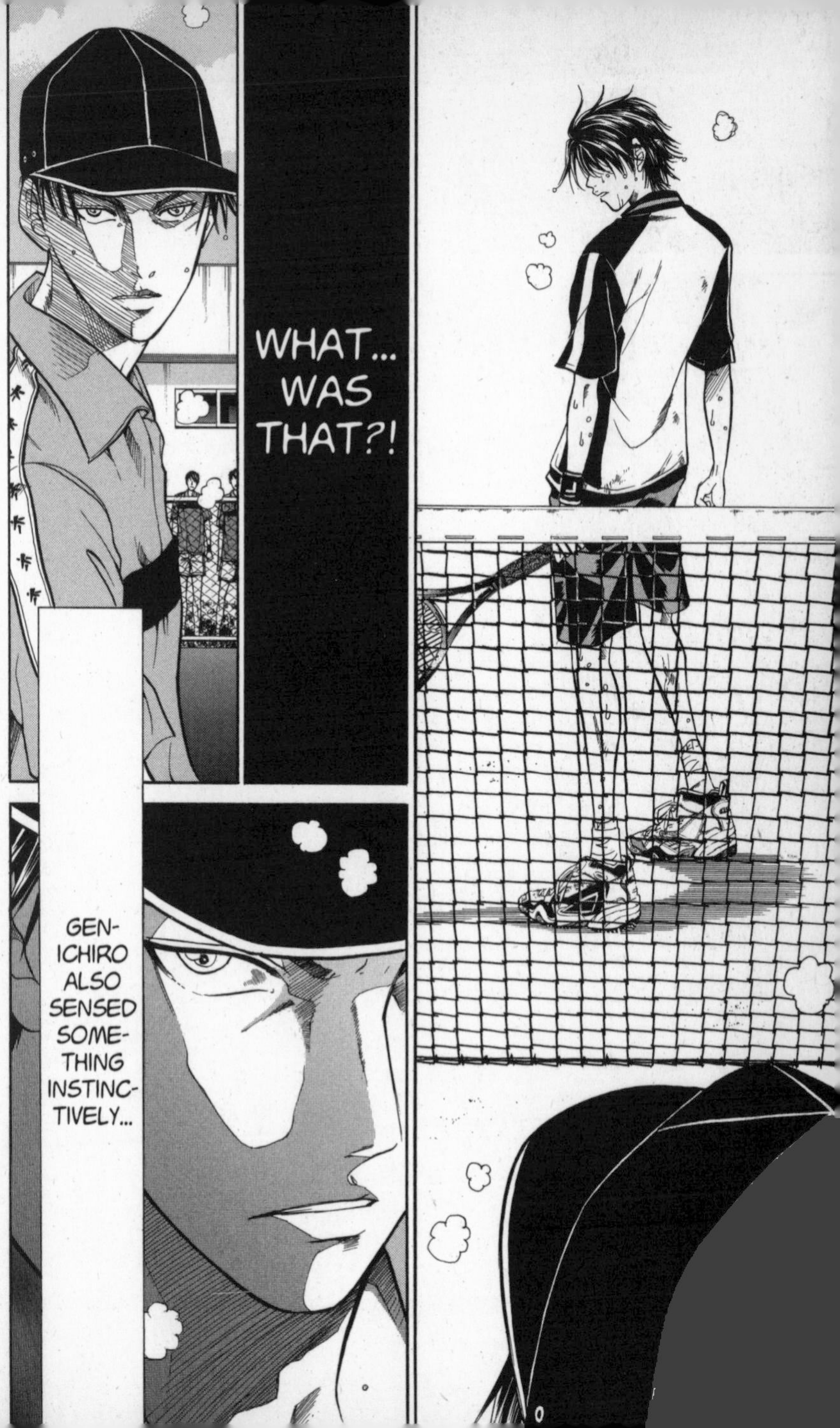
WHAT... WAS THAT?!
GEN-ICHIRO ALSO SENSED SOME-THING INSTINC-TIVELY...

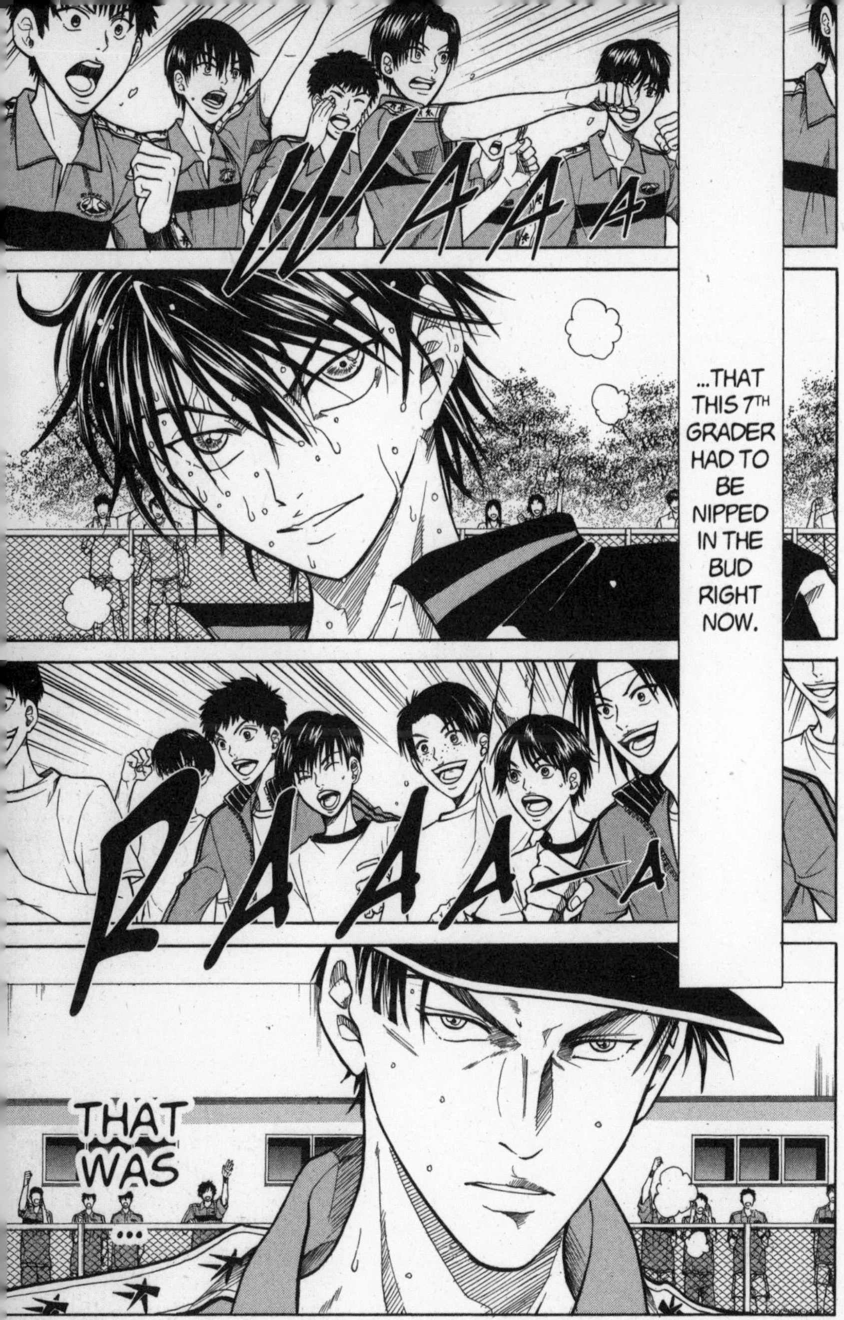

WAAA
...THAT THIS 7TH GRADER HAD TO BE NIPPED IN THE BUD RIGHT NOW.
RAAAA
THAT WAS
...

テニスの王子様

THE PRINCE OF TENNIS

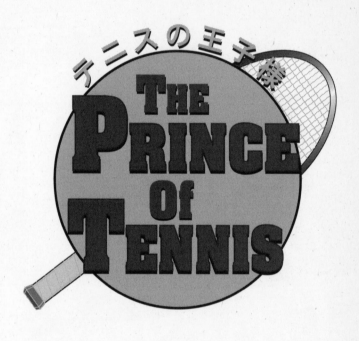

GENIUS 232: FLASHBACK

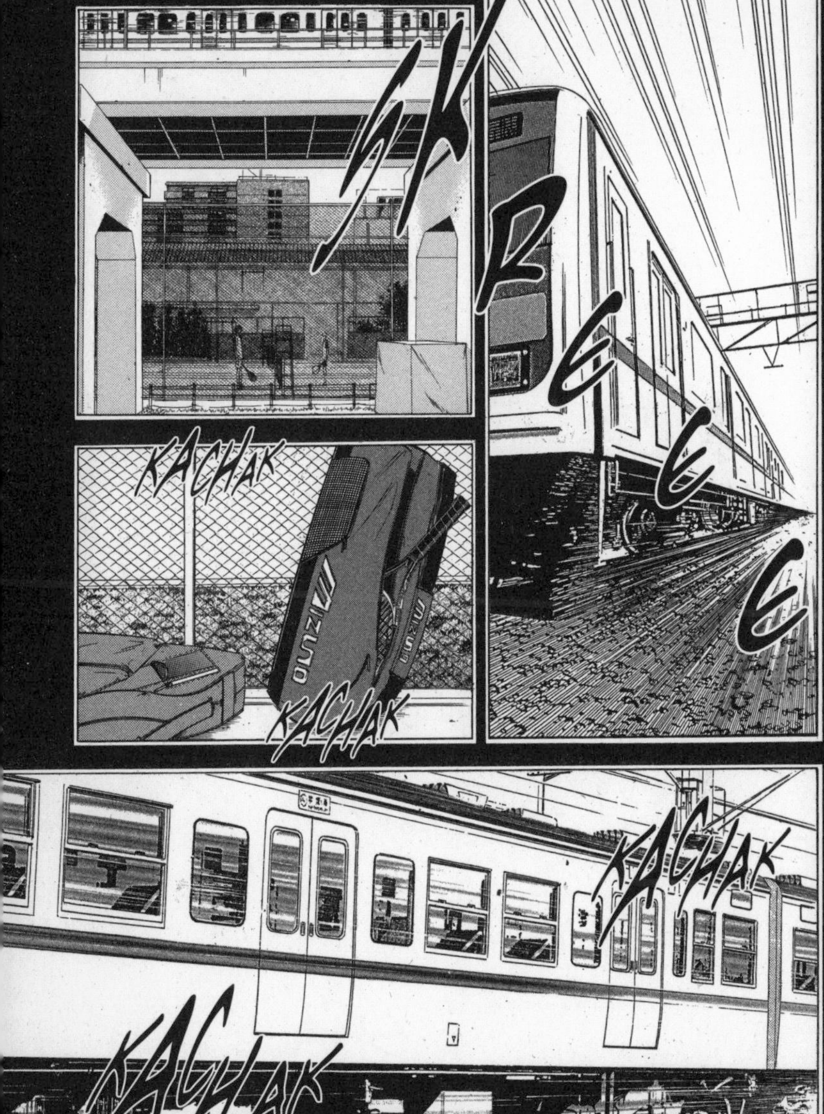
SKREEEEE
KACHAK
MIZUNO
KACHAK
KACHAK
KACHAK

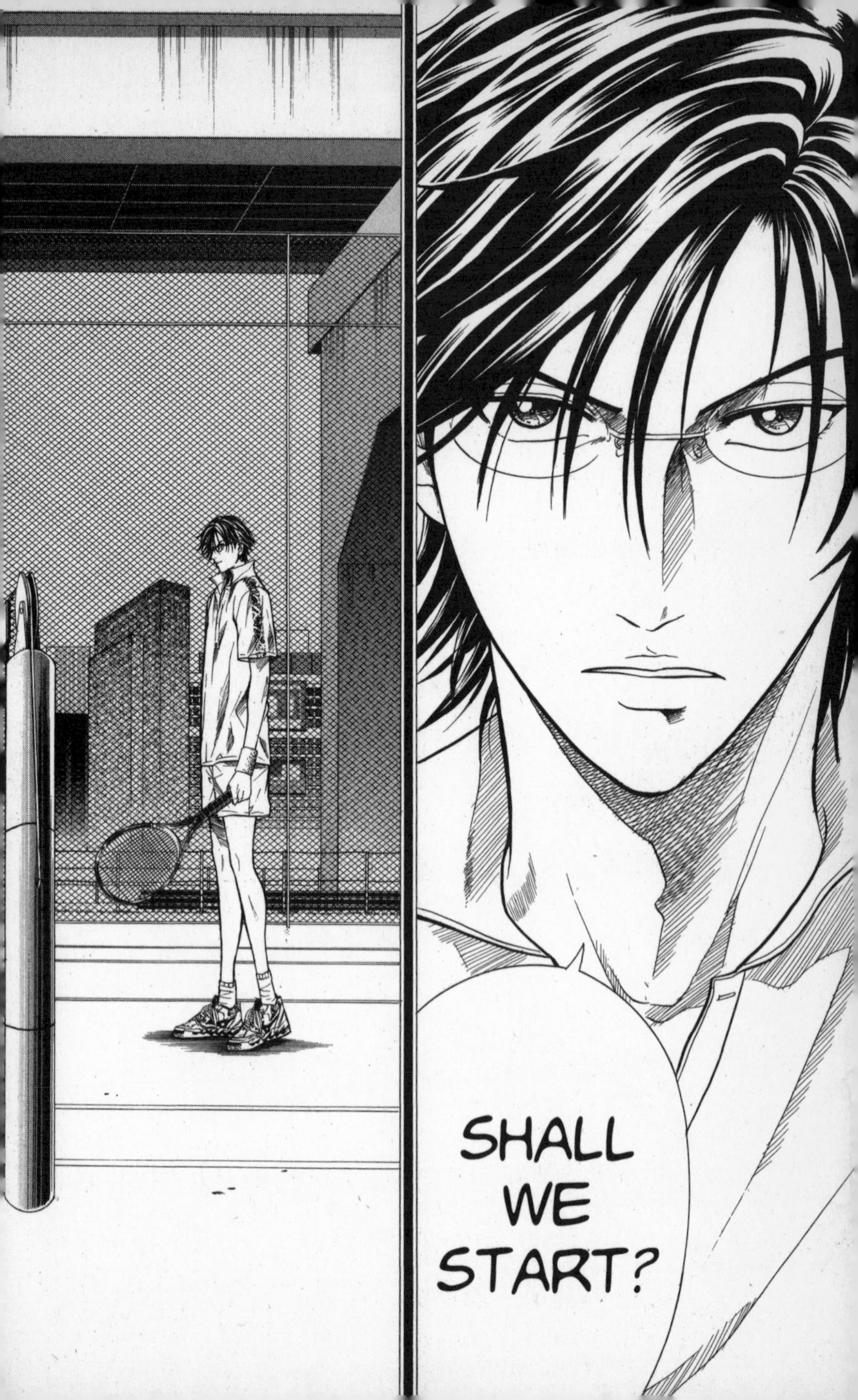
SHALL WE START?

GENIUS 232: FLASHBACK

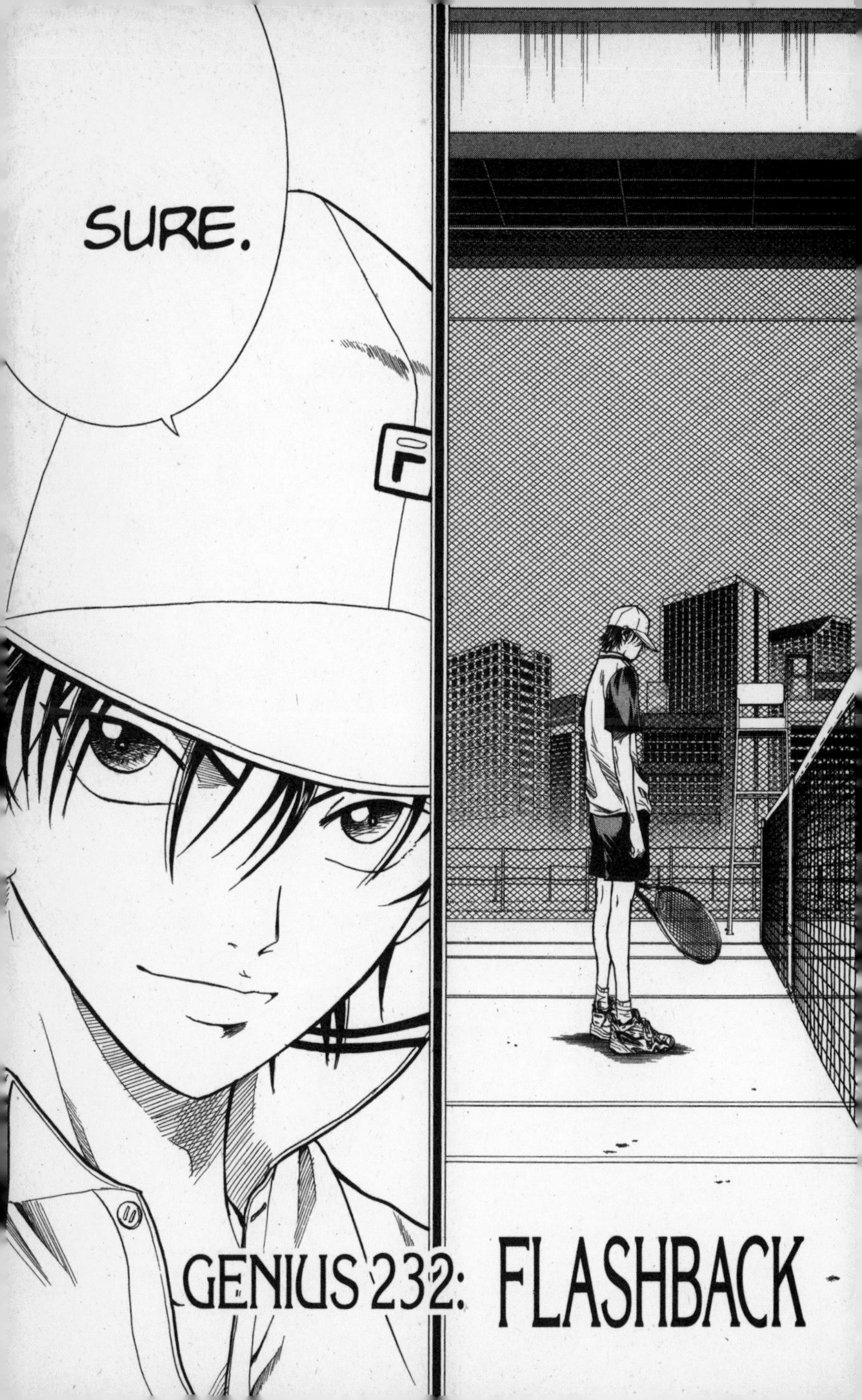
SURE.

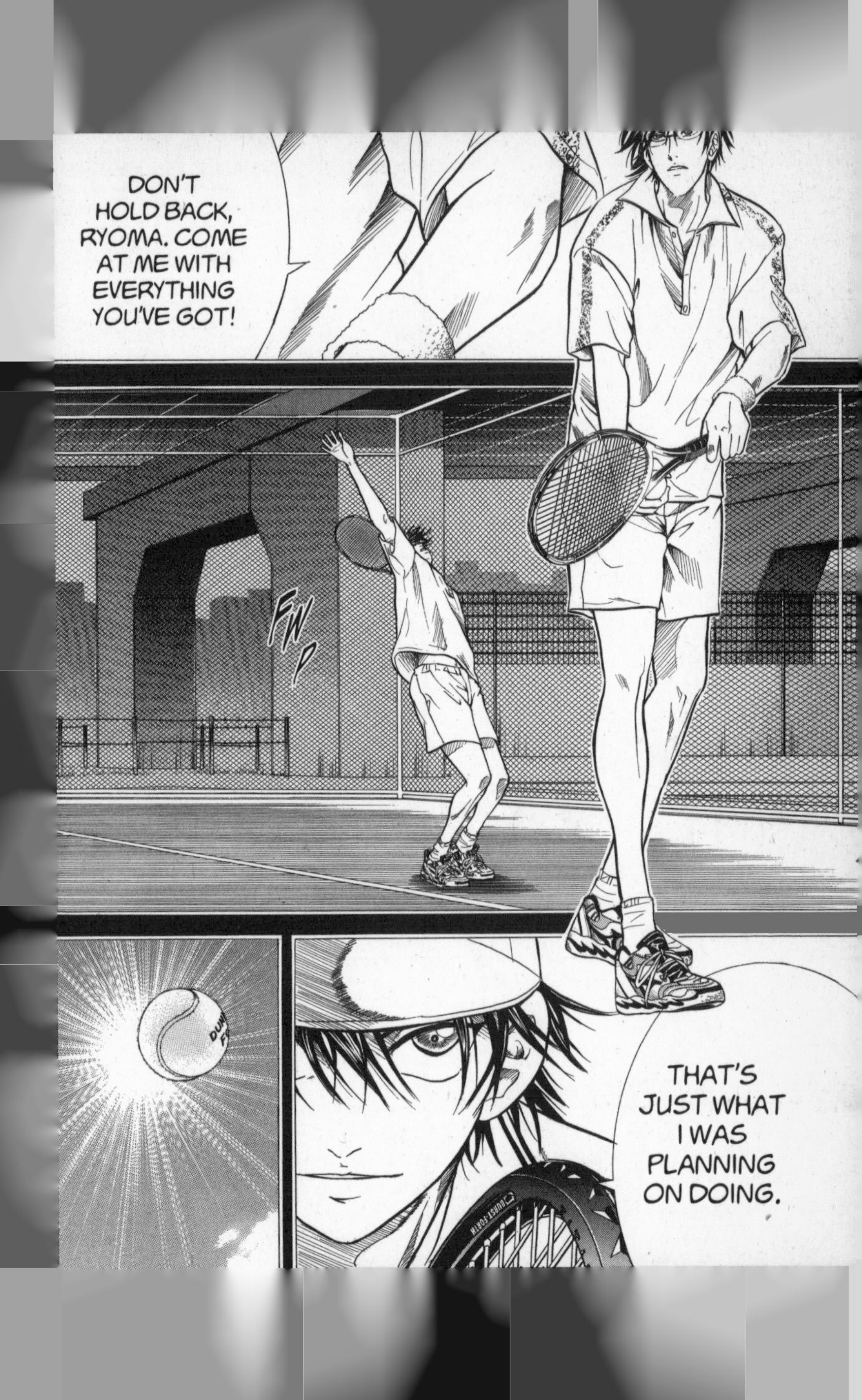
DON'T HOLD BACK, RYOMA. COME AT ME WITH EVERYTHING YOU'VE GOT!
FWP
THAT'S JUST WHAT I WAS PLANNING ON DOING.

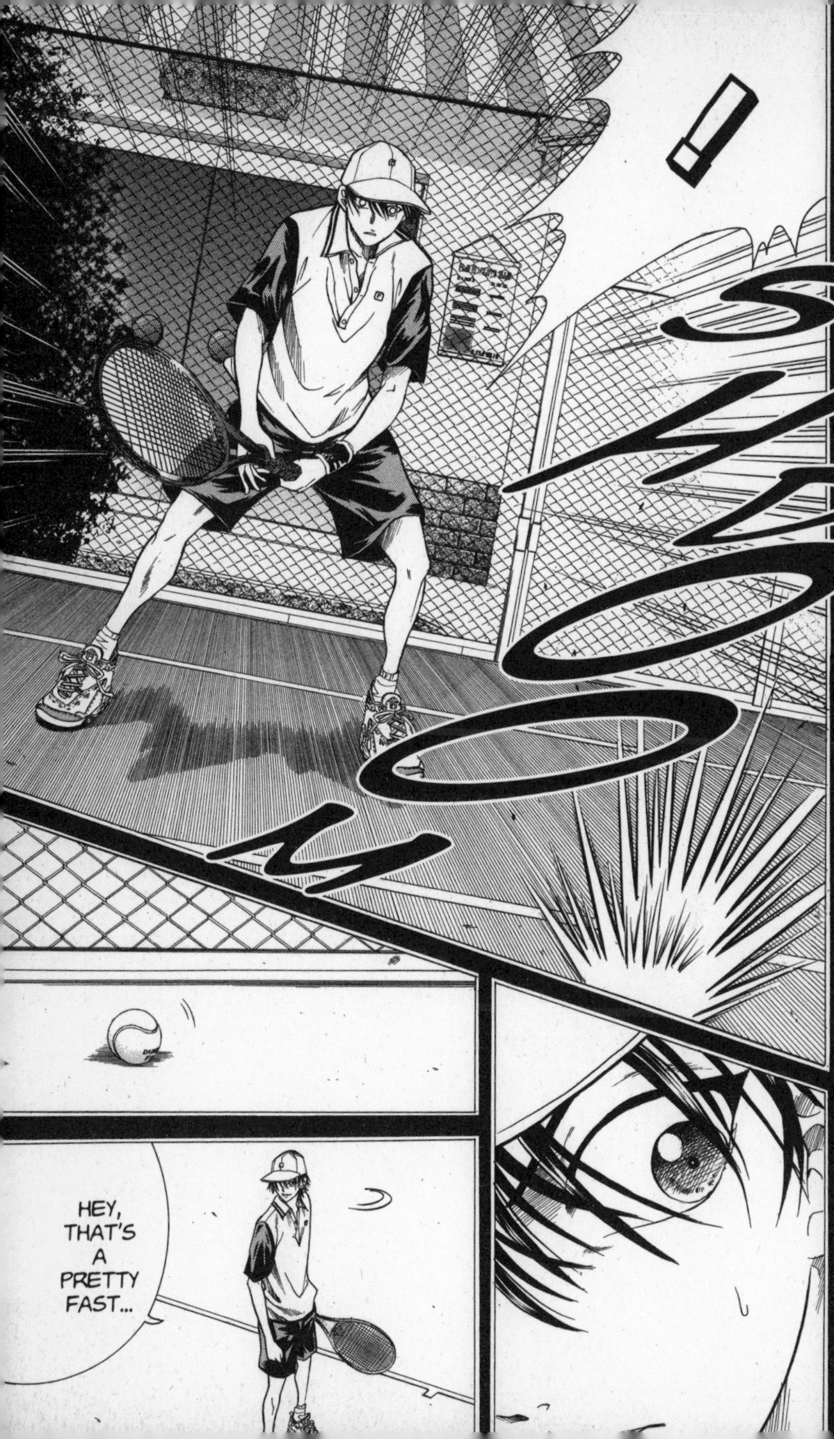
!
SHOOM
HEY, THAT'S A PRETTY FAST...

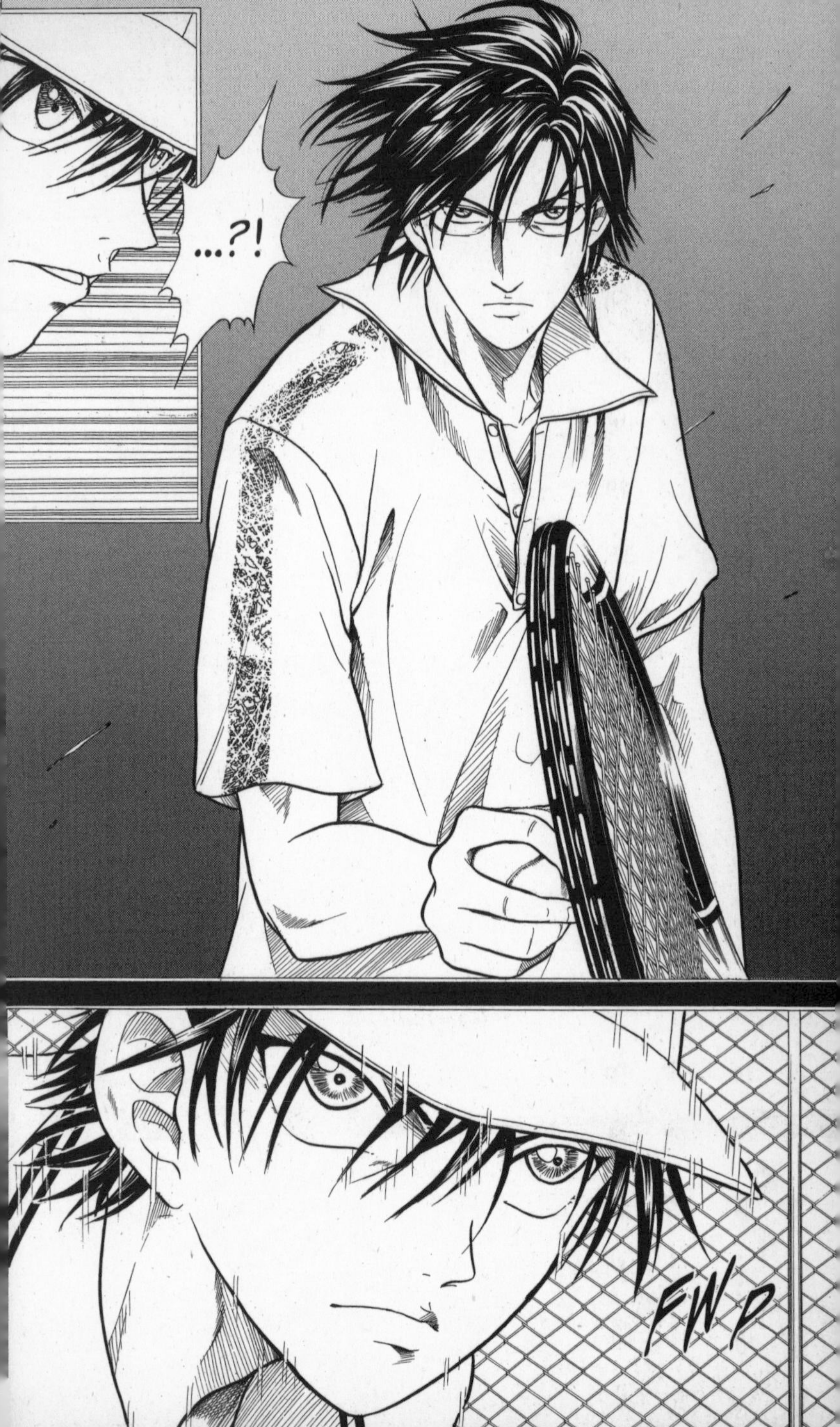
...?!
FWP

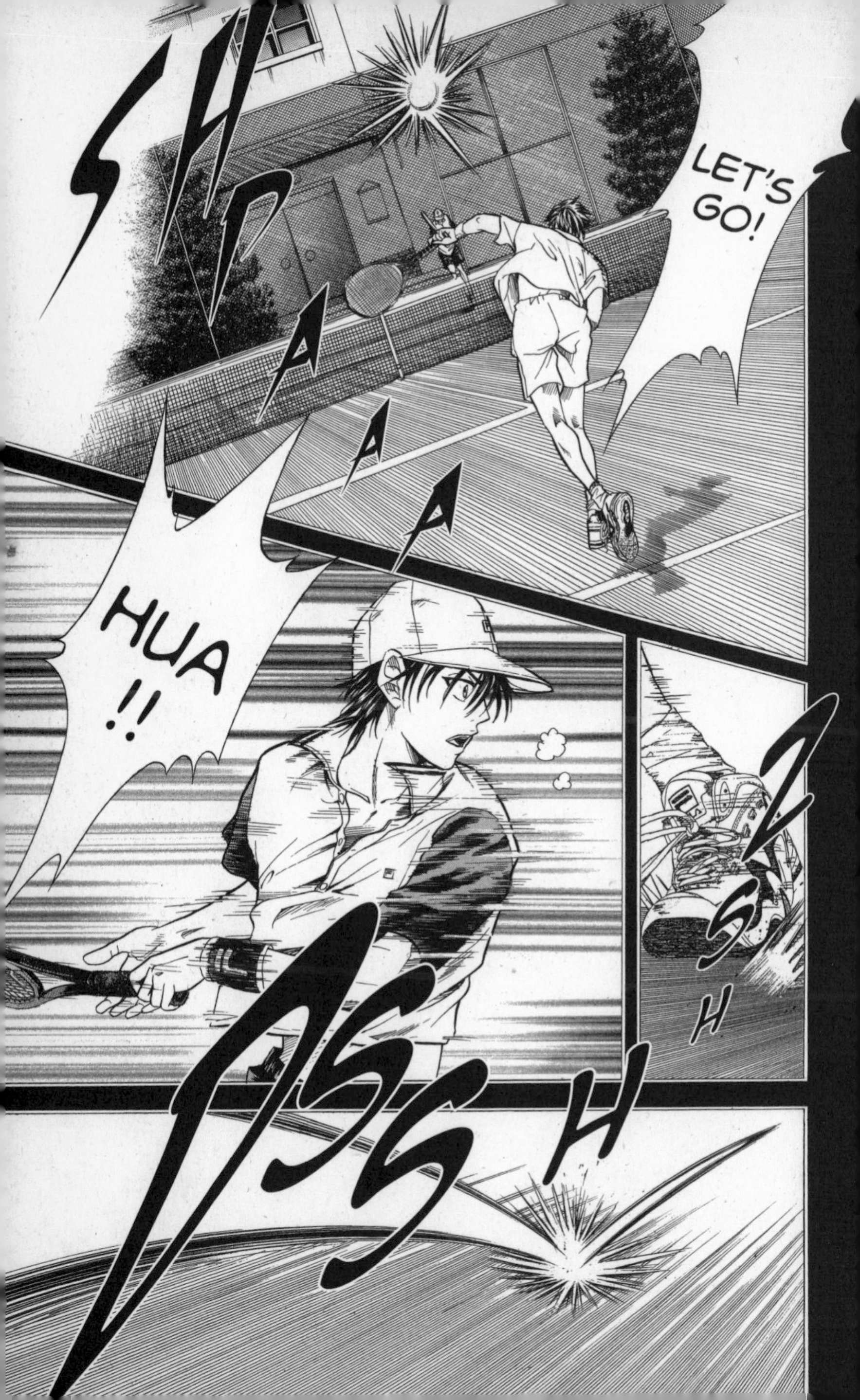
LET'S GO!
SHAAA
HUA!!

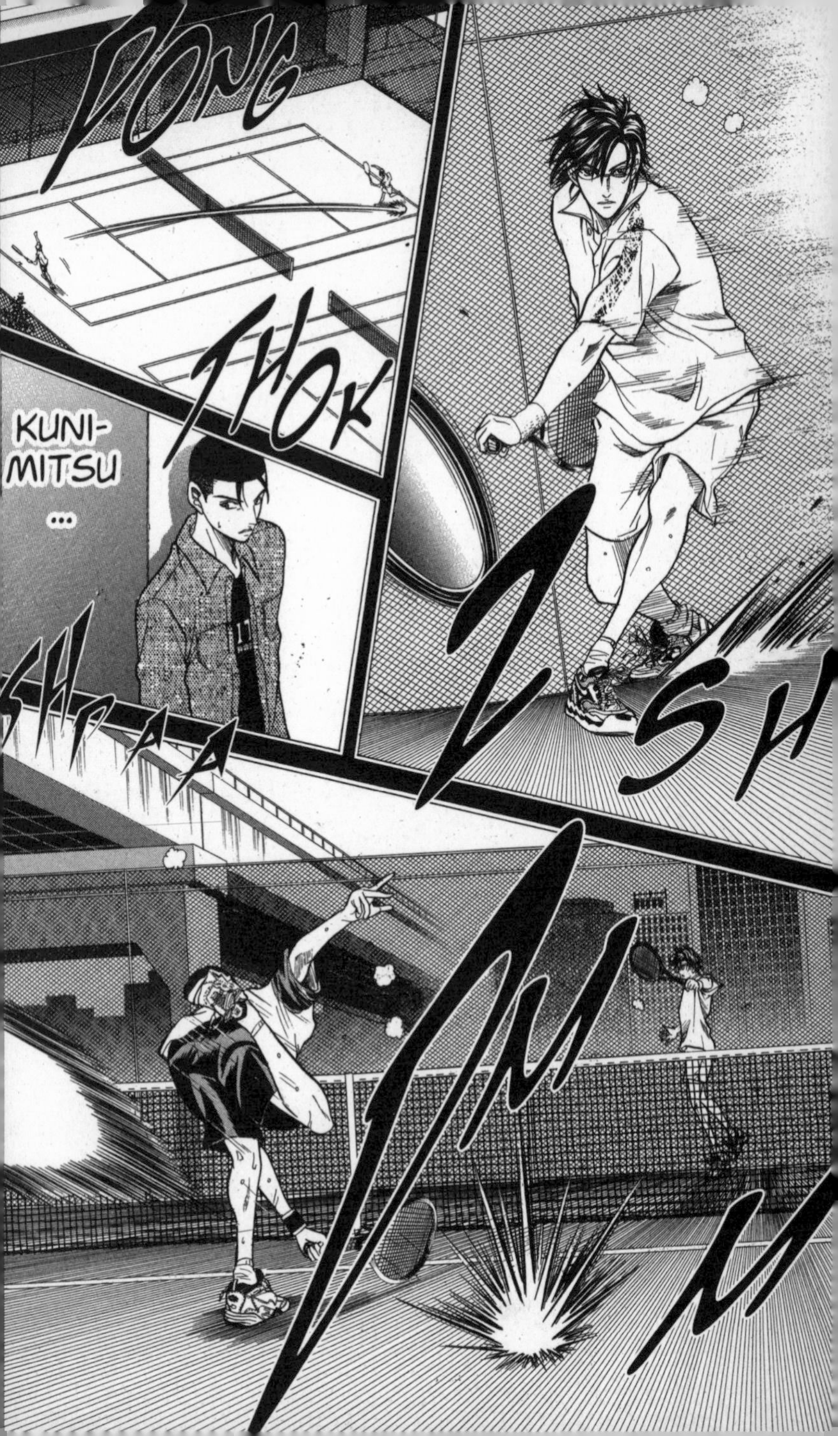
DONG
THOK
KUNI-MITSU...
SHPAAA

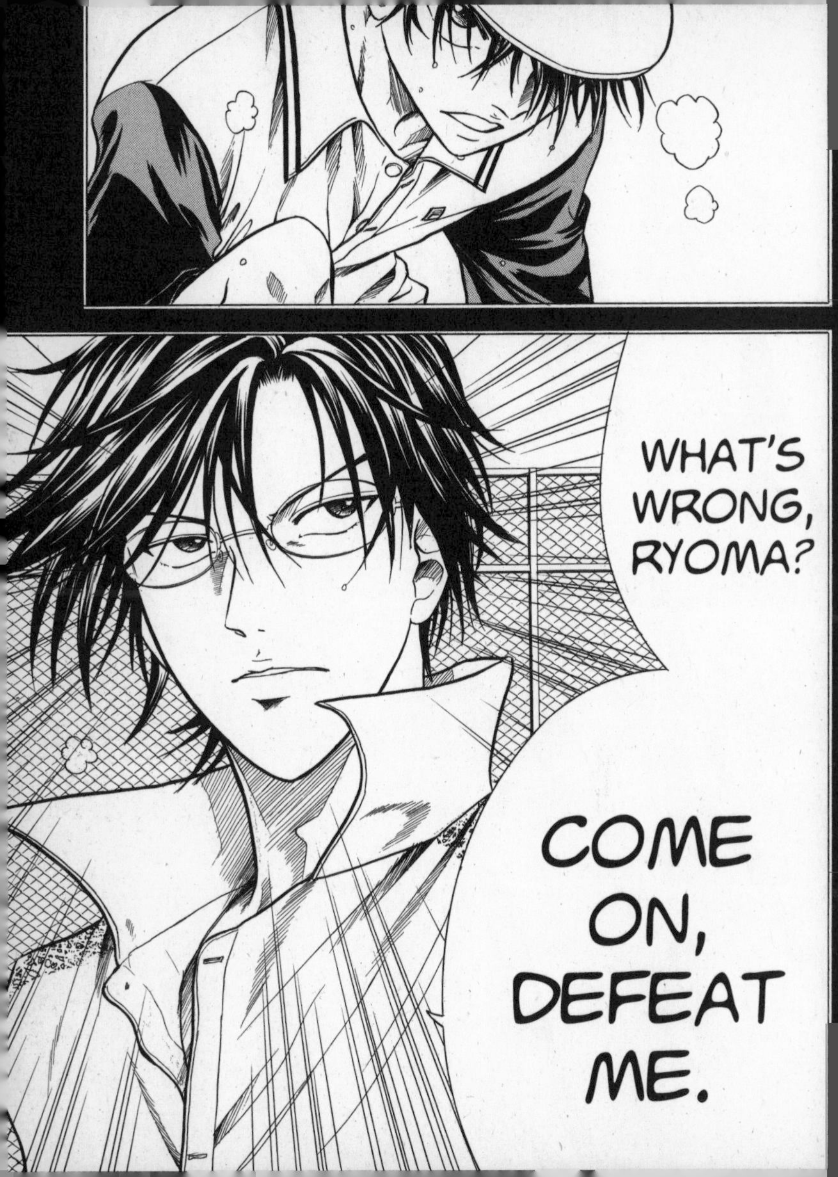
WHAT'S WRONG, RYOMA?
COME ON, DEFEAT ME.

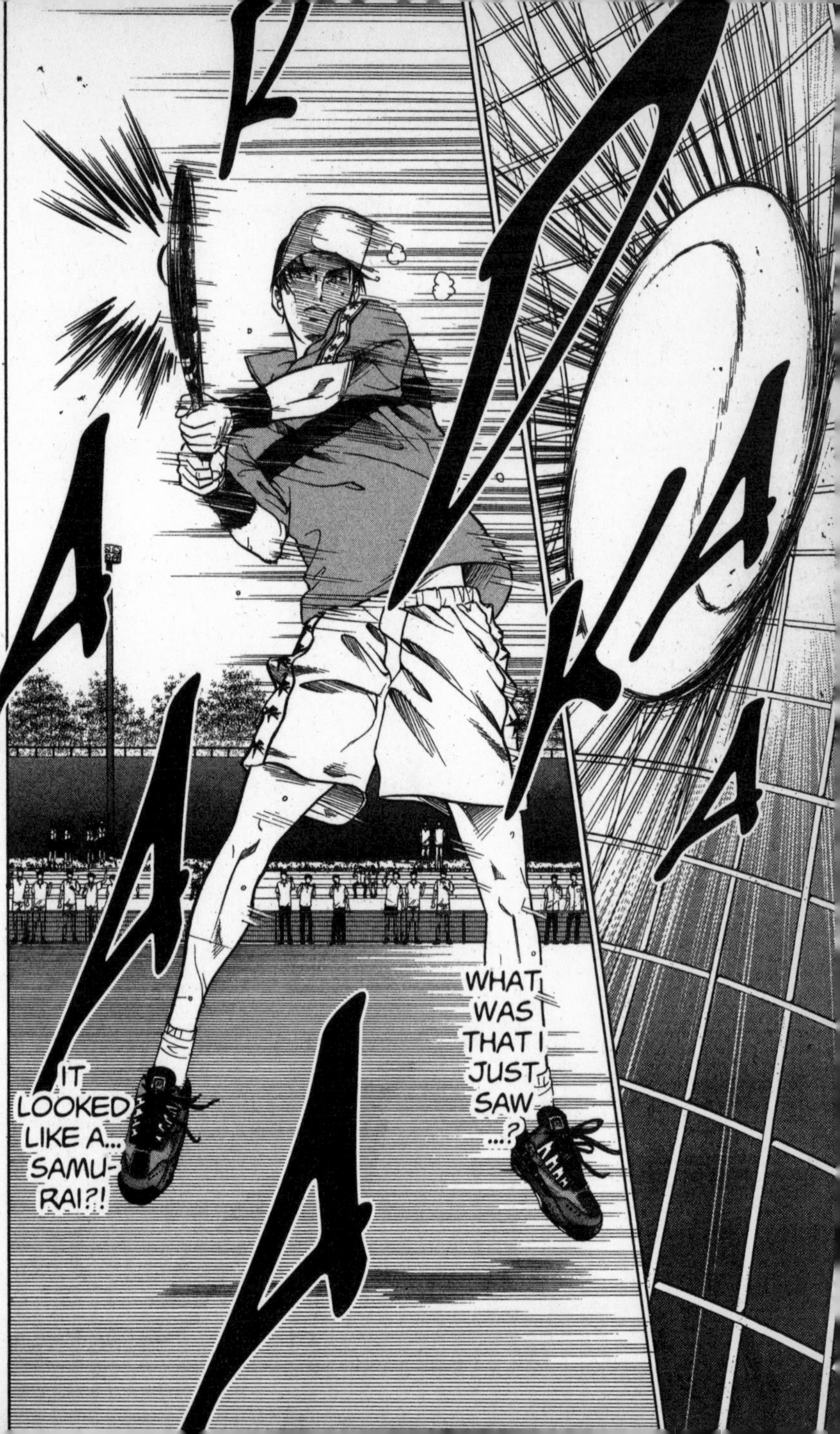
WHAT WAS THAT I JUST SAW...?
IT LOOKED LIKE A... SAMURAI?!

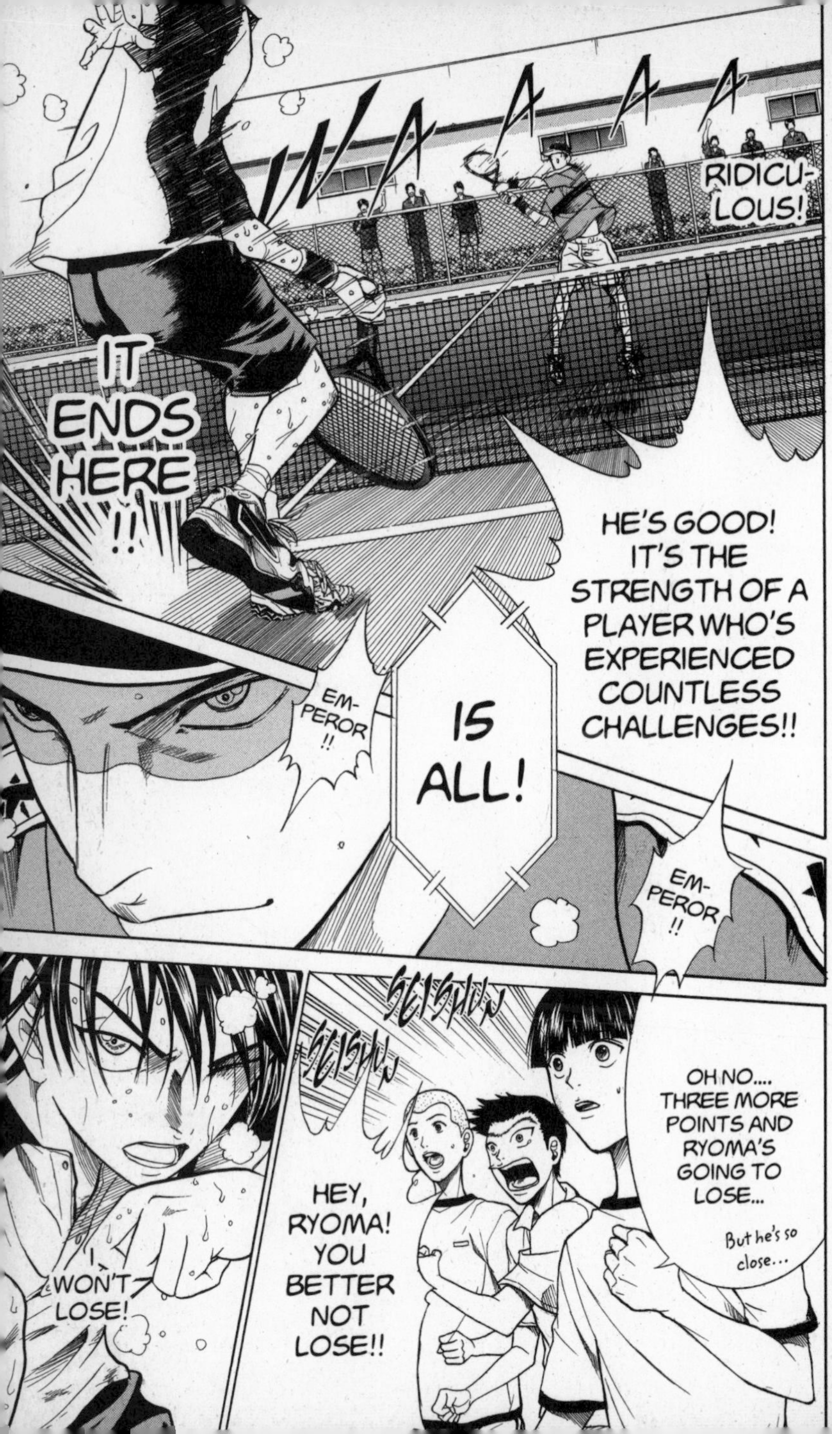
RIDICU-LOUS!
WAAAAA
IT ENDS HERE!!
HE'S GOOD! IT'S THE STRENGTH OF A PLAYER WHO'S EXPERIENCED COUNTLESS CHALLENGES!!
EM-PEROR!!
15 ALL!
EM-PEROR!!
OH NO.... THREE MORE POINTS AND RYOMA'S GOING TO LOSE...
But he's so close...
HEY, RYOMA! YOU BETTER NOT LOSE!!
SEISHUN
SEISHUN
I WON'T LOSE!

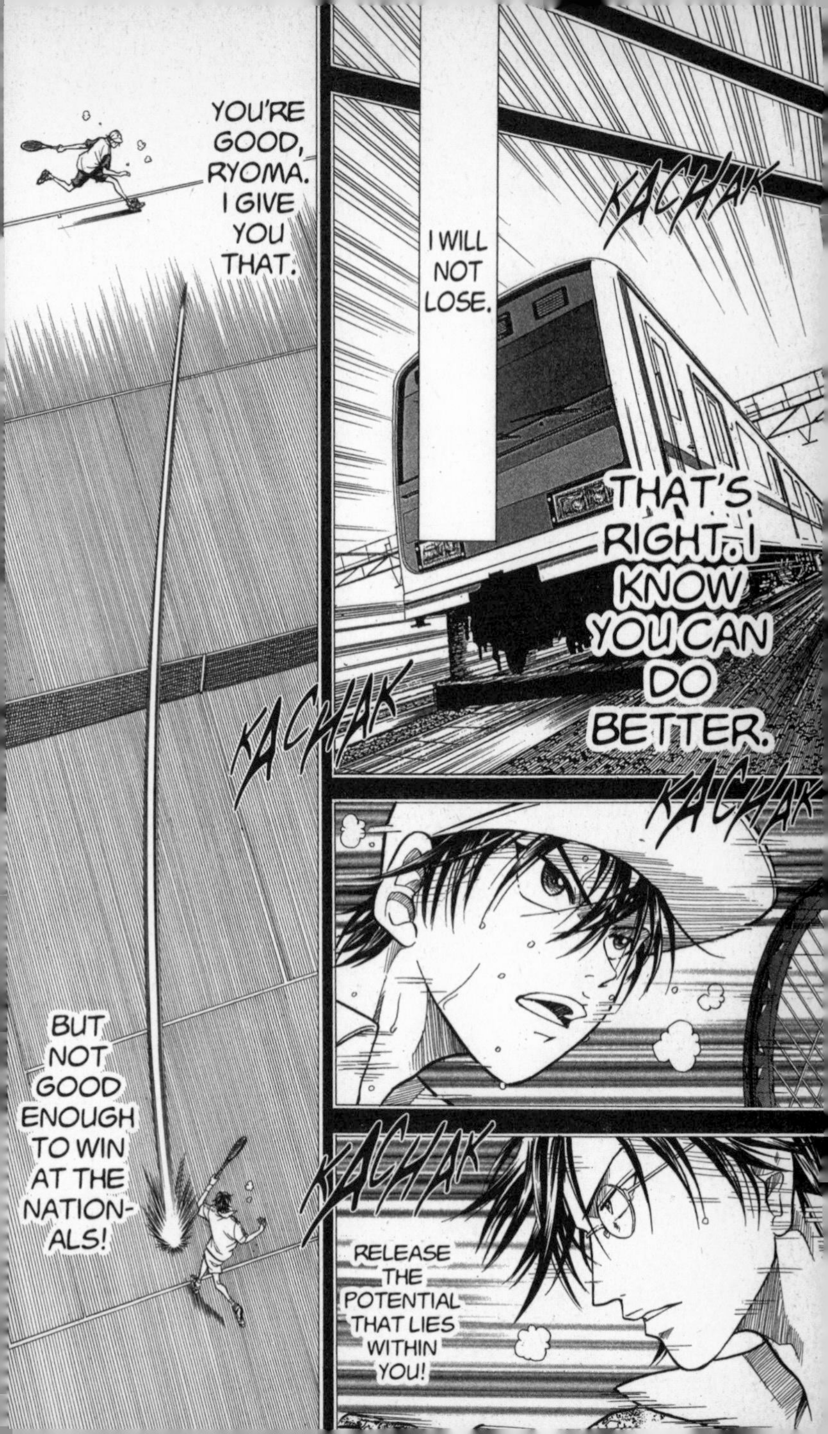
KACHAK
I WILL NOT LOSE.
THAT'S RIGHT. I KNOW YOU CAN DO BETTER.
KACHAK
KACHAK
KACHAK
RELEASE THE POTENTIAL THAT LIES WITHIN YOU!
YOU'RE GOOD, RYOMA. I GIVE YOU THAT.
BUT NOT GOOD ENOUGH TO WIN AT THE NATION-ALS!

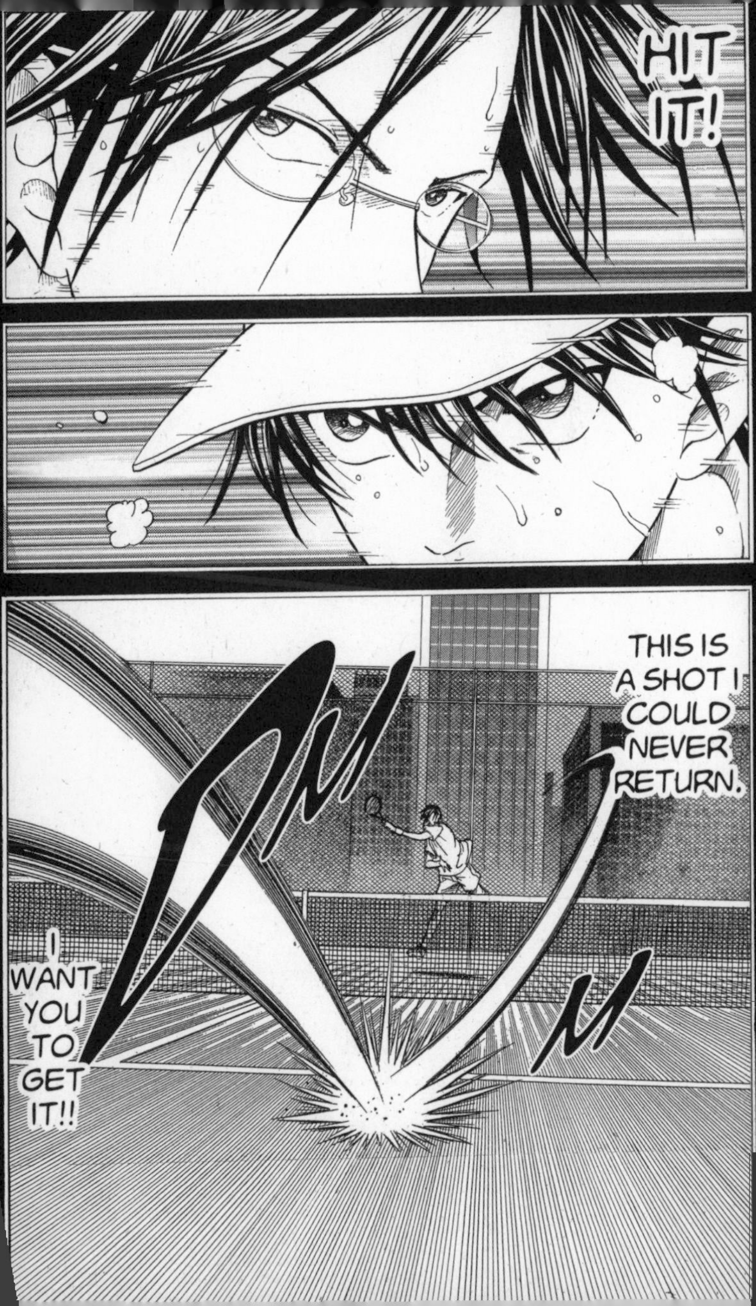
HIT IT!
THIS IS A SHOT I COULD NEVER RETURN.
I WANT YOU TO GET IT!!

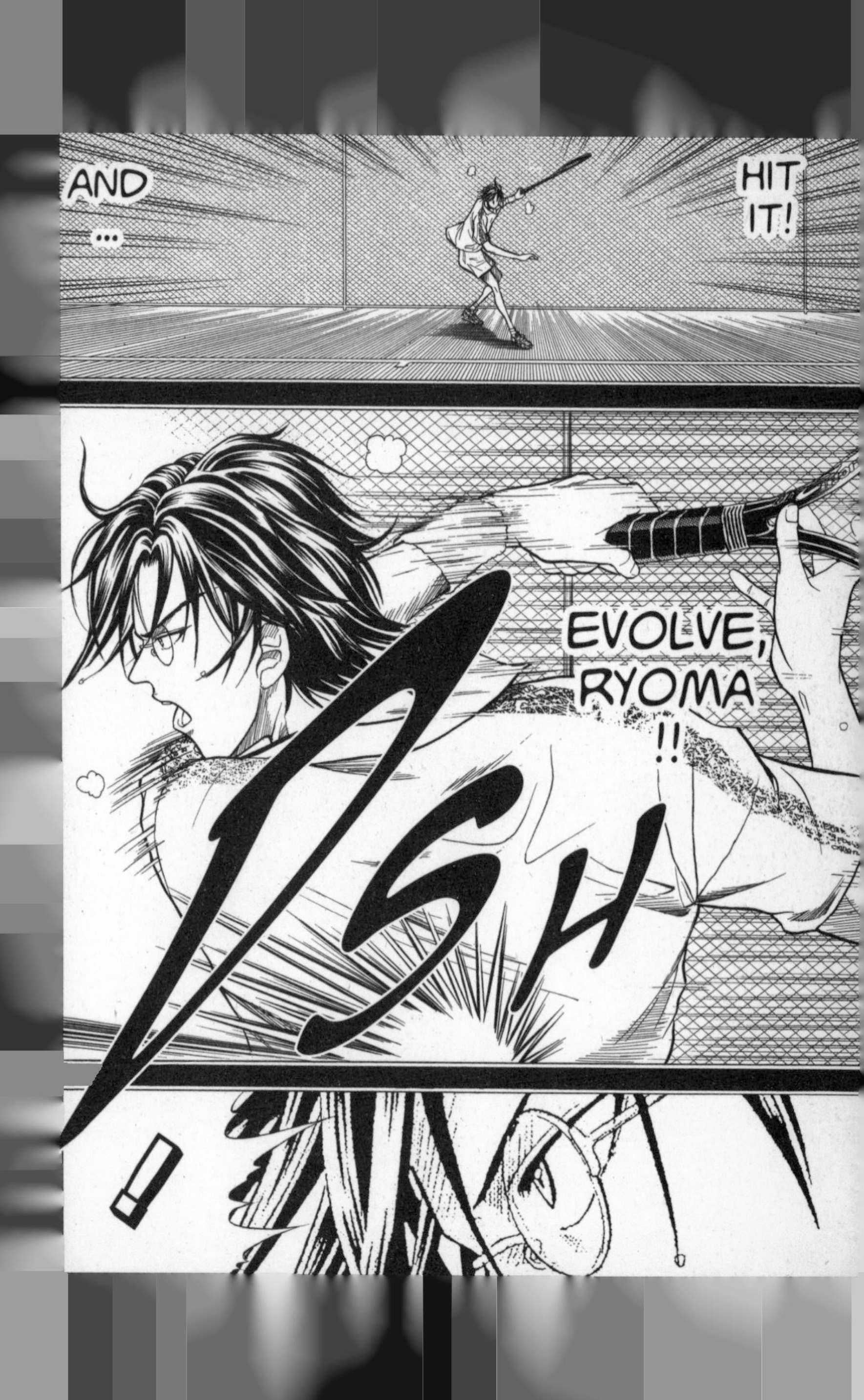
HIT IT!
AND ...
EVOLVE, RYOMA !!
VSH
!

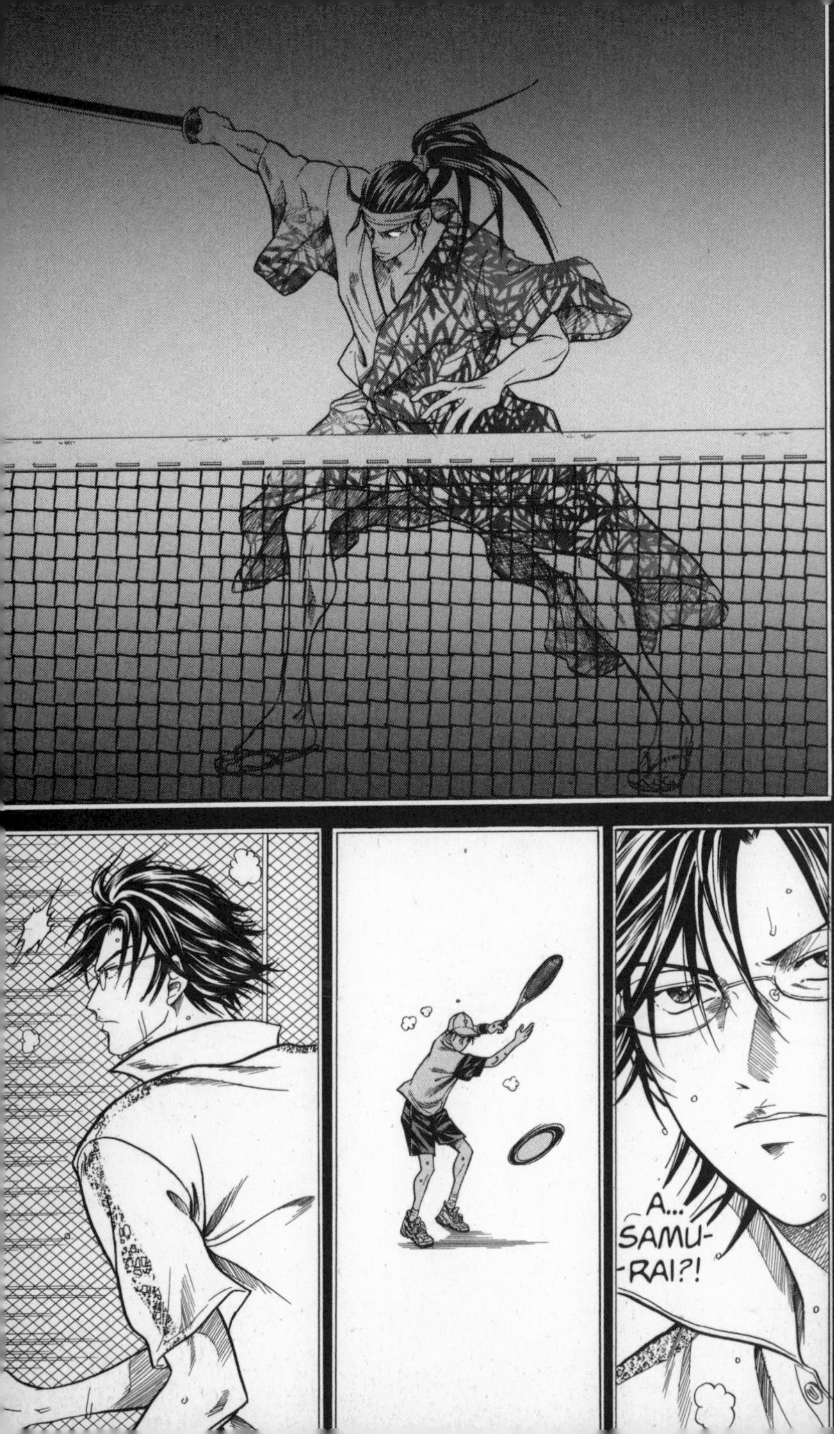
A... SAMU-RAI?!

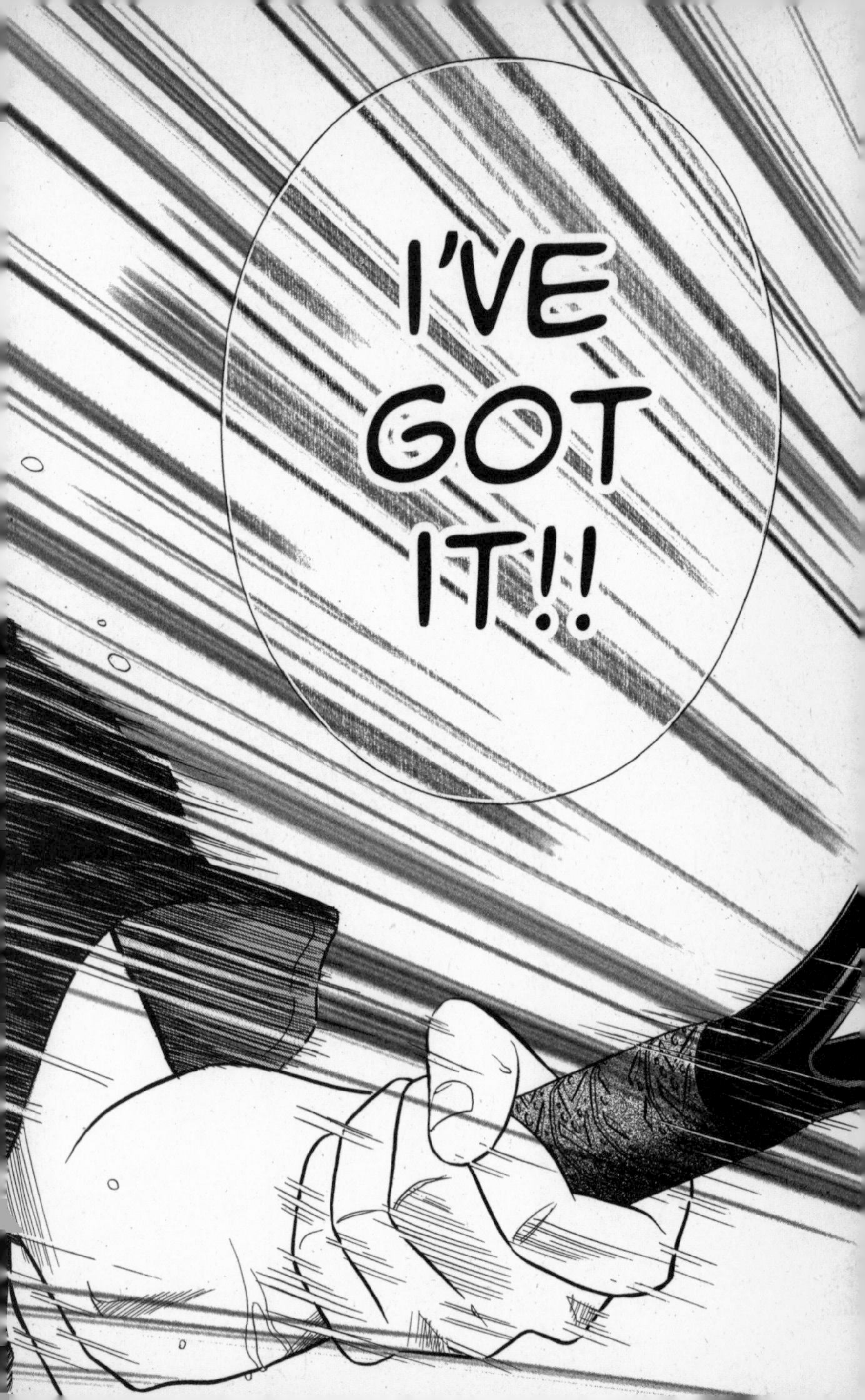
I'VE GOT IT!!

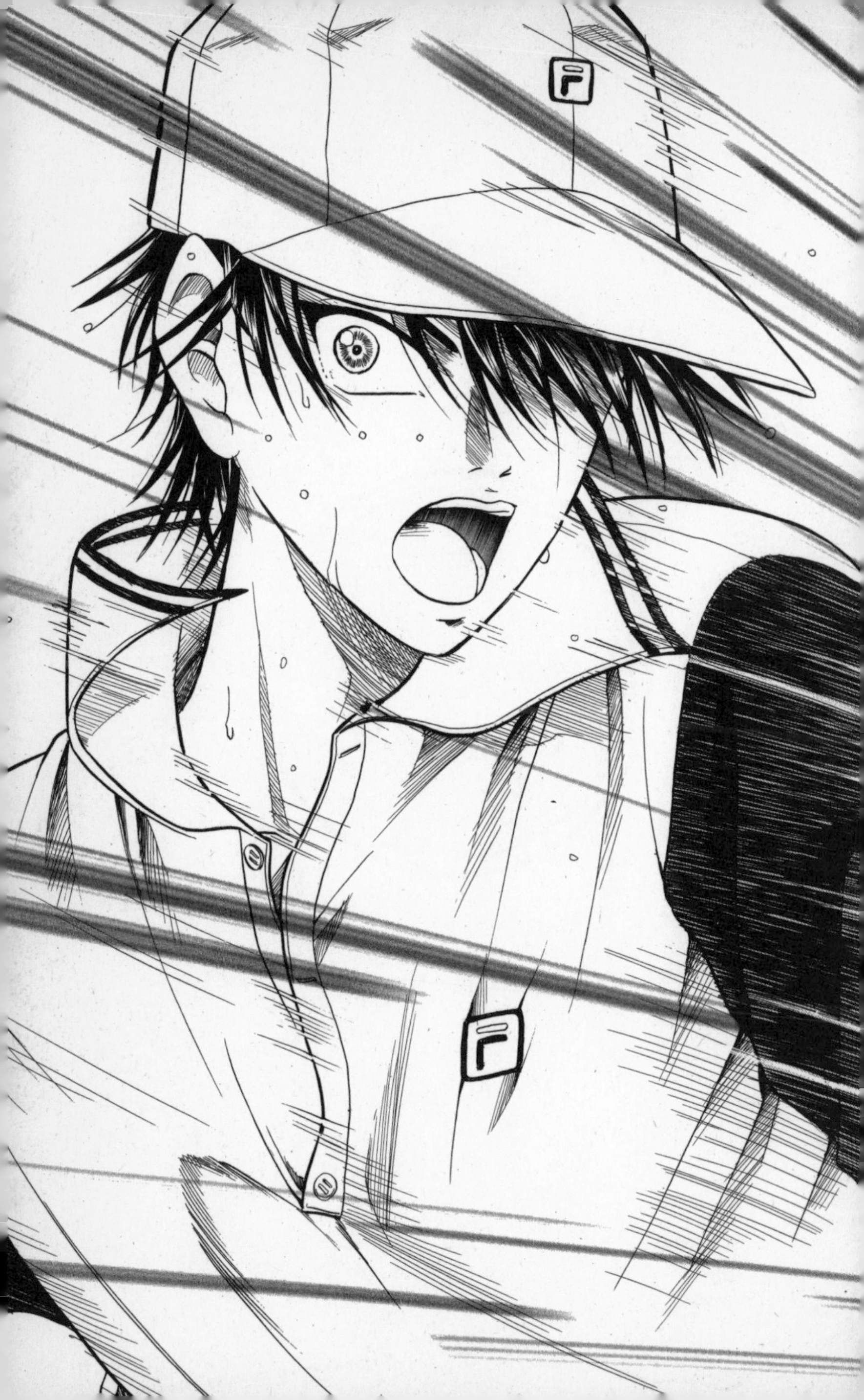

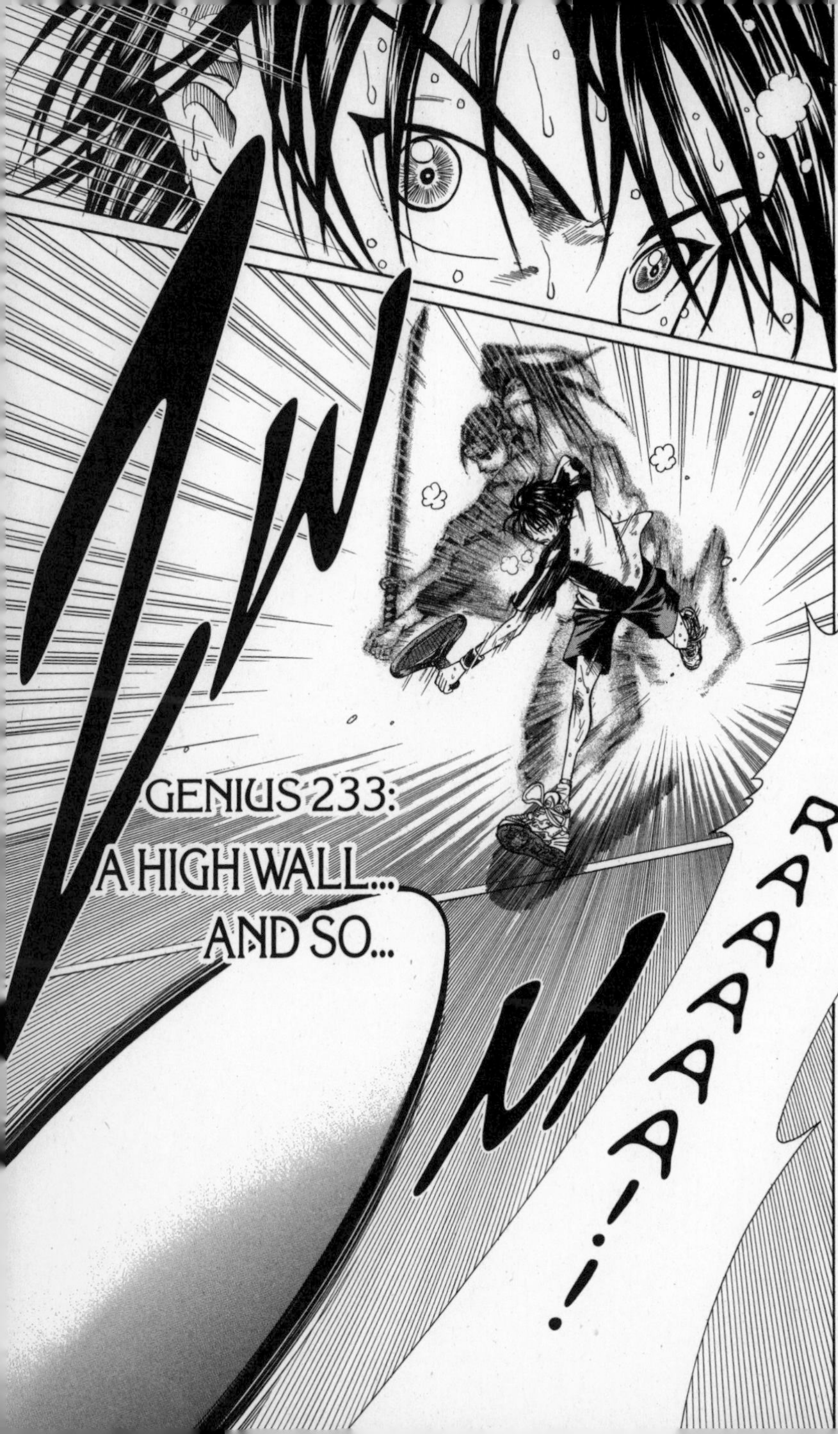
GENIUS 233:
A HIGH WALL...
AND SO...
RAAAAAA...!!

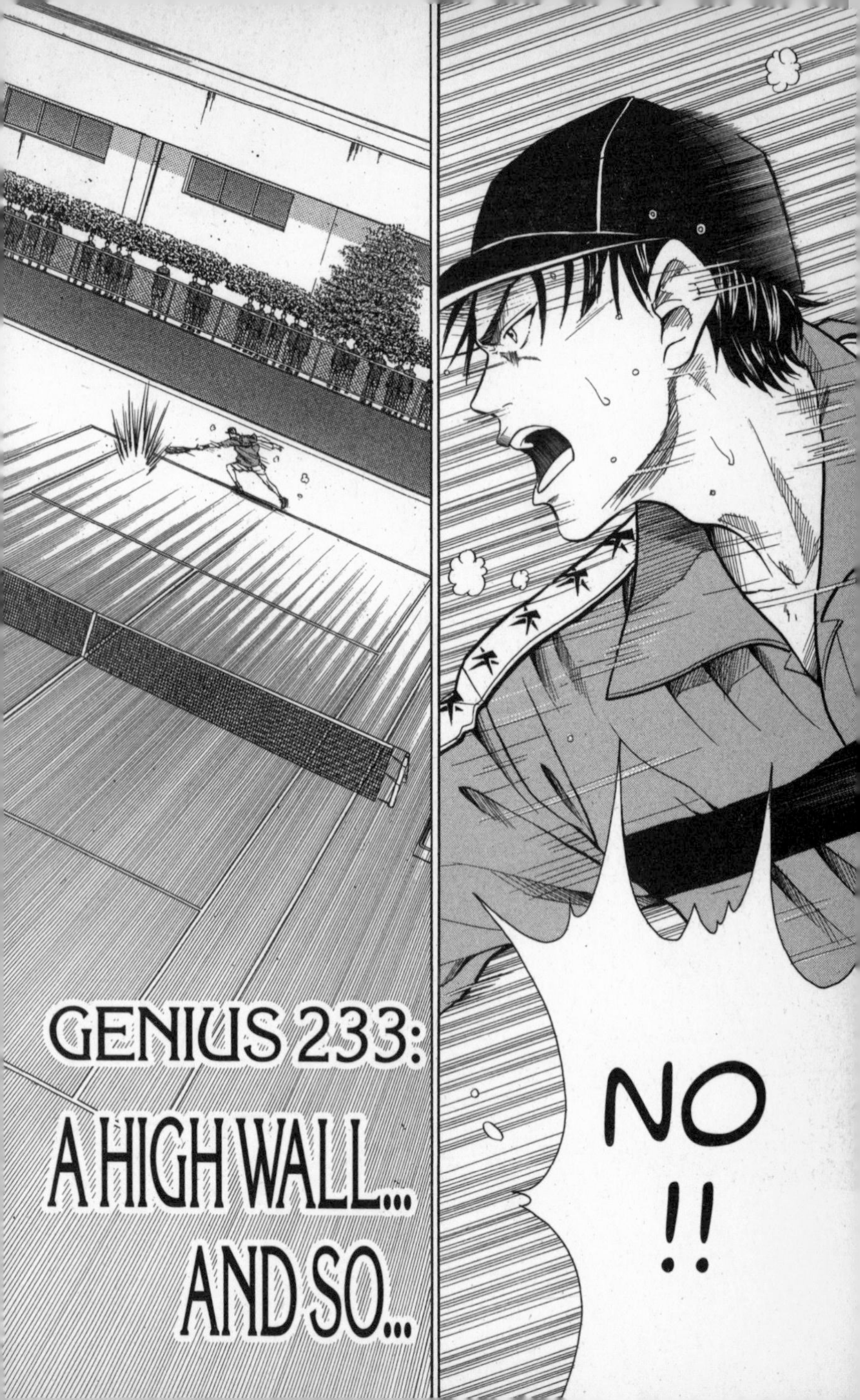
NO!!
GENIUS 233:
A HIGH WALL... AND SO...

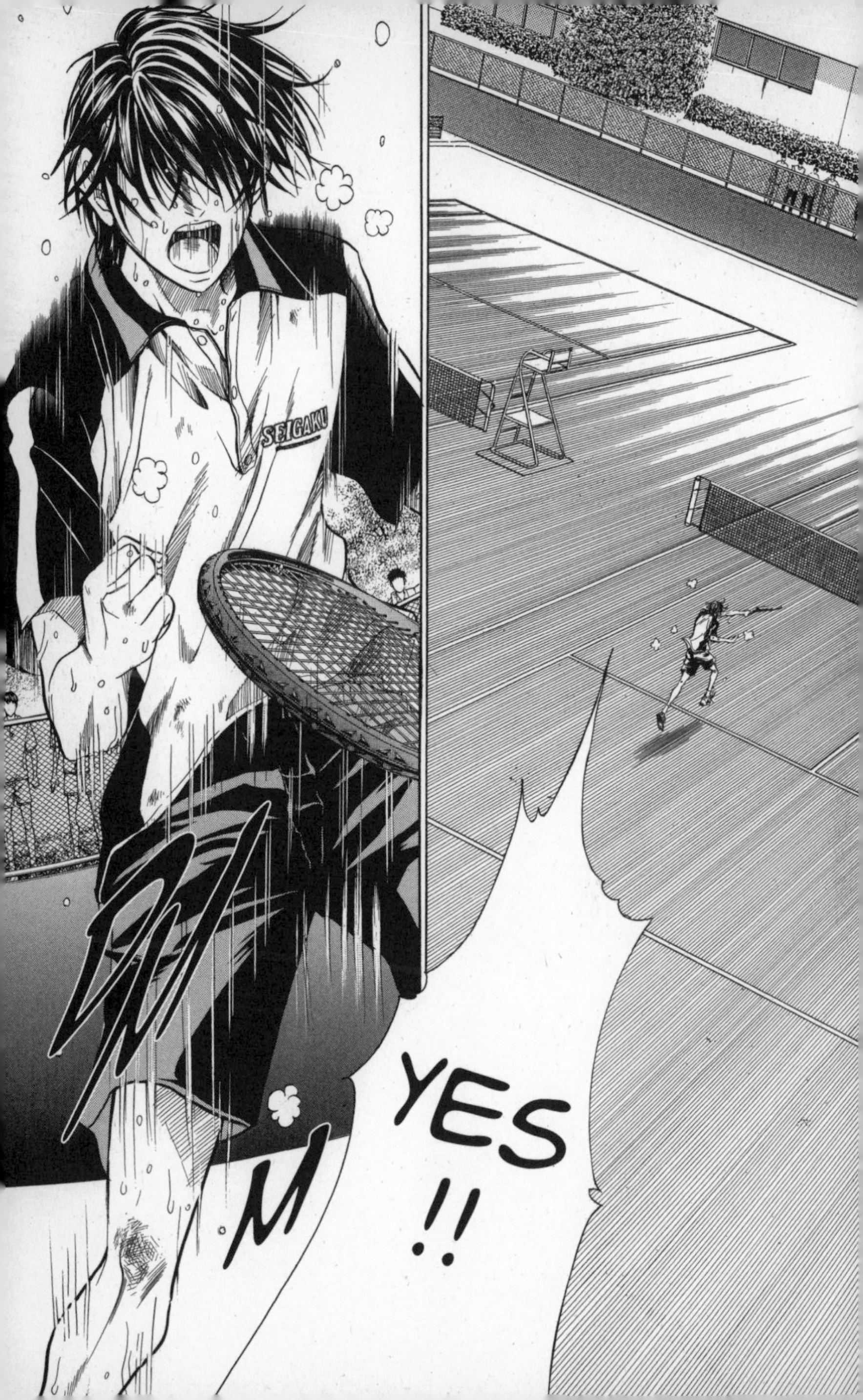
SEIGAKU
M YES!!

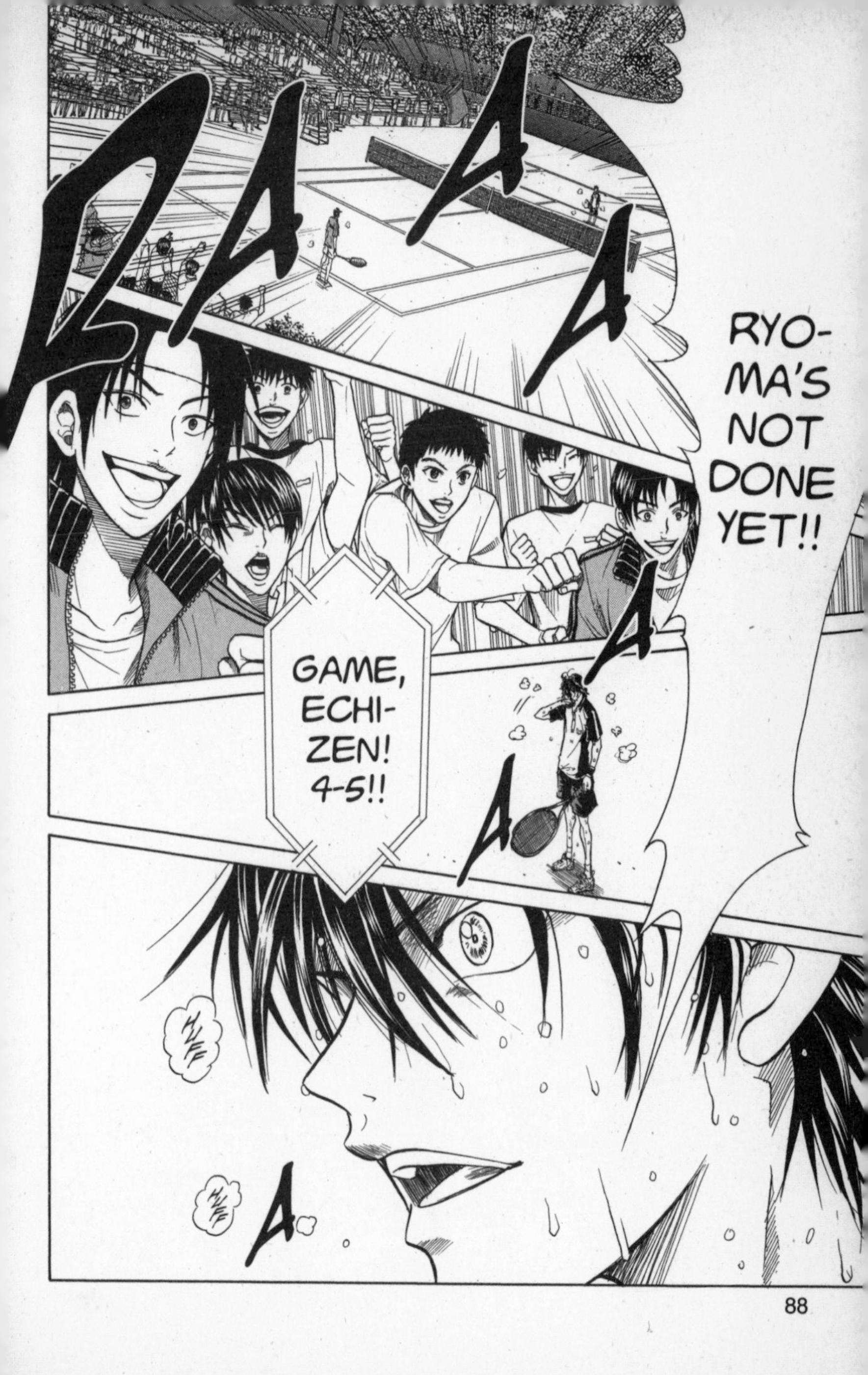
RYO-MA'S NOT DONE YET!!
GAME, ECHI-ZEN! 4-5!!
HUFF
HUFF

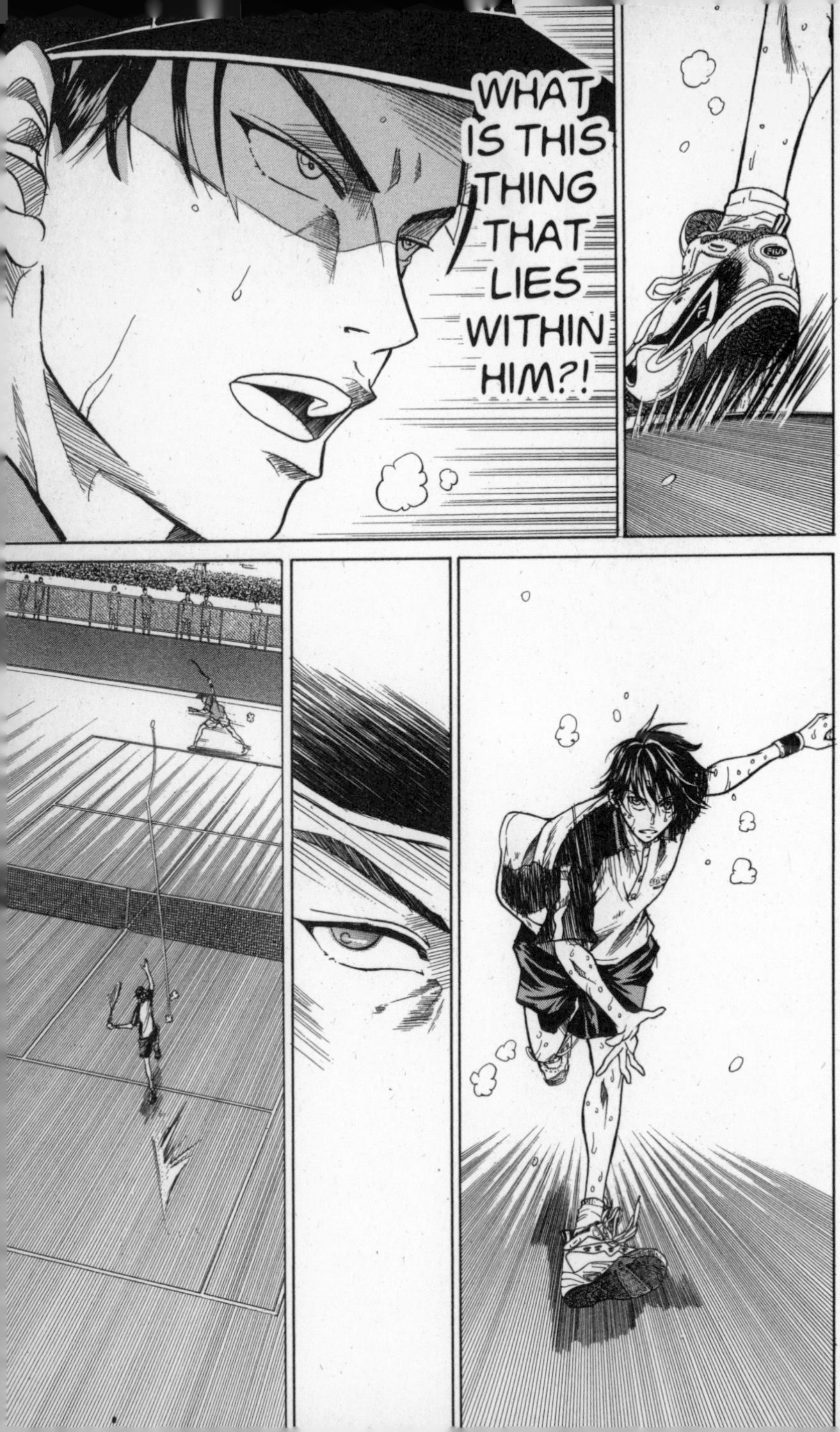
WHAT IS THIS THING THAT LIES WITHIN HIM?!

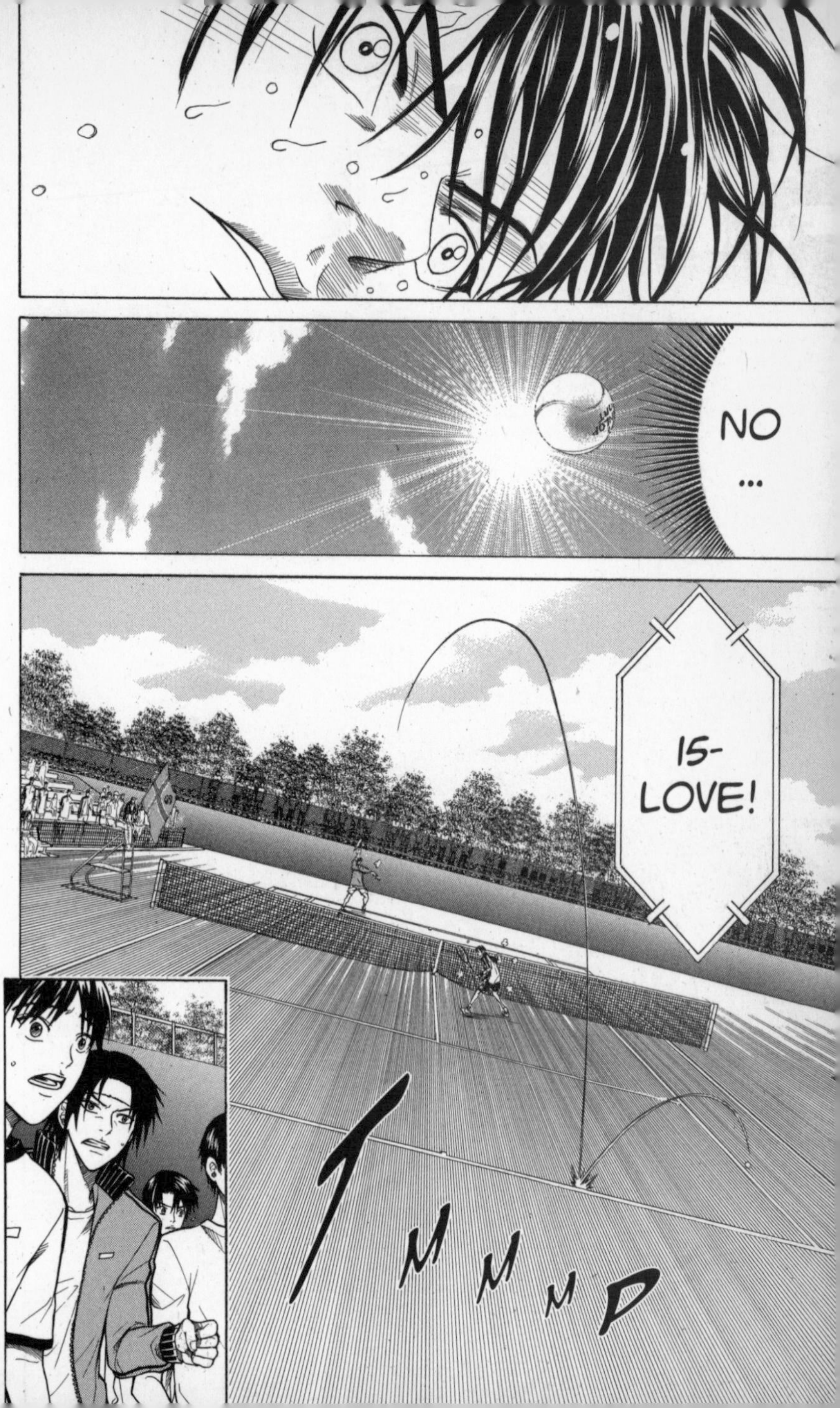
NO
...
15-LOVE!
TMMMD

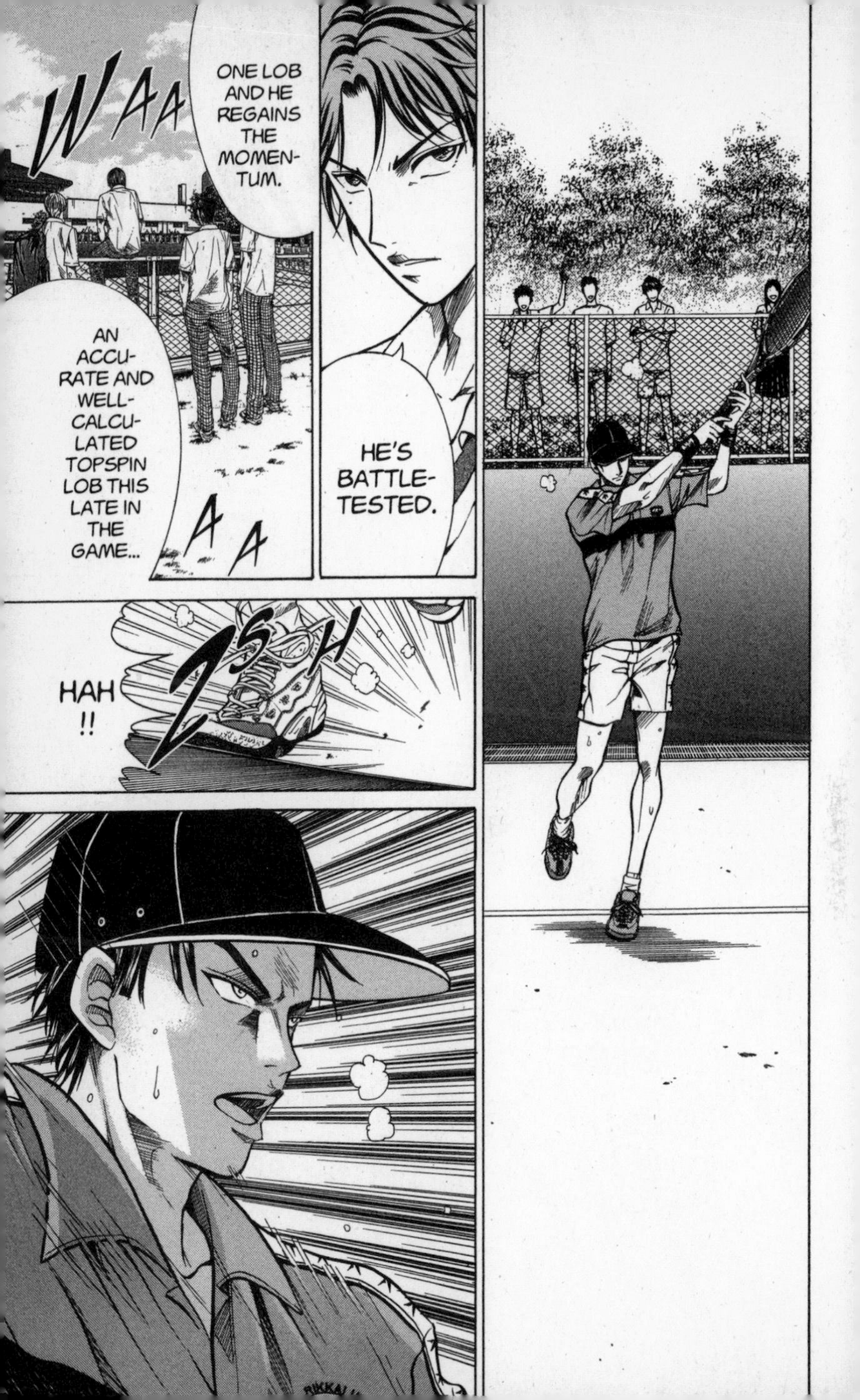
ONE LOB AND HE REGAINS THE MOMENTUM.
HE'S BATTLE-TESTED.
WAA
AN ACCURATE AND WELL-CALCULATED TOPSPIN LOB THIS LATE IN THE GAME...
AA
ZSH
HAH !!

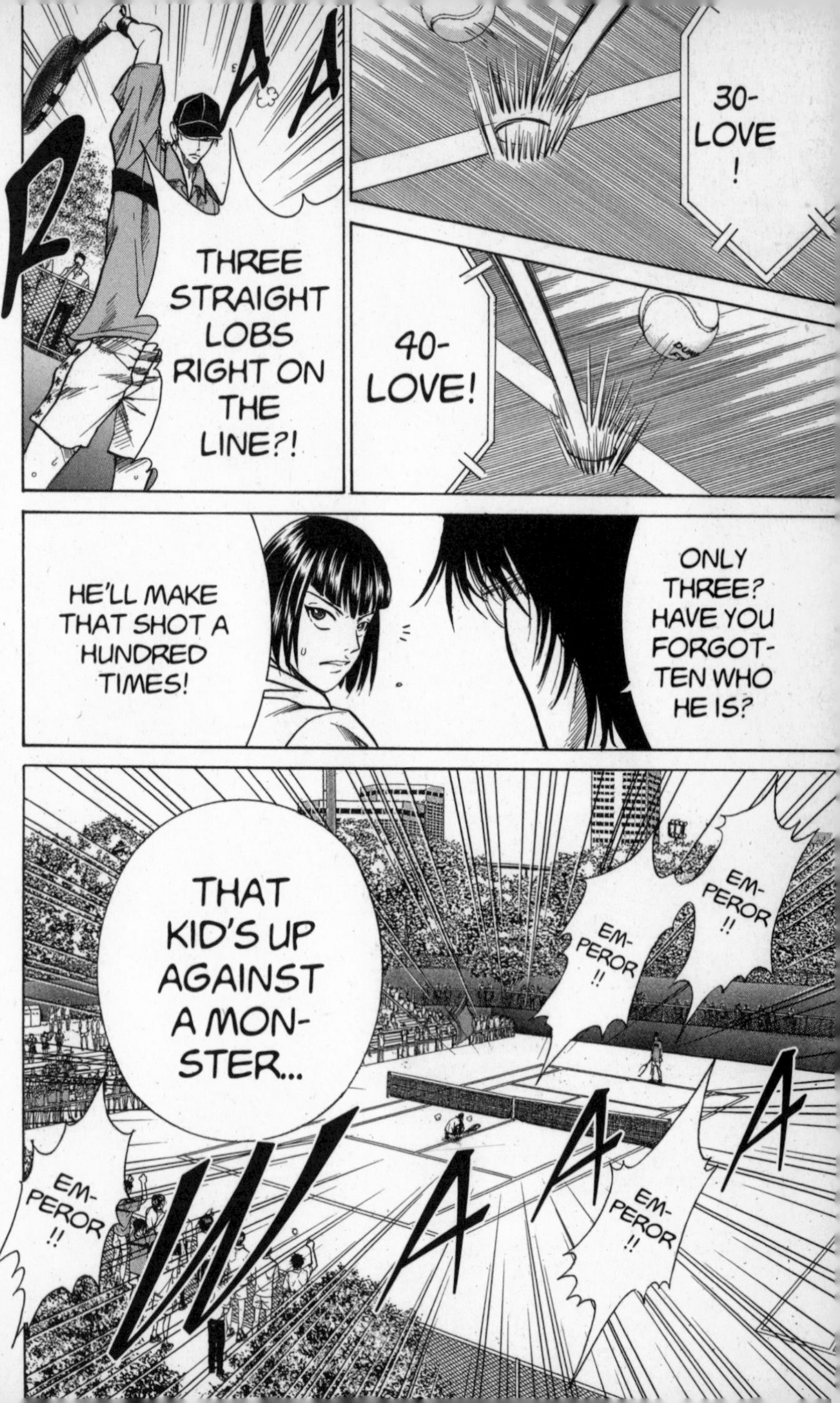
30-LOVE!
40-LOVE!
RAA
THREE STRAIGHT LOBS RIGHT ON THE LINE?!
ONLY THREE? HAVE YOU FORGOT-TEN WHO HE IS?
HE'LL MAKE THAT SHOT A HUNDRED TIMES!
EM-PEROR!!
EM-PEROR!!
THAT KID'S UP AGAINST A MON-STER...
EM-PEROR!!
EM-PEROR!!
WAAAA

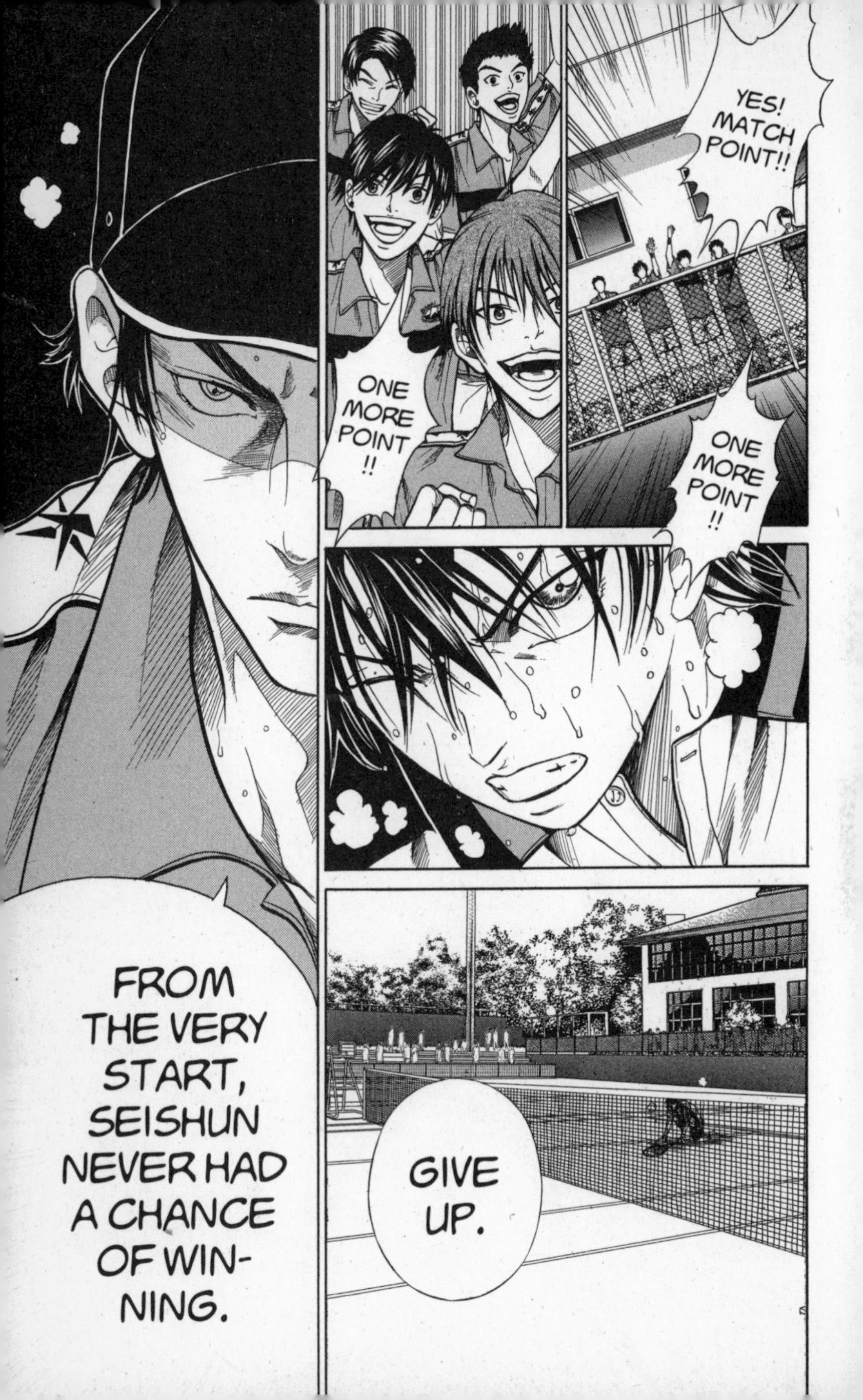
YES! MATCH POINT!!
ONE MORE POINT !!
ONE MORE POINT !!
GIVE UP.
FROM THE VERY START, SEISHUN NEVER HAD A CHANCE OF WIN-NING.

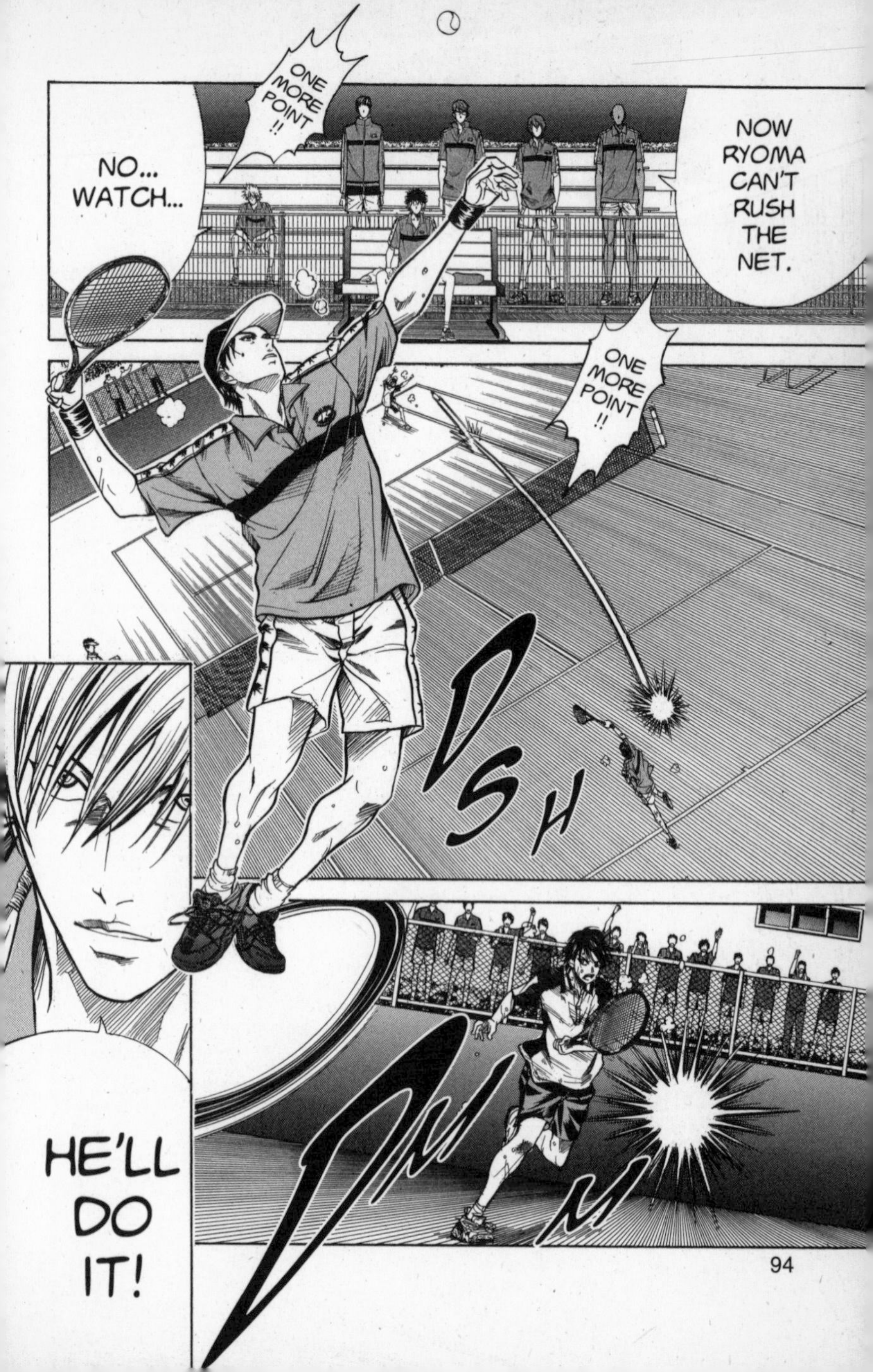
NOW RYOMA CAN'T RUSH THE NET.
ONE MORE POINT !!
NO... WATCH...
ONE MORE POINT !!
DSH
HE'LL DO IT!

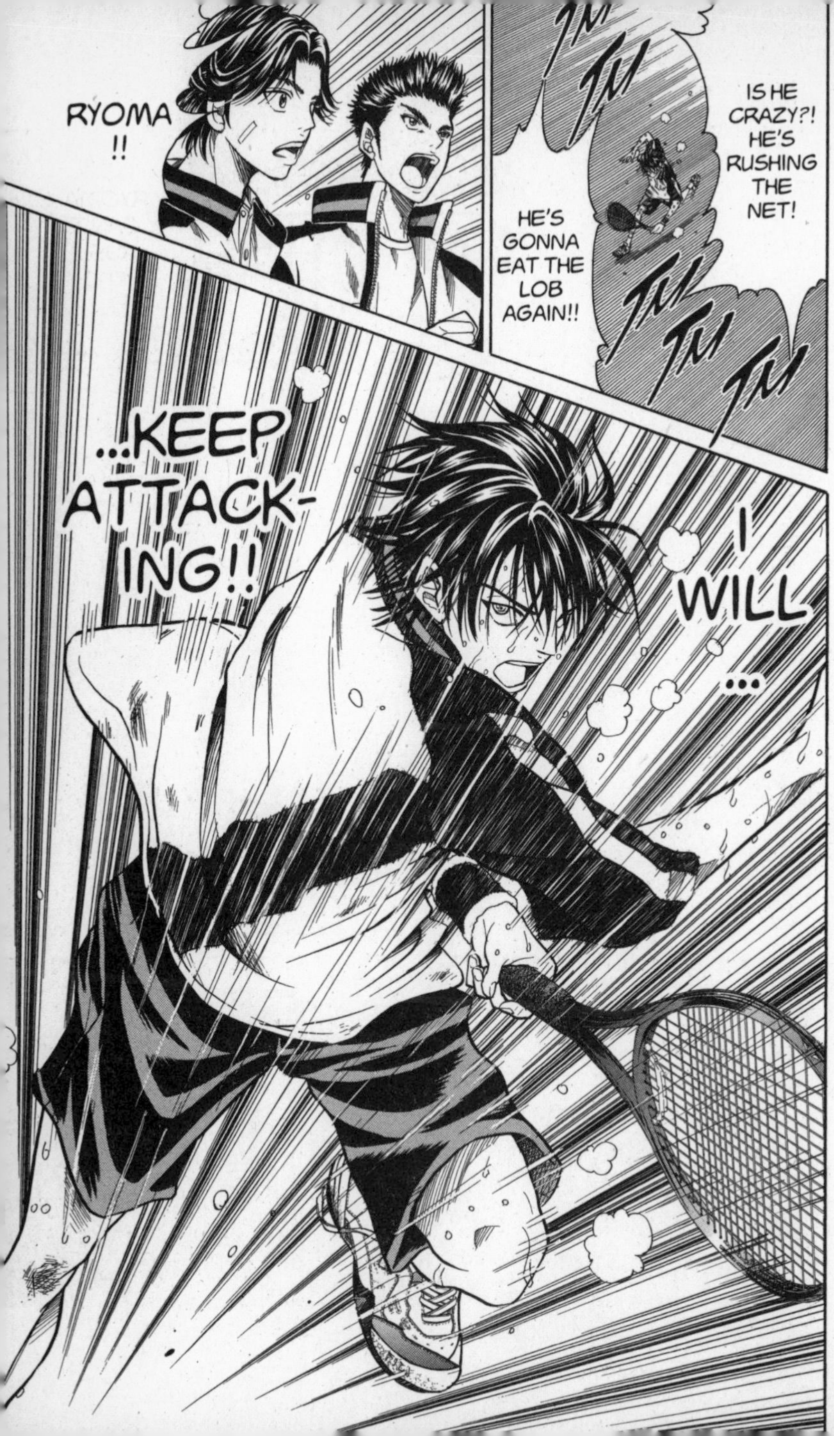
IS HE CRAZY?! HE'S RUSHING THE NET!
HE'S GONNA EAT THE LOB AGAIN!!
RYOMA !!
I WILL ...
...KEEP ATTACK-ING!!

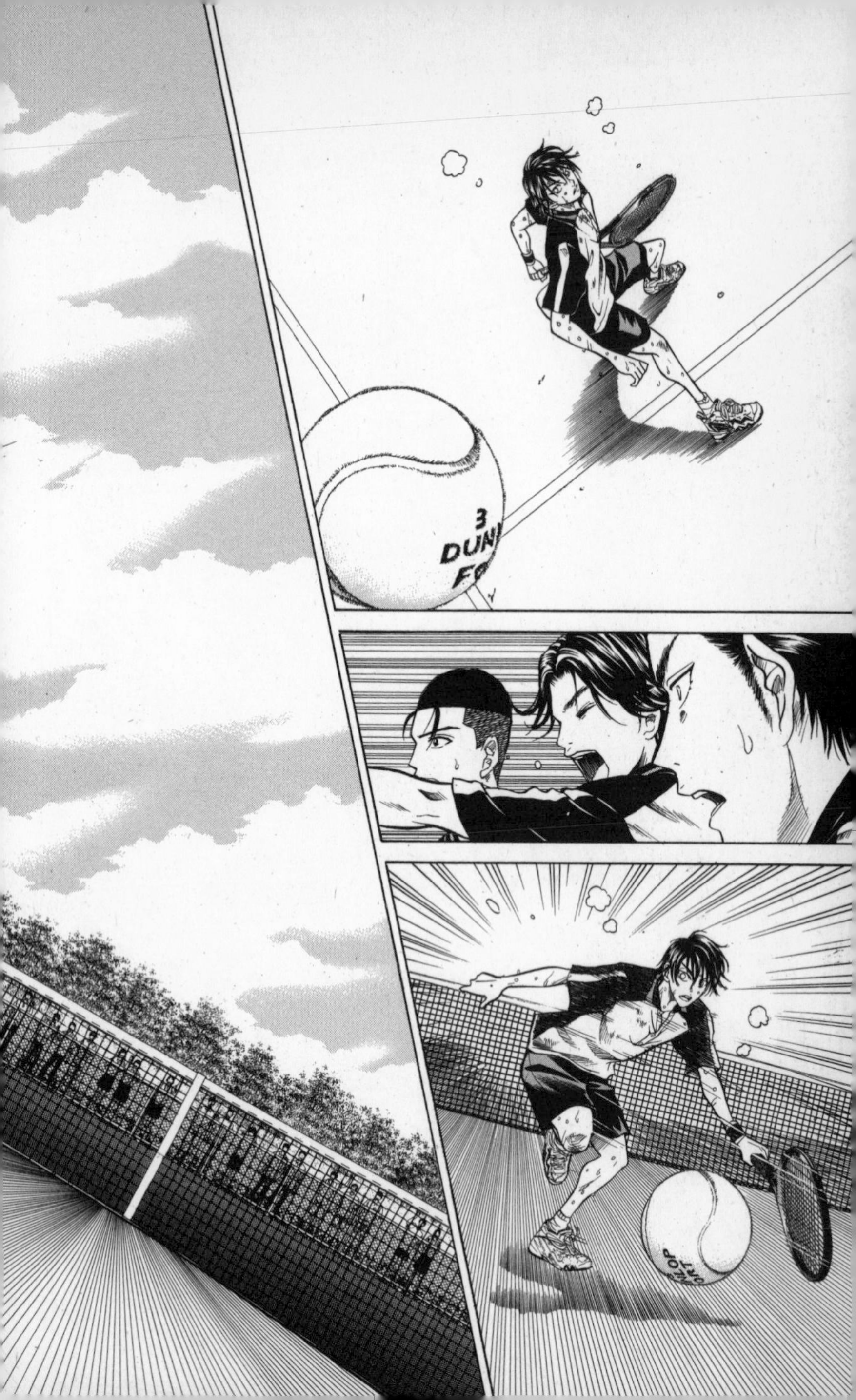

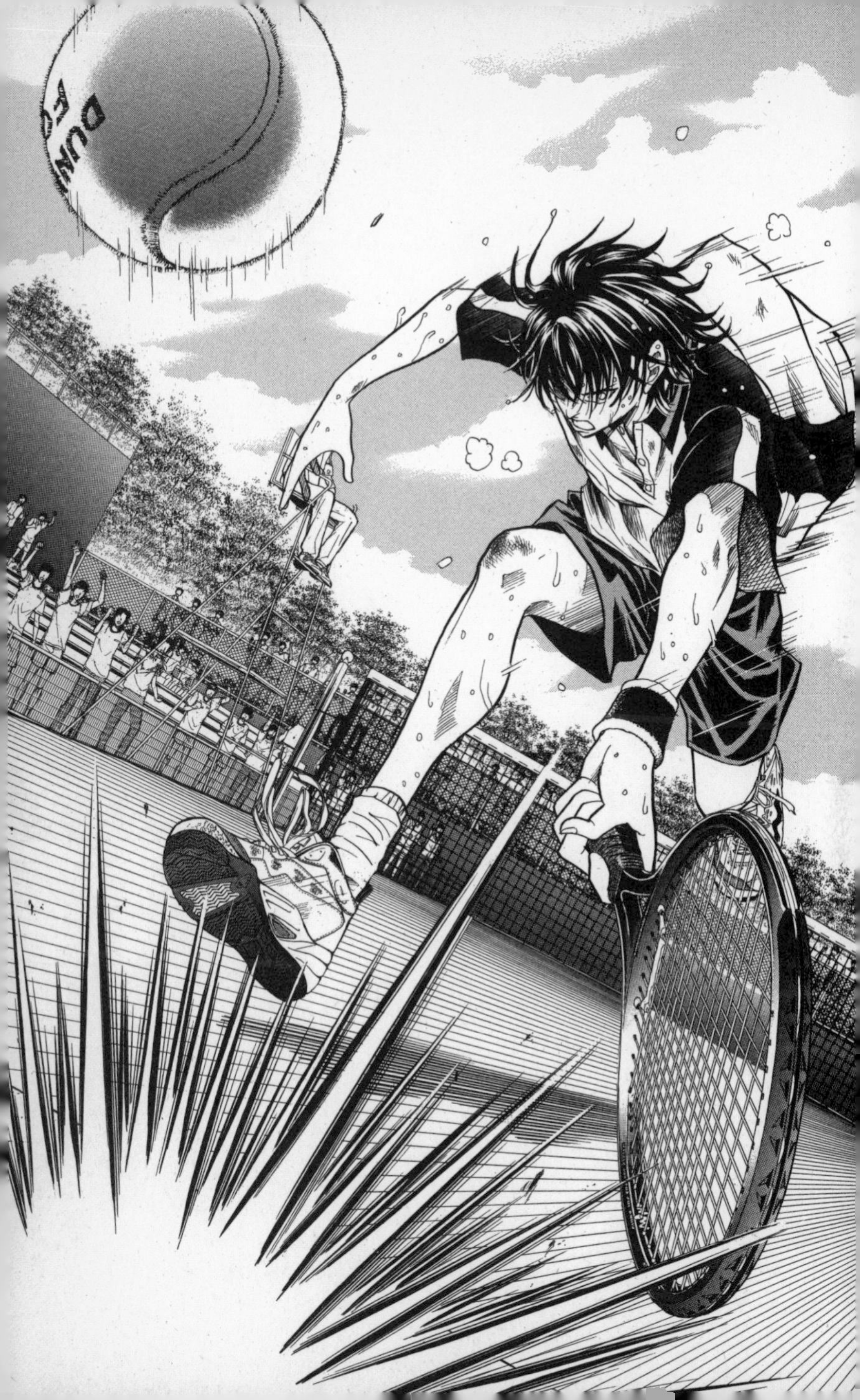

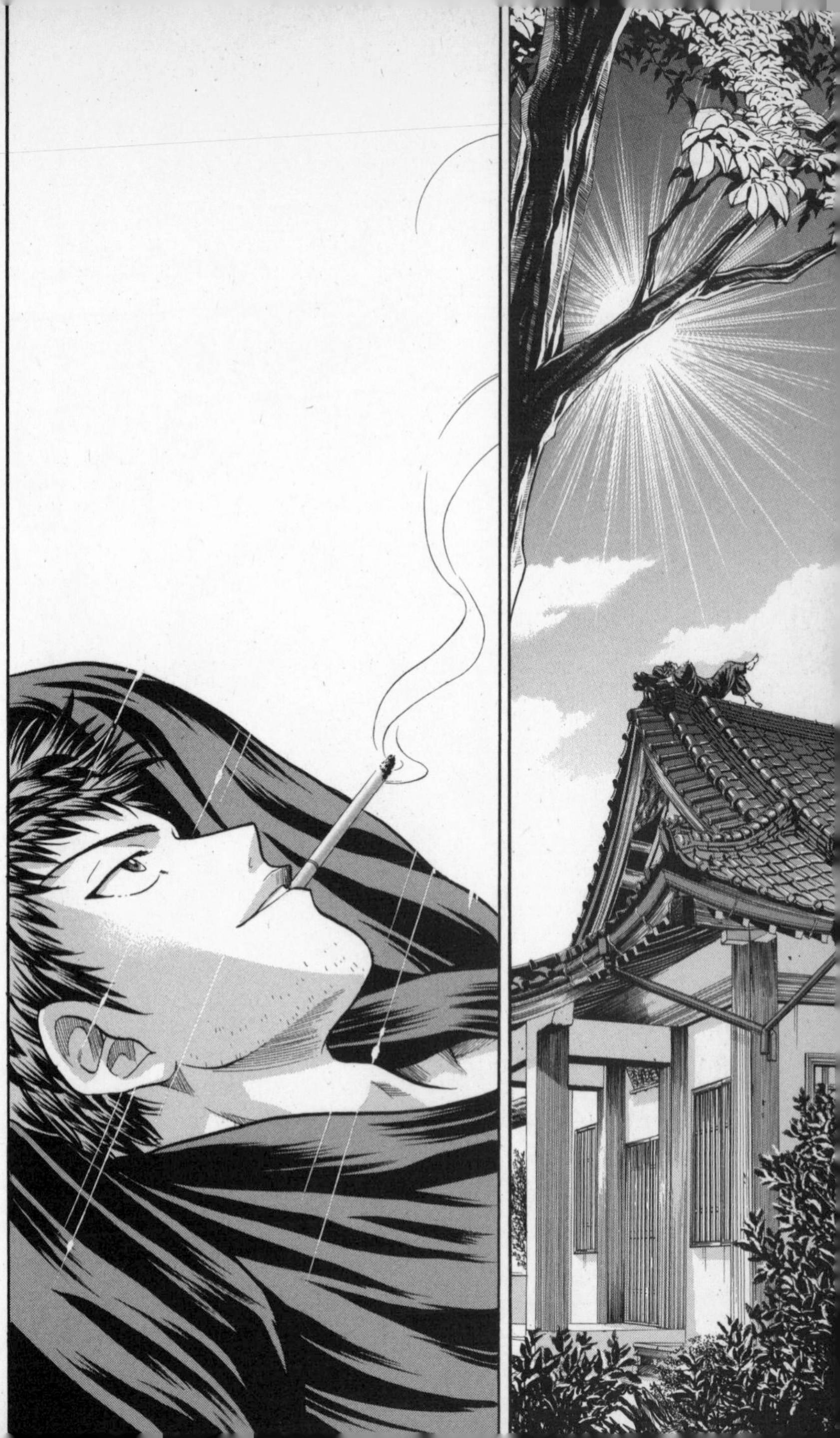

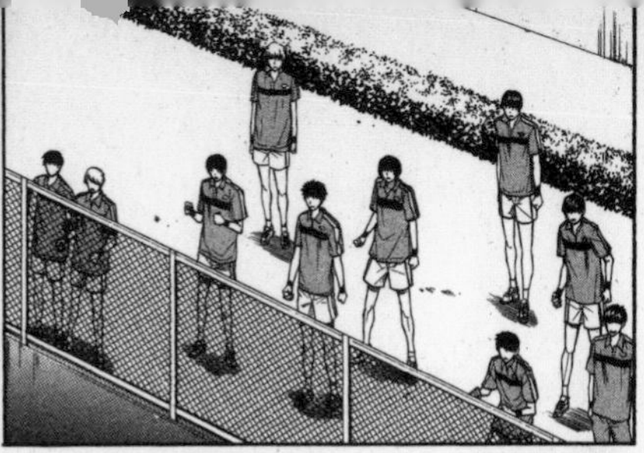

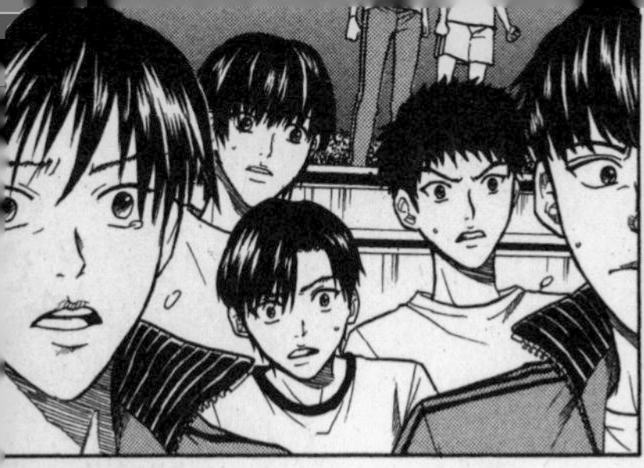

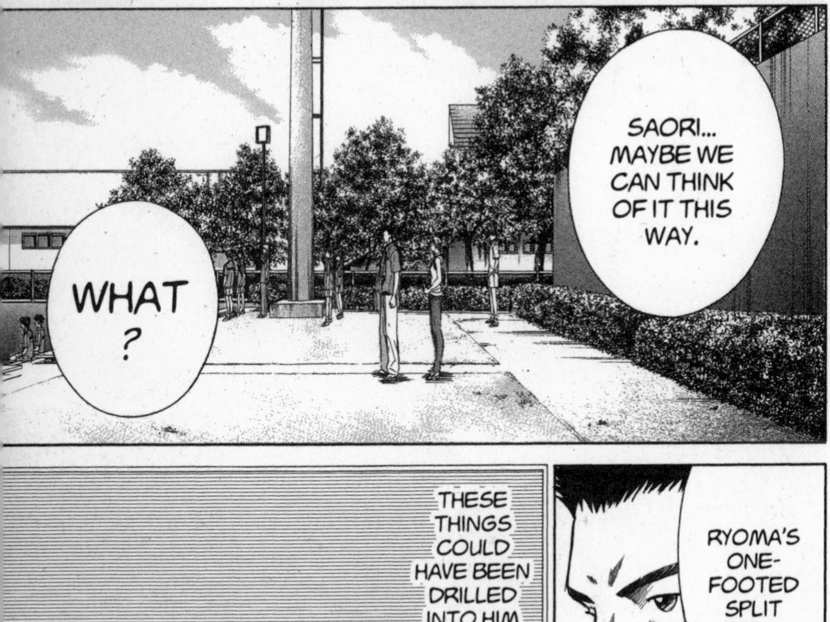
SAORI... MAYBE WE CAN THINK OF IT THIS WAY.
WHAT?

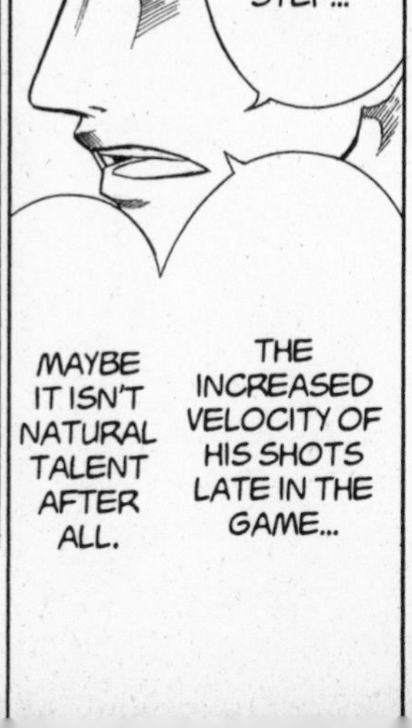
RYOMA'S ONE-FOOTED SPLIT STEP...
THE INCREASED VELOCITY OF HIS SHOTS LATE IN THE GAME...
MAYBE IT ISN'T NATURAL TALENT AFTER ALL.

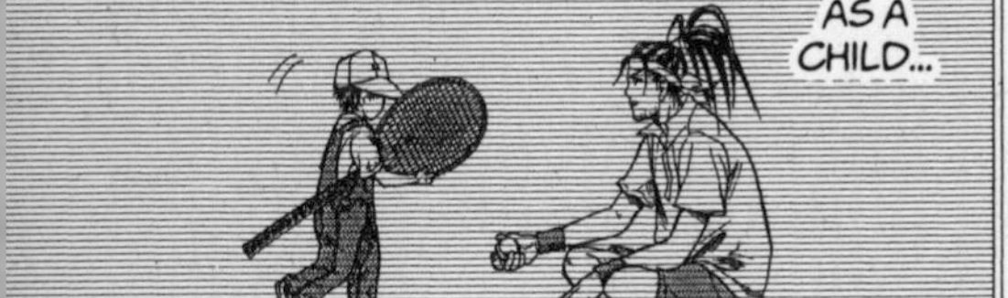
THESE THINGS COULD HAVE BEEN DRILLED INTO HIM AS A CHILD...
...WITHOUT HIM EVEN REALIZING IT.

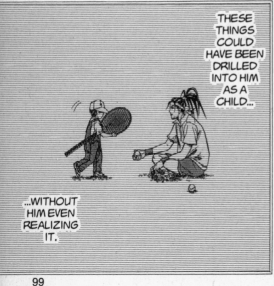

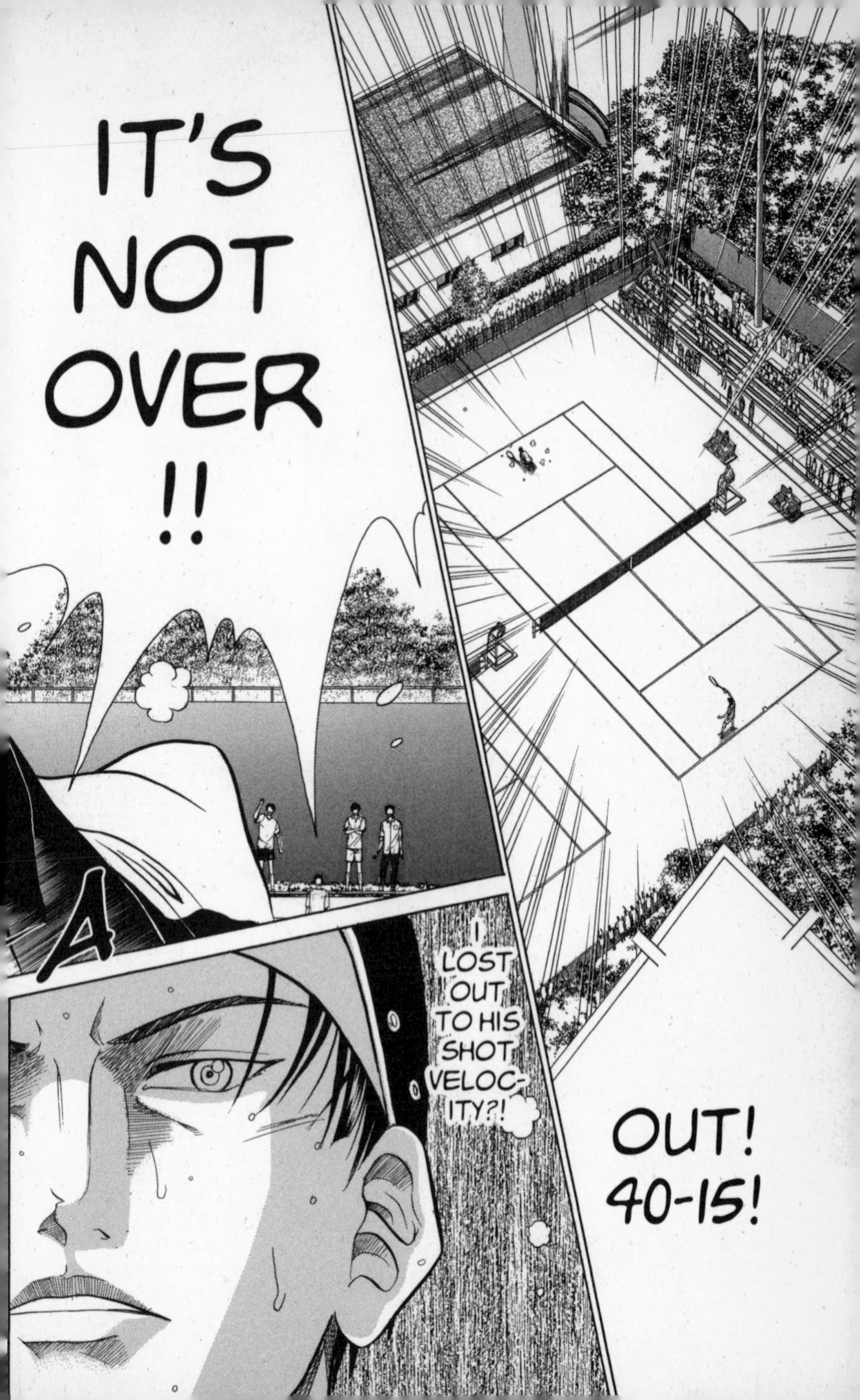
OUT! 40-15!
IT'S NOT OVER!!
I LOST OUT TO HIS SHOT VELOCITY?!

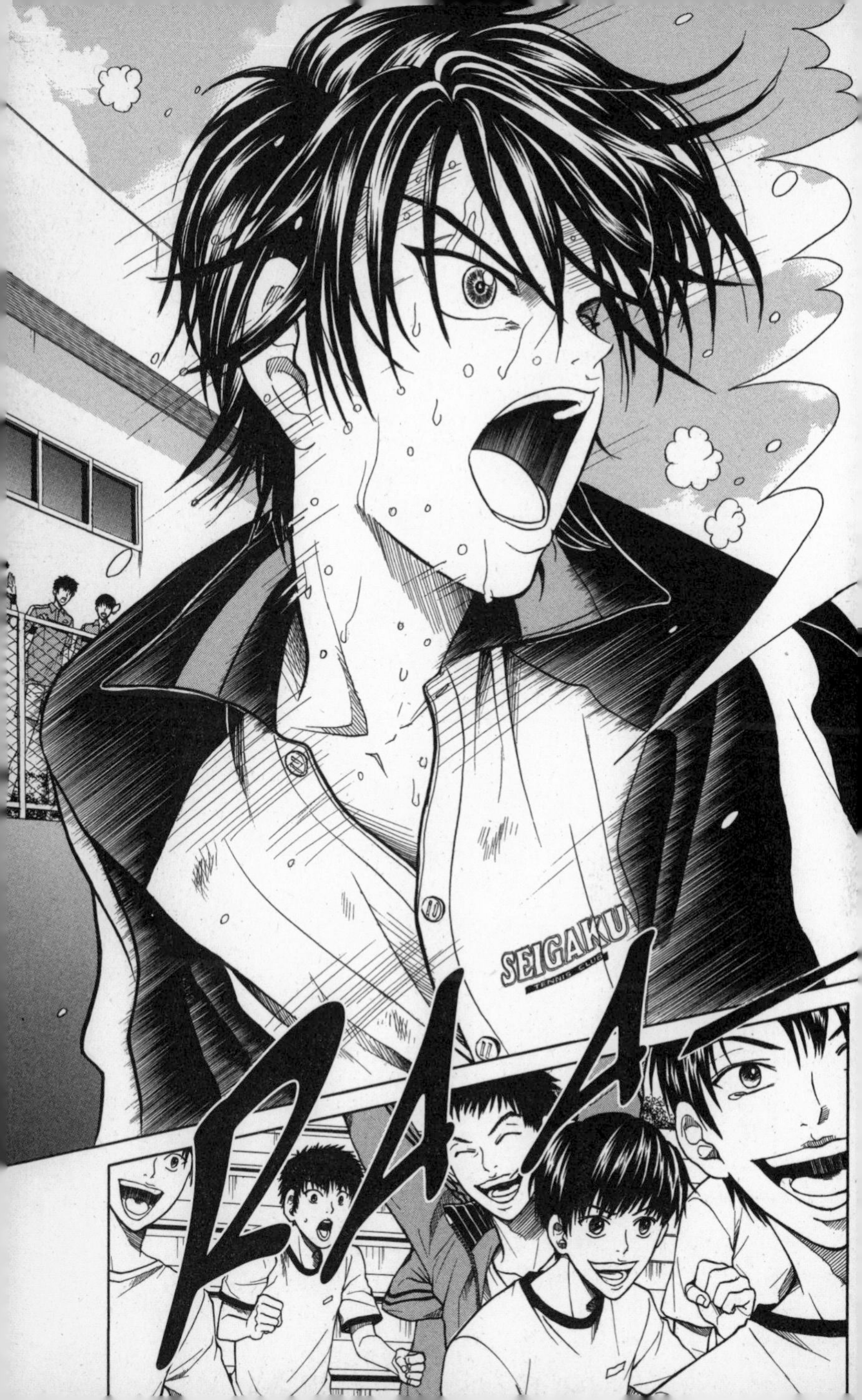
SEIGAKU
TENNIS CLUB

RIKKAI QUESTION CORNER

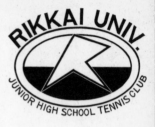

It's Back!!

Part 5

RIKKAI UNIV. JUNIOR HIGH SCHOOL TENNIS CLUB

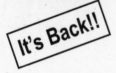

Back by popular demand! The guys from Rikkai aren't very forthcoming about themselves, are they? Well then, let's have them answer some of your questions!

Q: Who gets the best grades out of all the Rikkai starters?
(K.M., Asakuchi)

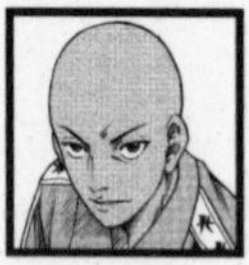

It's gotta be Renji, right? I think he had the best midterm scores.

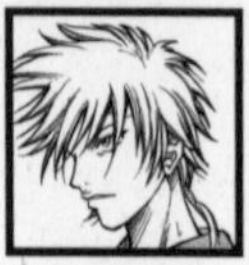

He's the brains of our team.

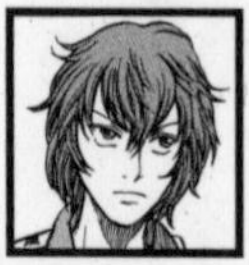

Yeah, but he's a grade grubber, isn't he?

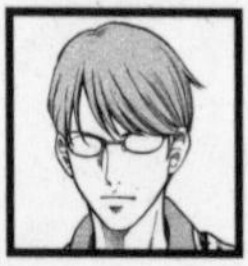

I get good grades, but I am *not* a grade grubber.
[Deafening silence]

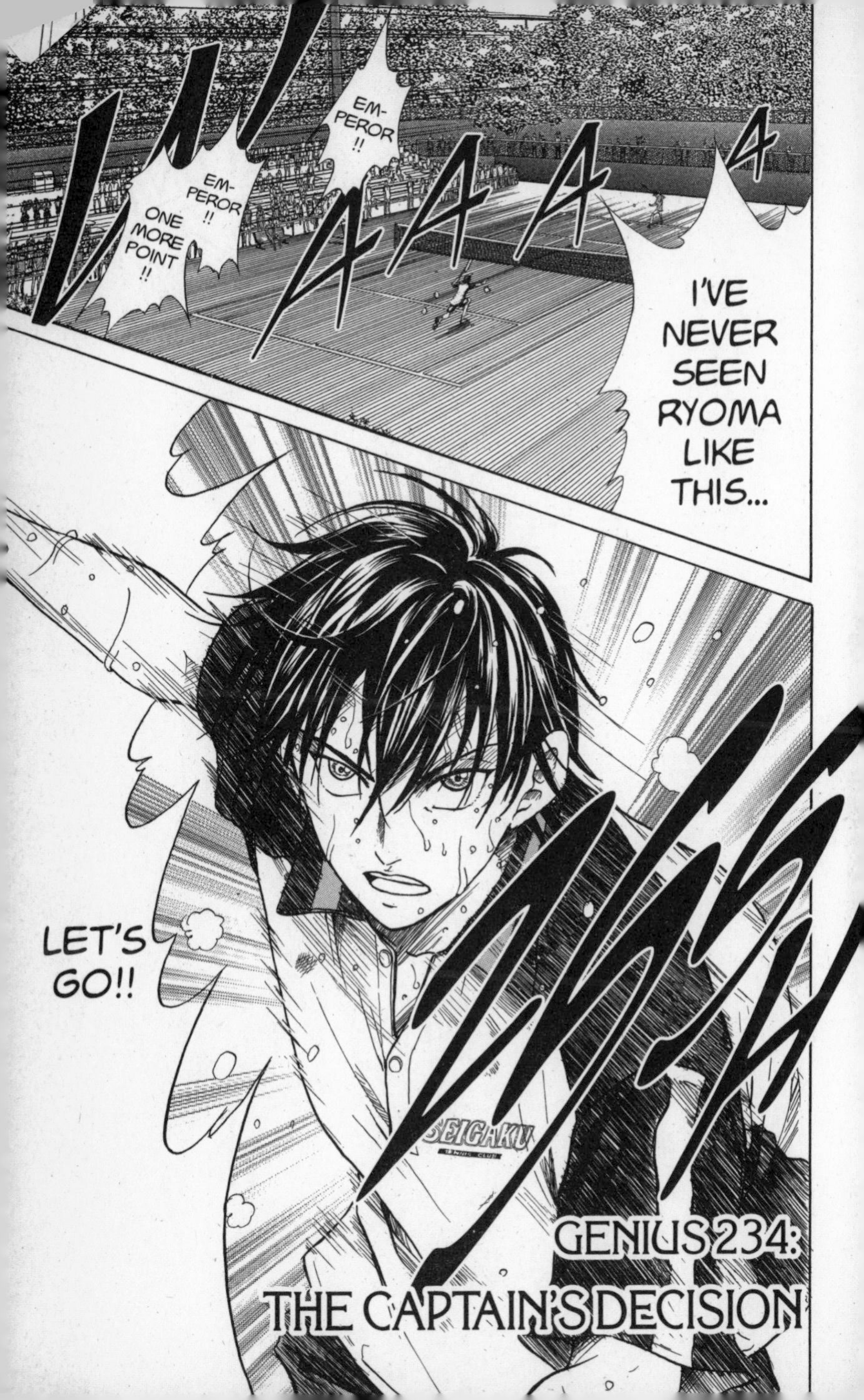
EM-PEROR!!
EM-PEROR!! ONE MORE POINT!!
I'VE NEVER SEEN RYOMA LIKE THIS...
LET'S GO!!
SEIGAKU

GENIUS 234: THE CAPTAIN'S DECISION

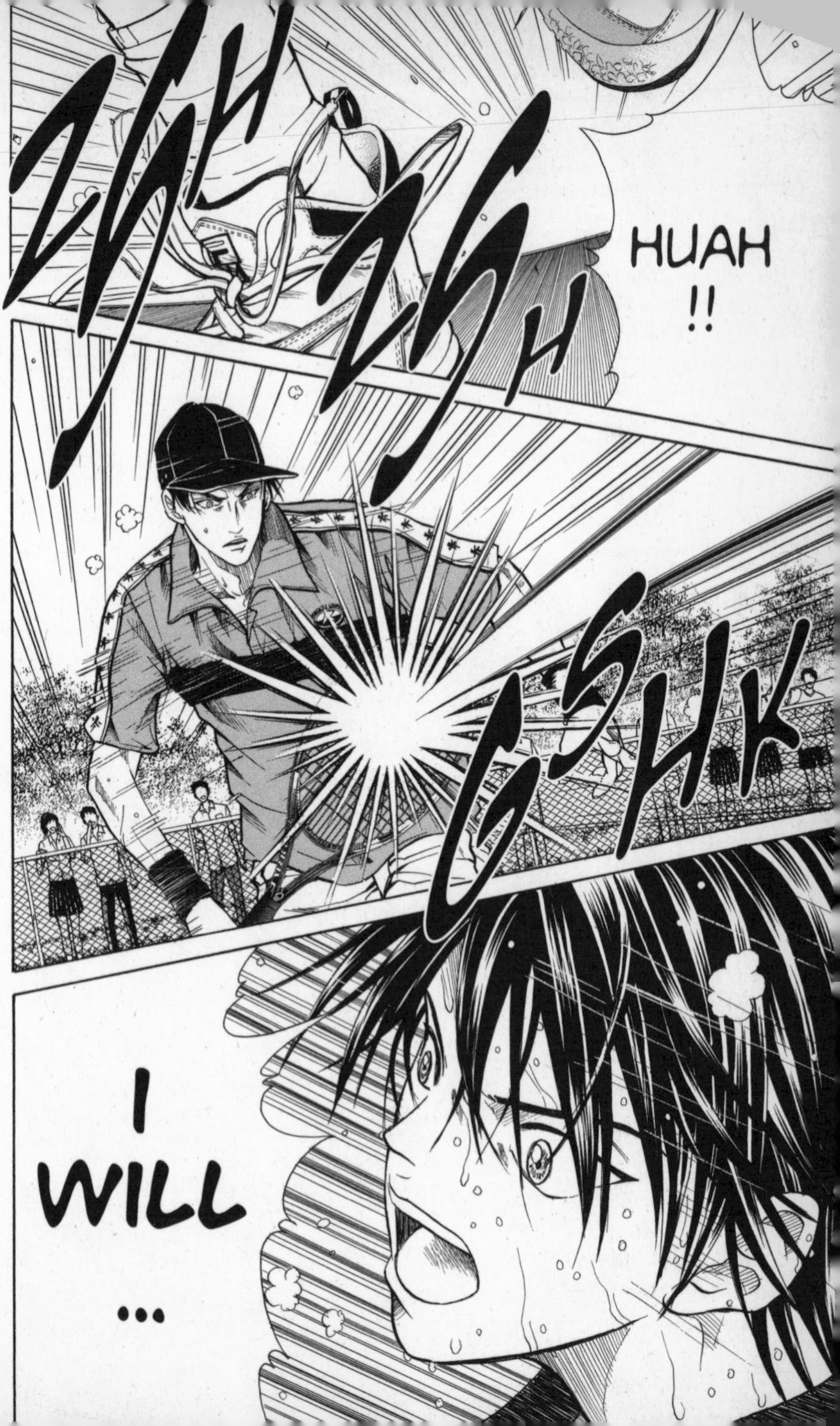
HUAH !!
GSHK
I WILL ...

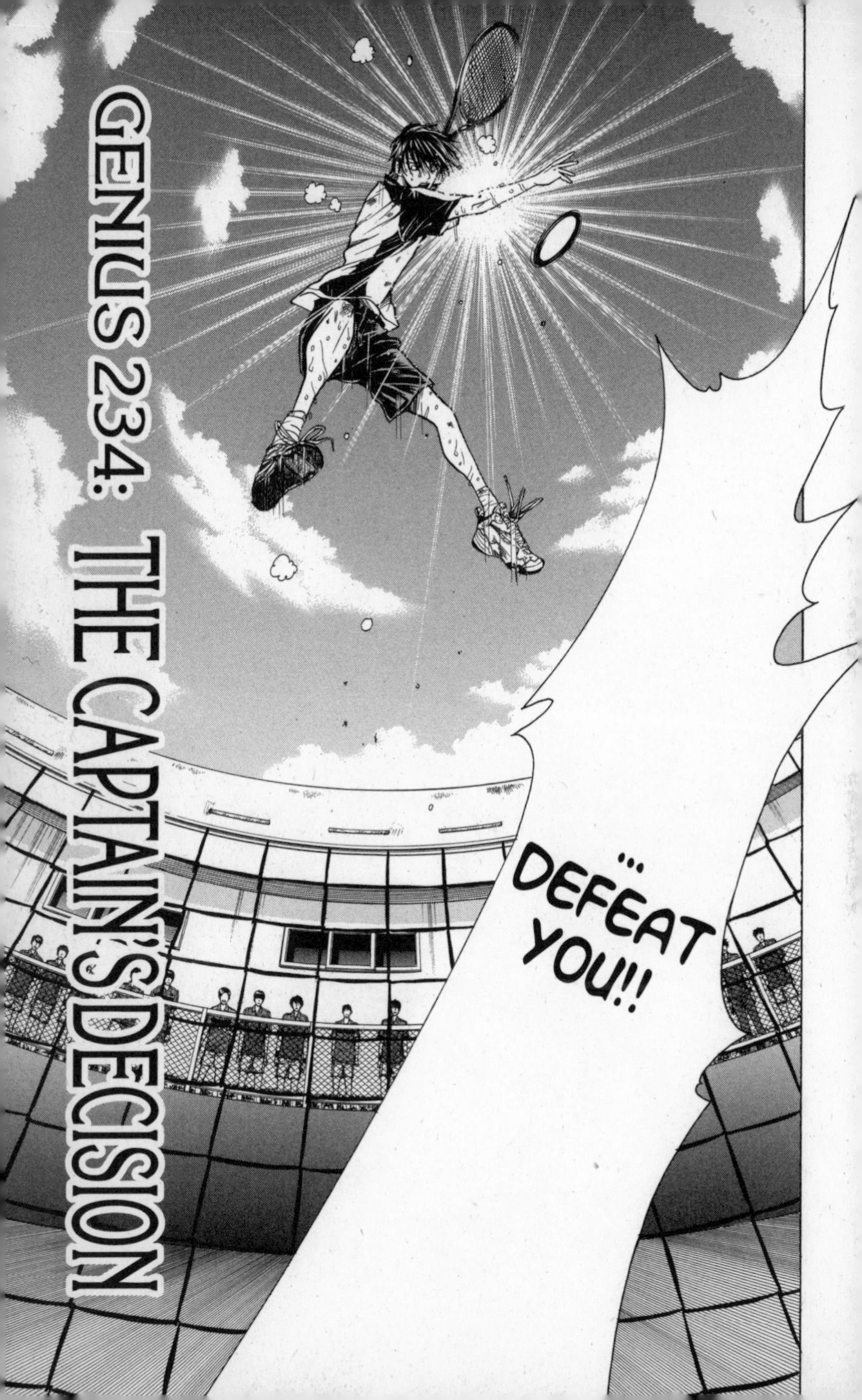
...DEFEAT YOU!!
GENIUS 234: THE CAPTAIN'S DECISION

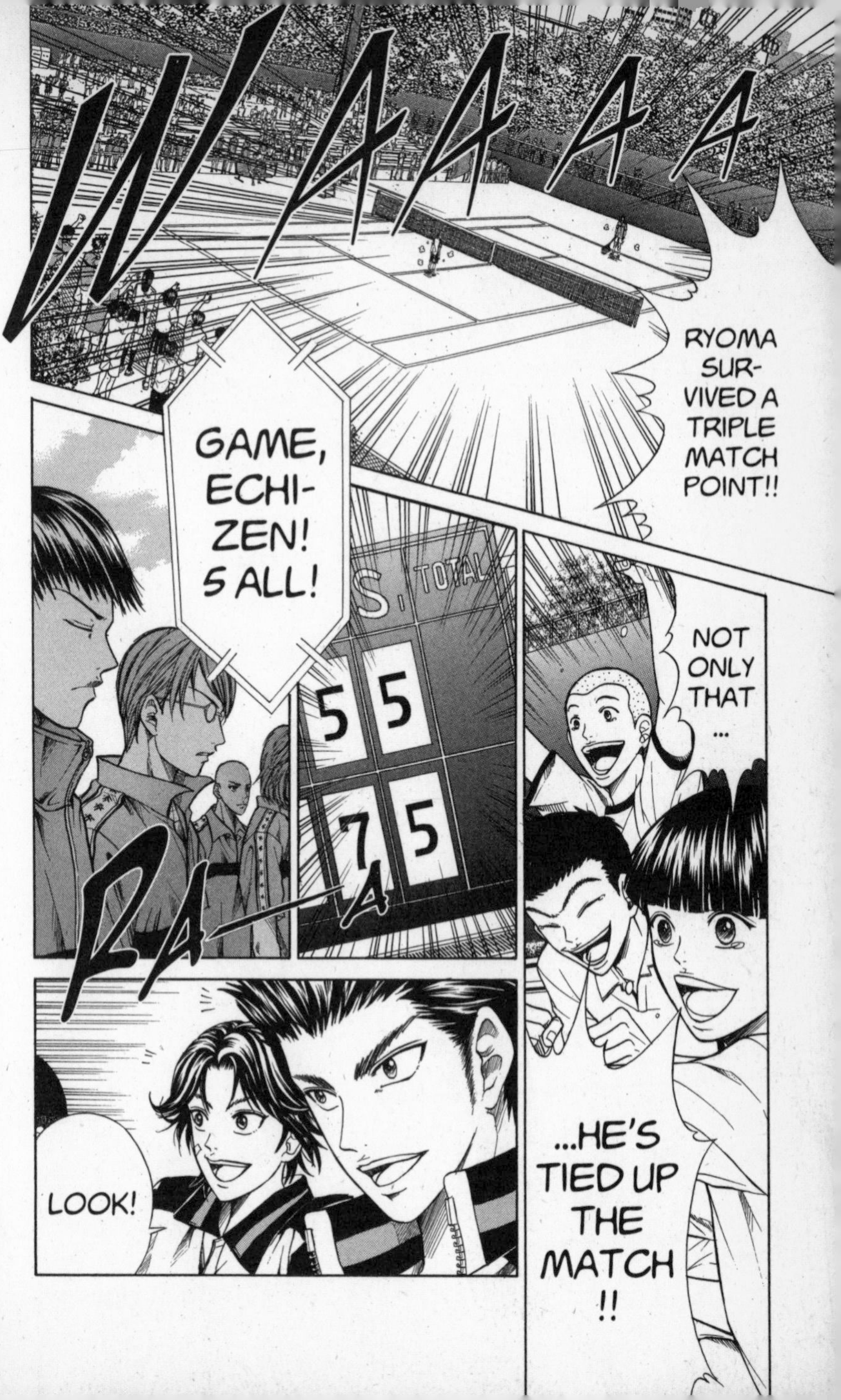
WAAAAA
RYOMA SURVIVED A TRIPLE MATCH POINT!!
GAME, ECHIZEN! 5 ALL!
NOT ONLY THAT...
...HE'S TIED UP THE MATCH!!
S. TOTAL
5 5
7 5
RAA
LOOK!

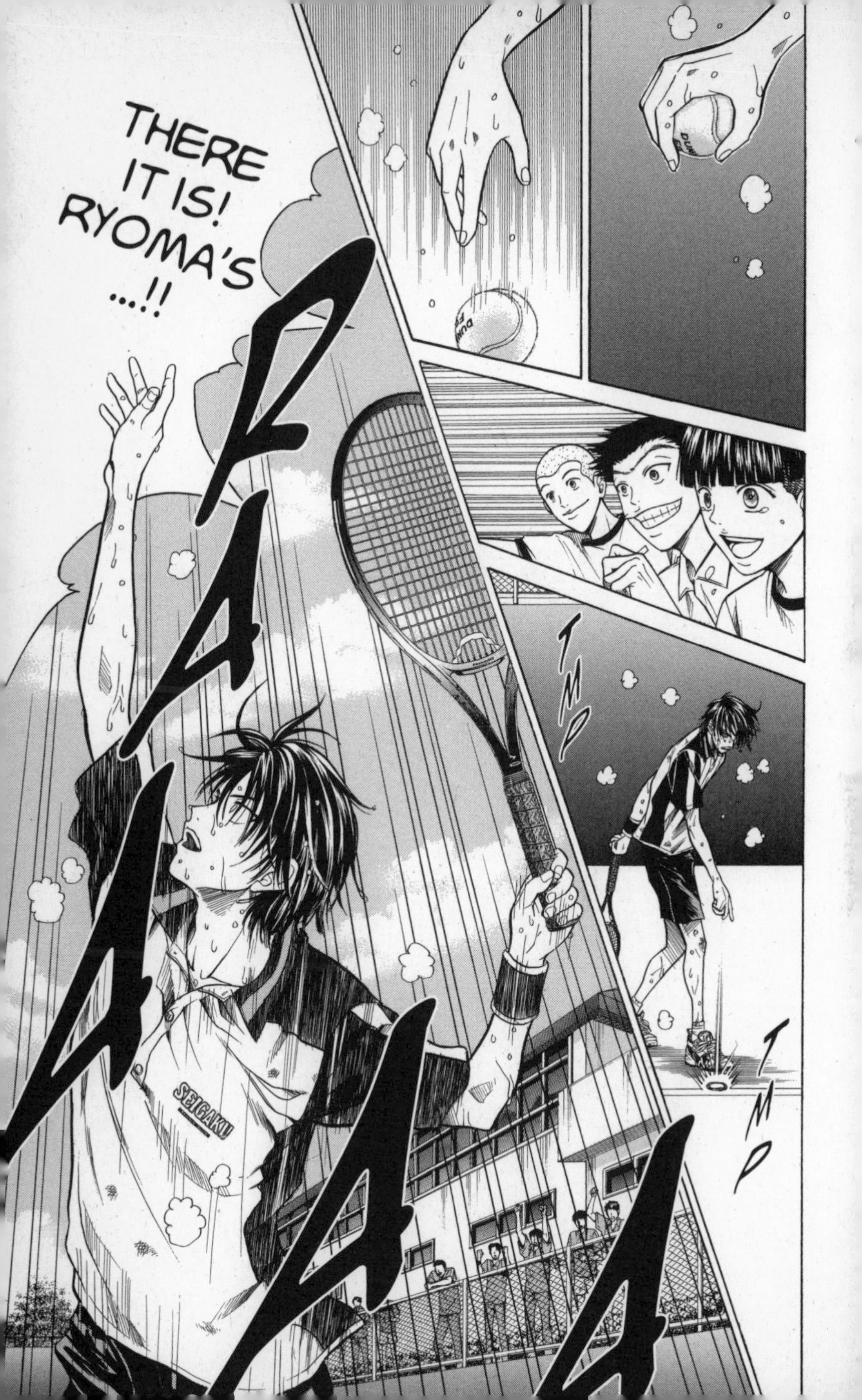
TMP
TMP
THERE IT IS! RYOMA'S ...!!

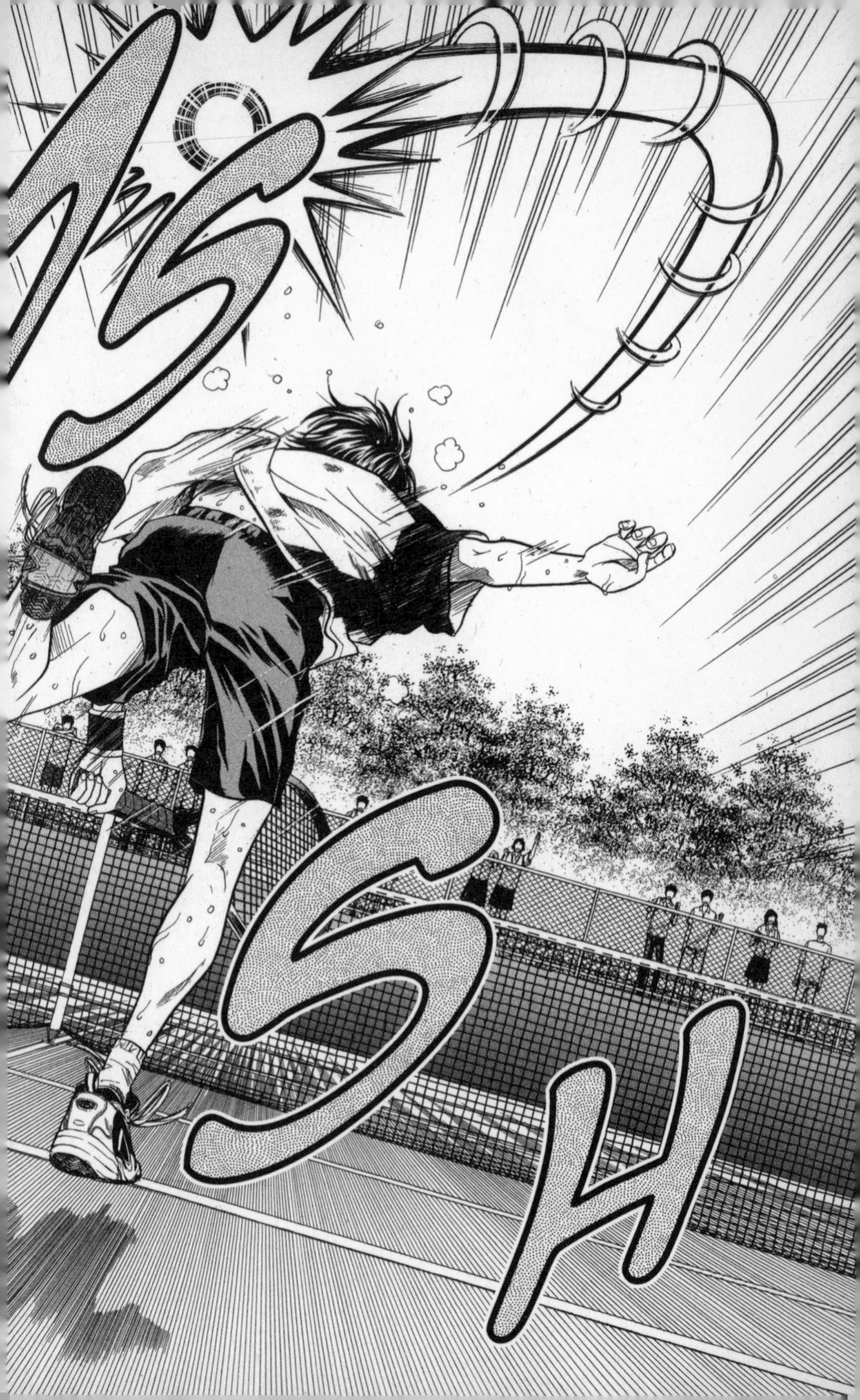
SSH

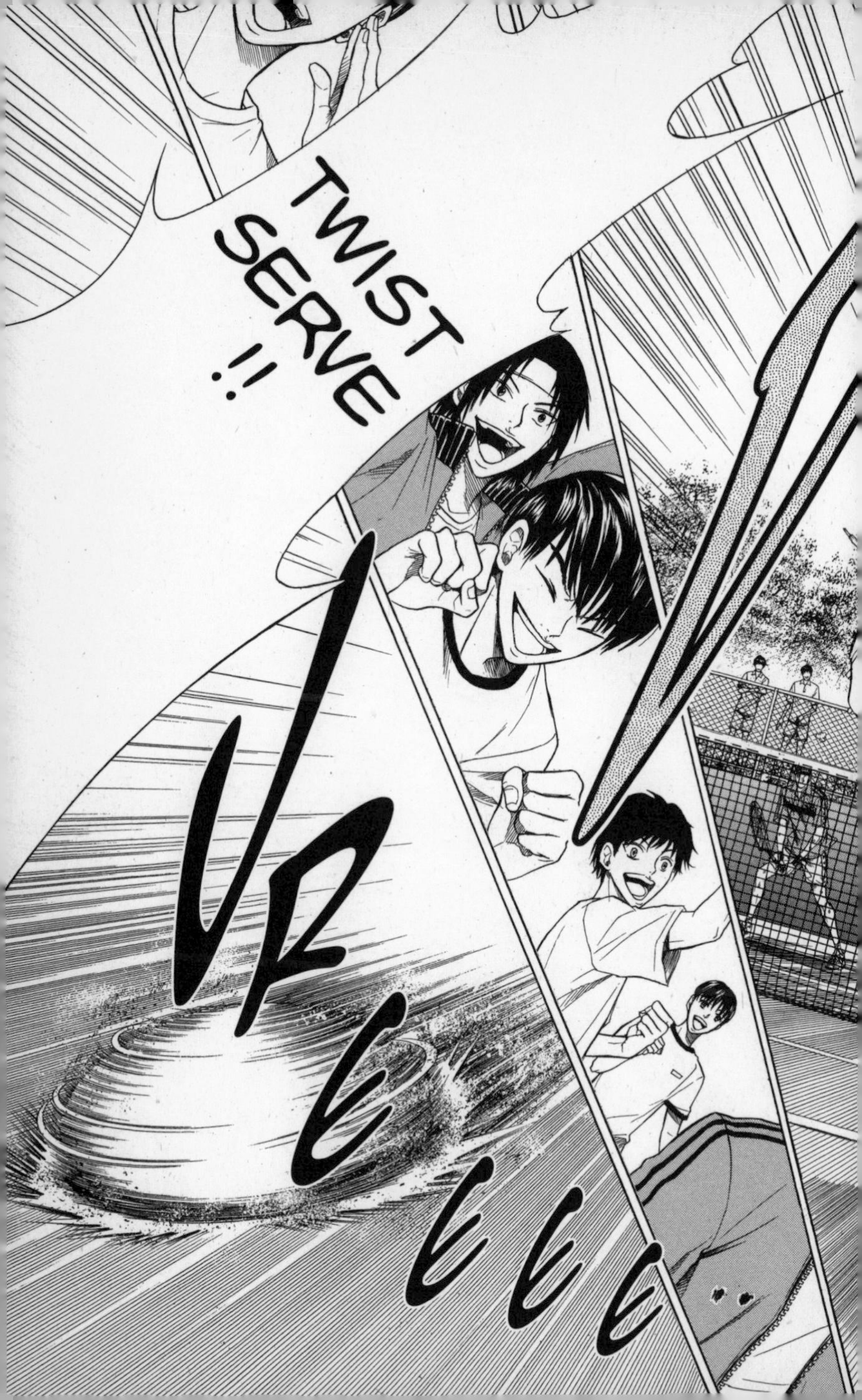
TWIST SERVE !!
VREEEEE

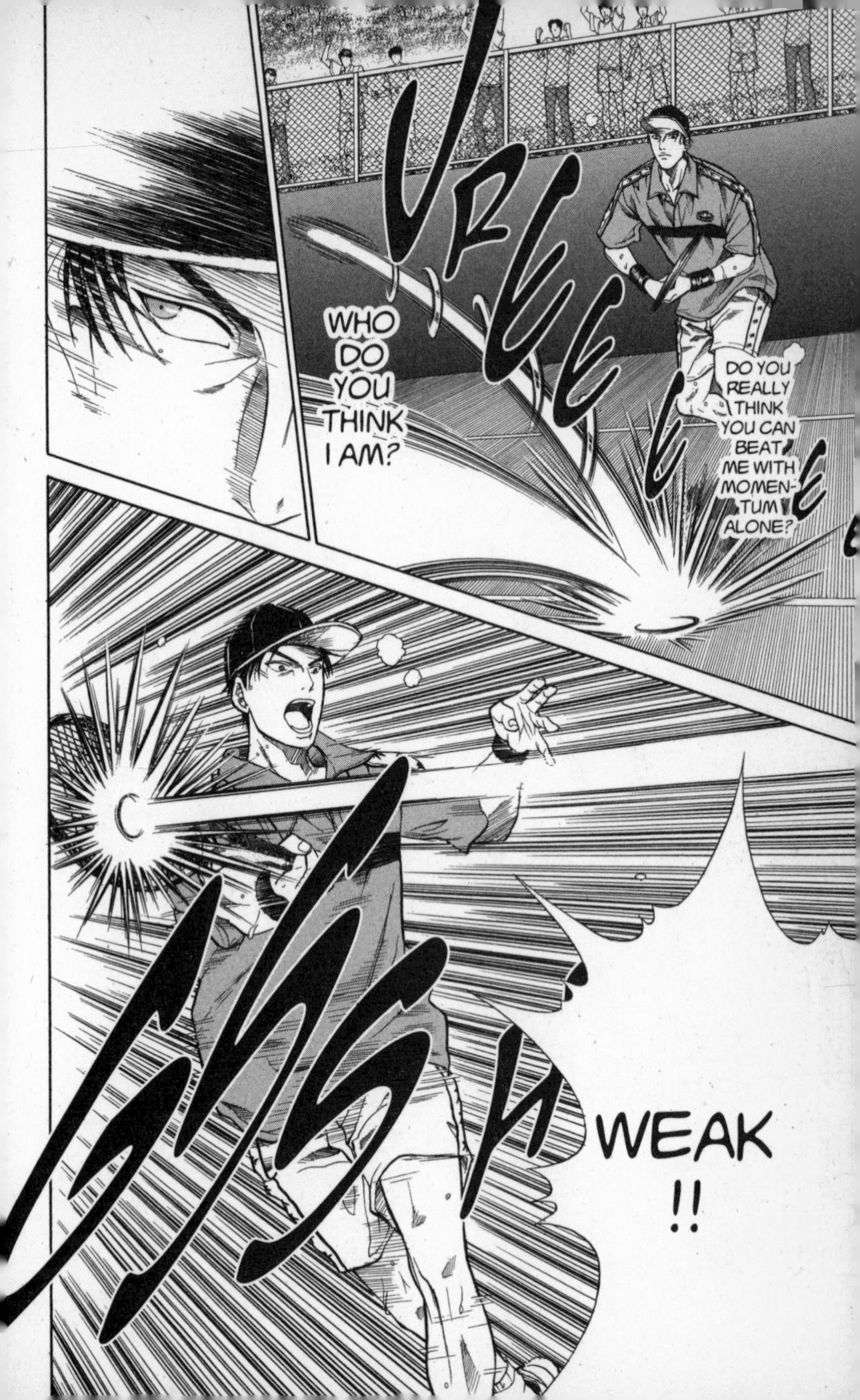
WHO DO YOU THINK I AM?
DO YOU REALLY THINK YOU CAN BEAT ME WITH MOMEN-TUM ALONE?
WEAK !!

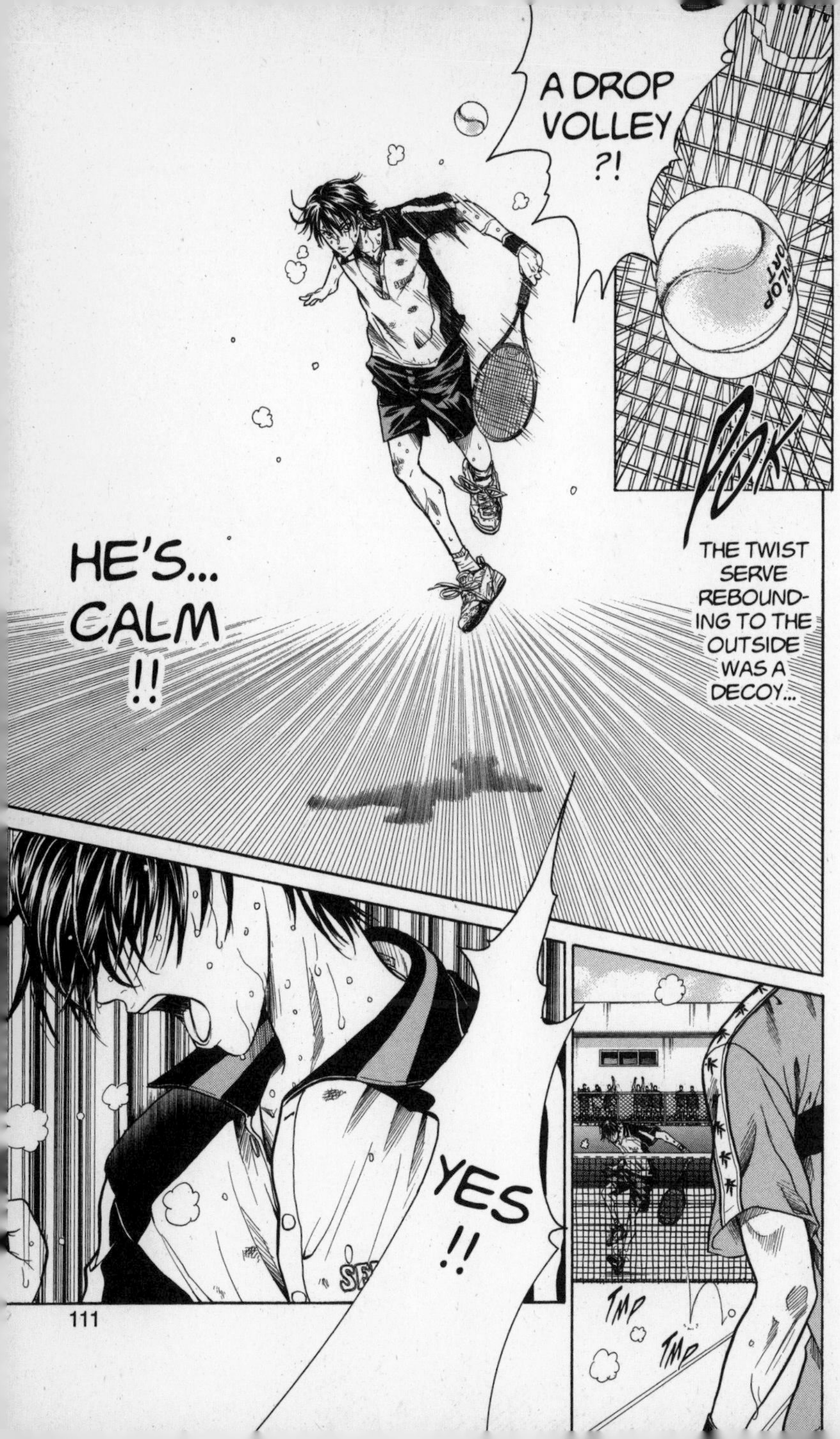
POK
THE TWIST SERVE REBOUNDING TO THE OUTSIDE WAS A DECOY...
A DROP VOLLEY ?!
HE'S... CALM !!
TMP
TMP
YES !!

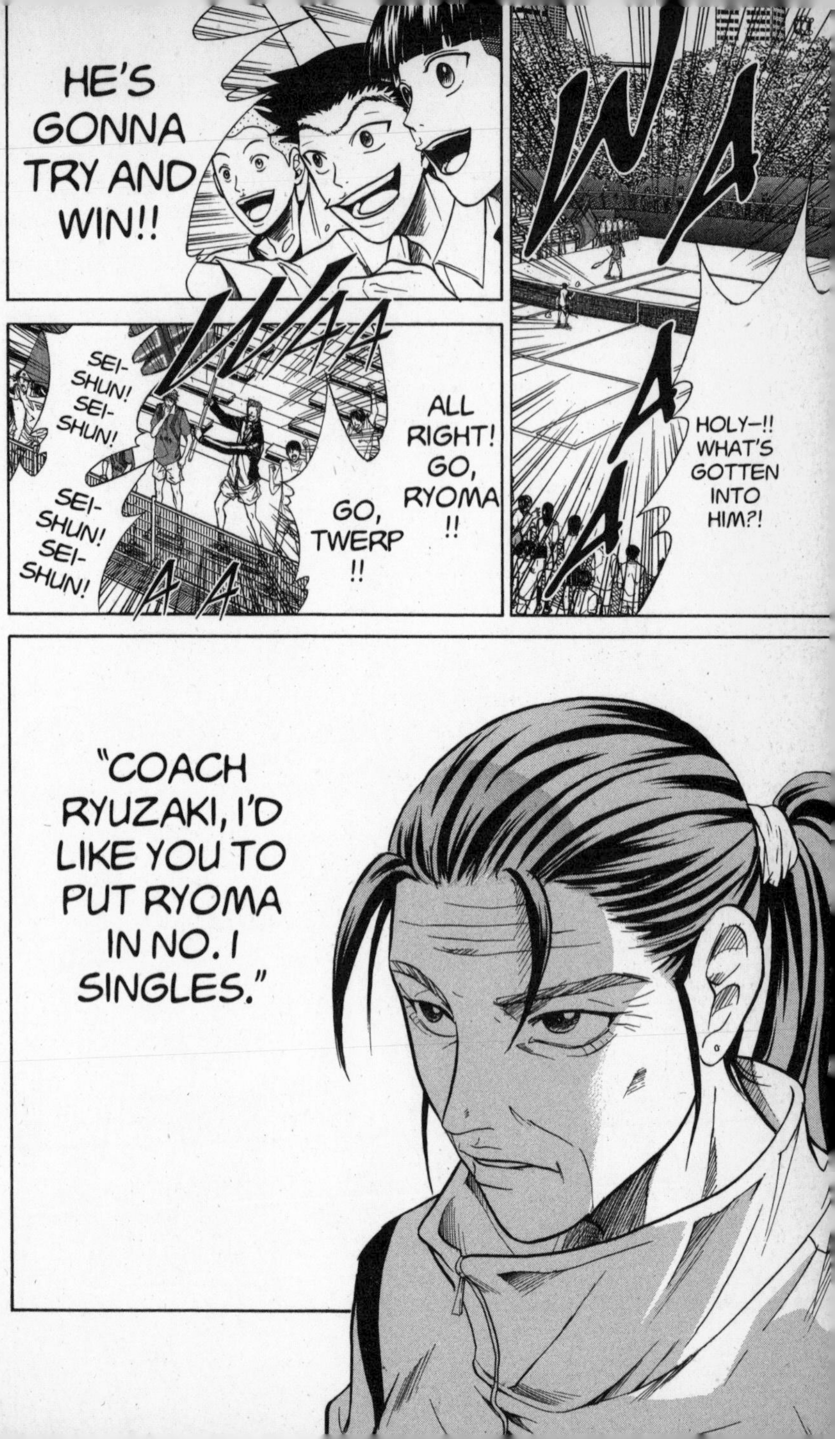

WAAAA
HOLY—!! WHAT'S GOTTEN INTO HIM?!
HE'S GONNA TRY AND WIN!!
WAA
AA
ALL RIGHT! GO, RYOMA!!
GO, TWERP!!
SEI-SHUN! SEI-SHUN!
SEI-SHUN! SEI-SHUN!
"COACH RYUZAKI, I'D LIKE YOU TO PUT RYOMA IN NO. 1 SINGLES."

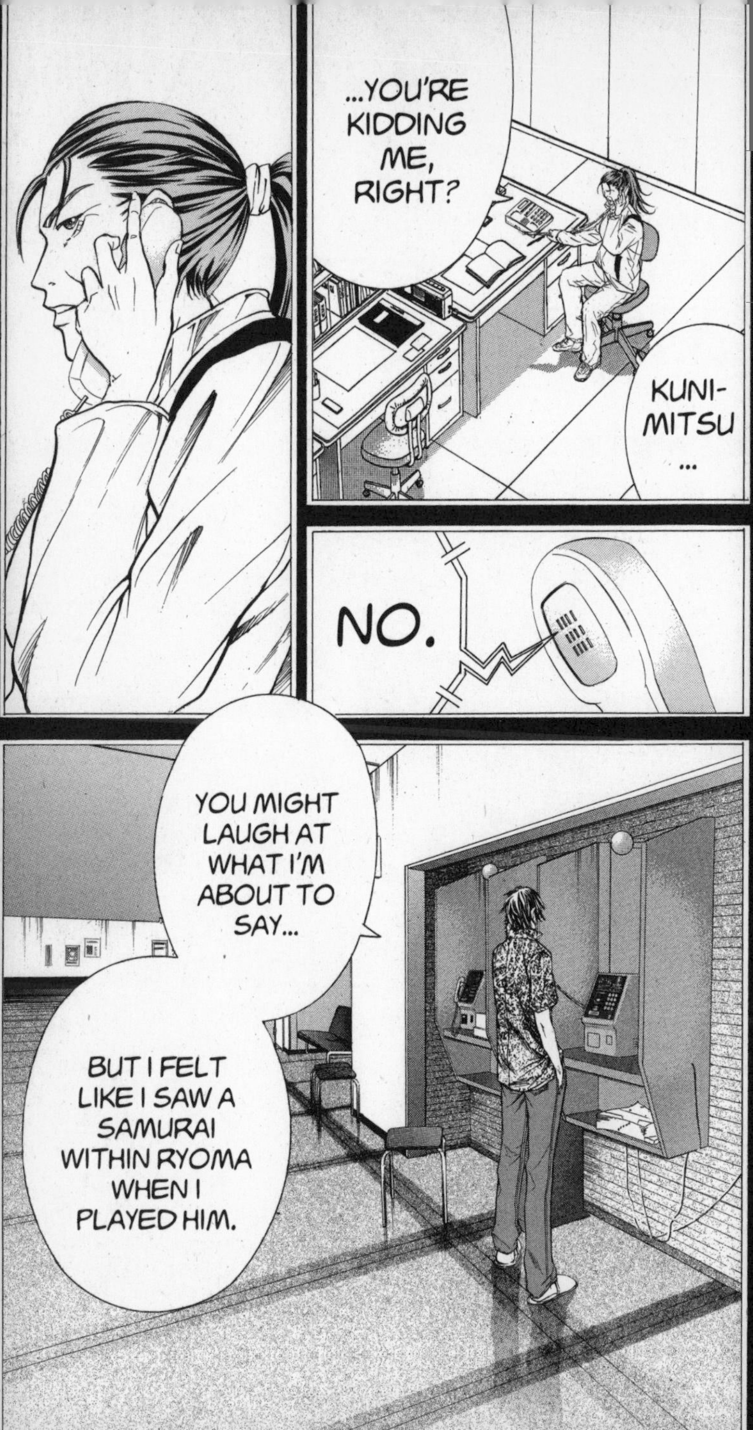
...YOU'RE KIDDING ME, RIGHT?
KUNI-MITSU ...
NO.
YOU MIGHT LAUGH AT WHAT I'M ABOUT TO SAY...
BUT I FELT LIKE I SAW A SAMURAI WITHIN RYOMA WHEN I PLAYED HIM.

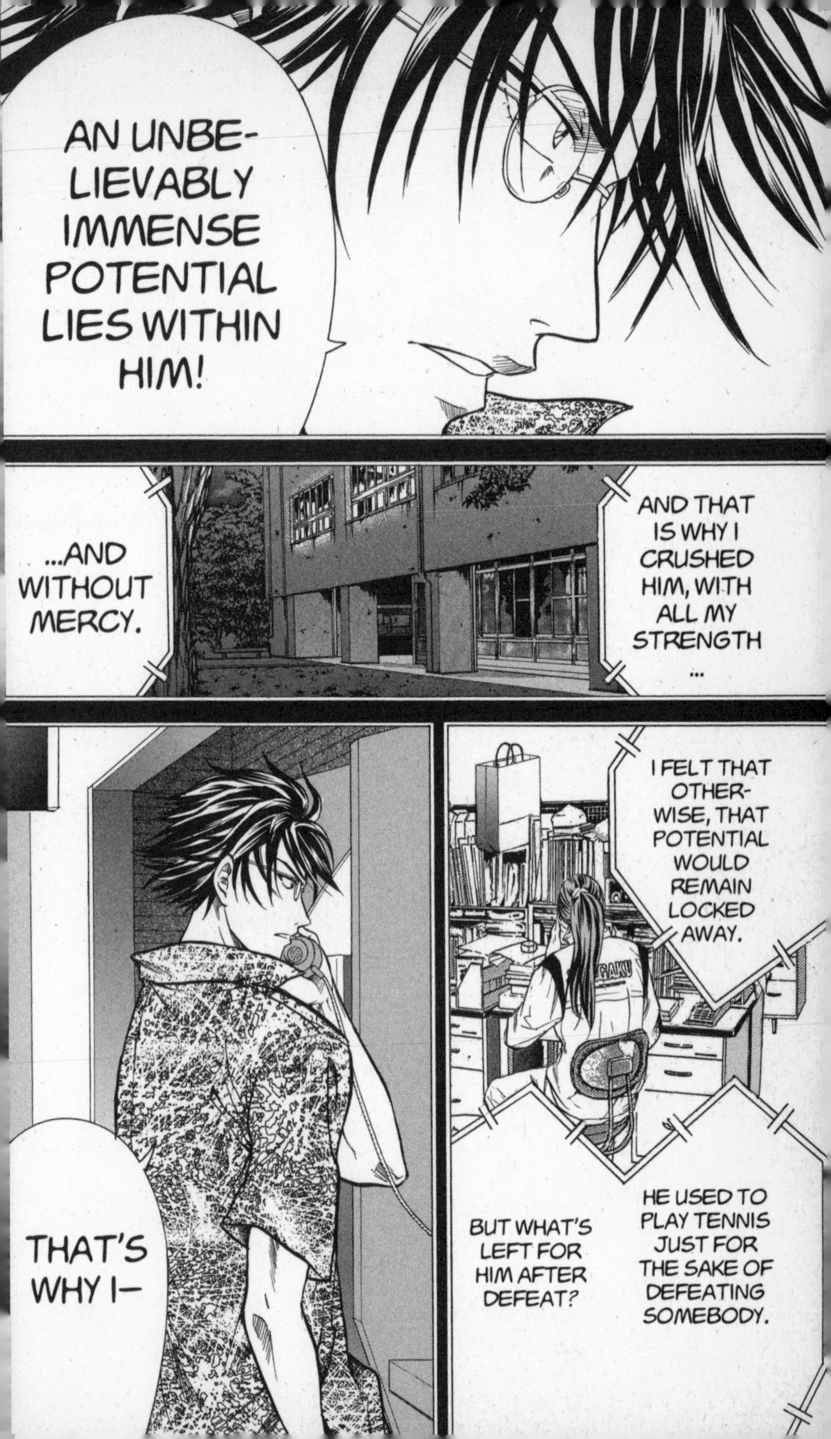
AN UNBELIEVABLY IMMENSE POTENTIAL LIES WITHIN HIM!
AND THAT IS WHY I CRUSHED HIM, WITH ALL MY STRENGTH...
...AND WITHOUT MERCY.
I FELT THAT OTHERWISE, THAT POTENTIAL WOULD REMAIN LOCKED AWAY.
HE USED TO PLAY TENNIS JUST FOR THE SAKE OF DEFEATING SOMEBODY.
BUT WHAT'S LEFT FOR HIM AFTER DEFEAT?
THAT'S WHY I—

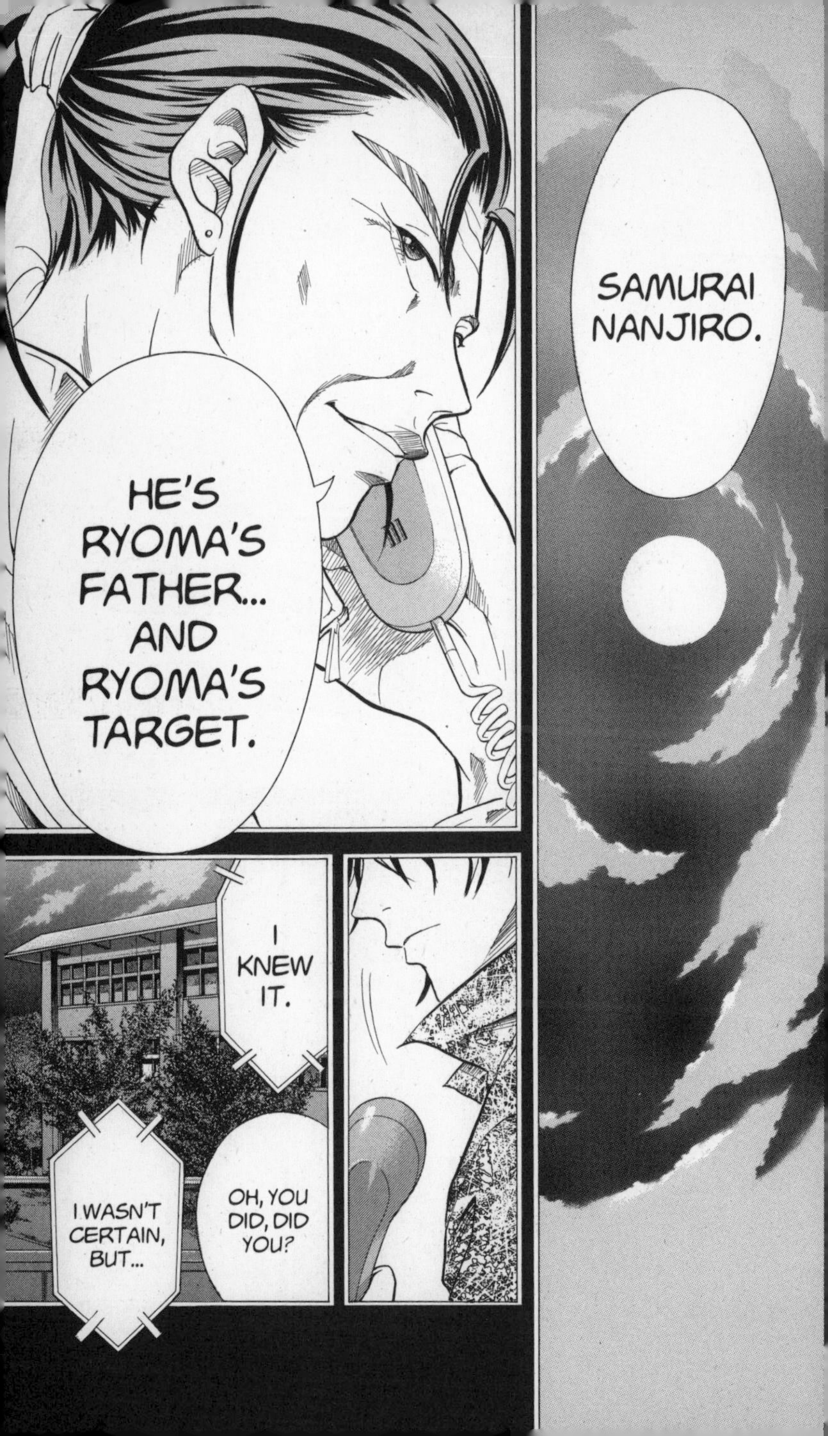
SAMURAI NANJIRO.
HE'S RYOMA'S FATHER... AND RYOMA'S TARGET.
I KNEW IT.
OH, YOU DID, DID YOU?
I WASN'T CERTAIN, BUT...

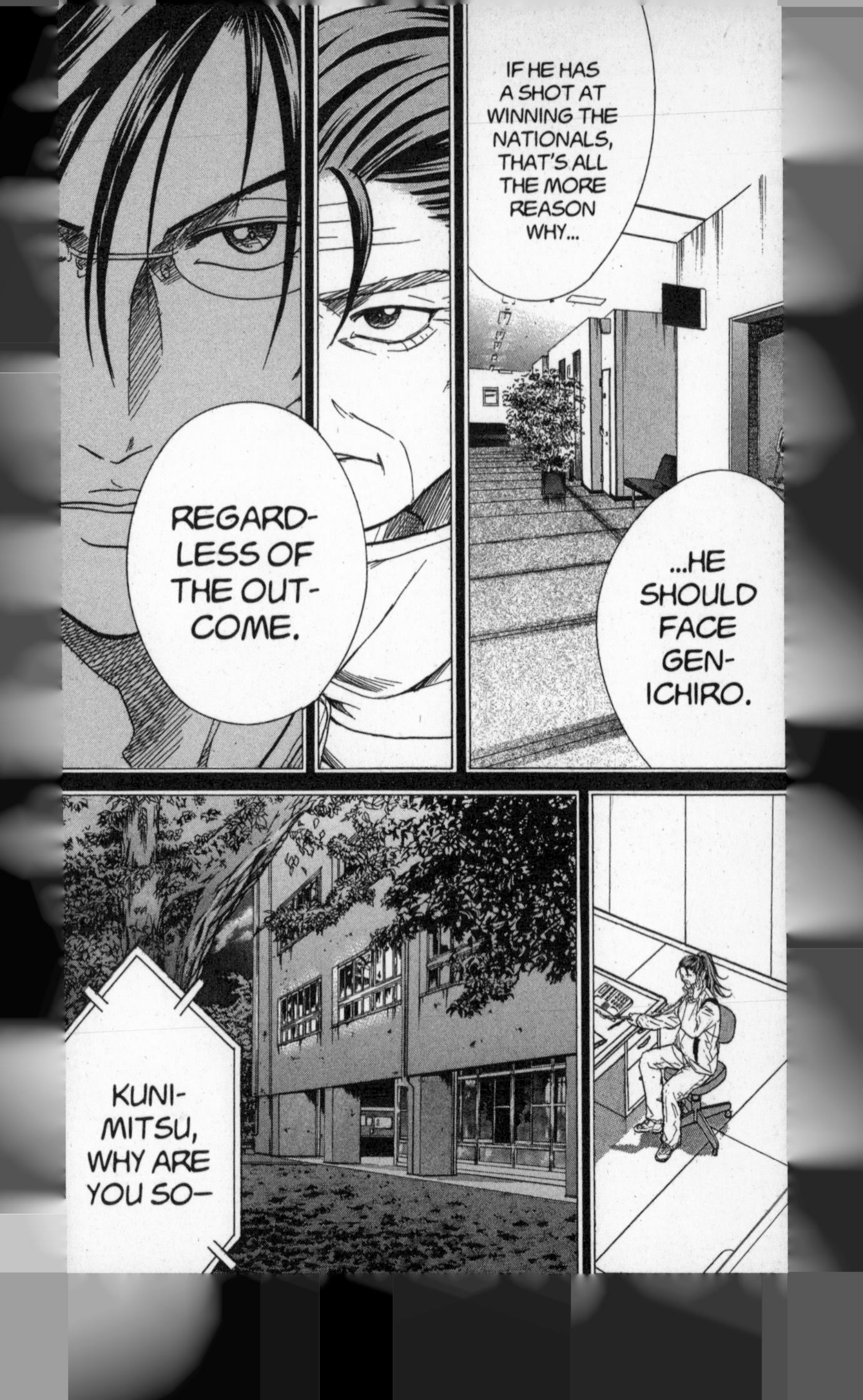
IF HE HAS A SHOT AT WINNING THE NATIONALS, THAT'S ALL THE MORE REASON WHY...
...HE SHOULD FACE GEN-ICHIRO.
REGARD-LESS OF THE OUT-COME.
KUNI-MITSU, WHY ARE YOU SO–

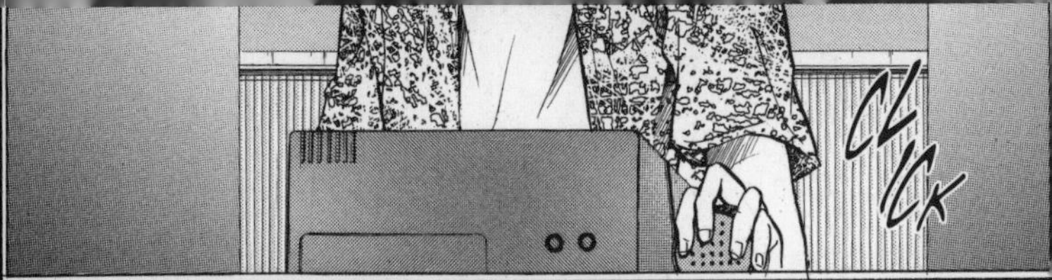
CLICK
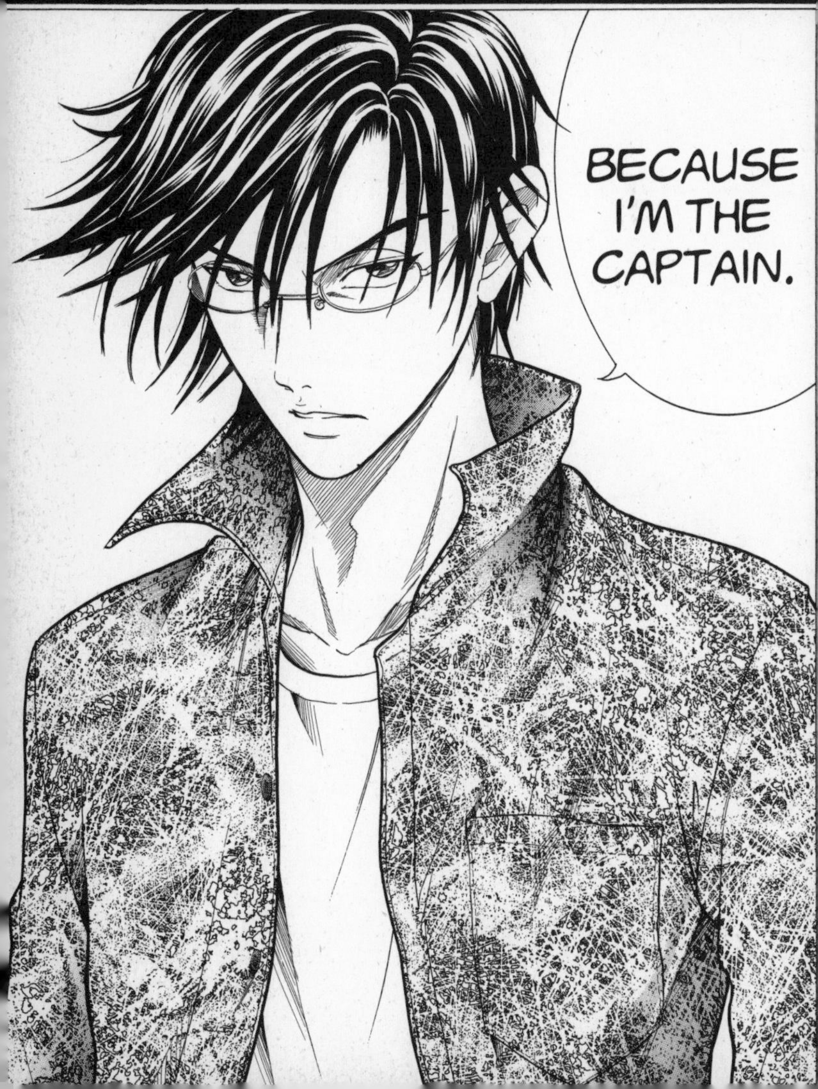
BECAUSE I'M THE CAPTAIN.

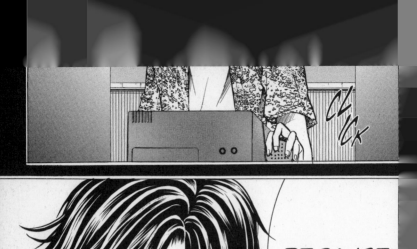

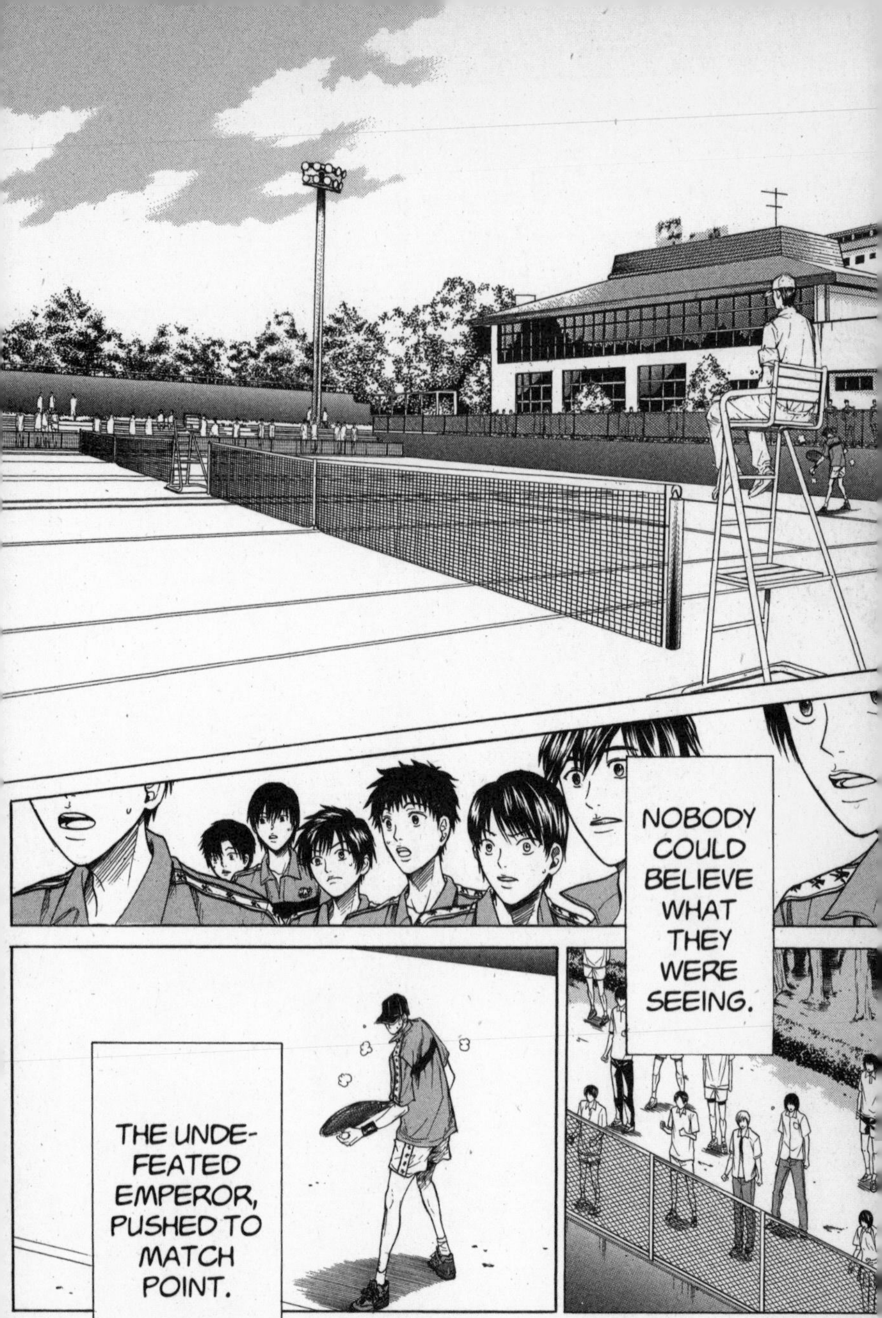
NOBODY COULD BELIEVE WHAT THEY WERE SEEING.
THE UNDE-FEATED EMPEROR, PUSHED TO MATCH POINT.

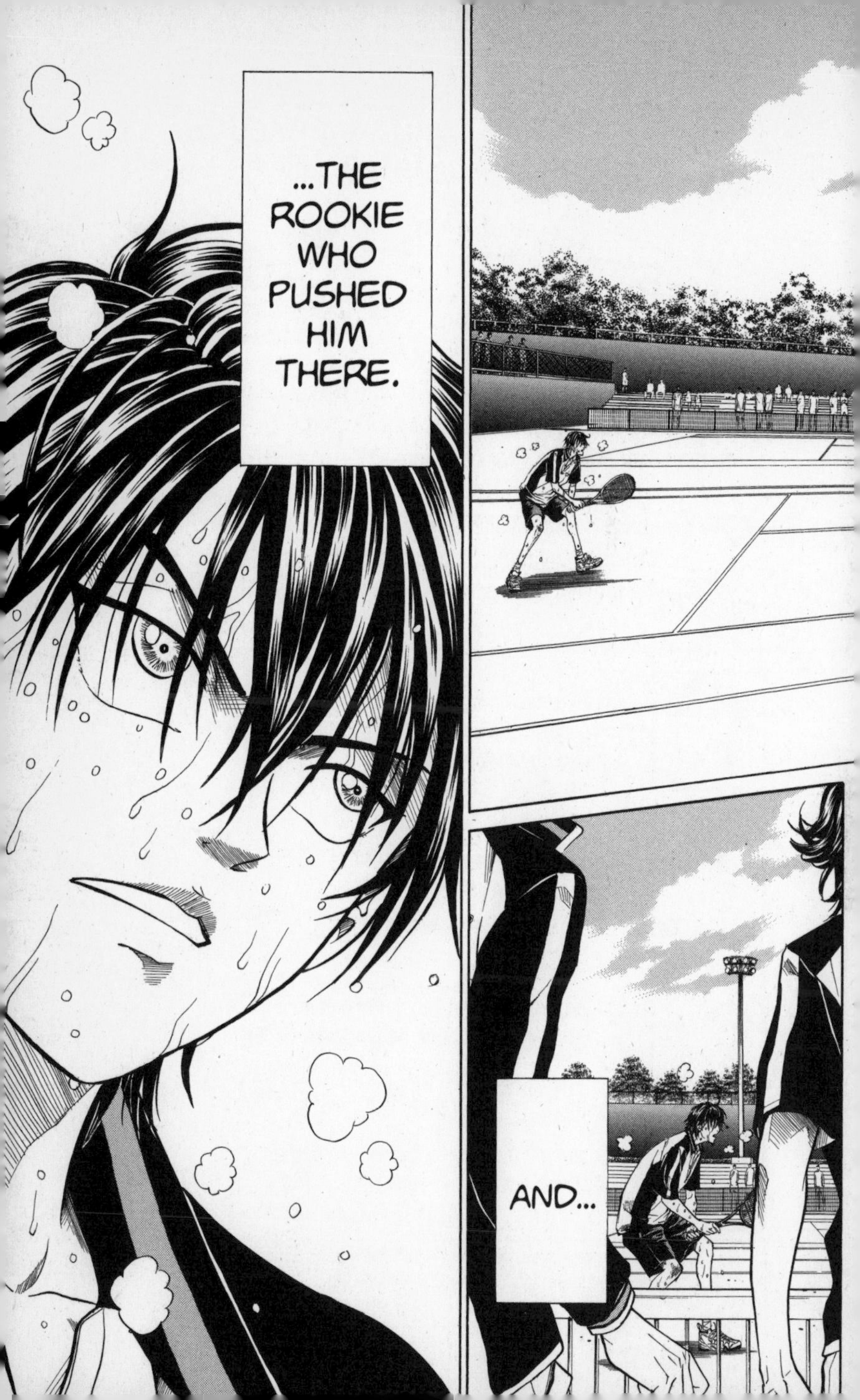
AND...
...THE ROOKIE WHO PUSHED HIM THERE.

RIKKAI QUESTION CORNER

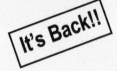

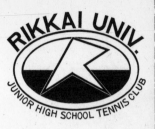

RIKKAI UNIV.
JUNIOR HIGH SCHOOL TENNIS CLUB

Part 6

It's Back!!

Back by popular demand! The guys from Rikkai aren't very forthcoming about themselves, are they? Well then, let's have them answer some of your questions!

Q: It's about Captain Yukimura's Guillain-Barré Syndrome. According to my friend, it can't be cured with surgery... I just hope he gets better soon. I'll be praying for him.
(R.O., Nagoya)

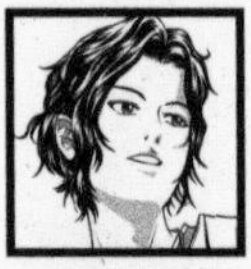

Thank you so much. I know a lot of people are worried about me, but I'll be fine! I'll be better in time for the Nationals.

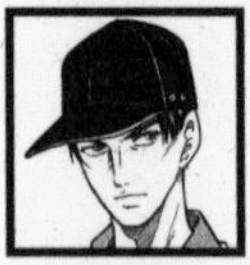

Seiichi's illness isn't Guillain-Barré Syndrome! It's just very similar to it...

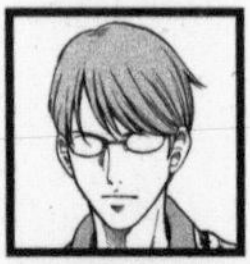

Indeed, Guillain-Barré Syndrome cannot be cured with surgery. I just hope he gets better soon.

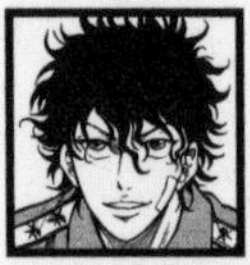

I hope I get to play you before you graduate. This time I'll win...

My deepest apology to all those suffering from Guillain-Barré Syndrome and to their families for misrepresenting the illness in volume 25.

Takeshi Konomi

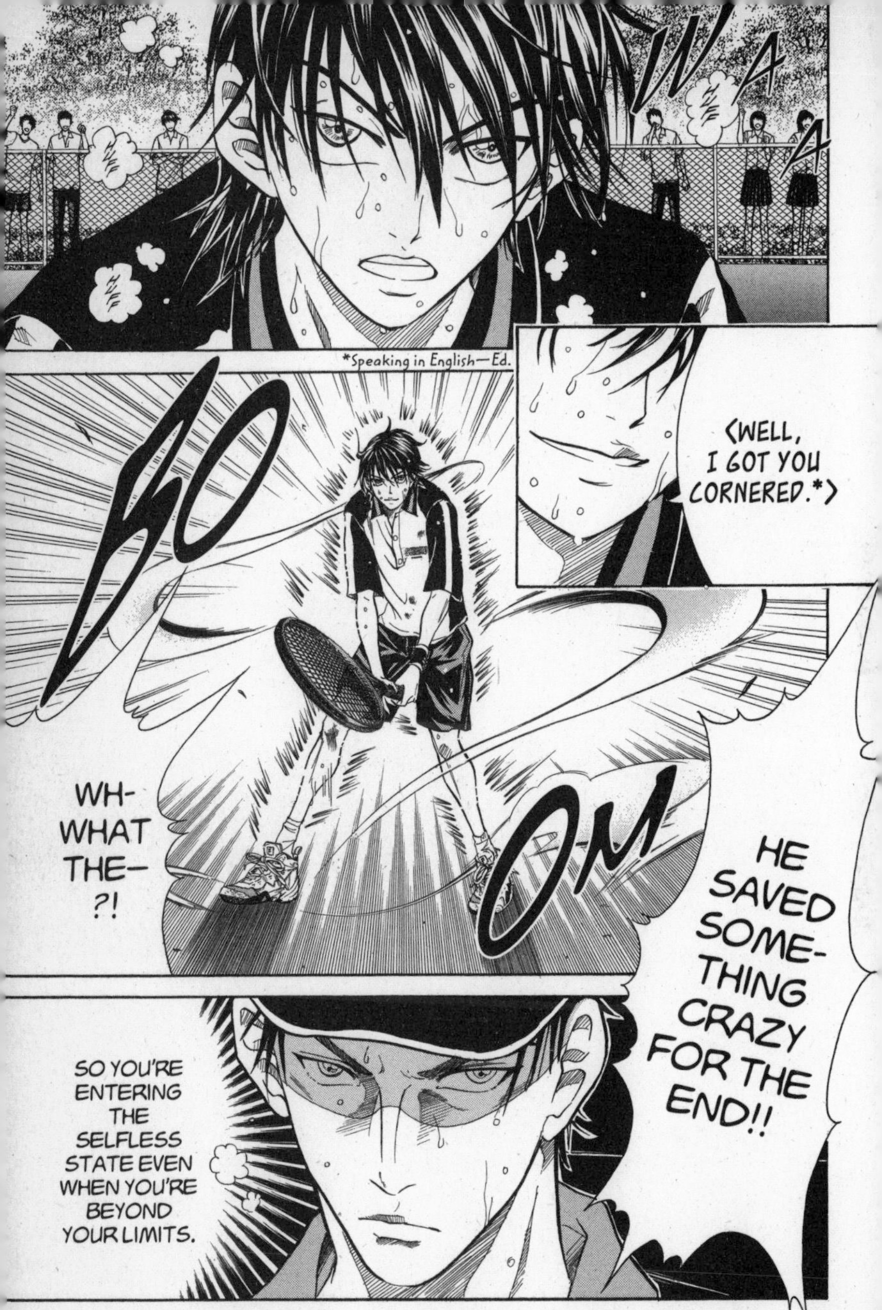
WA WA
*Speaking in English—Ed.
<WELL, I GOT YOU CORNERED.*>
ZOOM
HE SAVED SOMETHING CRAZY FOR THE END!!
WH-WHAT THE—?!
SO YOU'RE ENTERING THE SELFLESS STATE EVEN WHEN YOU'RE BEYOND YOUR LIMITS.

GENIUS 235: THE NO. 1 LOSS HATER

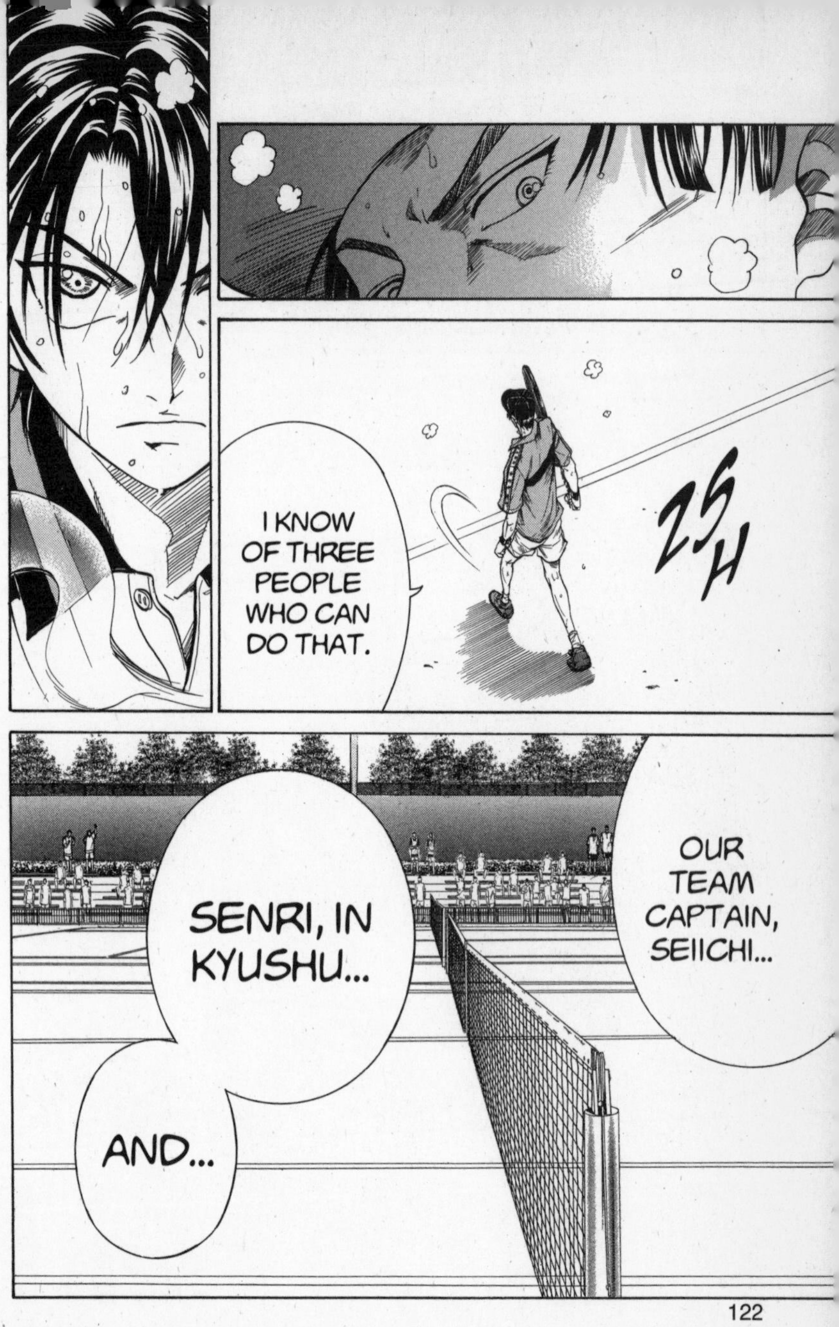
I KNOW OF THREE PEOPLE WHO CAN DO THAT.
ZSH
OUR TEAM CAPTAIN, SEIICHI...
SENRI, IN KYUSHU...
AND...

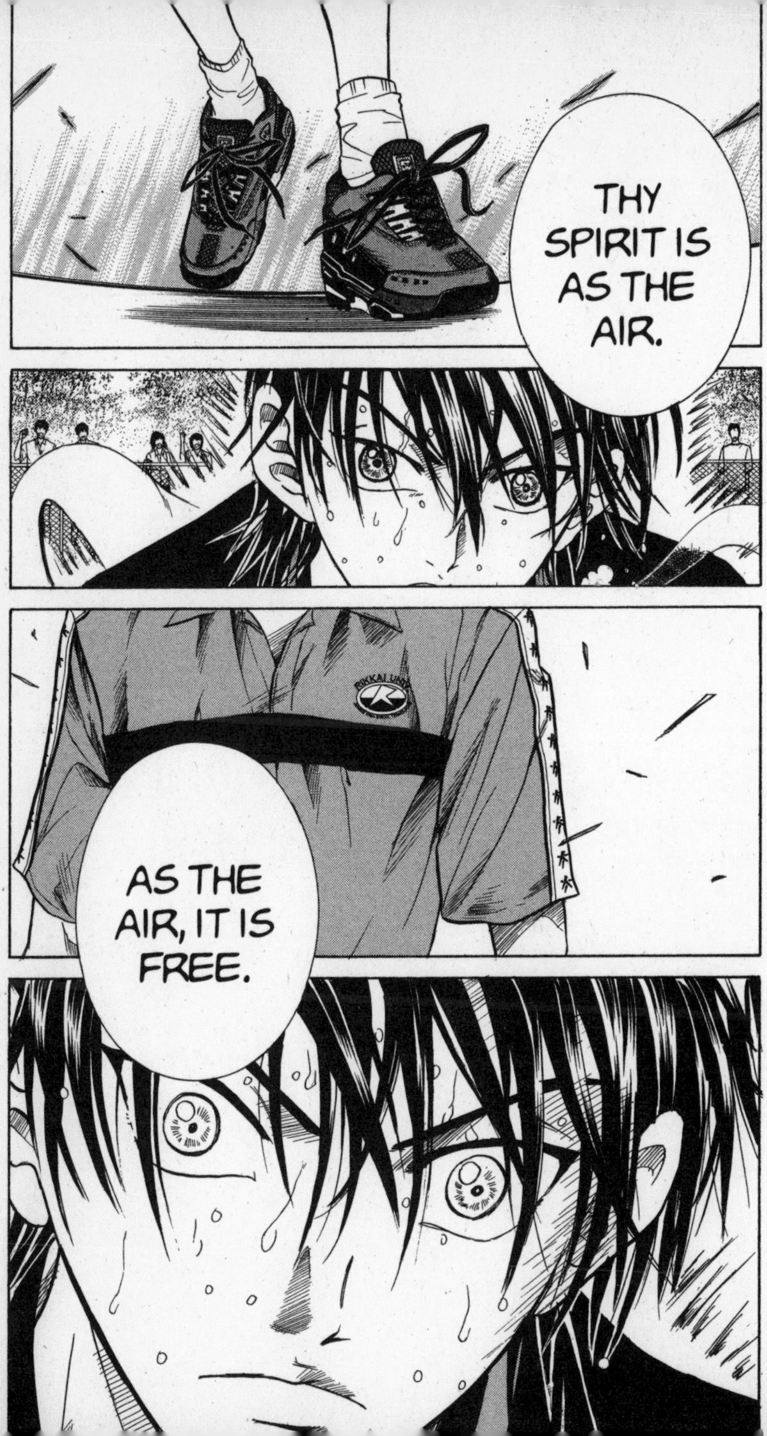
THY SPIRIT IS AS THE AIR.
RIKKAI UNIV
AS THE AIR, IT IS FREE.

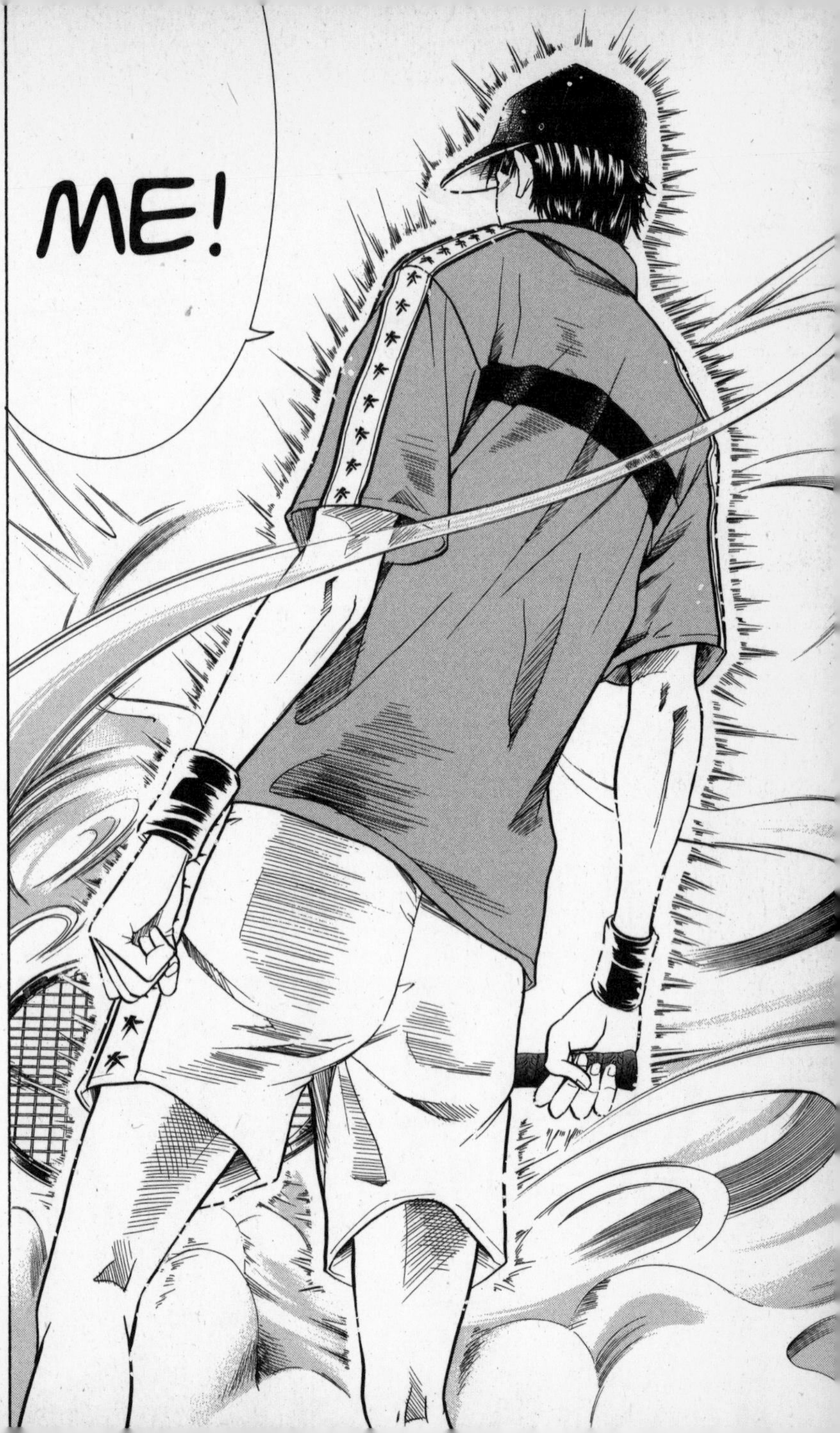
ME!

GENIUS 235: THE NO. 1 LOSS HATER

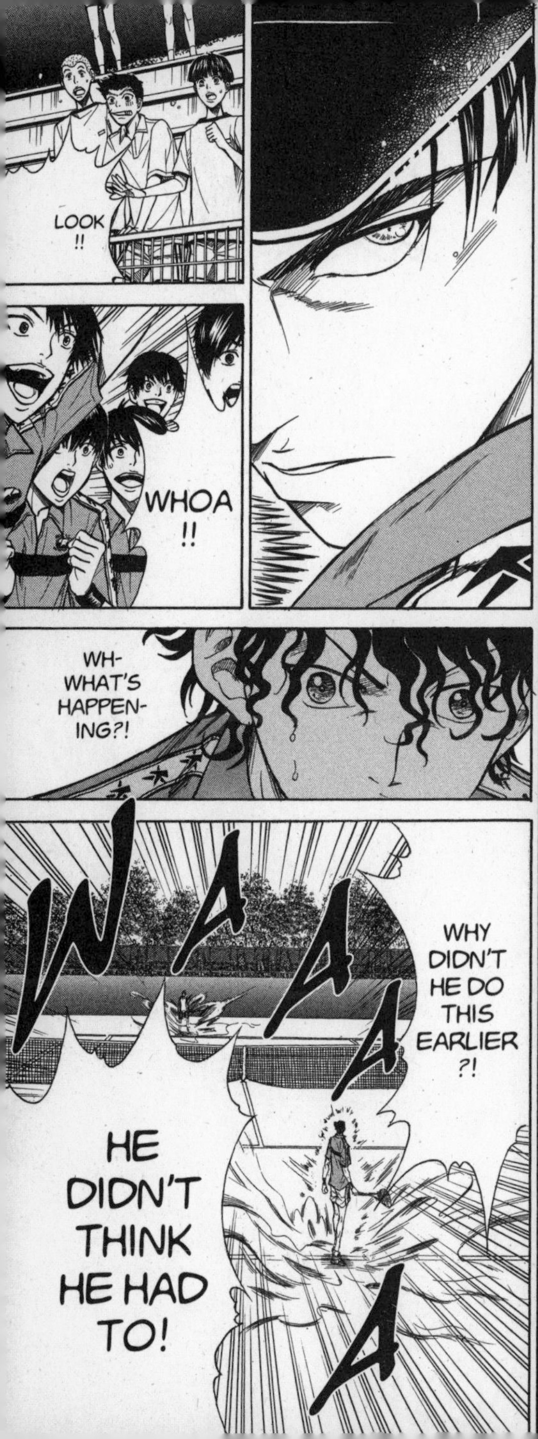

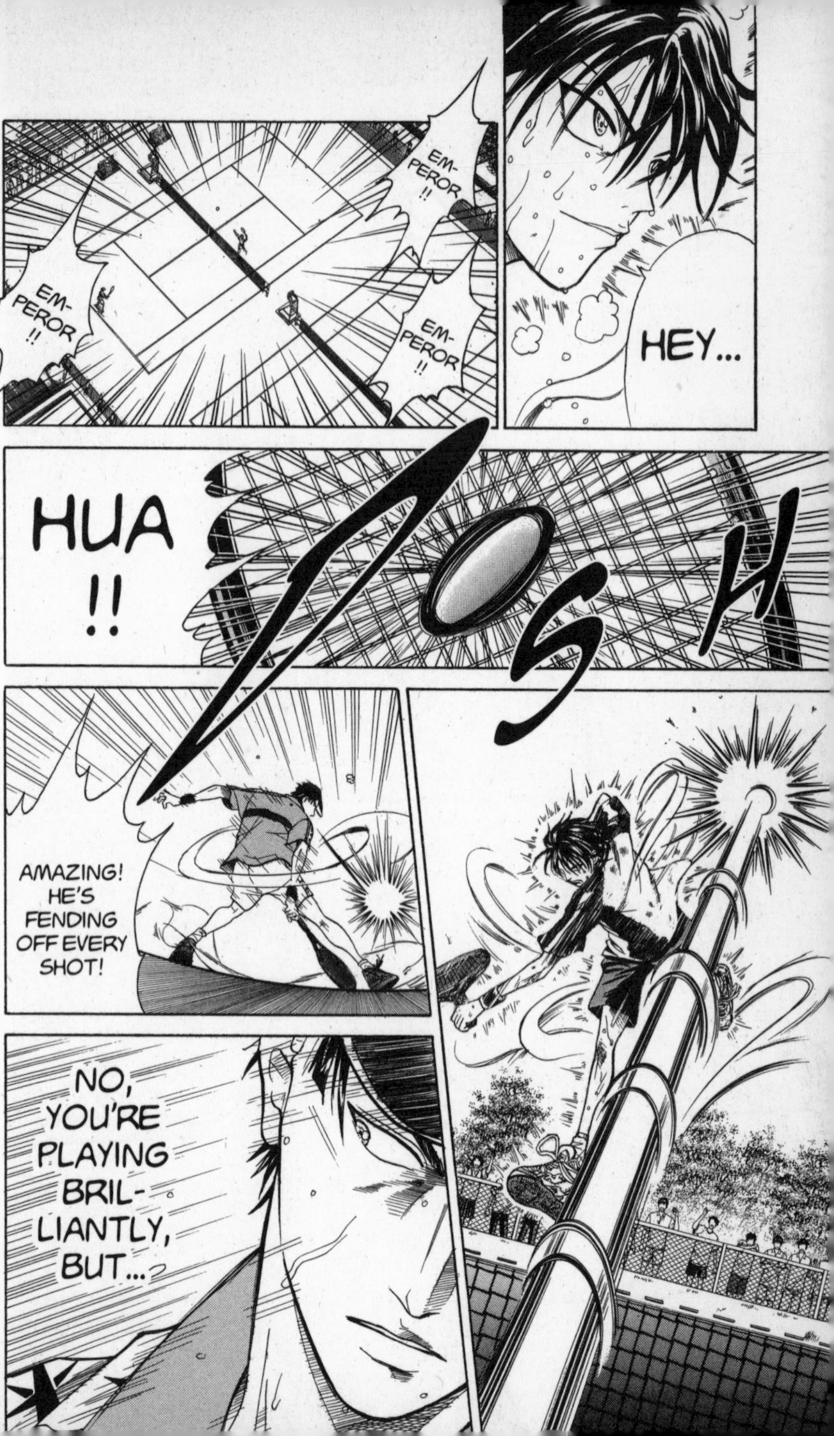
HEY...
EM-PEROR!!
EM-PEROR!!
EM-PEROR!!
HUA!!
WOSH
AMAZING! HE'S FENDING OFF EVERY SHOT!
NO, YOU'RE PLAYING BRIL-LIANTLY, BUT...

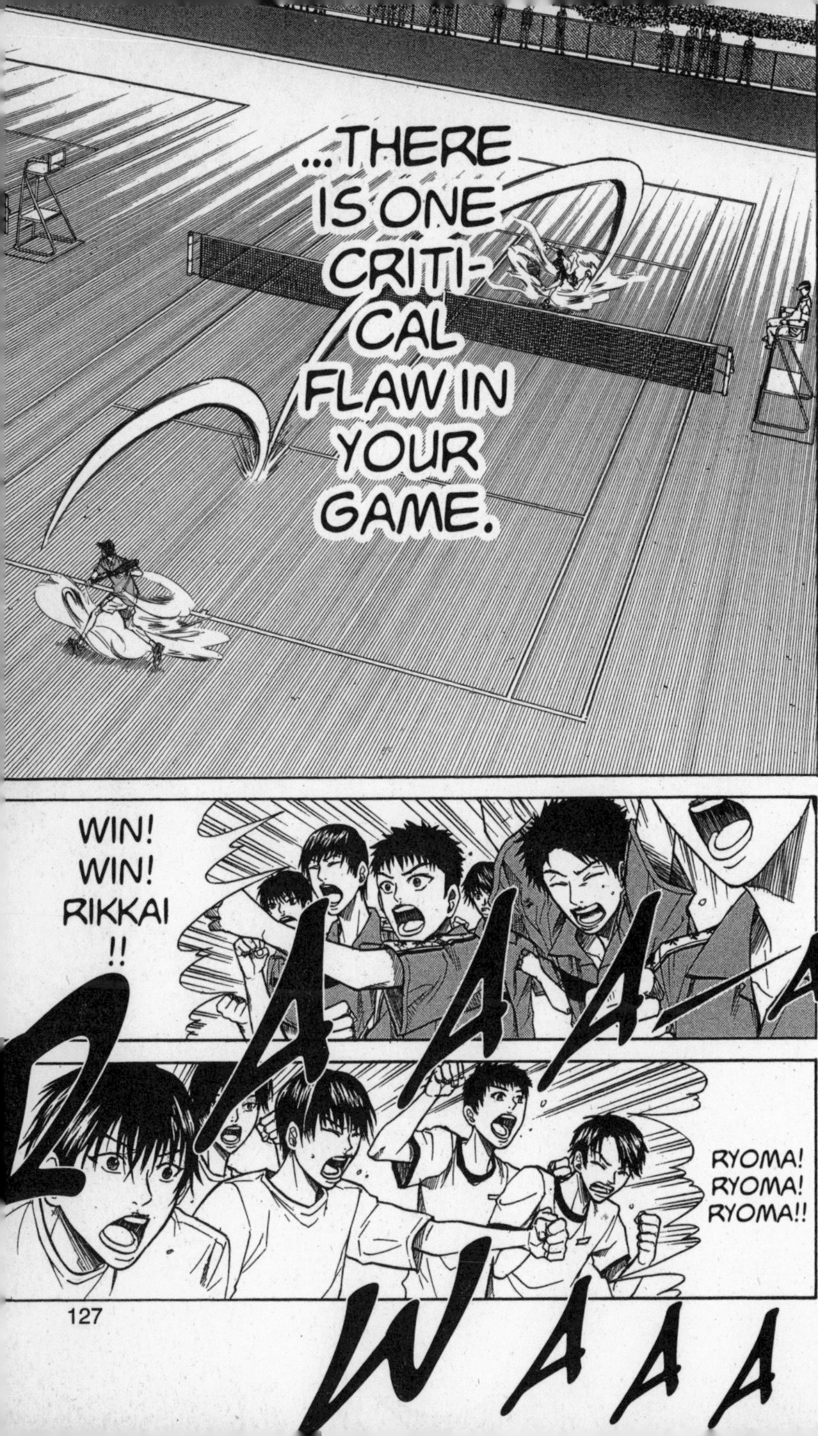
...THERE IS ONE CRITI- CAL FLAW IN YOUR GAME.
WIN! WIN! RIKKAI !!
WAAA-A
RYOMA! RYOMA! RYOMA!!
WAAA

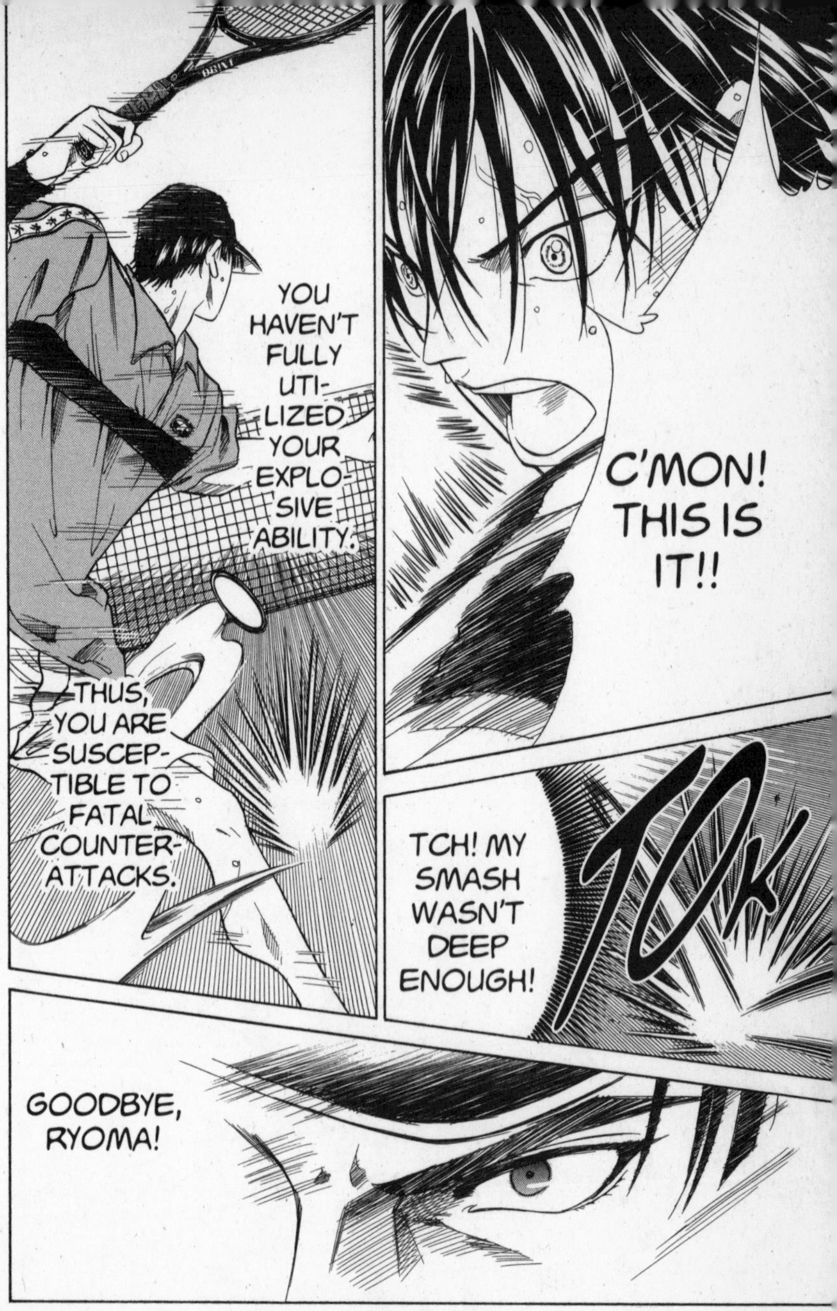
C'MON! THIS IS IT!!
TOK
TCH! MY SMASH WASN'T DEEP ENOUGH!
YOU HAVEN'T FULLY UTI-LIZED YOUR EXPLO-SIVE ABILITY.
THUS, YOU ARE SUSCEP-TIBLE TO FATAL COUNTER-ATTACKS.
GOODBYE, RYOMA!

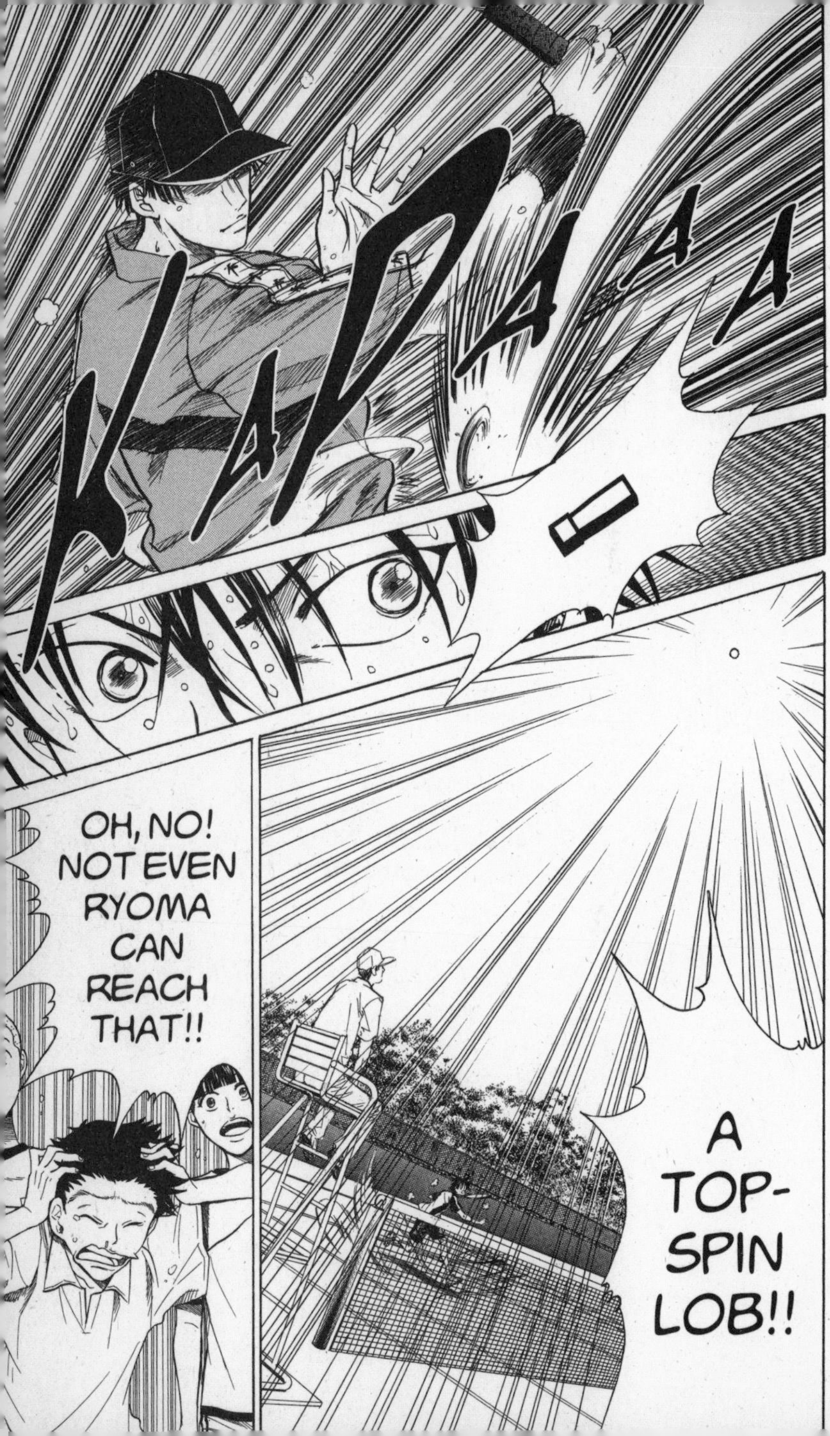
A TOP-SPIN LOB!!
OH, NO! NOT EVEN RYOMA CAN REACH THAT!!

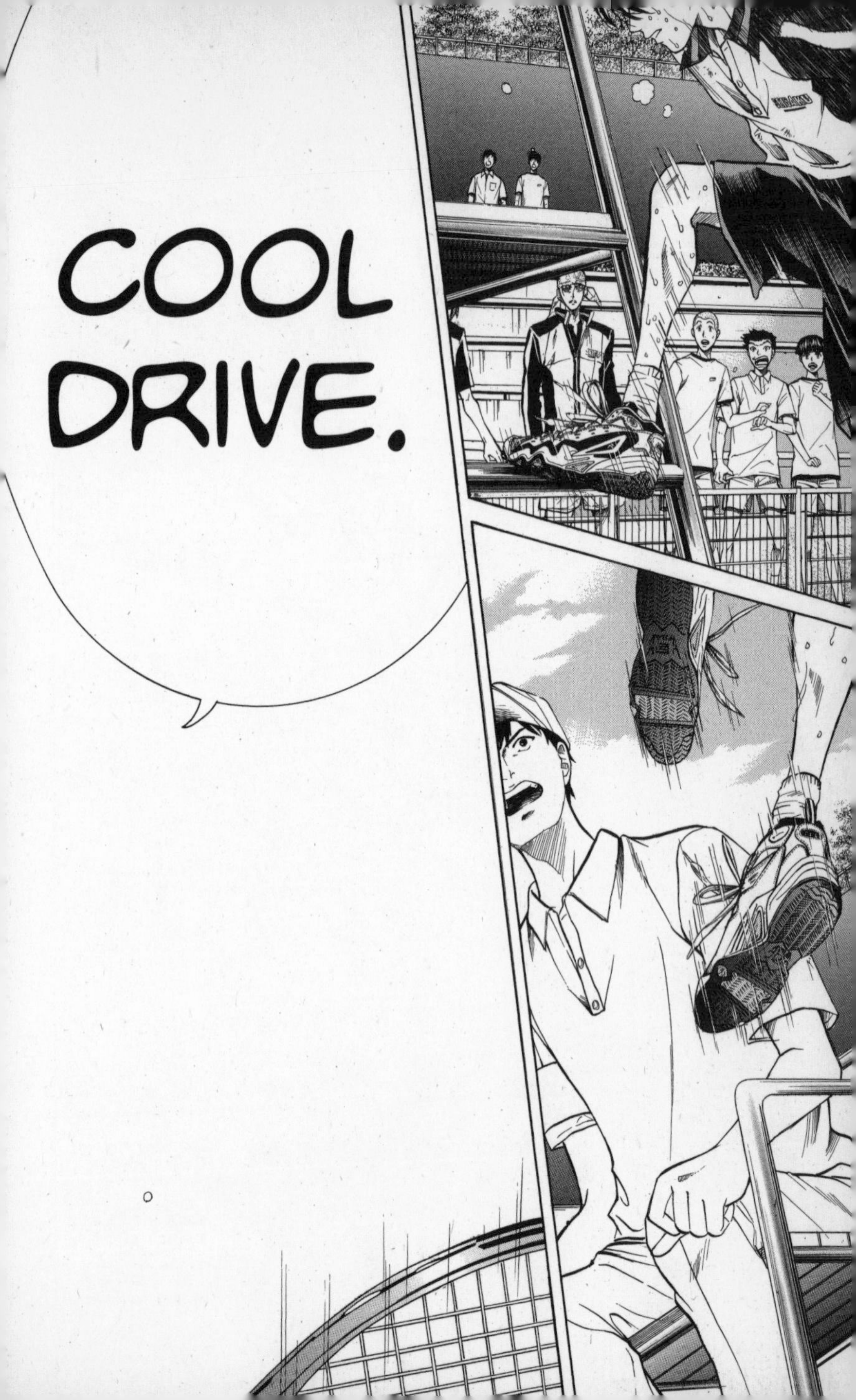
COOL DRIVE.

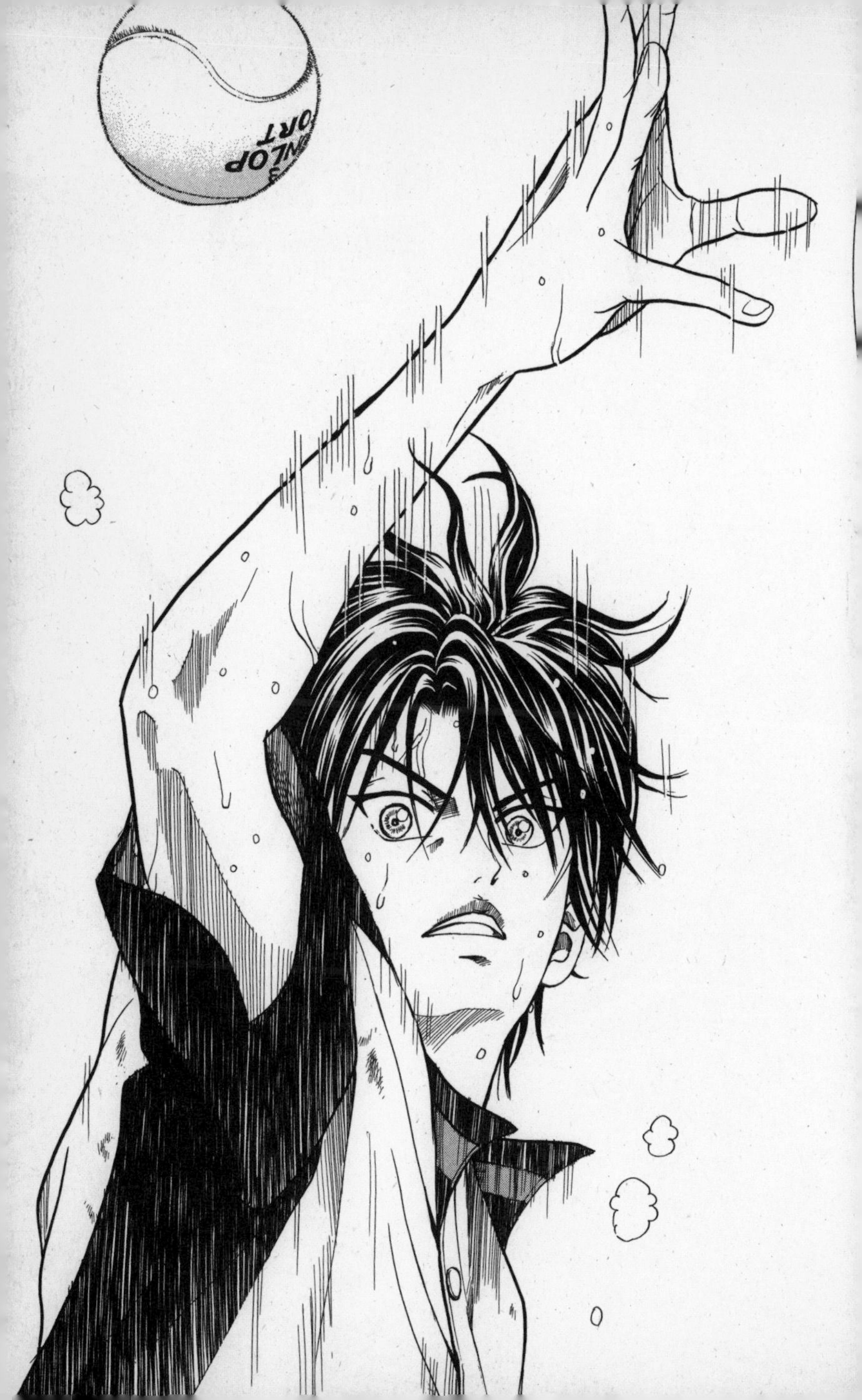

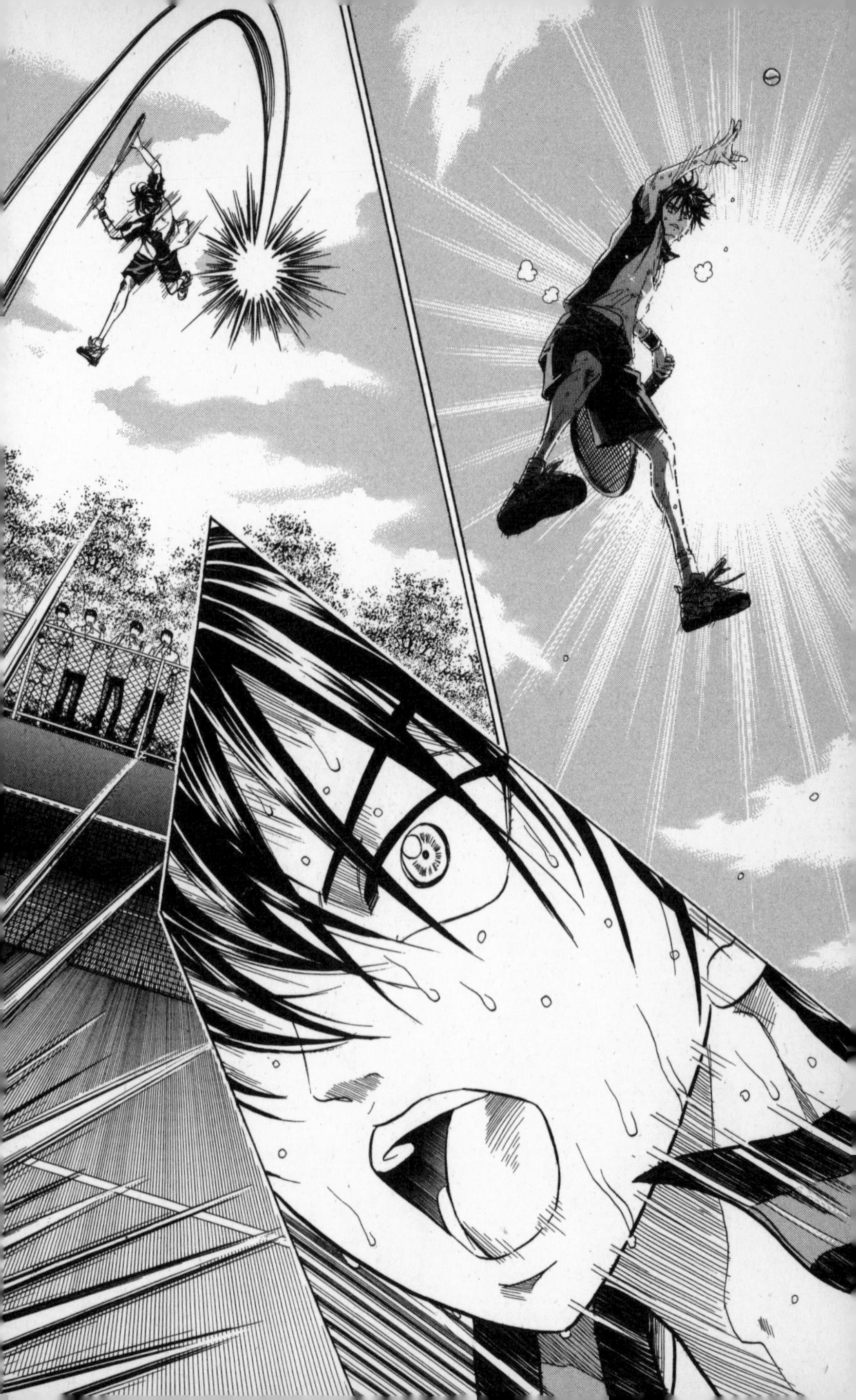

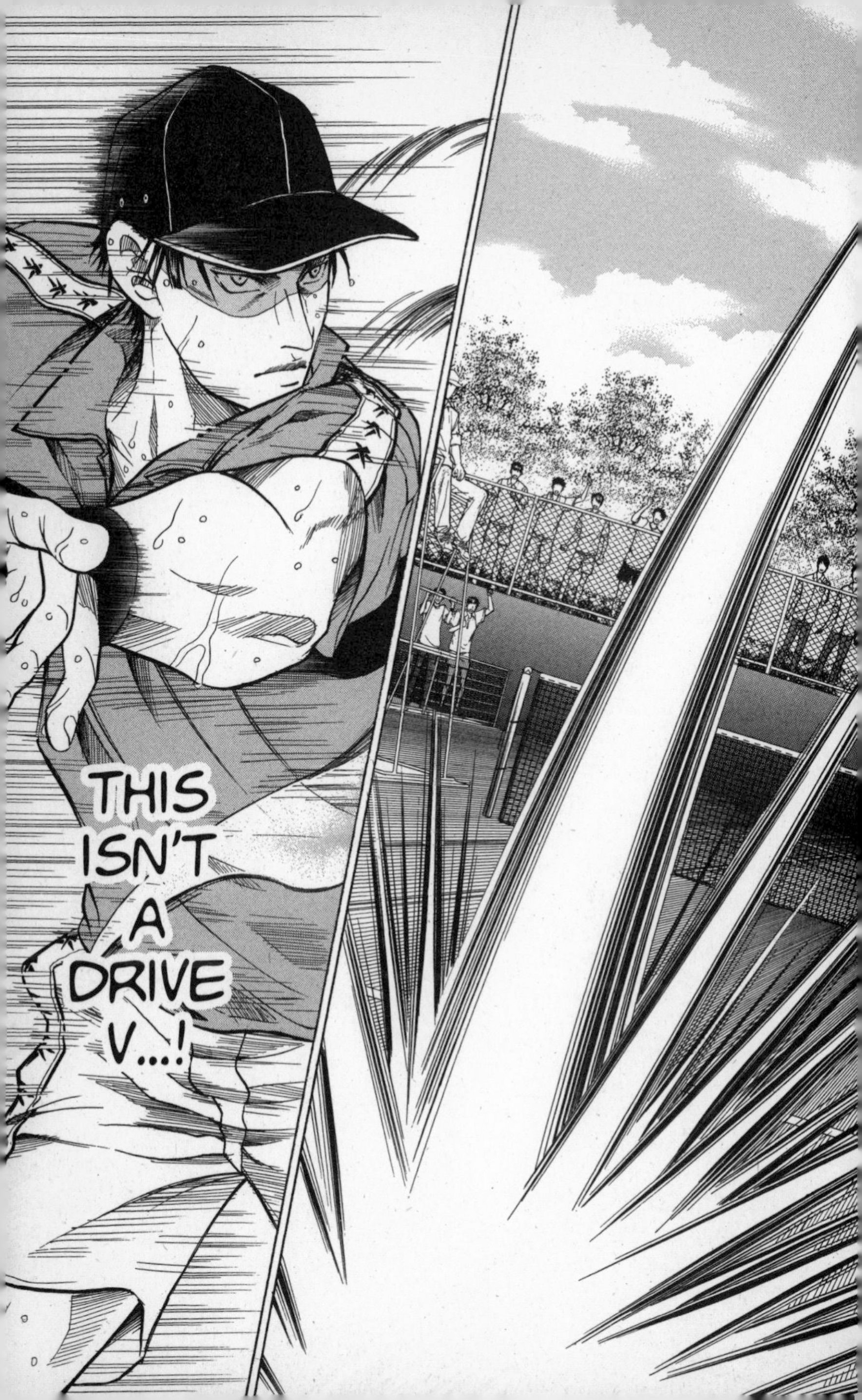
THIS ISN'T A DRIVE V...!

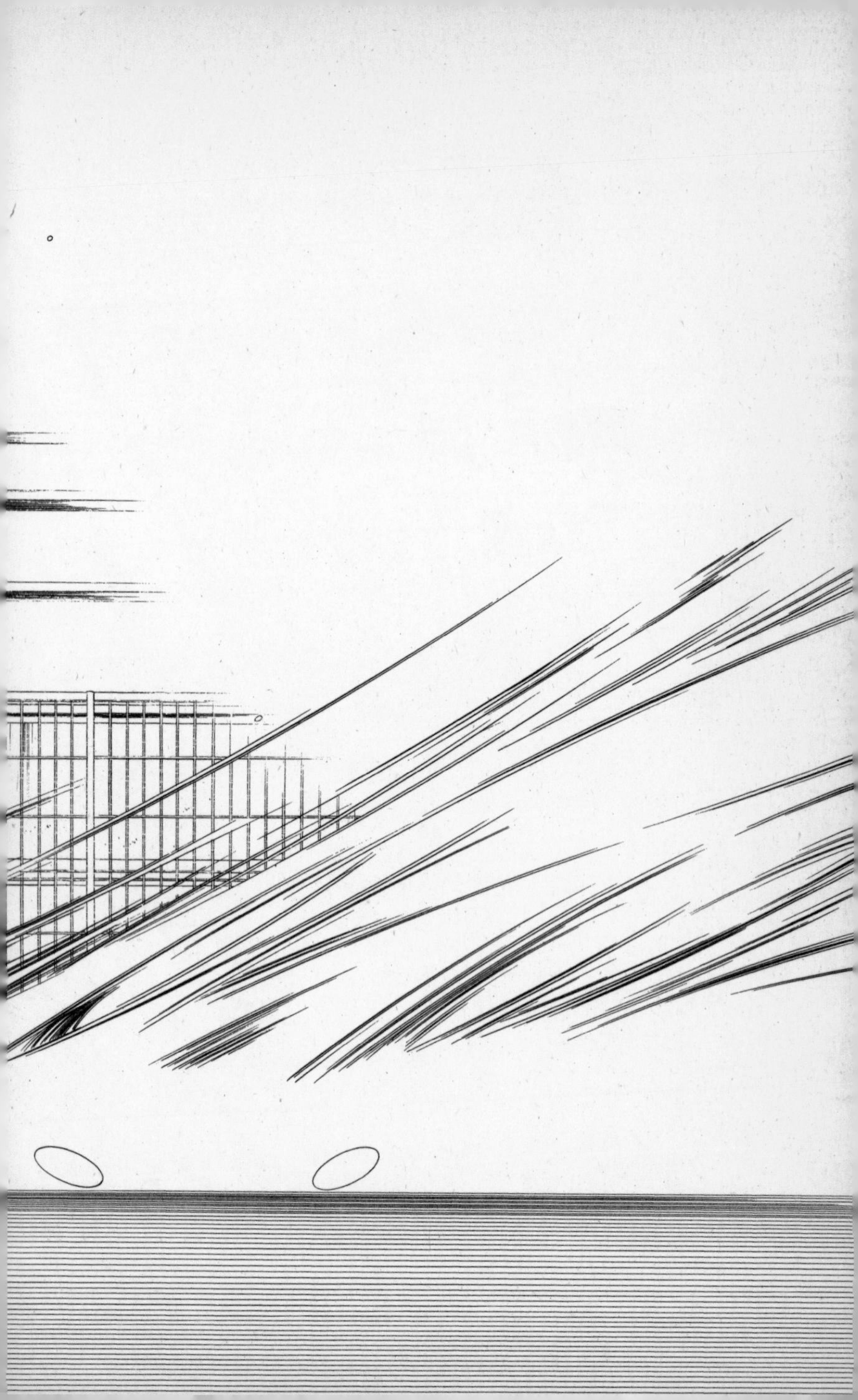

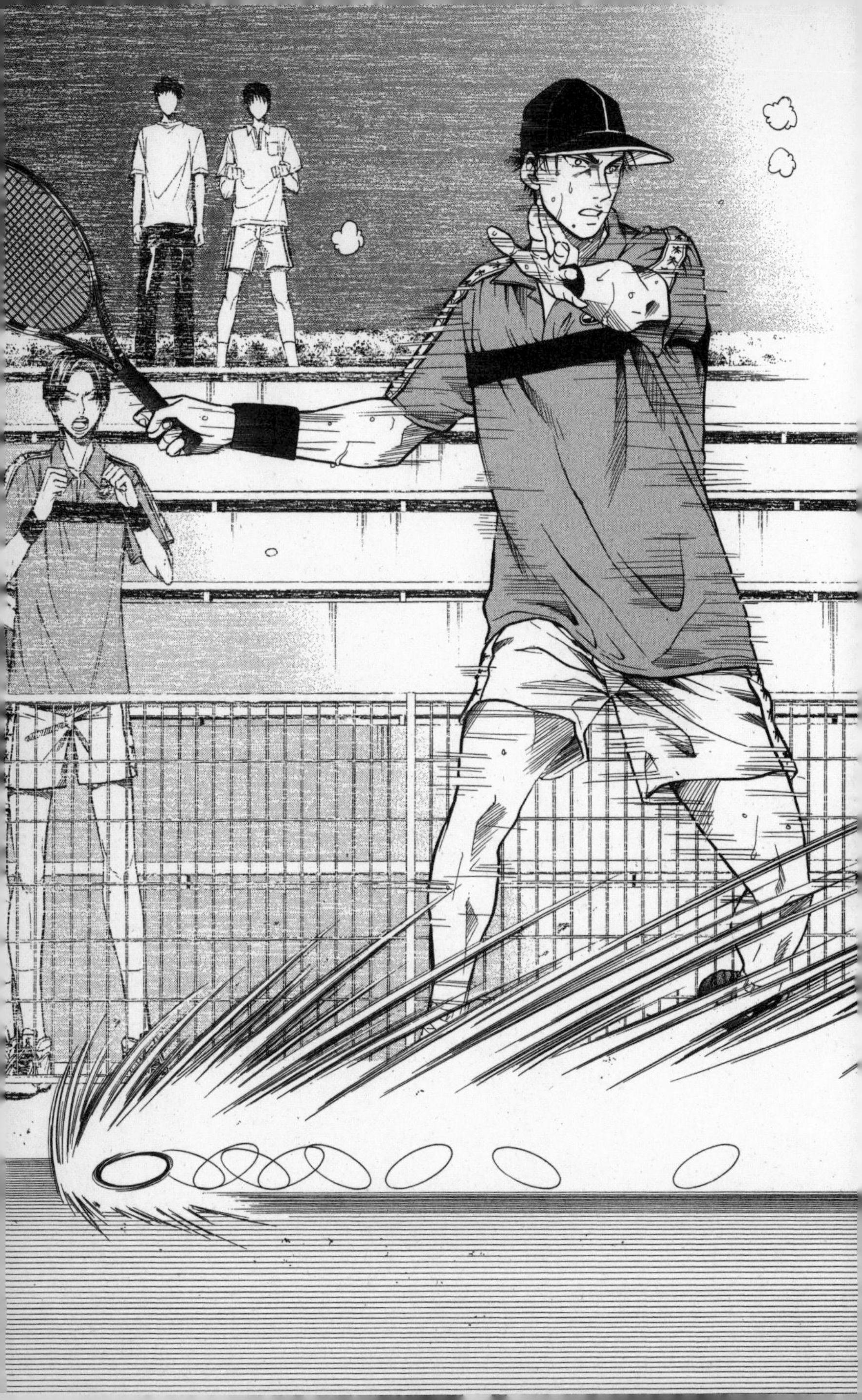

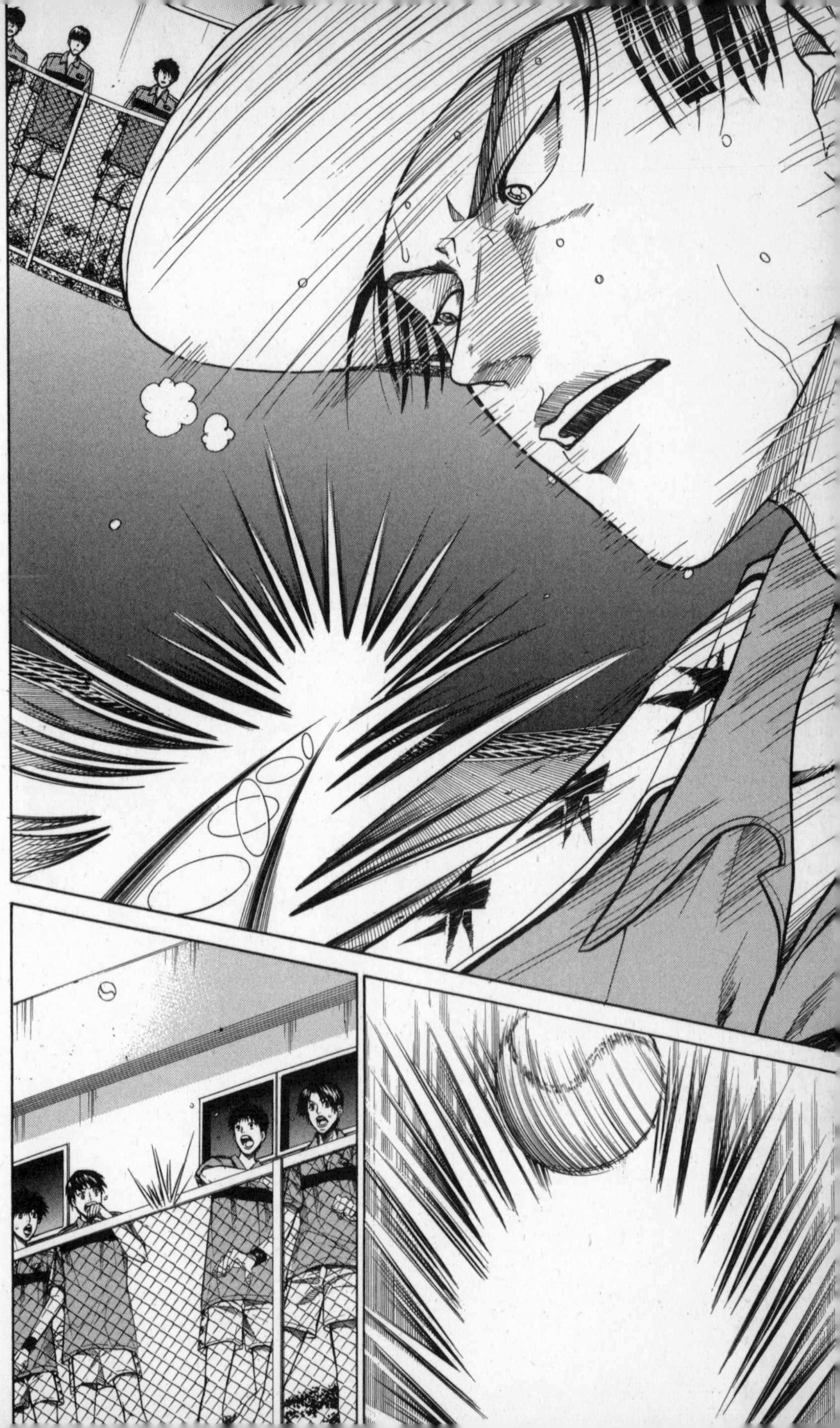

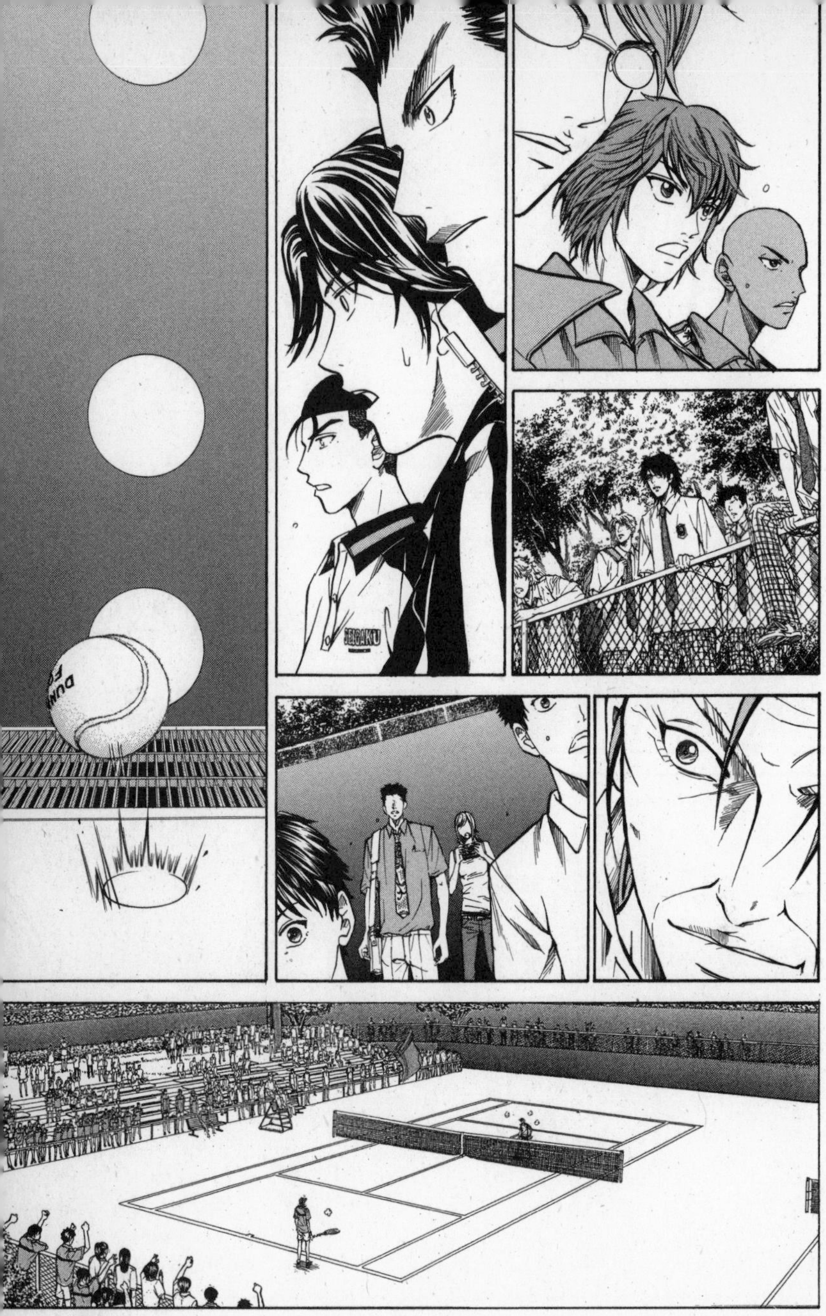
SEIGAKU

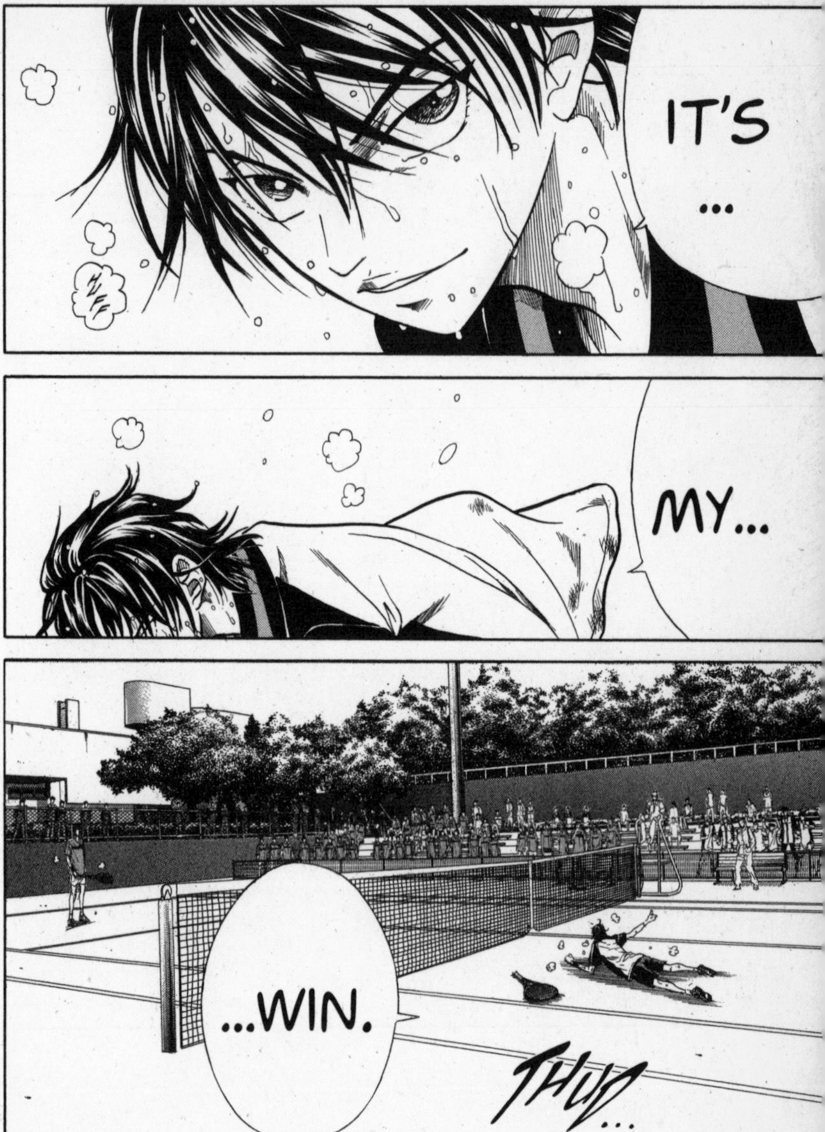
IT'S ...
HUFF
MY...
...WIN.
THUD...

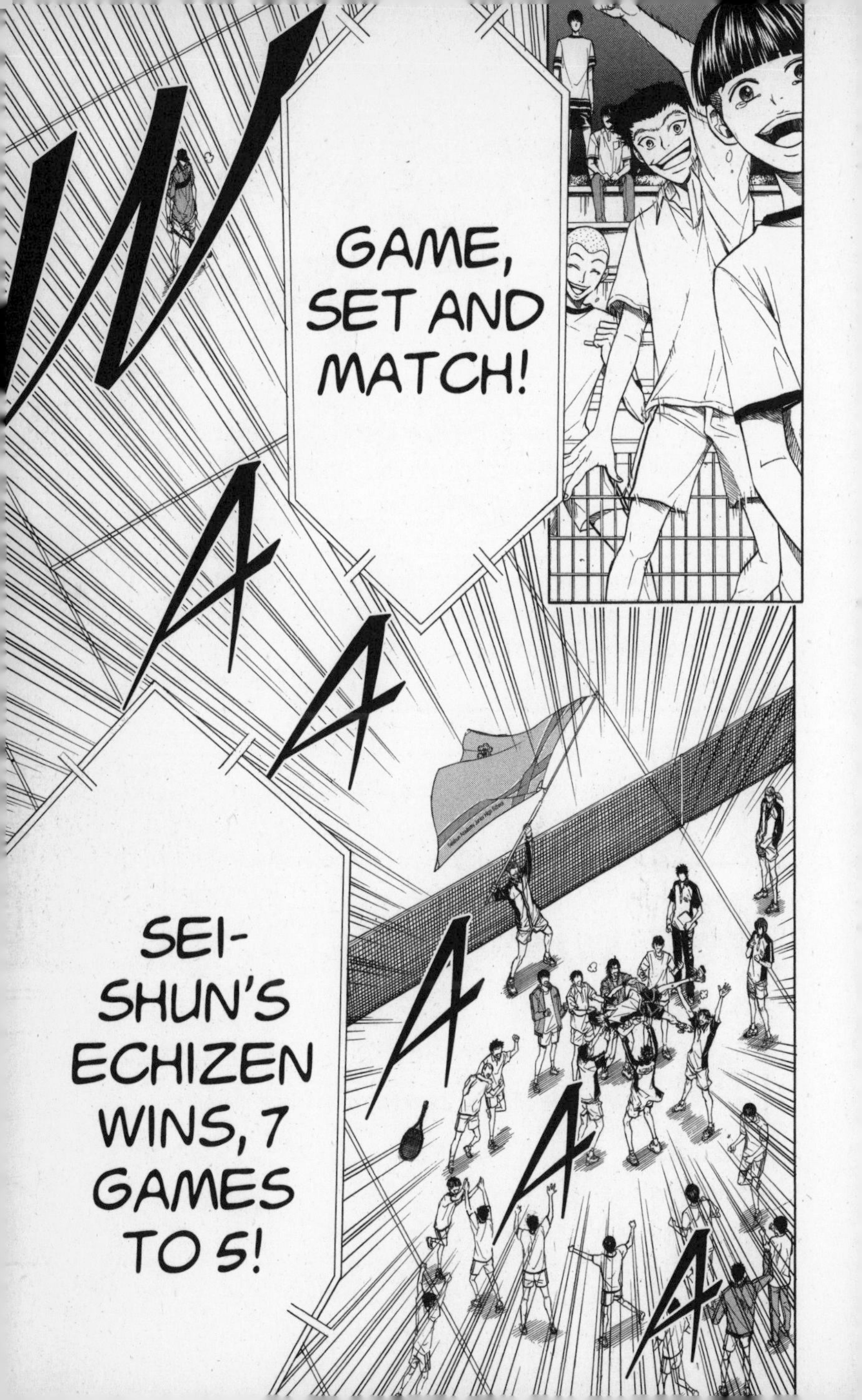
GAME, SET AND MATCH!
SEI-SHUN'S ECHIZEN WINS, 7 GAMES TO 5!
WAAAAAA

RIKKAI QUESTION CORNER

Part 7

RIKKAI UNIV.
JUNIOR HIGH SCHOOL TENNIS CLUB

Back by popular demand! The guys from Rikkai aren't very forthcoming about themselves, are they? Well then, let's have them answer some of your questions!

Q: I was surprised when Genichiro activated the Selfless State. As a fan of the Rikkai team, I wished he had done it earlier. Why didn't he?

(Y.K., Isezaki)

Yeah, that was totally crazy. And by the way, I can do it too [smirk].

WHACK [hit by Genichiro] Ow!

Why should I mimic the actions of low-level players?

Snap.

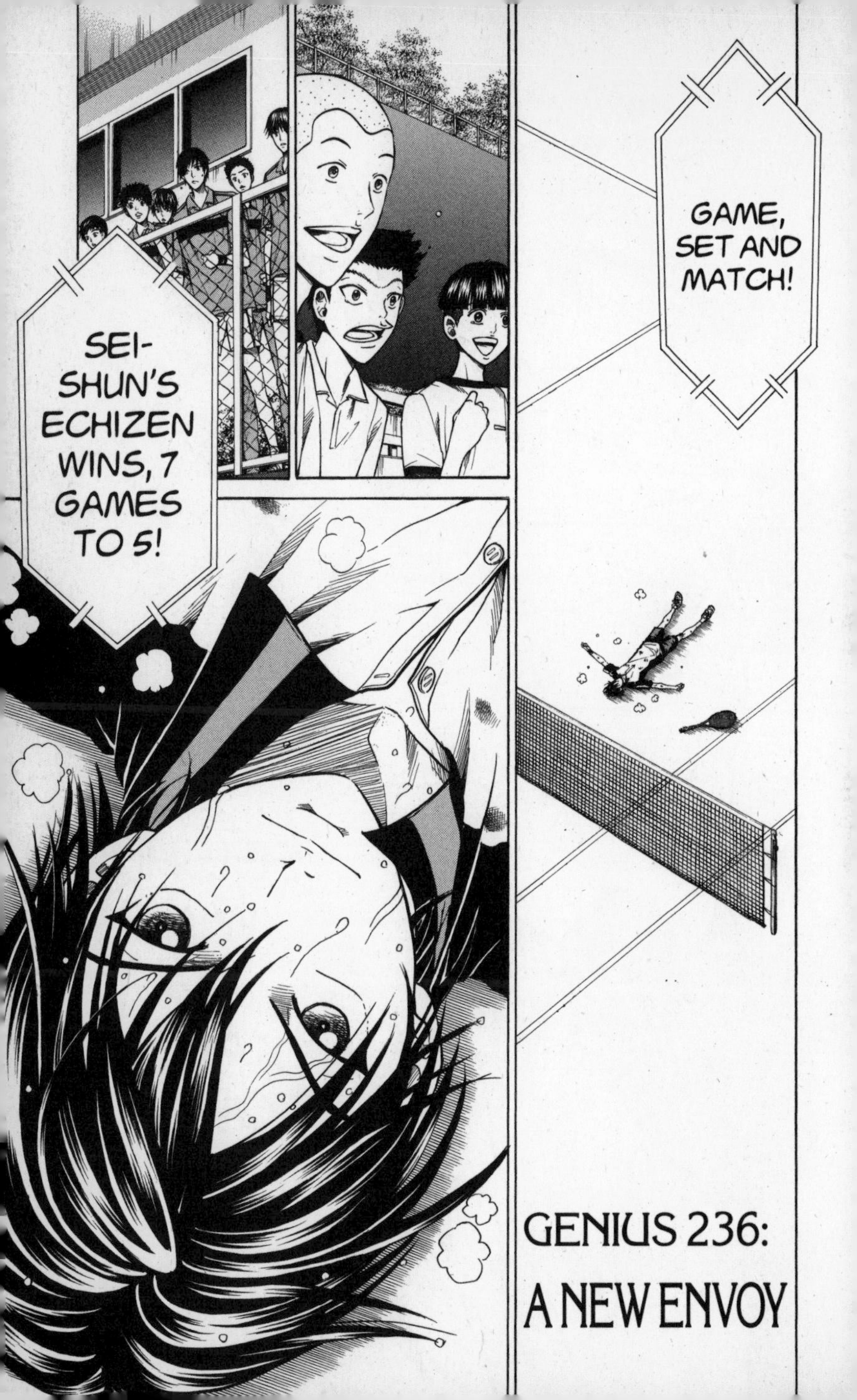
GAME, SET AND MATCH!
GENIUS 236: A NEW ENVOY
SEI-SHUN'S ECHIZEN WINS, 7 GAMES TO 5!

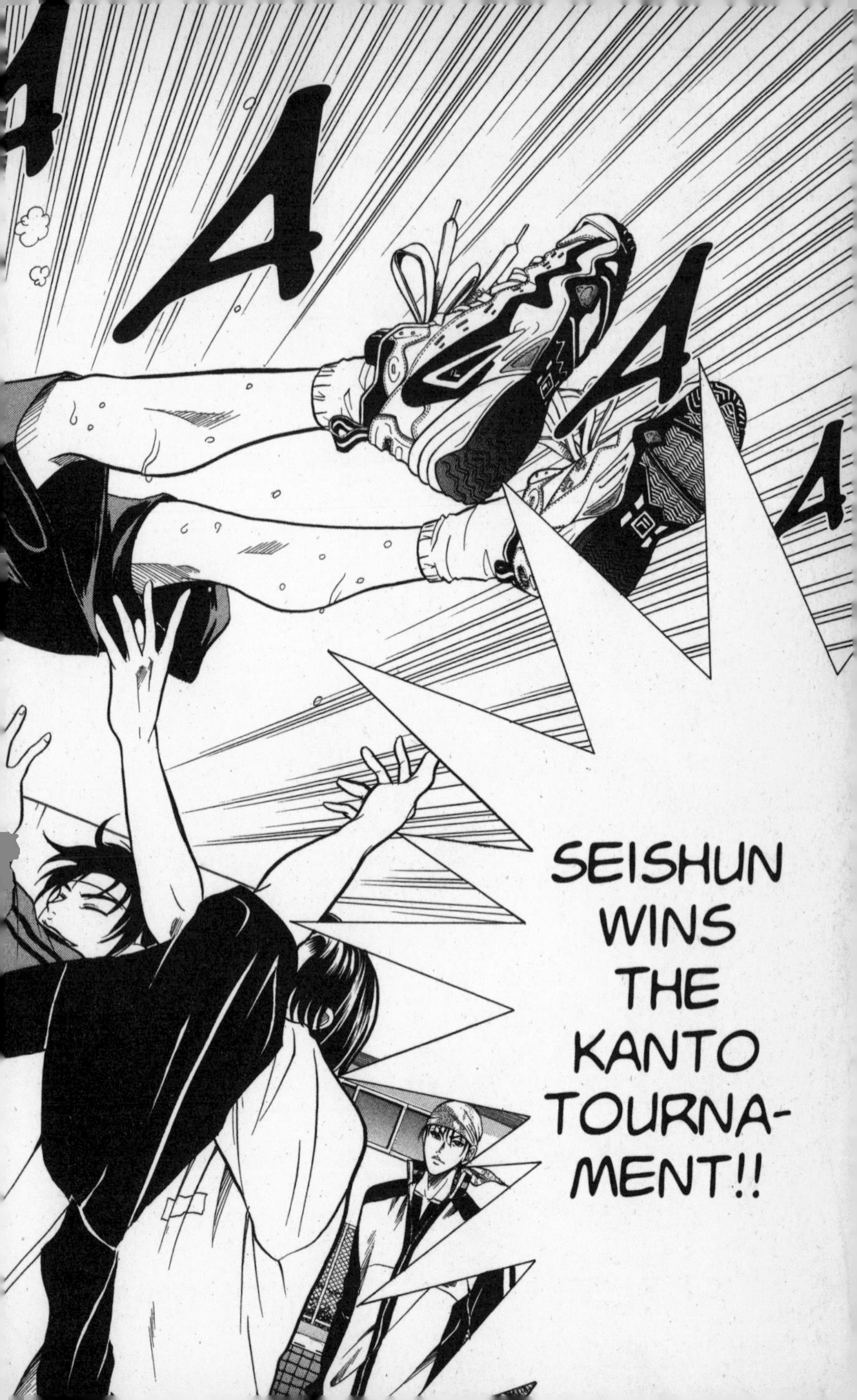
AAAAA
SEISHUN WINS THE KANTO TOURNA- MENT!!

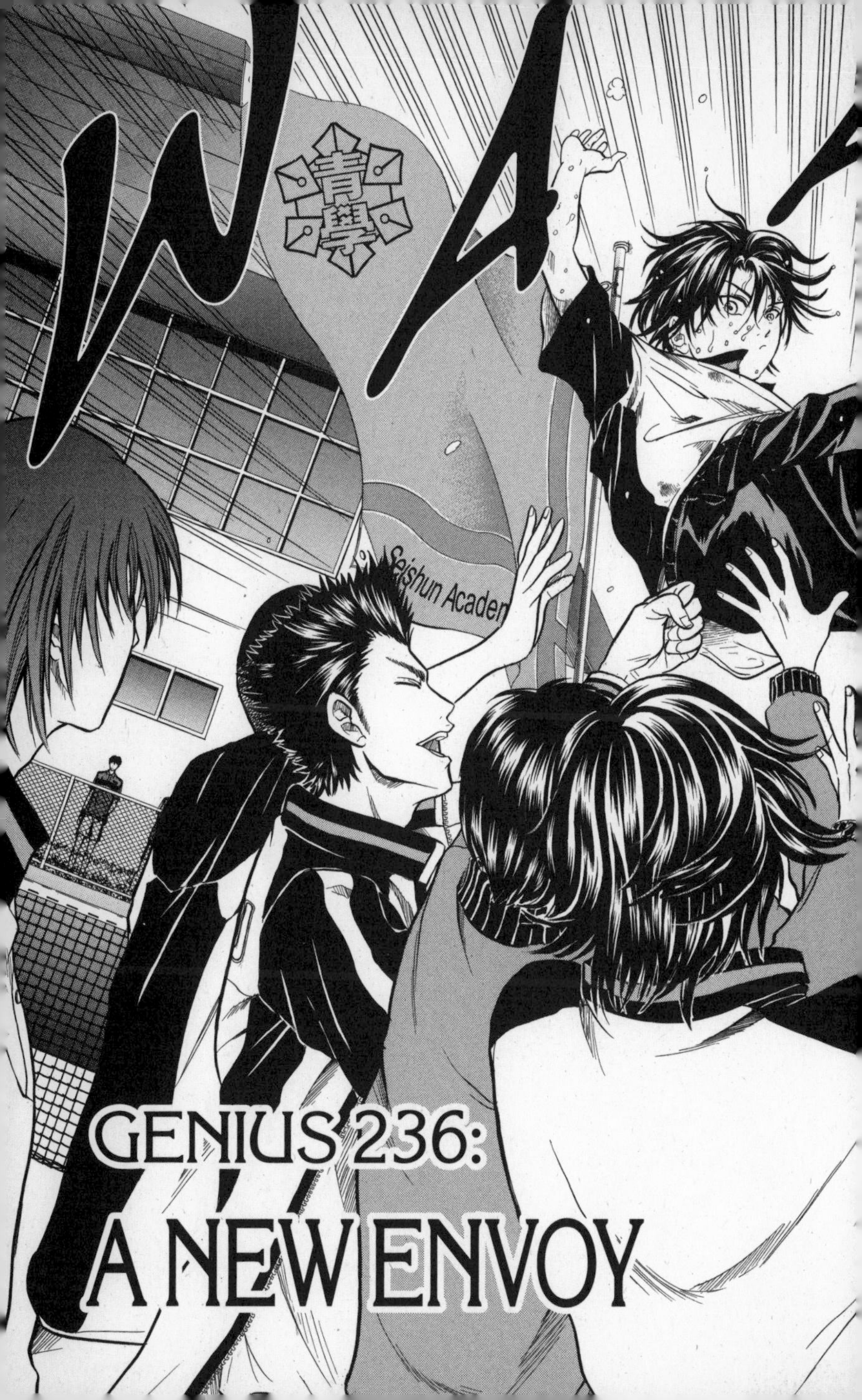
WAA
青學

GENIUS 236: A NEW ENVOY

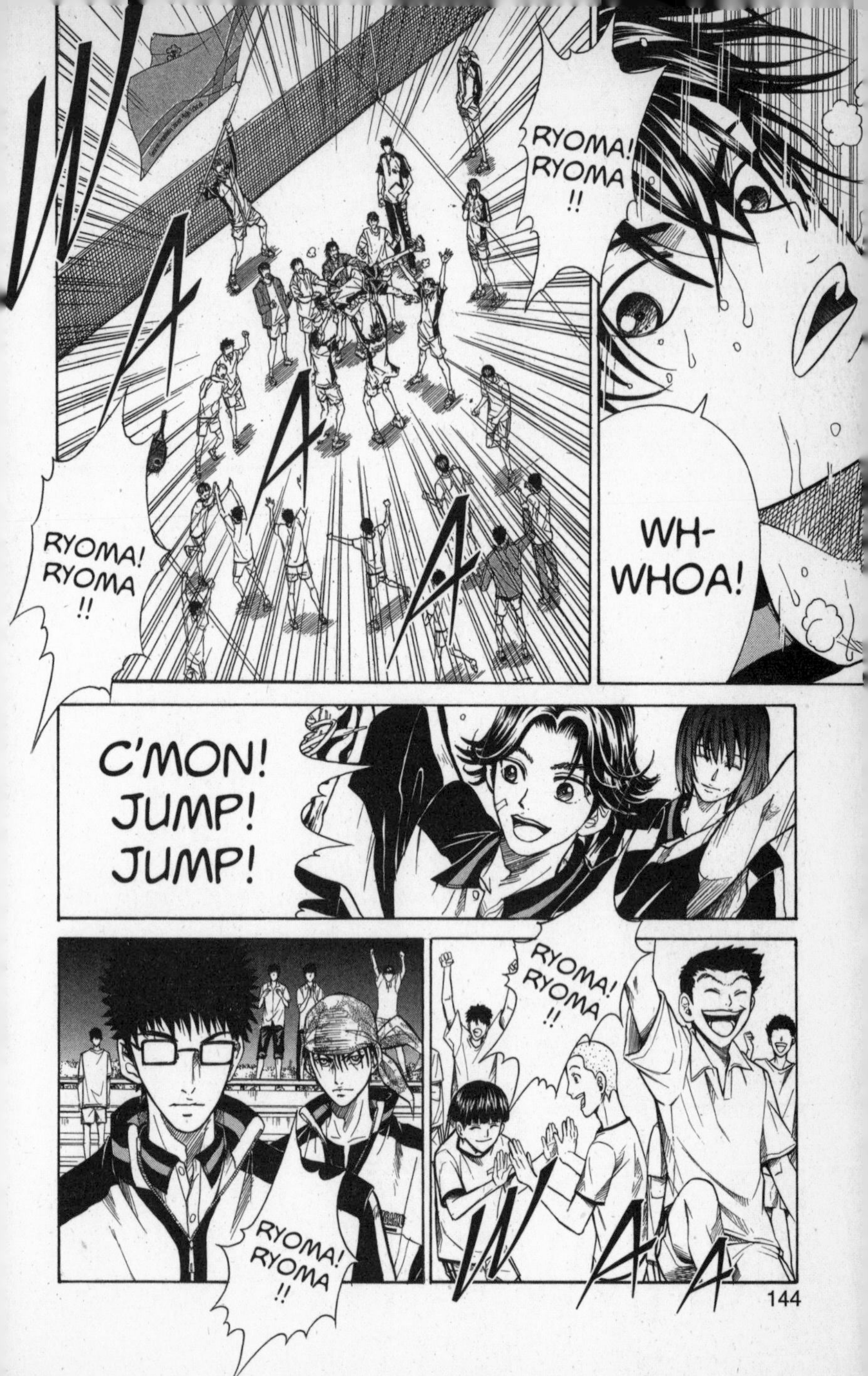
WH-WHOA!
RYOMA! RYOMA!!
WAAAA
RYOMA! RYOMA!!
C'MON! JUMP! JUMP!
RYOMA! RYOMA!!
WAAA
RYOMA! RYOMA!!

READ THIS WAY

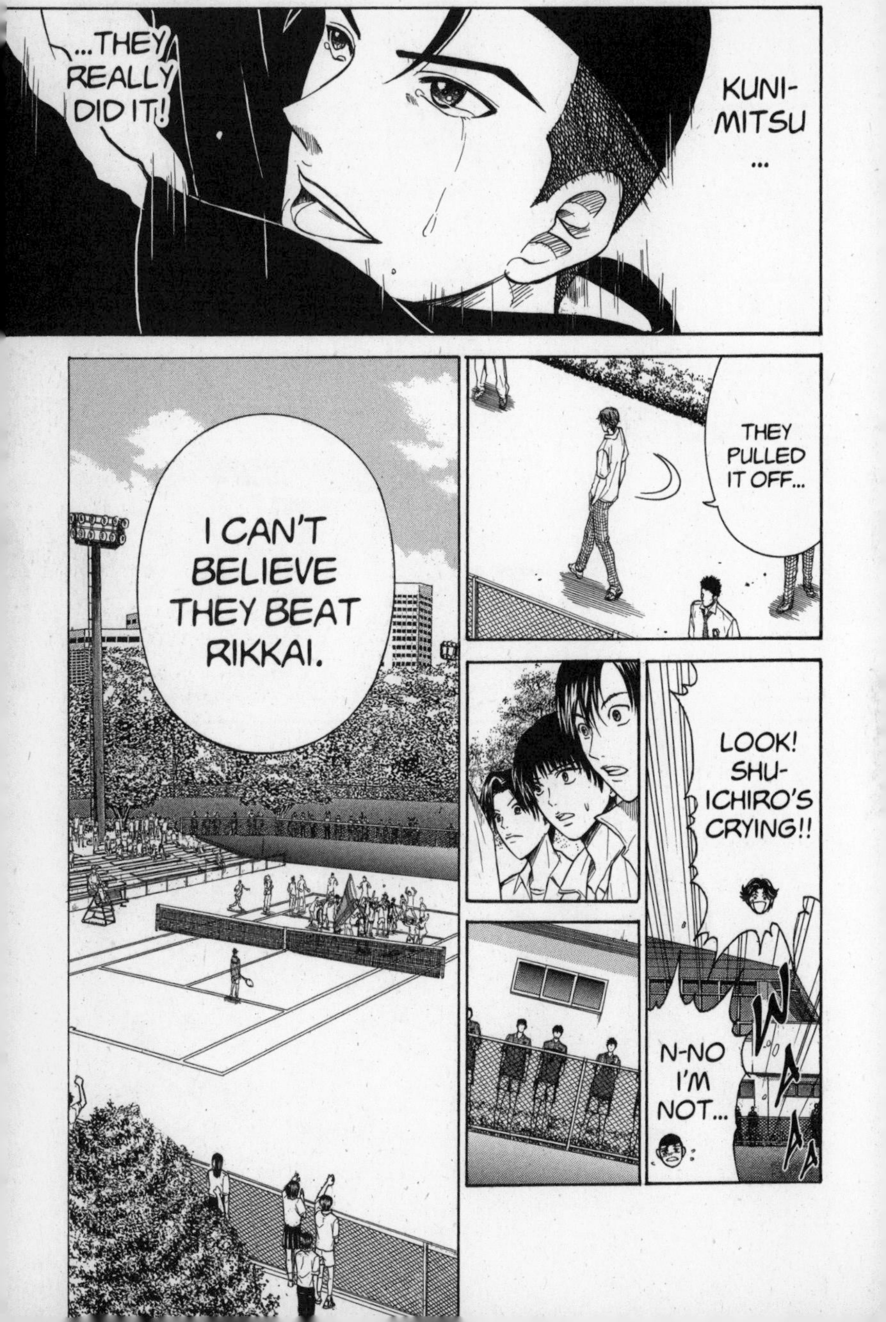
KUNI-MITSU...
...THEY REALLY DID IT!
THEY PULLED IT OFF...
LOOK! SHU-ICHIRO'S CRYING!!
N-NO I'M NOT...
WAAA
I CAN'T BELIEVE THEY BEAT RIKKAI.

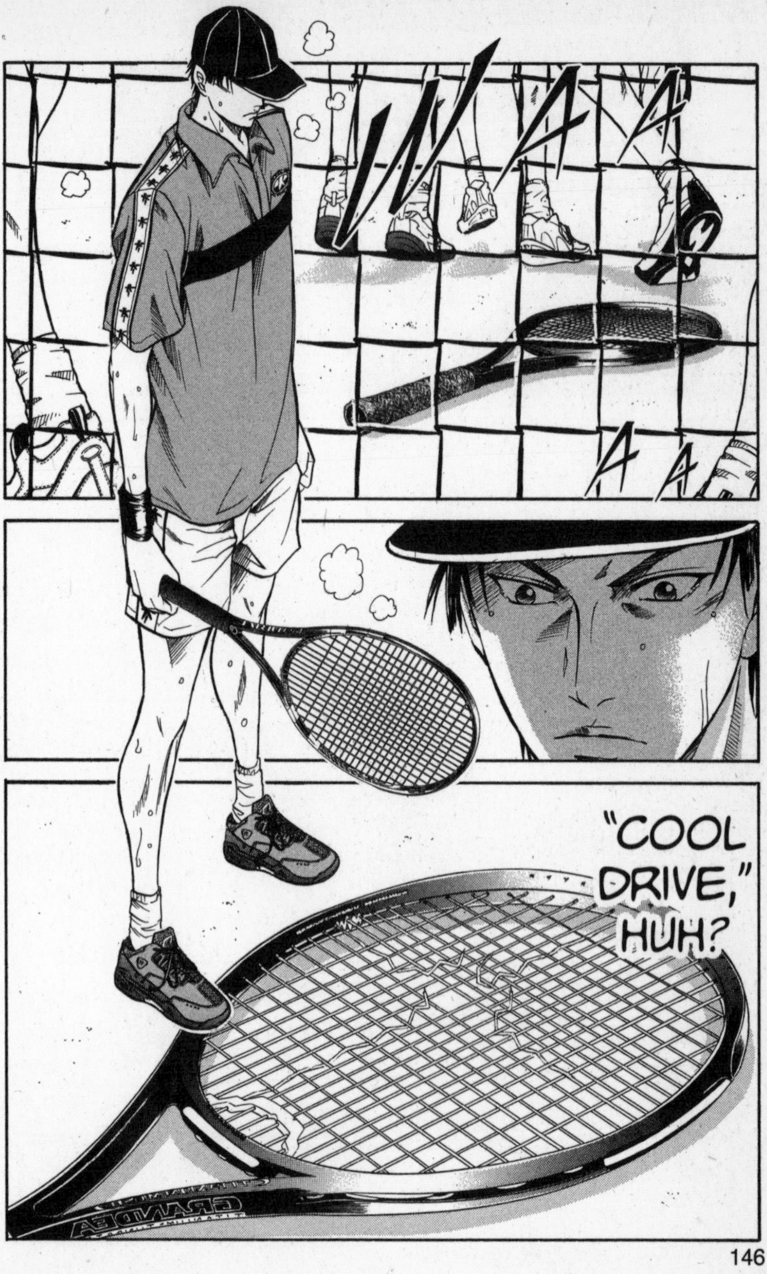
WAA
AA
"COOL DRIVE," HUH?
GRANDEA

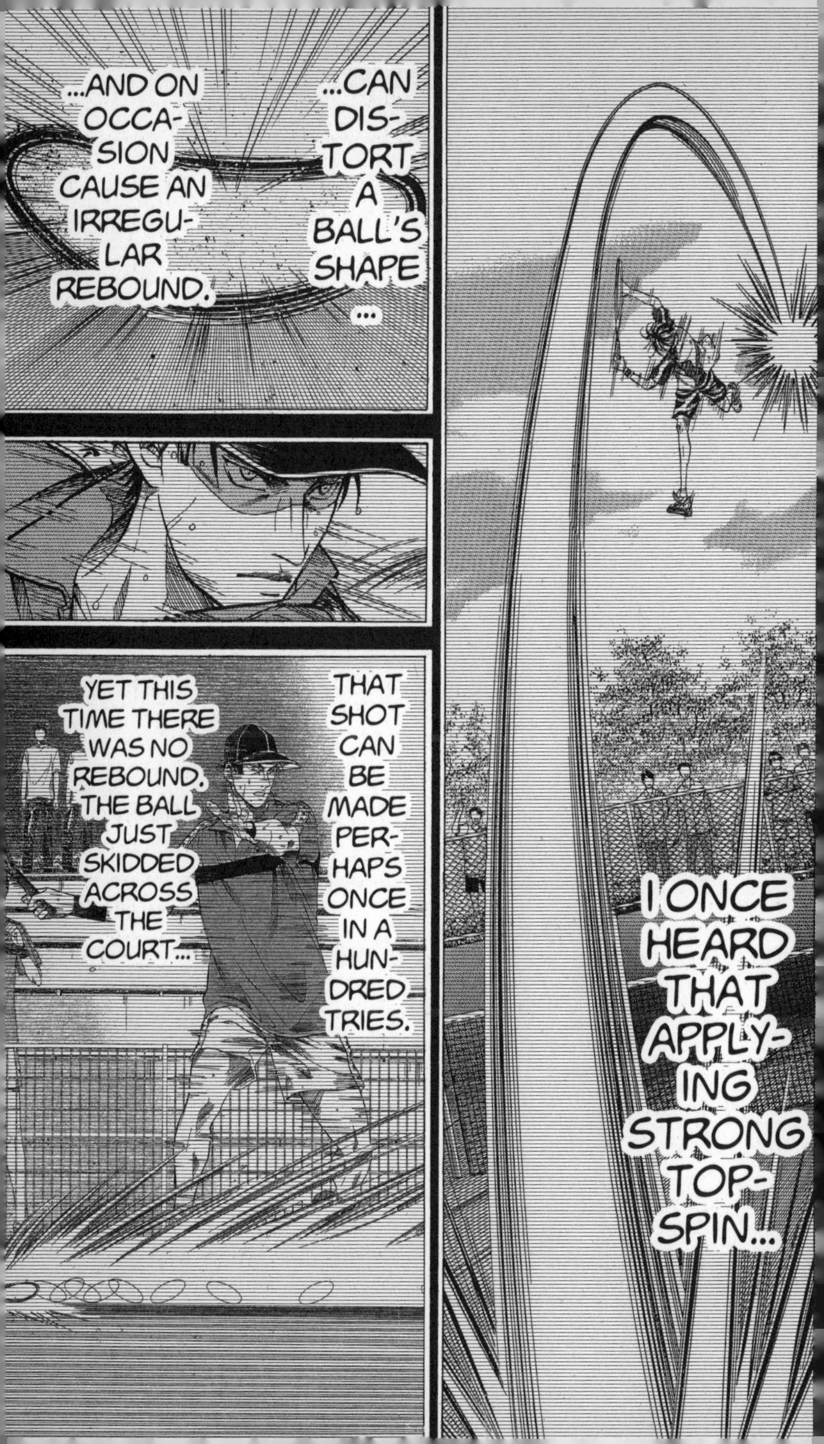
I ONCE HEARD THAT APPLYING STRONG TOPSPIN...
...CAN DISTORT A BALL'S SHAPE...
...AND ON OCCASION CAUSE AN IRREGULAR REBOUND.
THAT SHOT CAN BE MADE PERHAPS ONCE IN A HUNDRED TRIES.
YET THIS TIME THERE WAS NO REBOUND. THE BALL JUST SKIDDED ACROSS THE COURT...

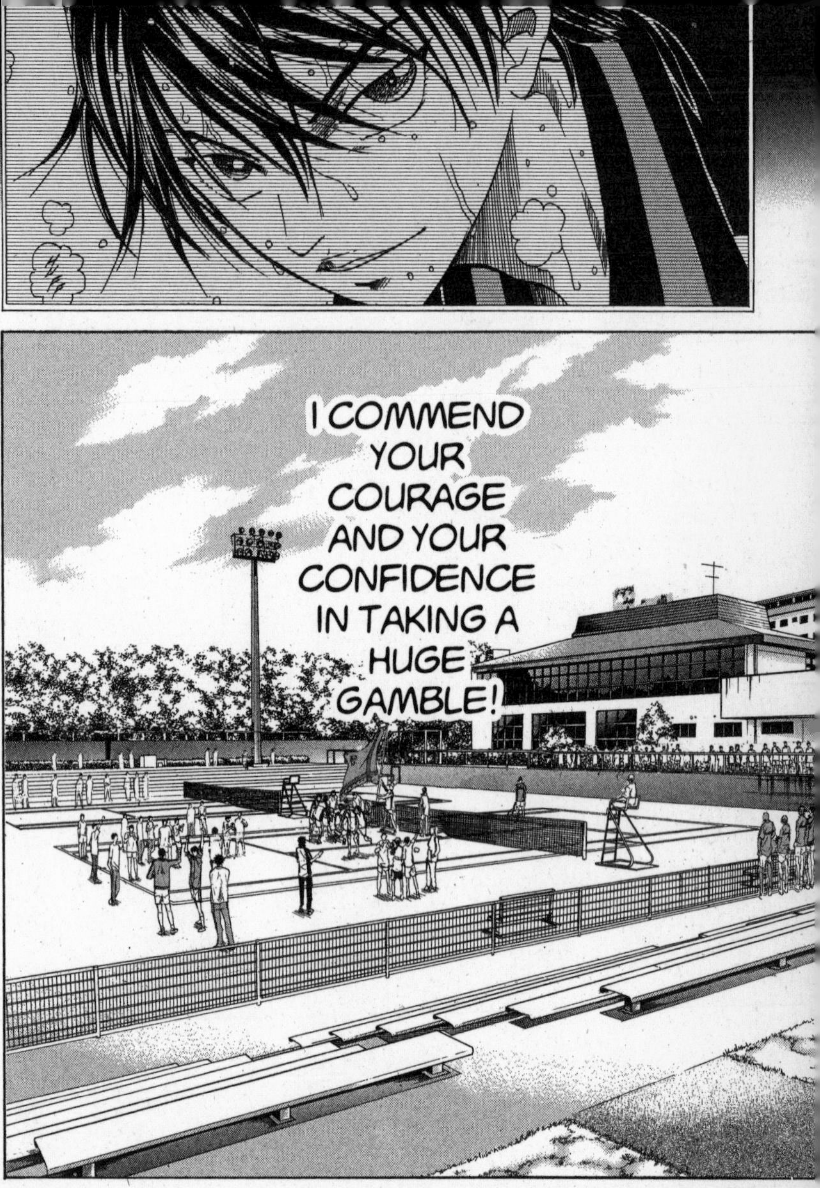
I COMMEND YOUR COURAGE AND YOUR CONFIDENCE IN TAKING A HUGE GAMBLE!

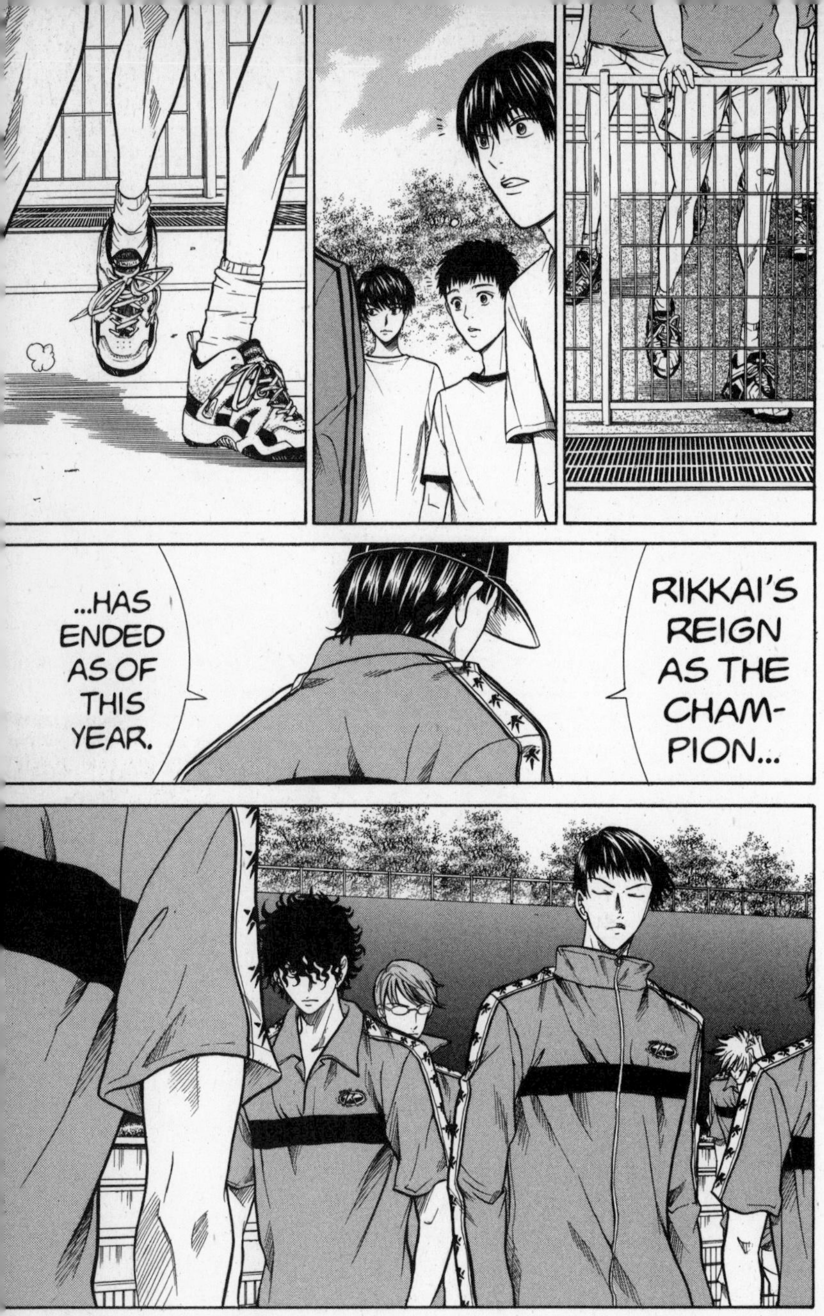
RIKKAI'S REIGN AS THE CHAMPION...
...HAS ENDED AS OF THIS YEAR.

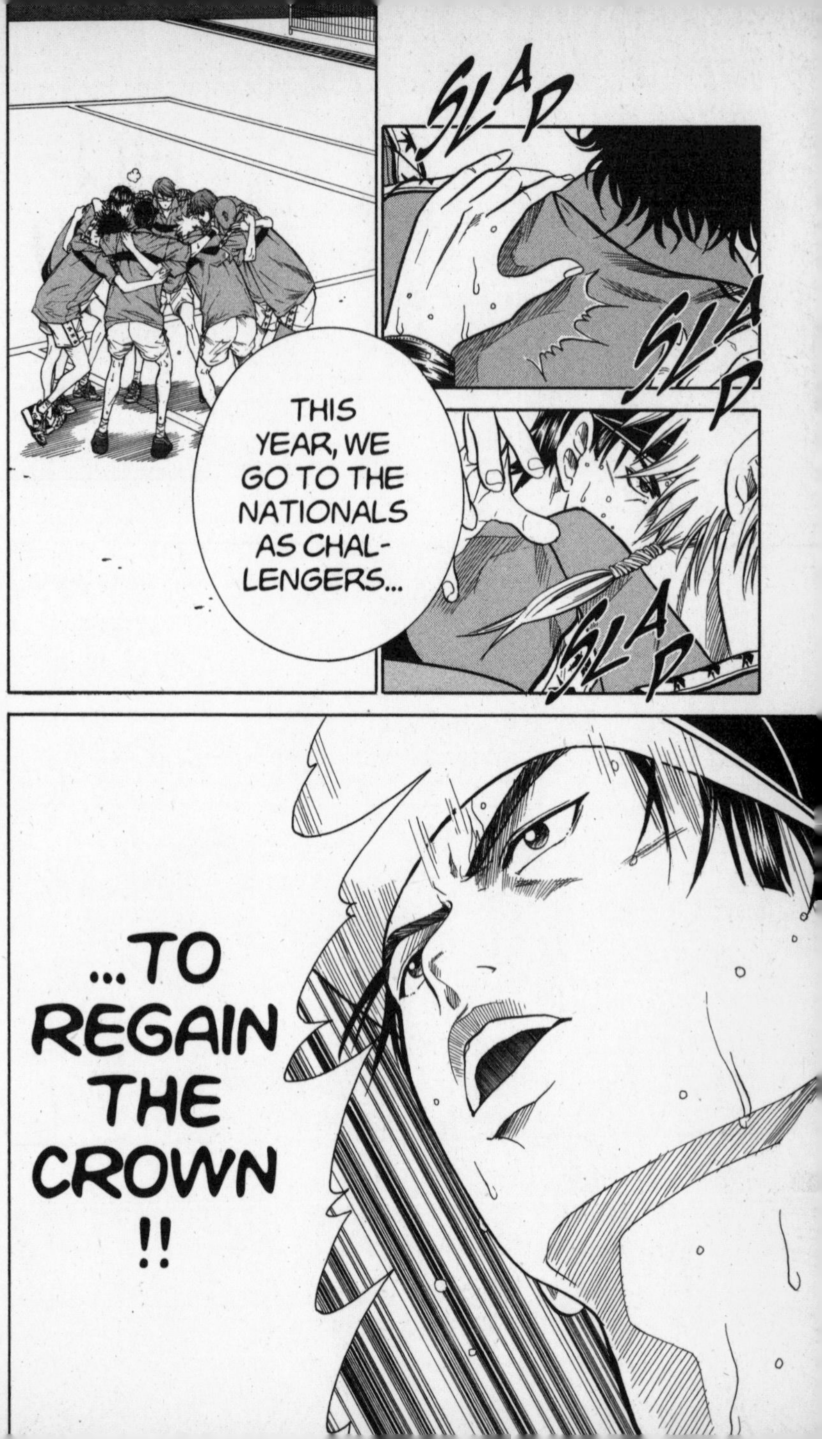
SLAP
SLAP
SLAP
THIS YEAR, WE GO TO THE NATIONALS AS CHAL-LENGERS...
...TO REGAIN THE CROWN!!

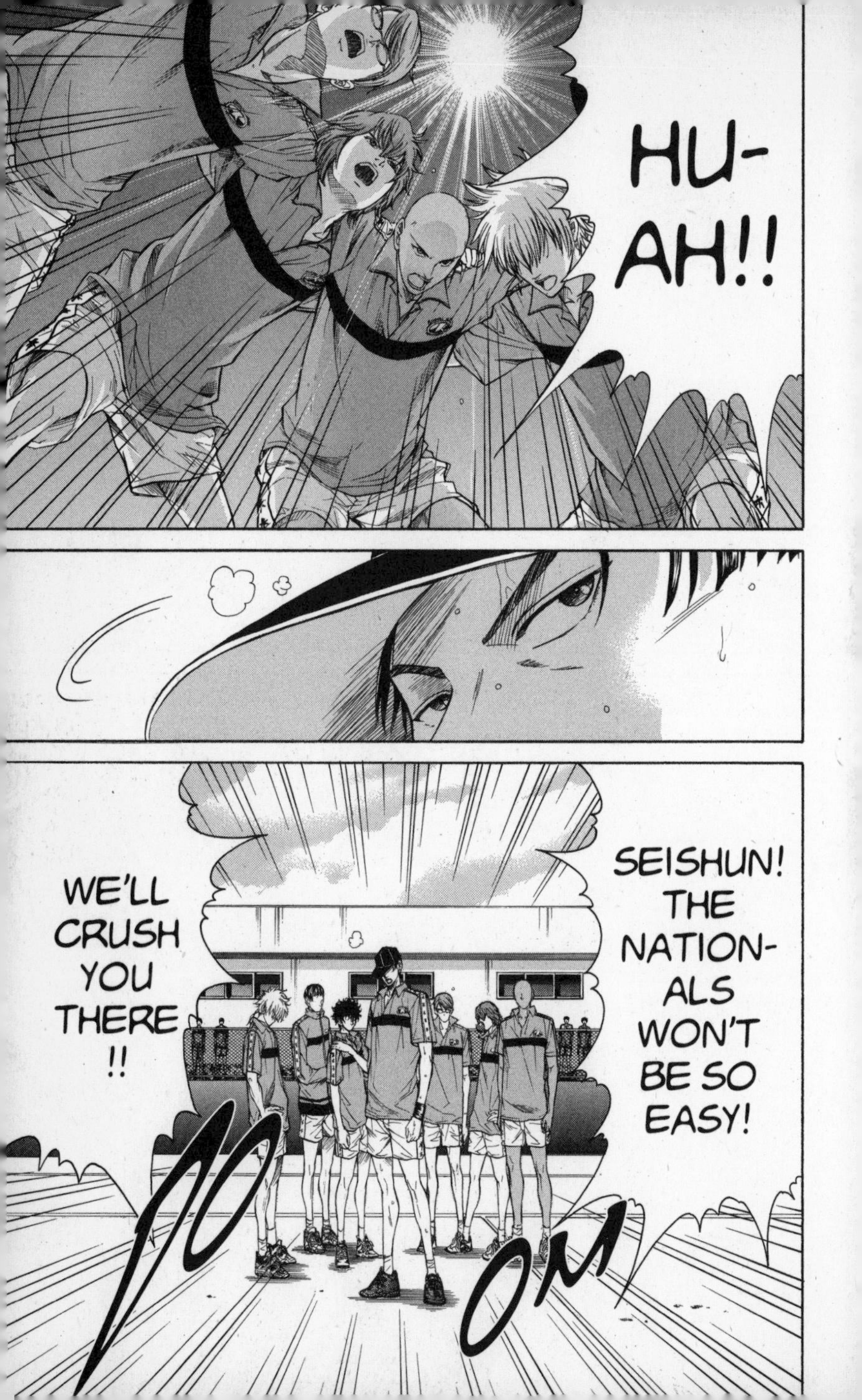
HU-
AH!!
SEISHUN! THE NATION-ALS WON'T BE SO EASY!
WE'LL CRUSH YOU THERE !!
MOOM

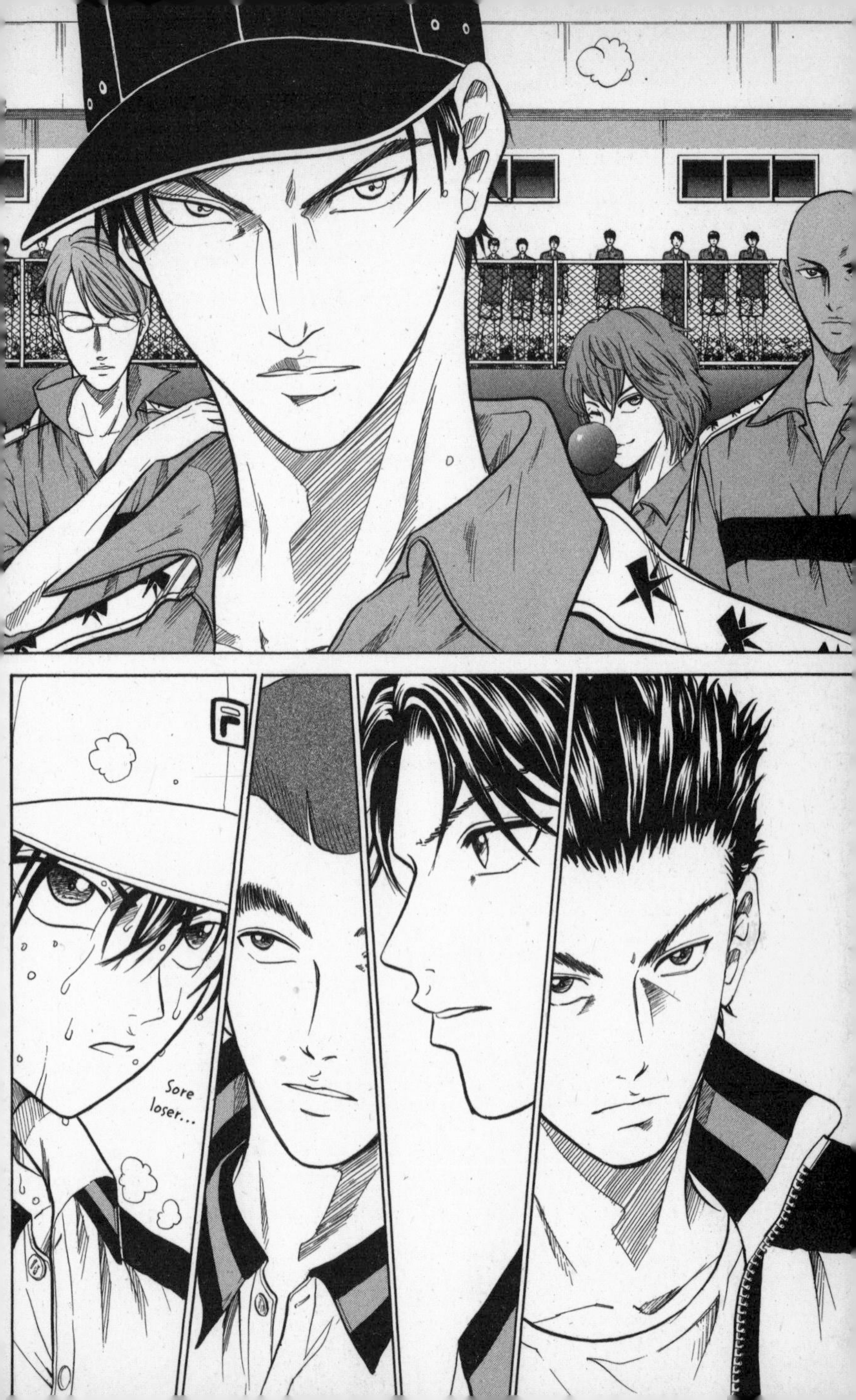
Sore loser...

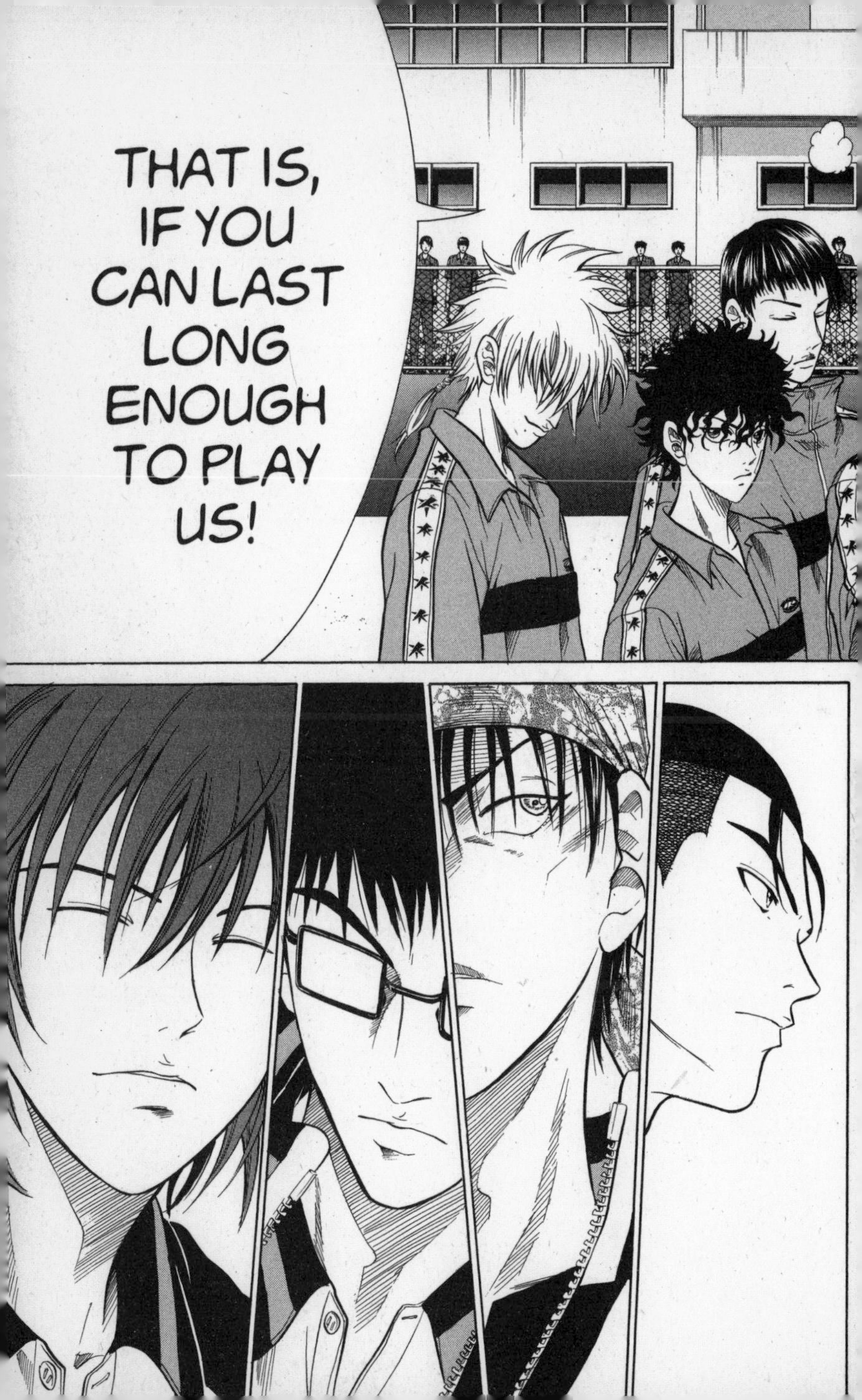
THAT IS, IF YOU CAN LAST LONG ENOUGH TO PLAY US!

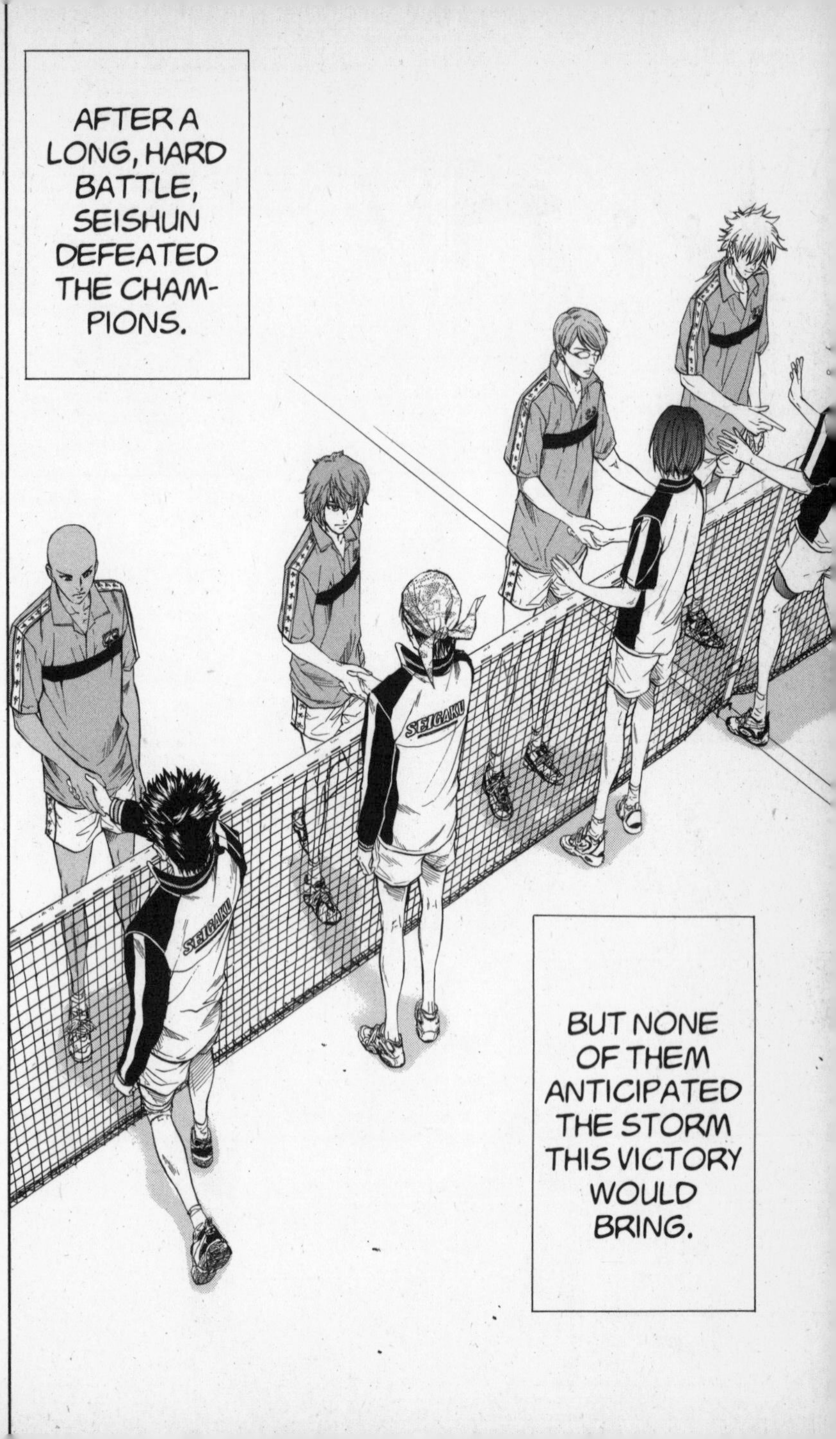
AFTER A LONG, HARD BATTLE, SEISHUN DEFEATED THE CHAMPIONS.
SEIGAKU
SEIGAKU
BUT NONE OF THEM ANTICIPATED THE STORM THIS VICTORY WOULD BRING.

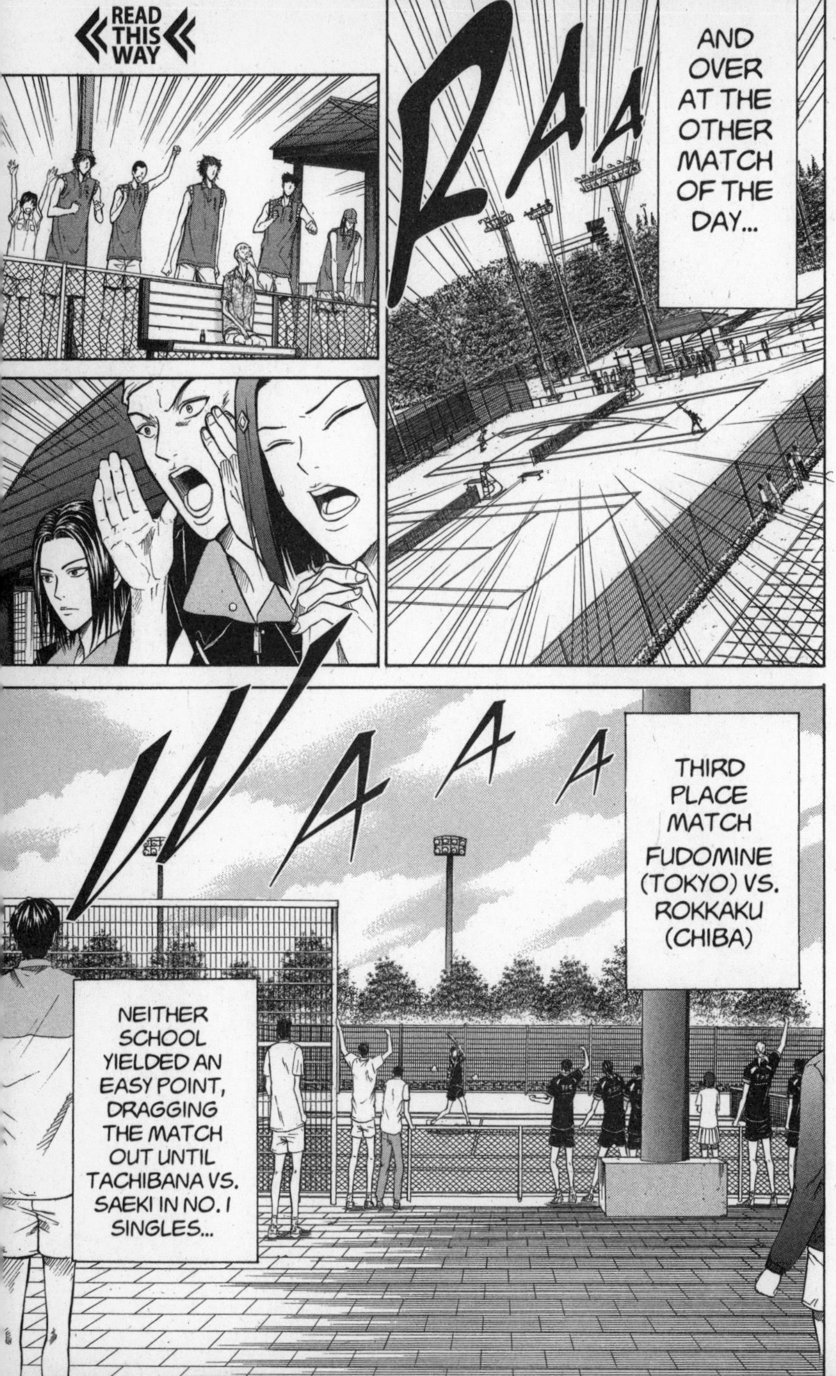
READ THIS WAY
AND OVER AT THE OTHER MATCH OF THE DAY...
RAA
WAAA
THIRD PLACE MATCH FUDOMINE (TOKYO) VS. ROKKAKU (CHIBA)
NEITHER SCHOOL YIELDED AN EASY POINT, DRAGGING THE MATCH OUT UNTIL TACHIBANA VS. SAEKI IN NO. 1 SINGLES...

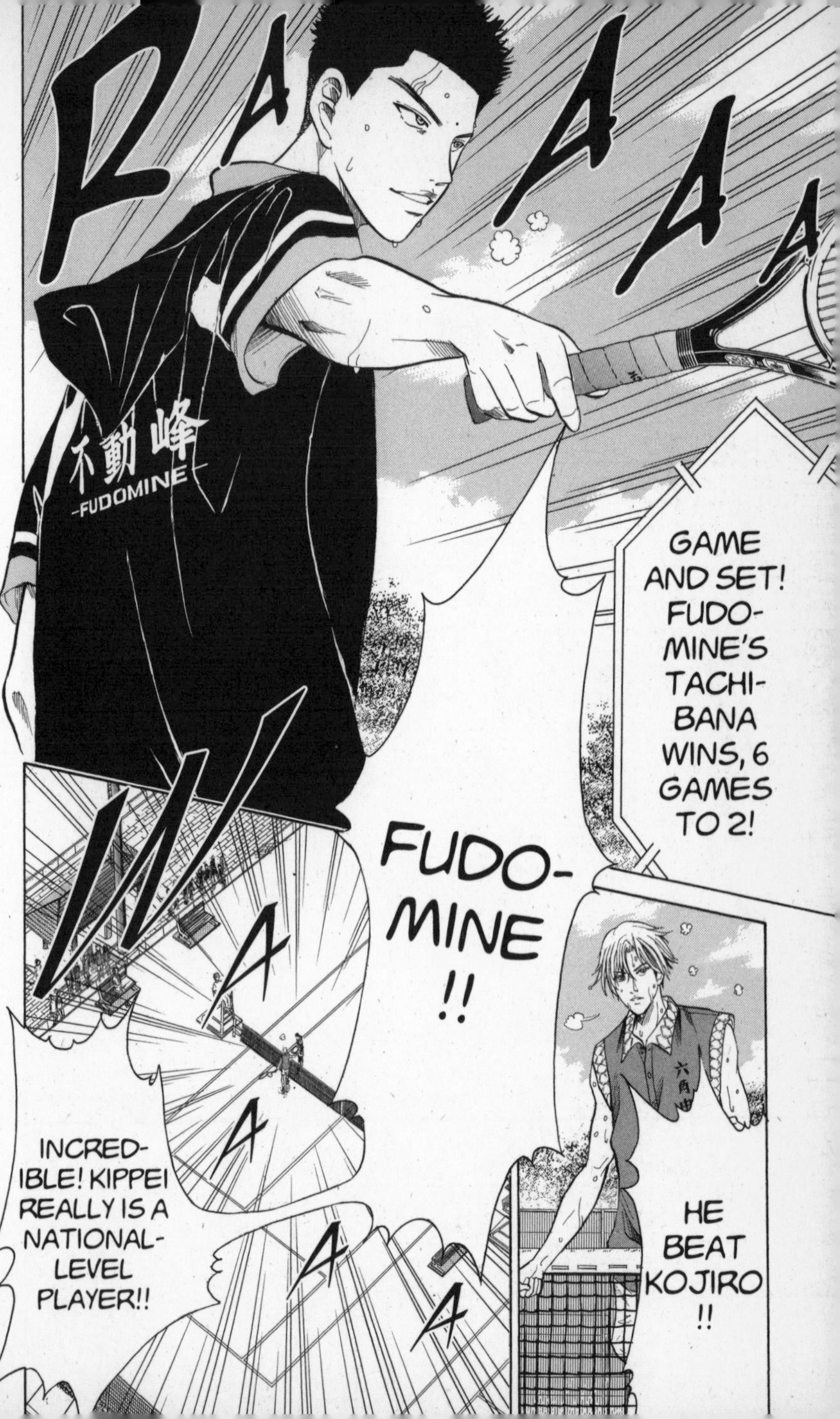
RAAAAA
不動峰
-FUDOMINE-
GAME AND SET! FUDOMINE'S TACHIBANA WINS, 6 GAMES TO 2!
FUDOMINE!!
WAAAAA
HE BEAT KOJIRO!!
INCREDIBLE! KIPPEI REALLY IS A NATIONAL-LEVEL PLAYER!!

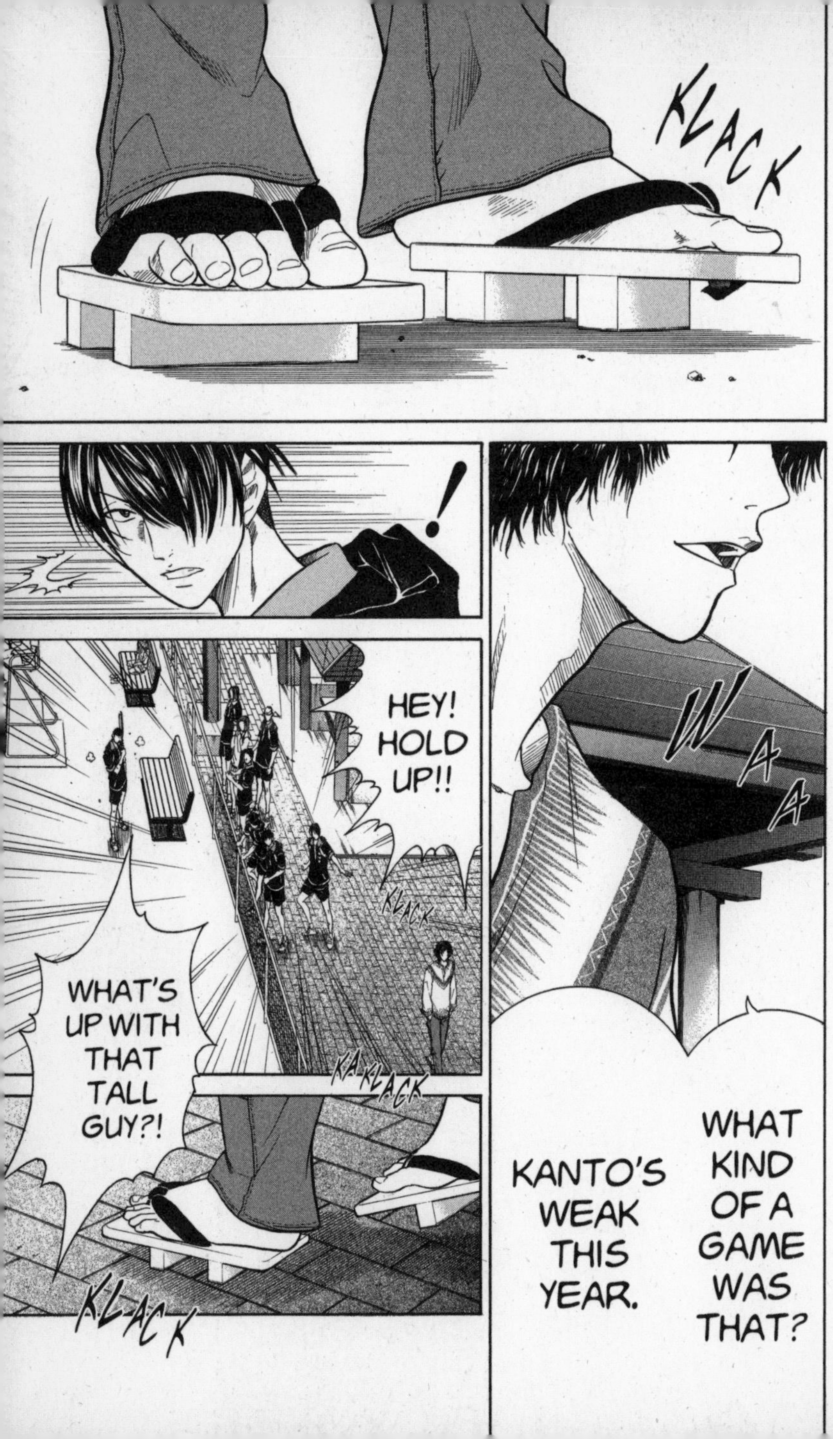
KLACK
WAA
WHAT KIND OF A GAME WAS THAT?
KANTO'S WEAK THIS YEAR.
!
HEY! HOLD UP!!
KLACK
WHAT'S UP WITH THAT TALL GUY?!
KA-KLACK
KLACK

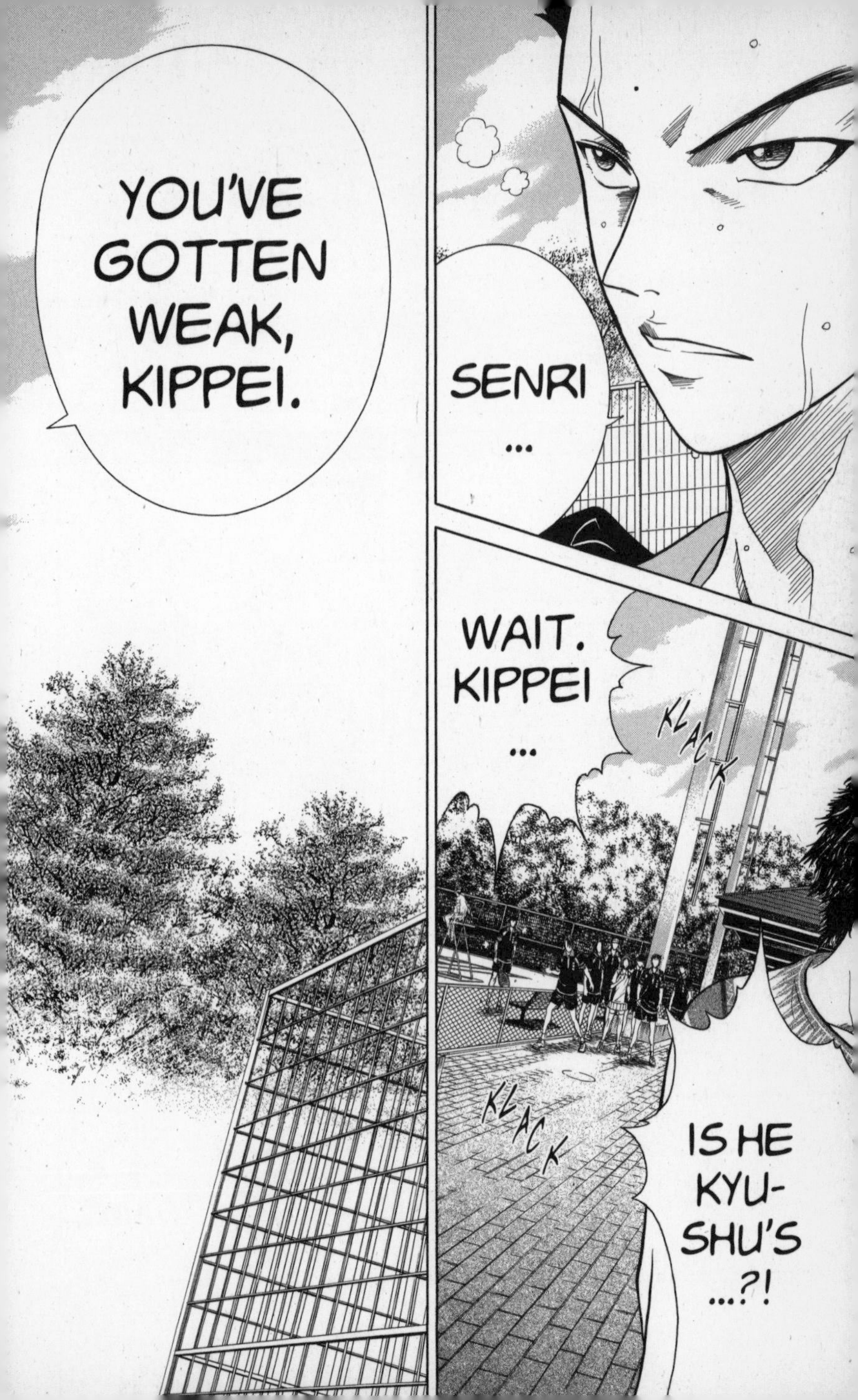
SENRI ...
WAIT. KIPPEI ...
KLACK
KLACK
IS HE KYU-SHU'S ...?!
YOU'VE GOTTEN WEAK, KIPPEI.

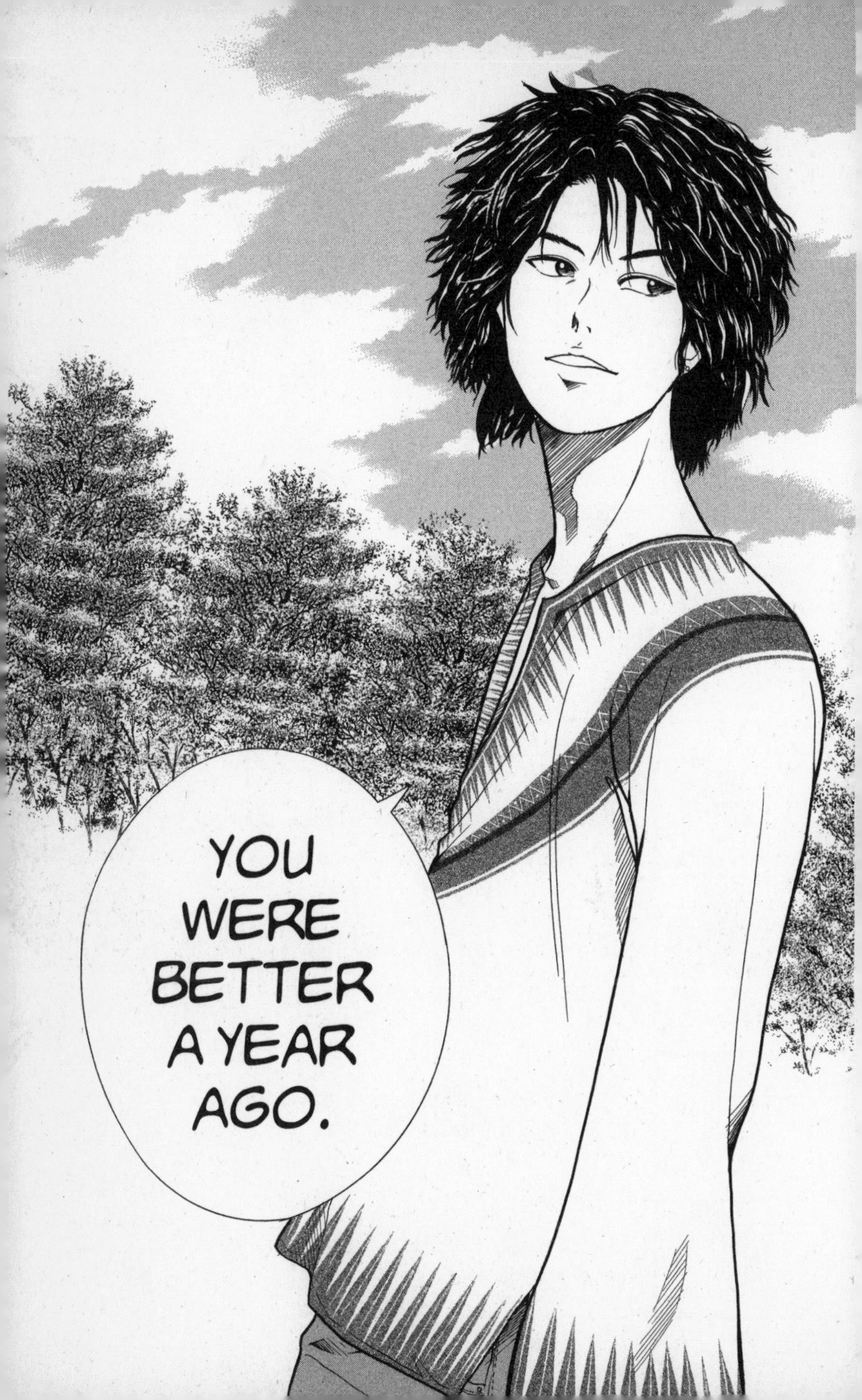
YOU WERE BETTER A YEAR AGO.

RIKKAI QUESTION CORNER

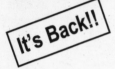

It's Back!!

Part 8

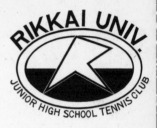

RIKKAI UNIV.
JUNIOR HIGH SCHOOL TENNIS CLUB

Back by popular demand! The guys from Rikkai aren't very forthcoming about themselves, are they? Well then, let's have them answer some of your questions!

Q: Which Rikkai starter is the most popular with the girls?
(S.N., Yokohama)

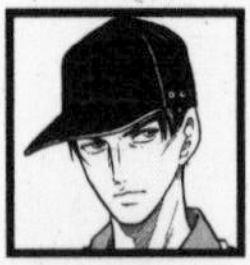

What a dumb question! [Brow twitches.]

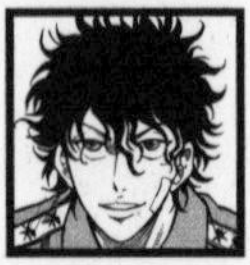

Me, of course! That "good-looking guy" you keep hearing about is me!

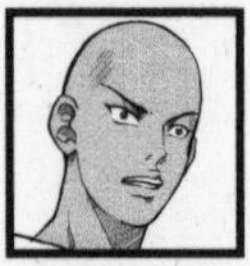

Whatever! Seiichi or Bunta, or even Masaharu or Hiroshi, are more popular than you...

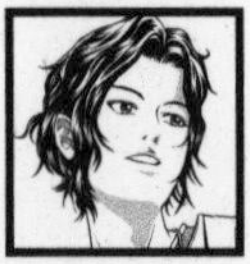

But Jackal, you're not that popular either... Heheh!
[Deafening silence]

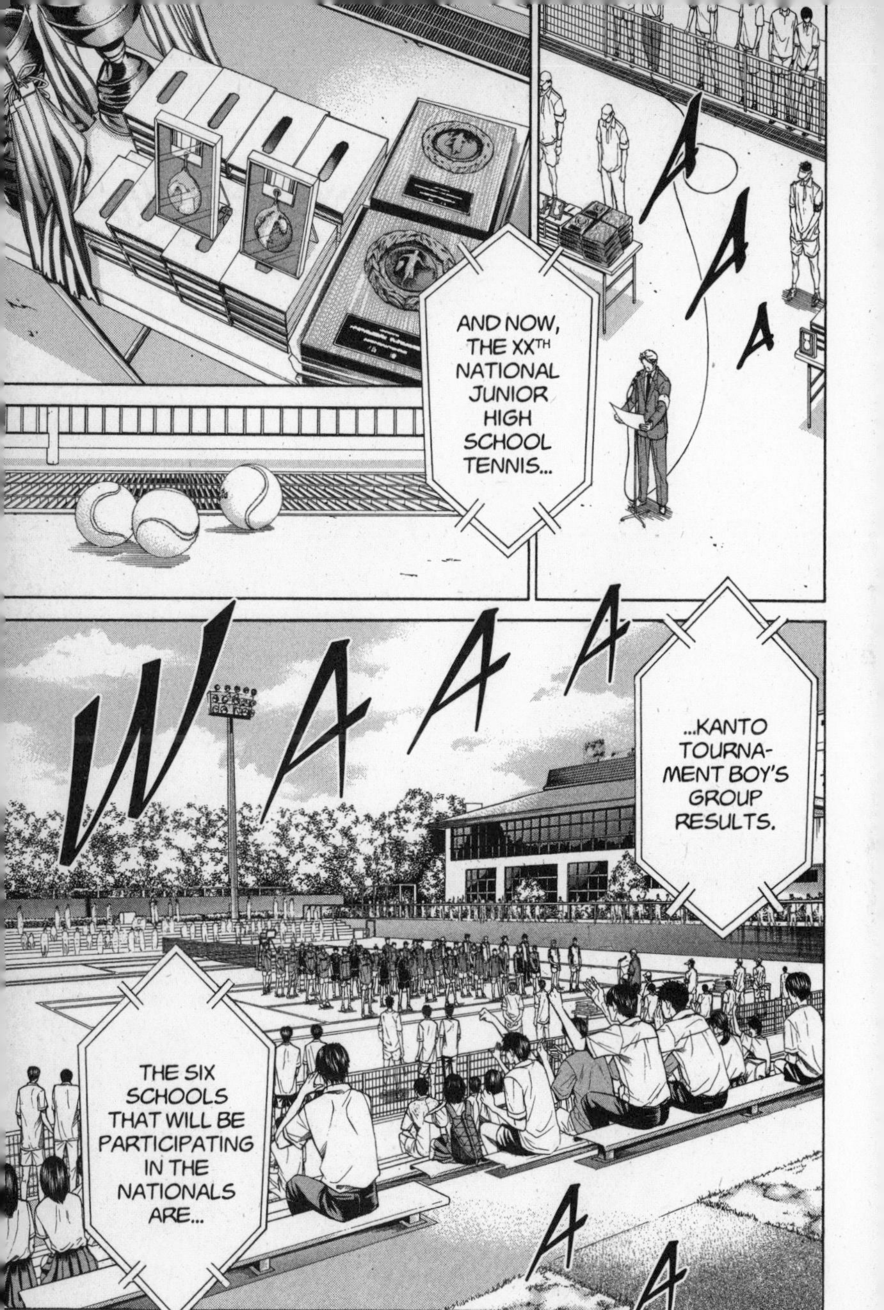
AAAA
AND NOW, THE XXTH NATIONAL JUNIOR HIGH SCHOOL TENNIS...
WAAAA
...KANTO TOURNA-MENT BOY'S GROUP RESULTS.
THE SIX SCHOOLS THAT WILL BE PARTICIPATING IN THE NATIONALS ARE...
AA

GENIUS 237: SEISHUN'S SUMMER BREAK

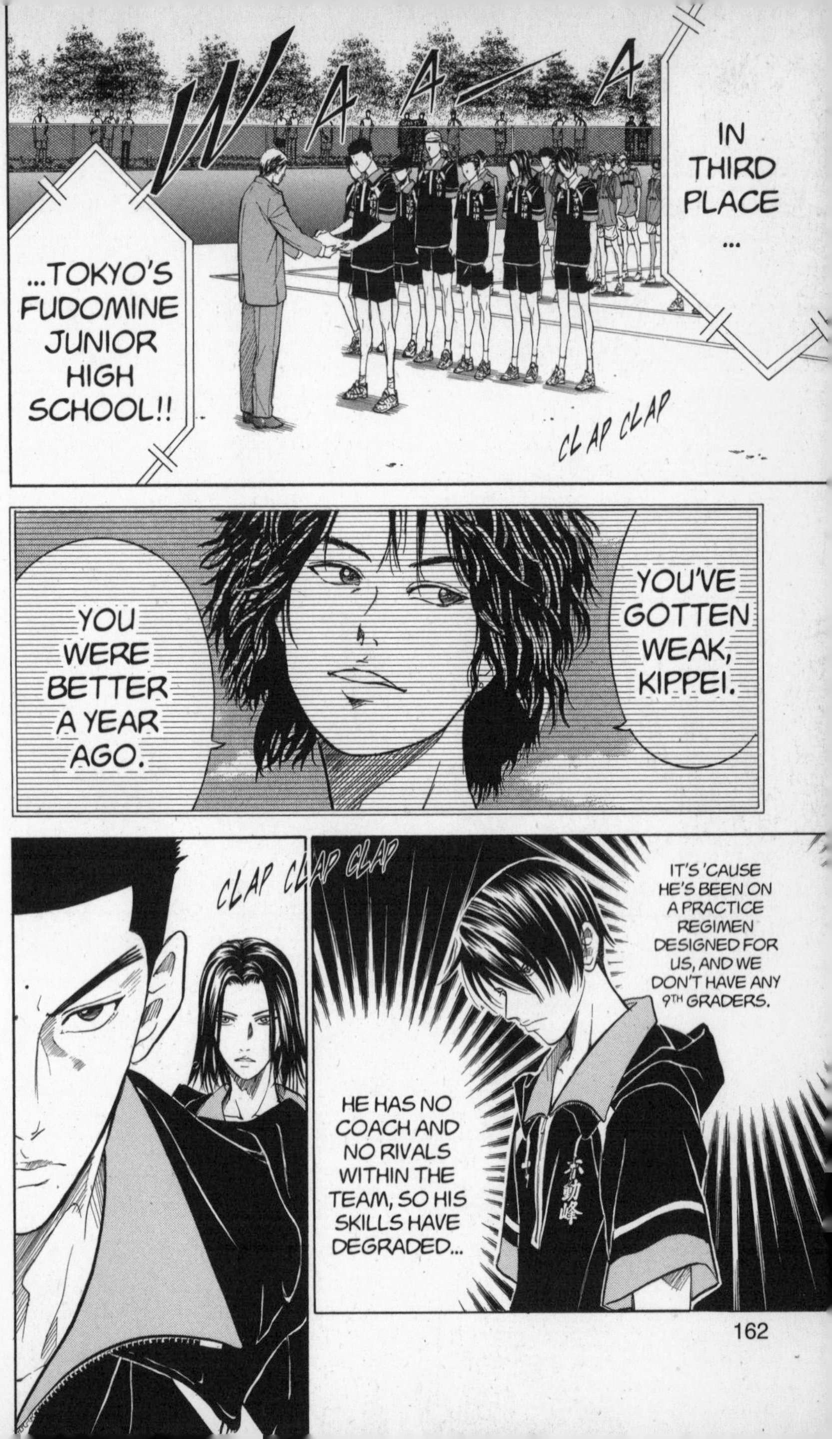
WAA—A
IN THIRD PLACE ...
...TOKYO'S FUDOMINE JUNIOR HIGH SCHOOL!!
CLAP CLAP
YOU'VE GOTTEN WEAK, KIPPEI.
YOU WERE BETTER A YEAR AGO.
IT'S 'CAUSE HE'S BEEN ON A PRACTICE REGIMEN DESIGNED FOR US, AND WE DON'T HAVE ANY 9TH GRADERS.
HE HAS NO COACH AND NO RIVALS WITHIN THE TEAM, SO HIS SKILLS HAVE DEGRADED...
CLAP CLAP CLAP CLAP

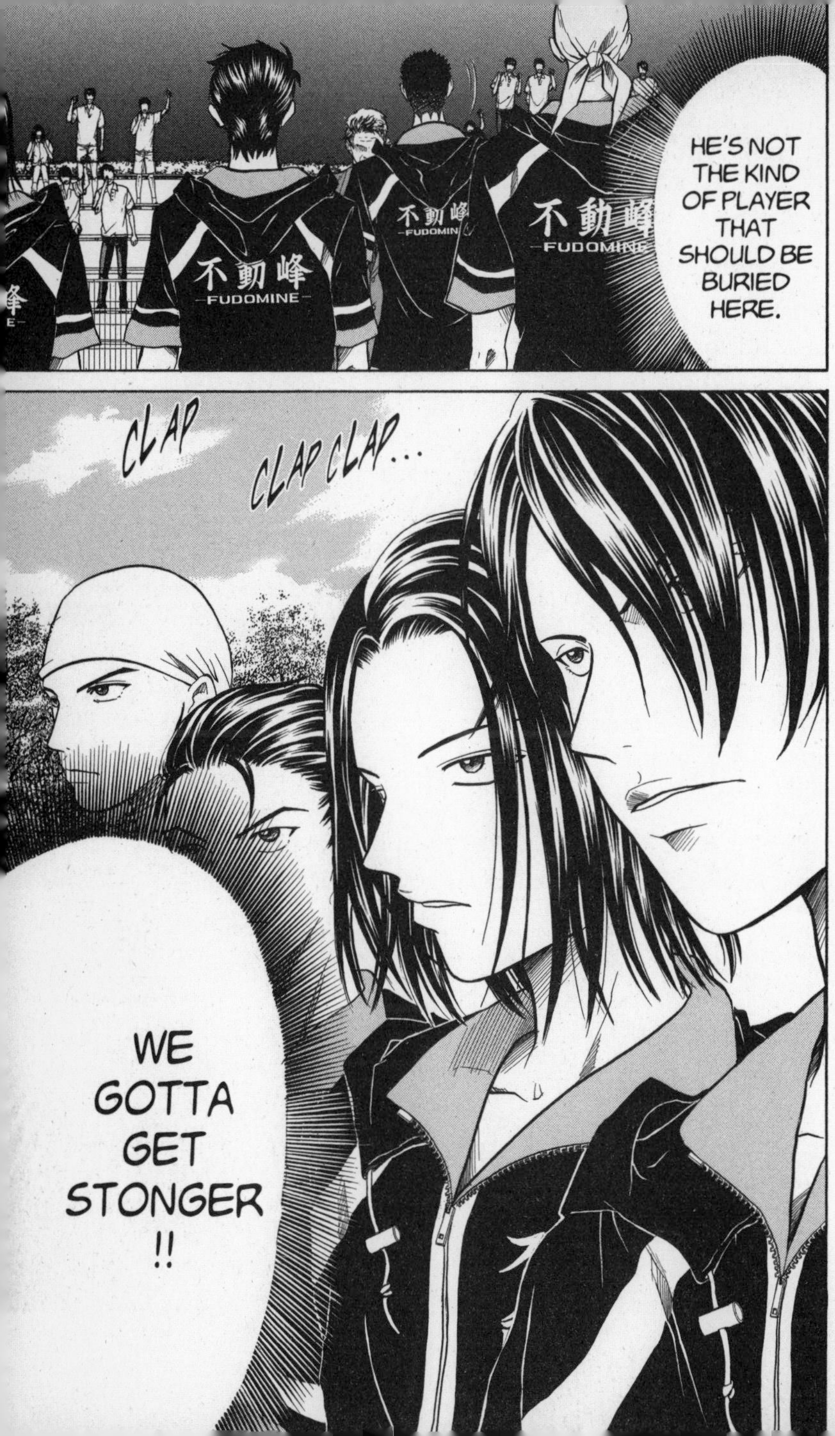

HE'S NOT THE KIND OF PLAYER THAT SHOULD BE BURIED HERE.
不動峰 —FUDOMINE—
不動峰 —FUDOMINE—
不動峰 —FUDOMINE—
CLAP CLAP...
CLAP
WE GOTTA GET STONGER !!

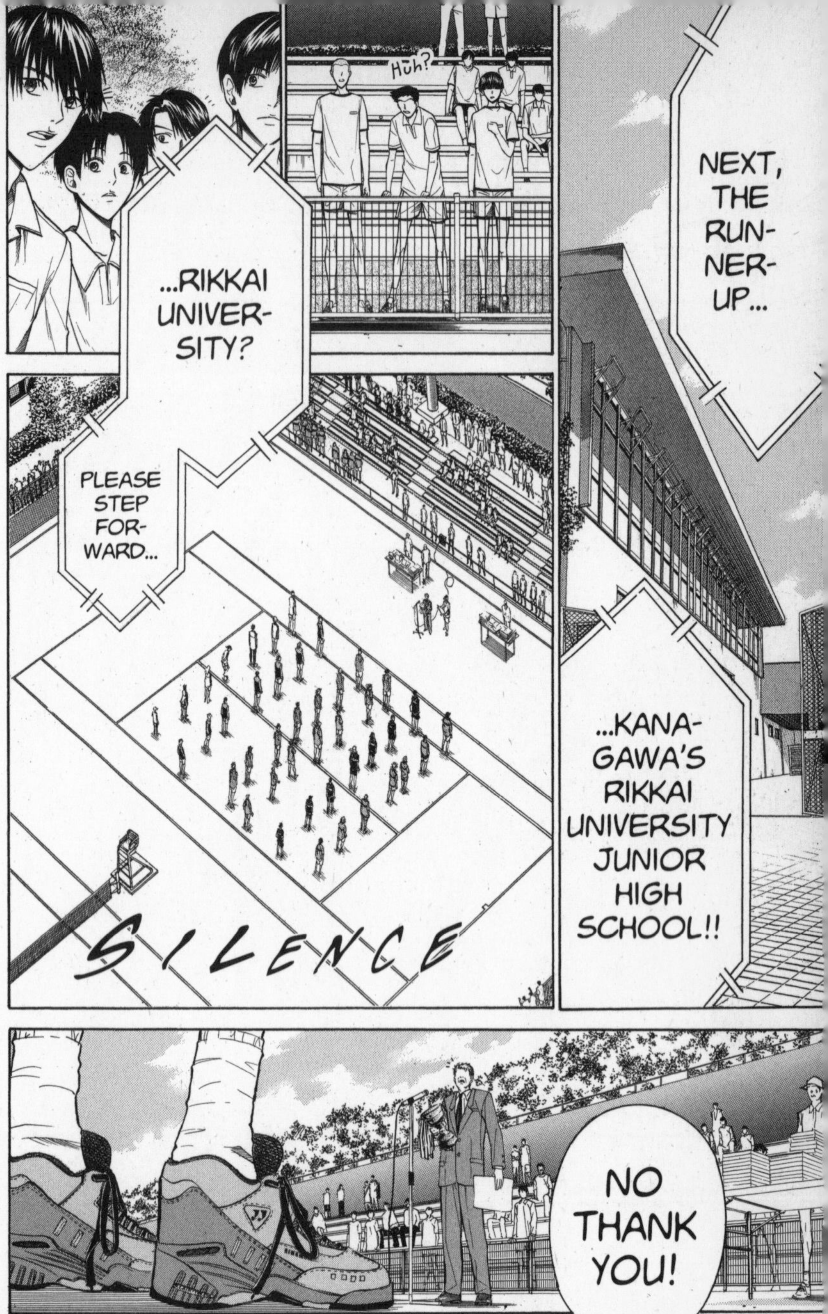
NEXT, THE RUNNER-UP...
...KANAGAWA'S RIKKAI UNIVERSITY JUNIOR HIGH SCHOOL!!
Huh?
...RIKKAI UNIVERSITY?
PLEASE STEP FORWARD...
SILENCE
NO THANK YOU!

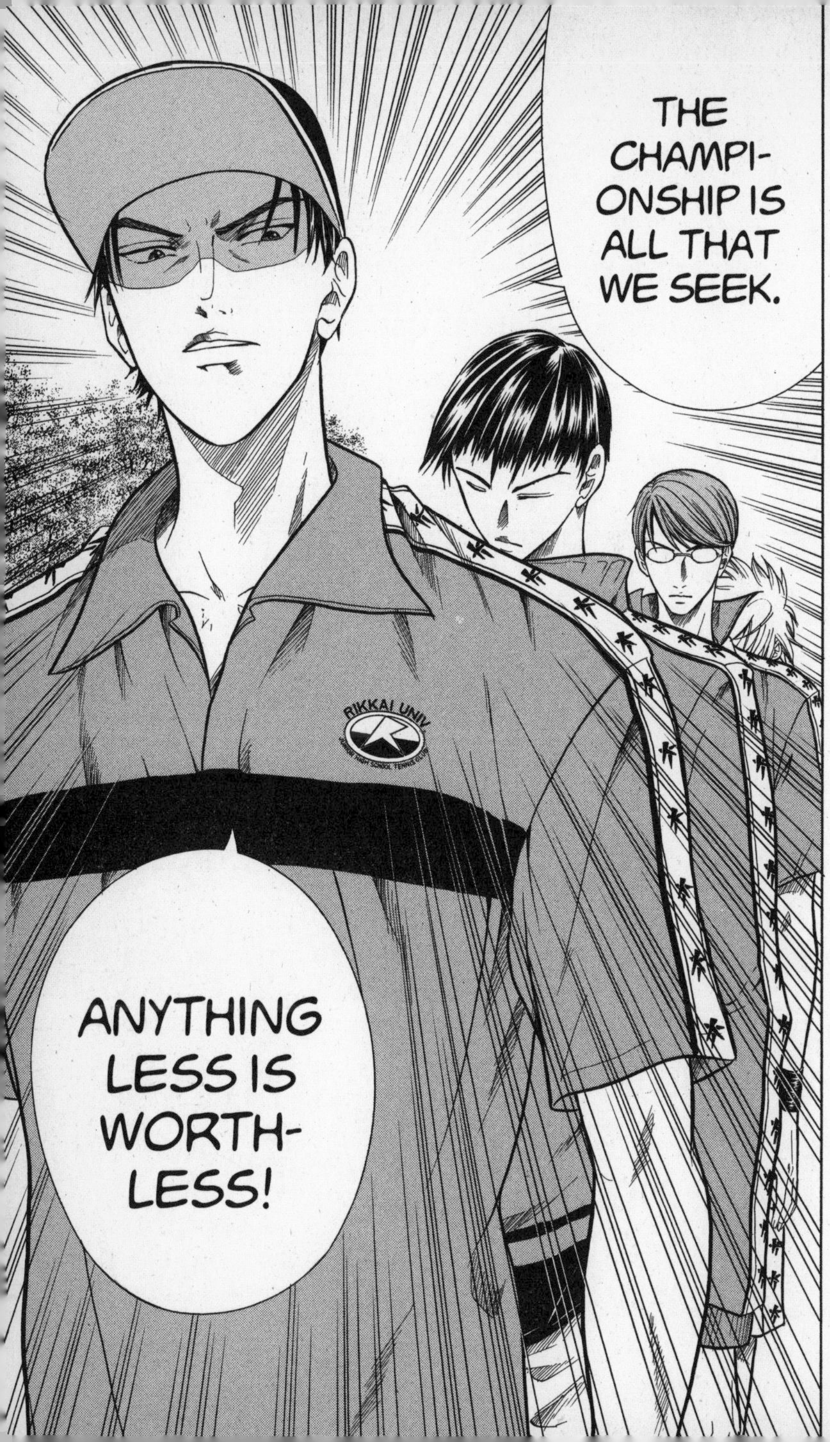
THE CHAMPIONSHIP IS ALL THAT WE SEEK.
RIKKAI UNIV
ANYTHING LESS IS WORTHLESS!

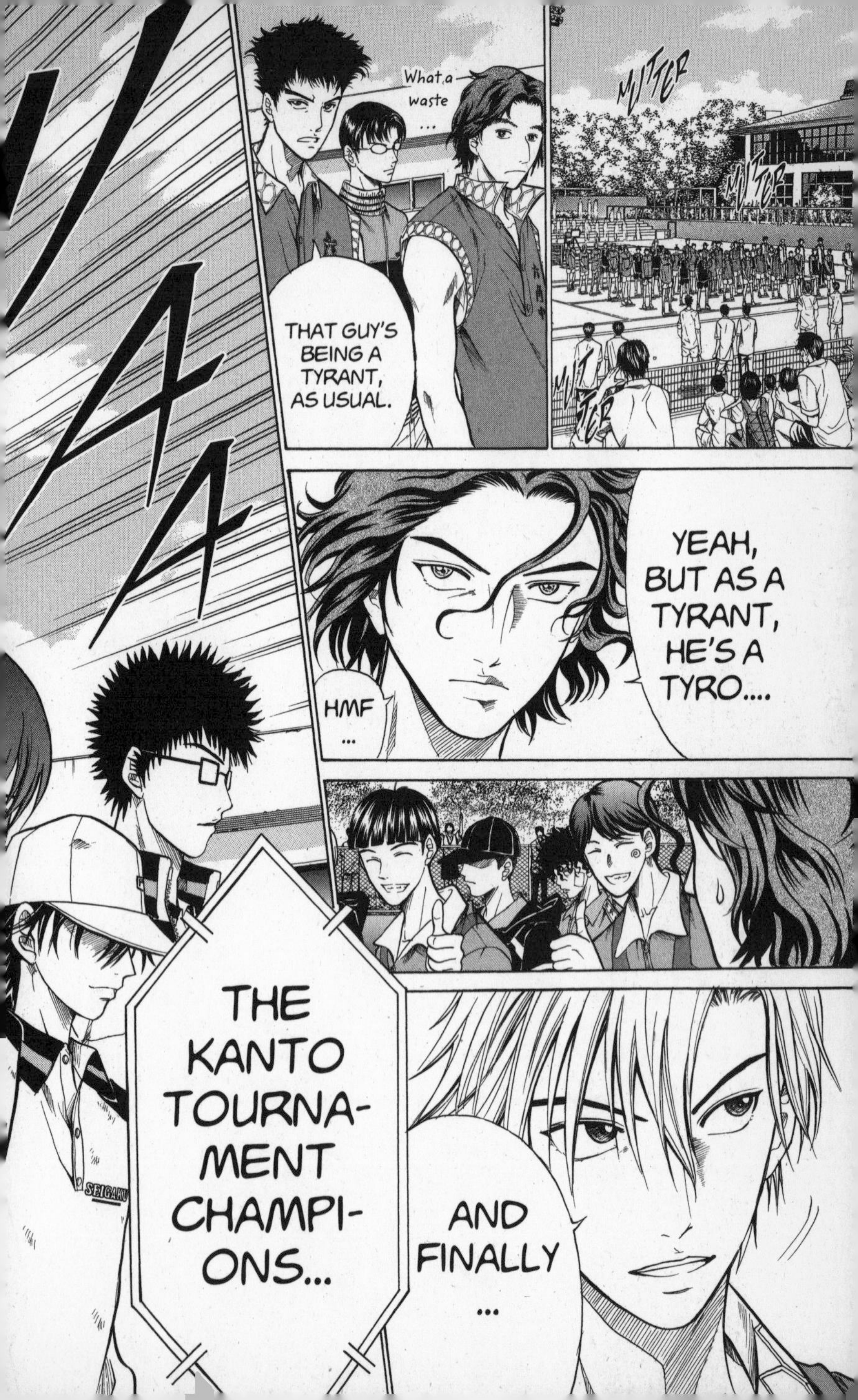
MUTTER
MUTTER
MUTTER
What a waste ...
THAT GUY'S BEING A TYRANT, AS USUAL.
WAA
YEAH, BUT AS A TYRANT, HE'S A TYRO....
HMF ...
AND FINALLY ...
THE KANTO TOURNAMENT CHAMPIONS...
SEIGAKU

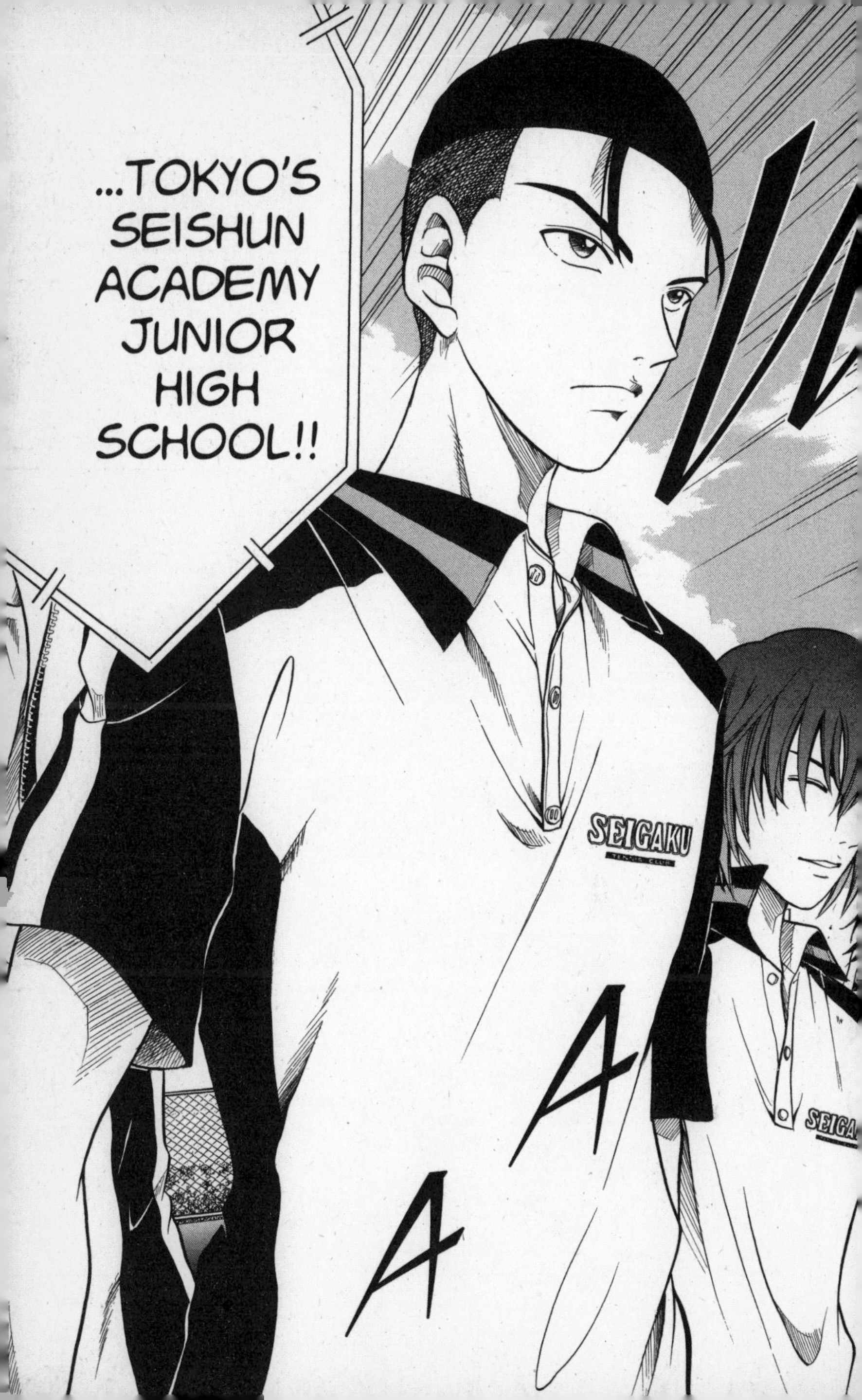
...TOKYO'S SEISHUN ACADEMY JUNIOR HIGH SCHOOL!!
SEIGAKU
SEIGA

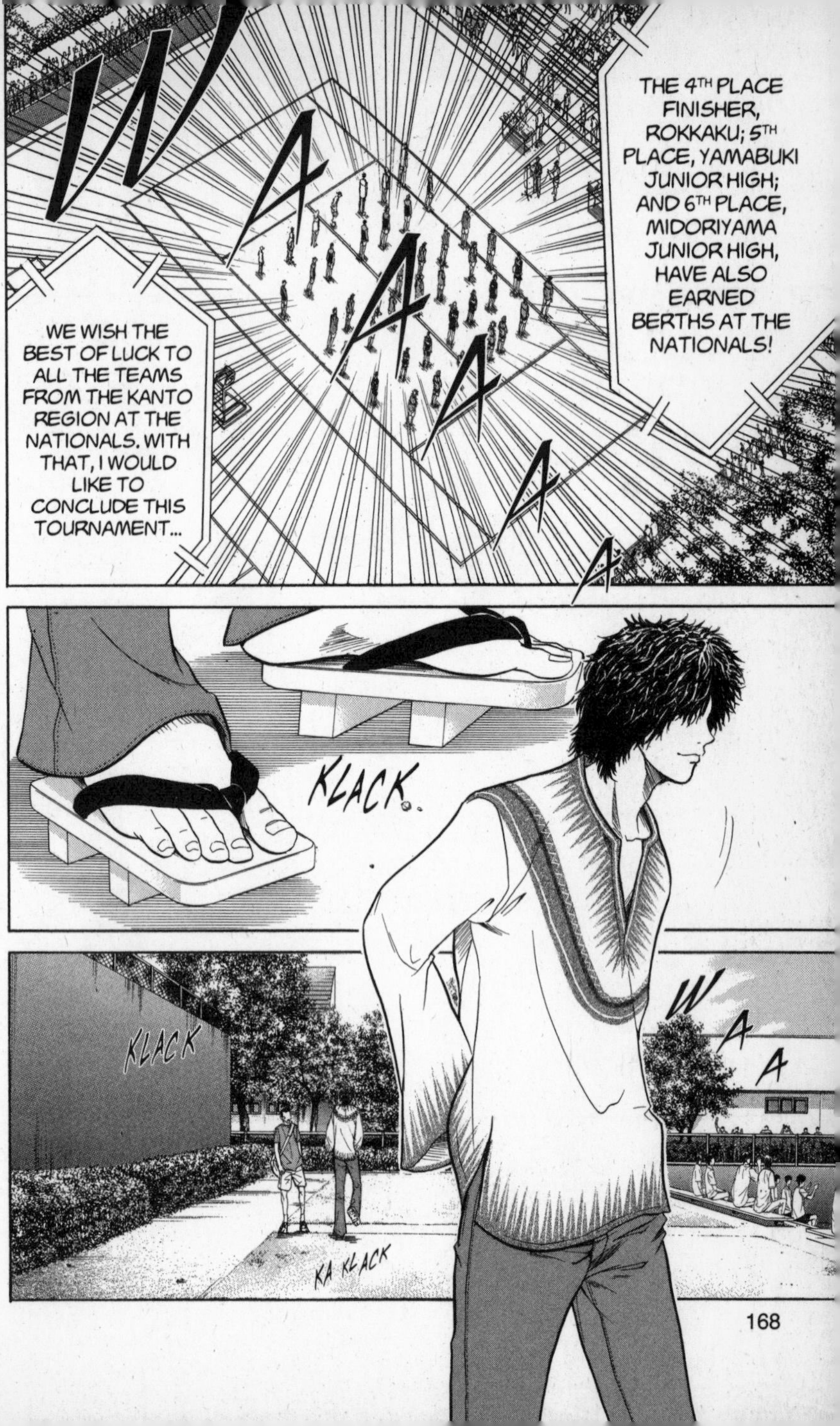
THE 4TH PLACE FINISHER, ROKKAKU; 5TH PLACE, YAMABUKI JUNIOR HIGH; AND 6TH PLACE, MIDORIYAMA JUNIOR HIGH, HAVE ALSO EARNED BERTHS AT THE NATIONALS!
WE WISH THE BEST OF LUCK TO ALL THE TEAMS FROM THE KANTO REGION AT THE NATIONALS. WITH THAT, I WOULD LIKE TO CONCLUDE THIS TOURNAMENT...
WAAAAAA
KLACK
WAA
KLACK
KA KLACK

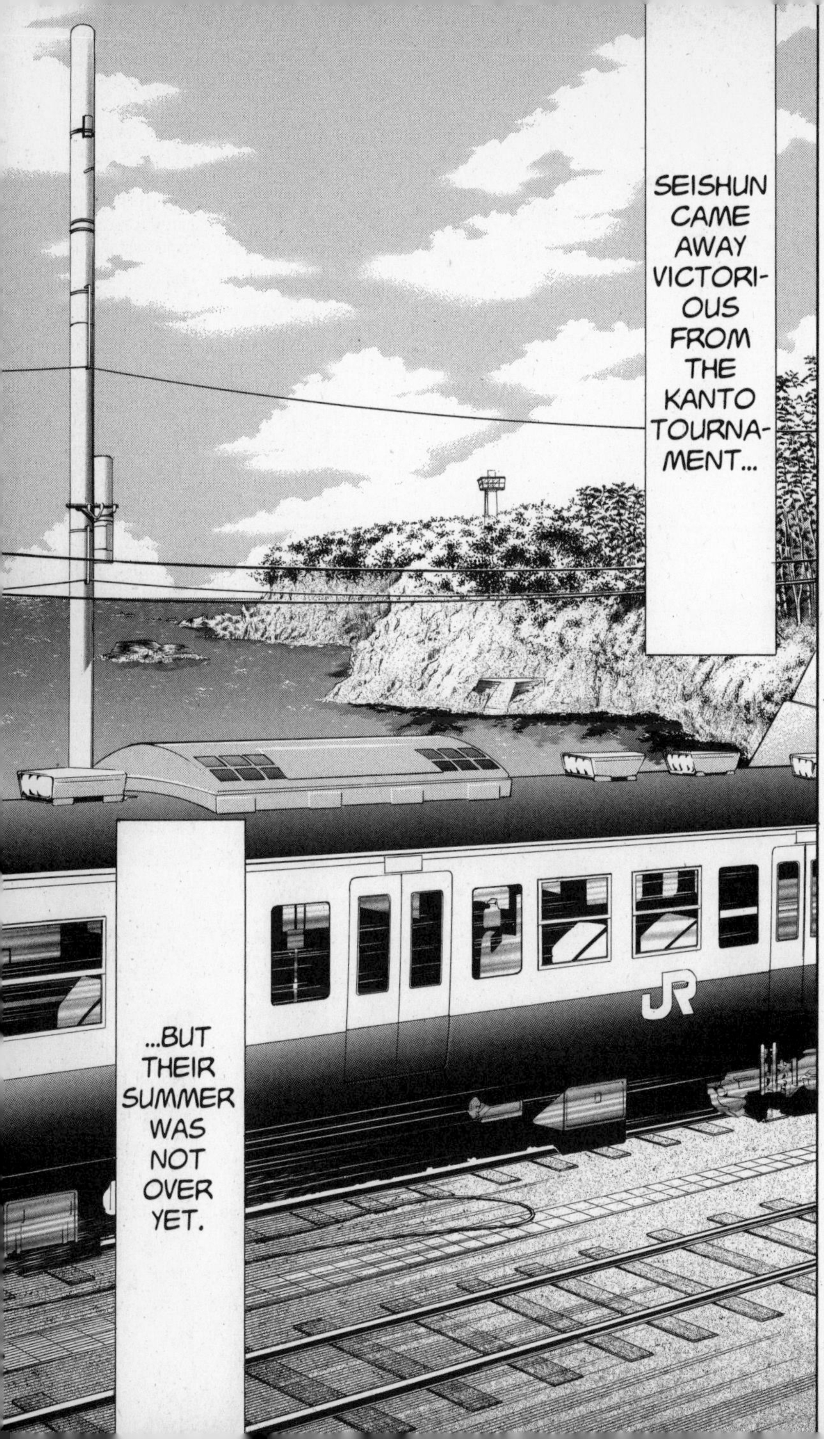
SEISHUN CAME AWAY VICTORIOUS FROM THE KANTO TOURNAMENT...
...BUT THEIR SUMMER WAS NOT OVER YET.
JR

GENIUS 237: SEISHUN'S SUMMER BREAK

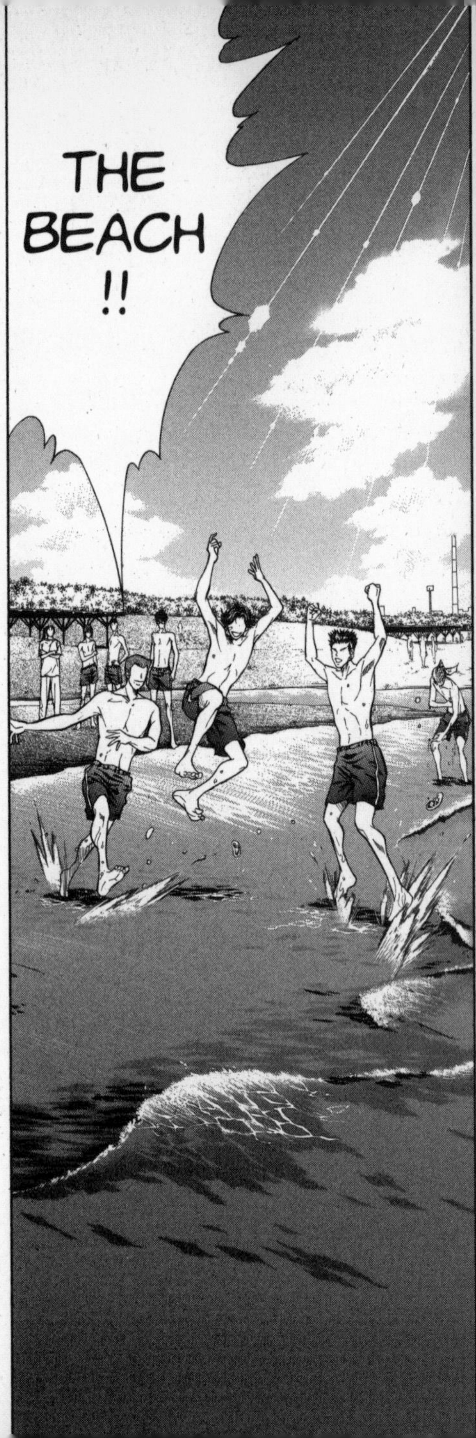
THE BEACH !!

READ THIS WAY

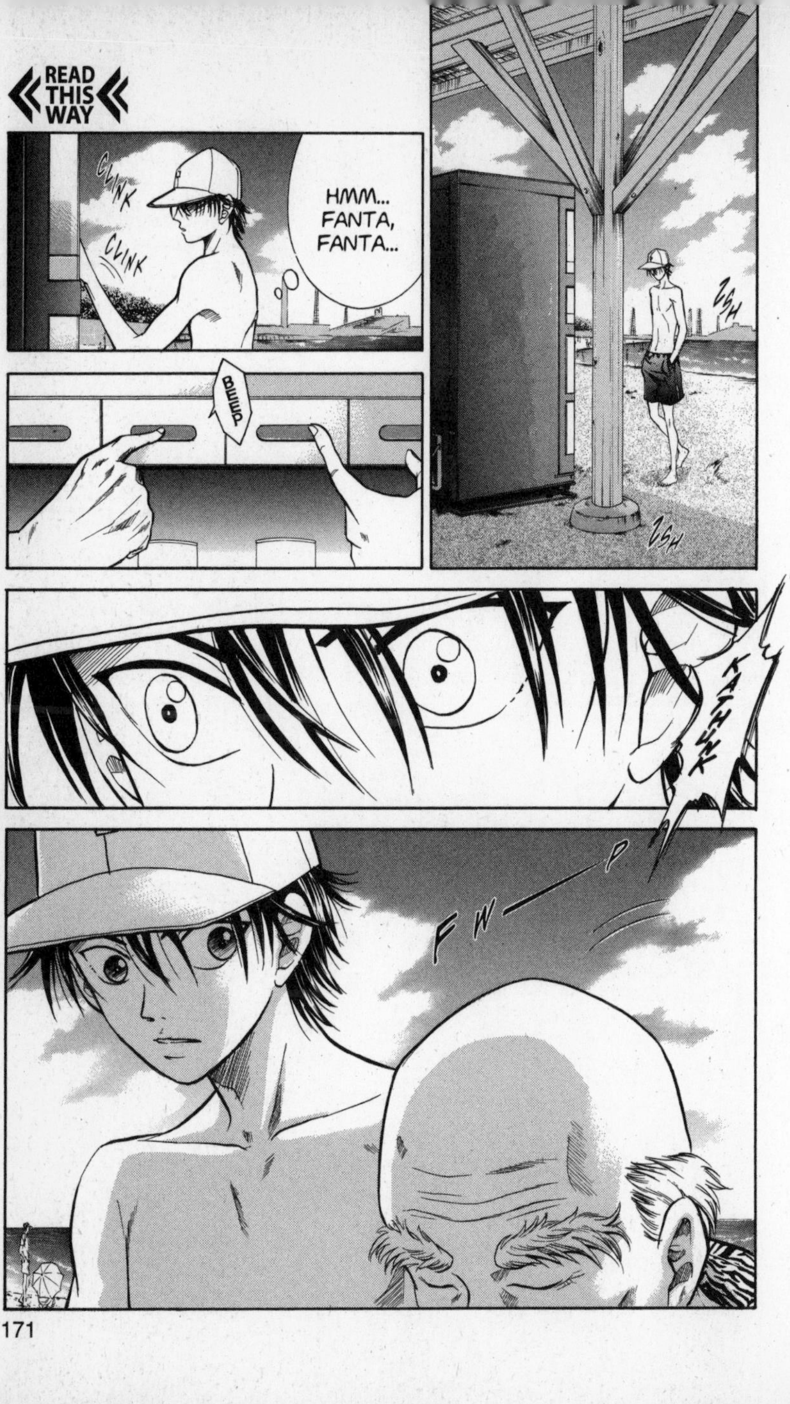
ZSH
ZSH
CLINK
CLINK
HMM... FANTA, FANTA...
BEEP
KATHUNK
FW—P

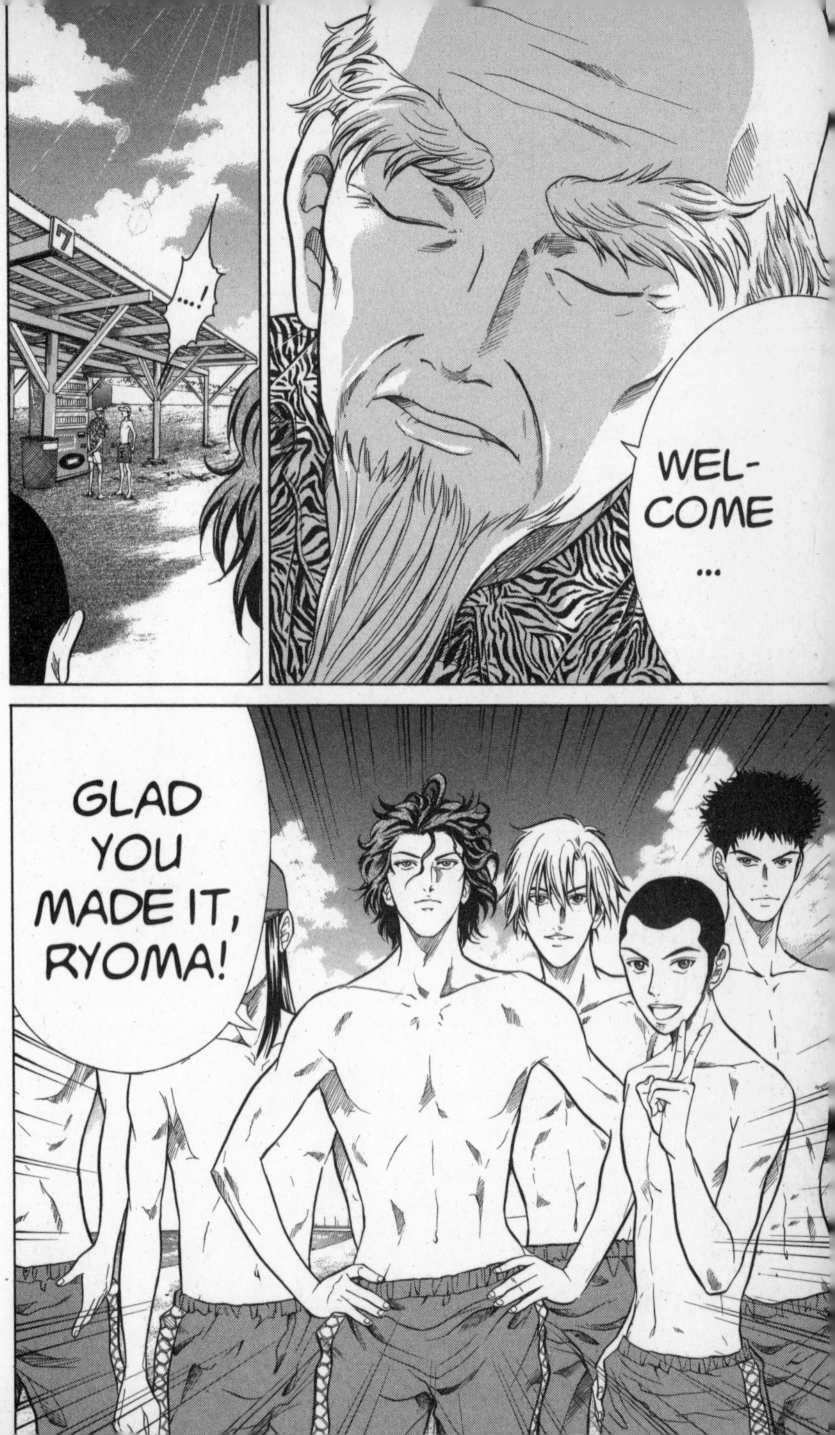
WEL-
COME
...
...!
GLAD YOU MADE IT, RYOMA!

READ THIS WAY

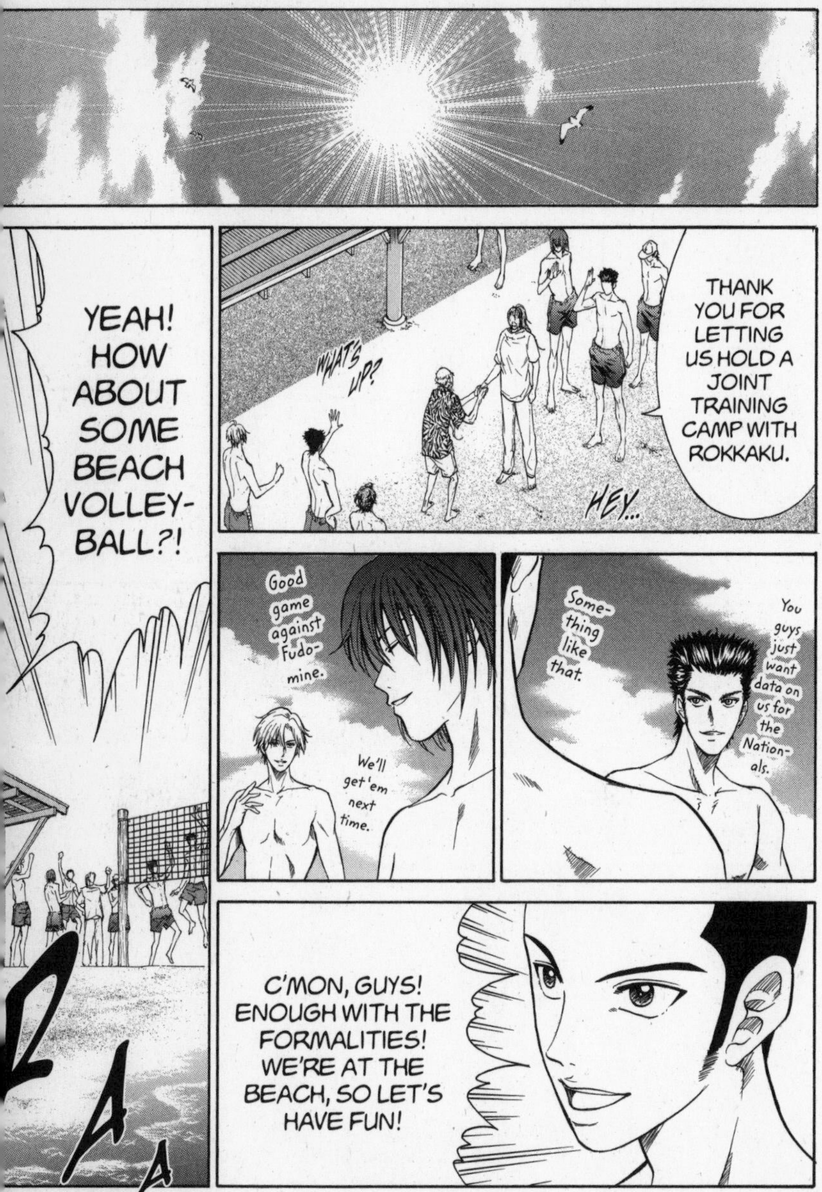
THANK YOU FOR LETTING US HOLD A JOINT TRAINING CAMP WITH ROKKAKU.
HEY...
WHAT'S UP?
You guys just want data on us for the Nationals.
Something like that.
Good game against Fudomine.
We'll get 'em next time.
C'MON, GUYS! ENOUGH WITH THE FORMALITIES! WE'RE AT THE BEACH, SO LET'S HAVE FUN!
YEAH! HOW ABOUT SOME BEACH VOLLEYBALL?!

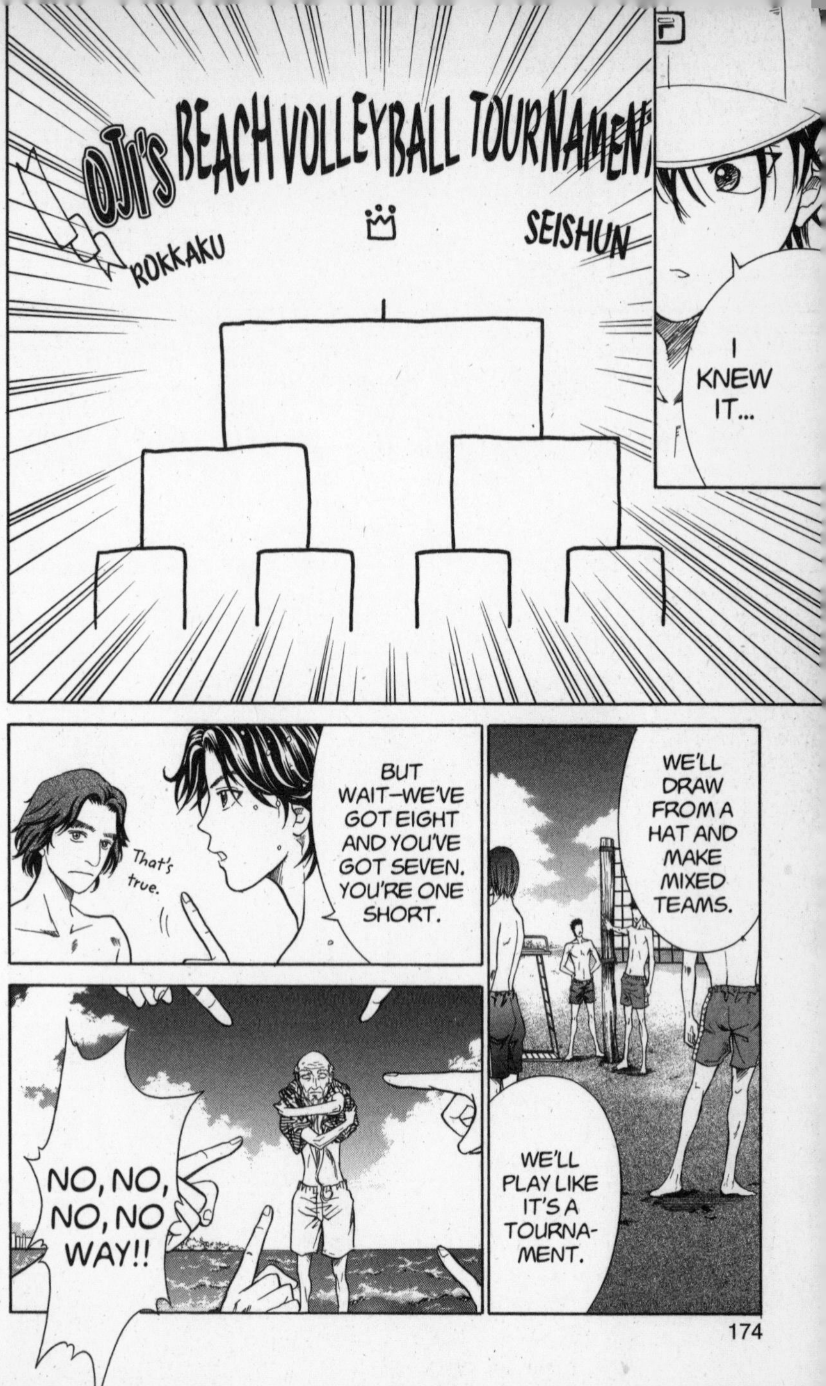
I KNEW IT...
OJI'S BEACH VOLLEYBALL TOURNAMENT
ROKKAKU
SEISHUN
WE'LL DRAW FROM A HAT AND MAKE MIXED TEAMS.
WE'LL PLAY LIKE IT'S A TOURNA-MENT.
BUT WAIT—WE'VE GOT EIGHT AND YOU'VE GOT SEVEN. YOU'RE ONE SHORT.
That's true.
NO, NO, NO, NO WAY!!

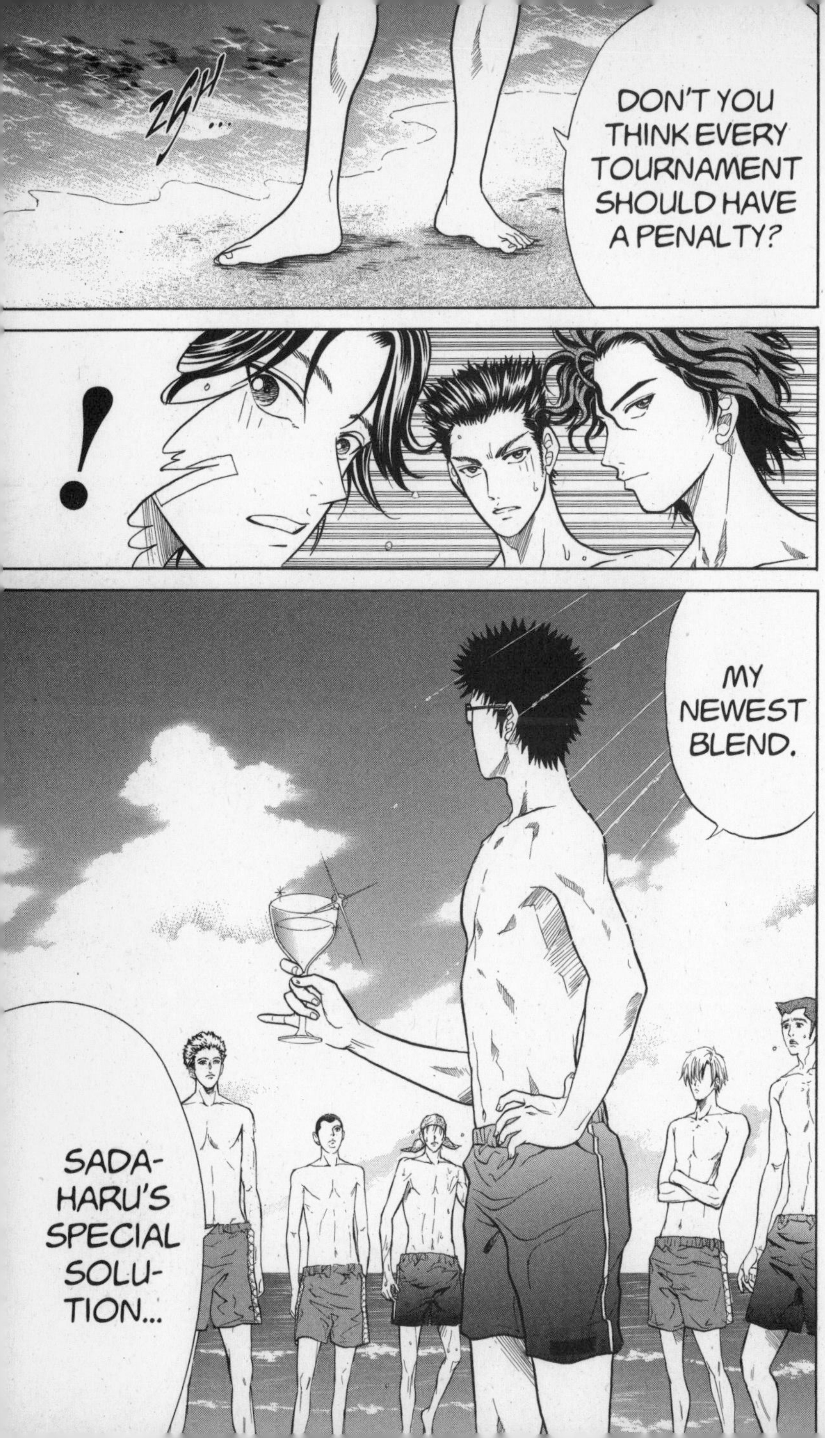
DON'T YOU THINK EVERY TOURNAMENT SHOULD HAVE A PENALTY?
ZSH...
!
MY NEWEST BLEND.
SADA-HARU'S SPECIAL SOLU-TION...

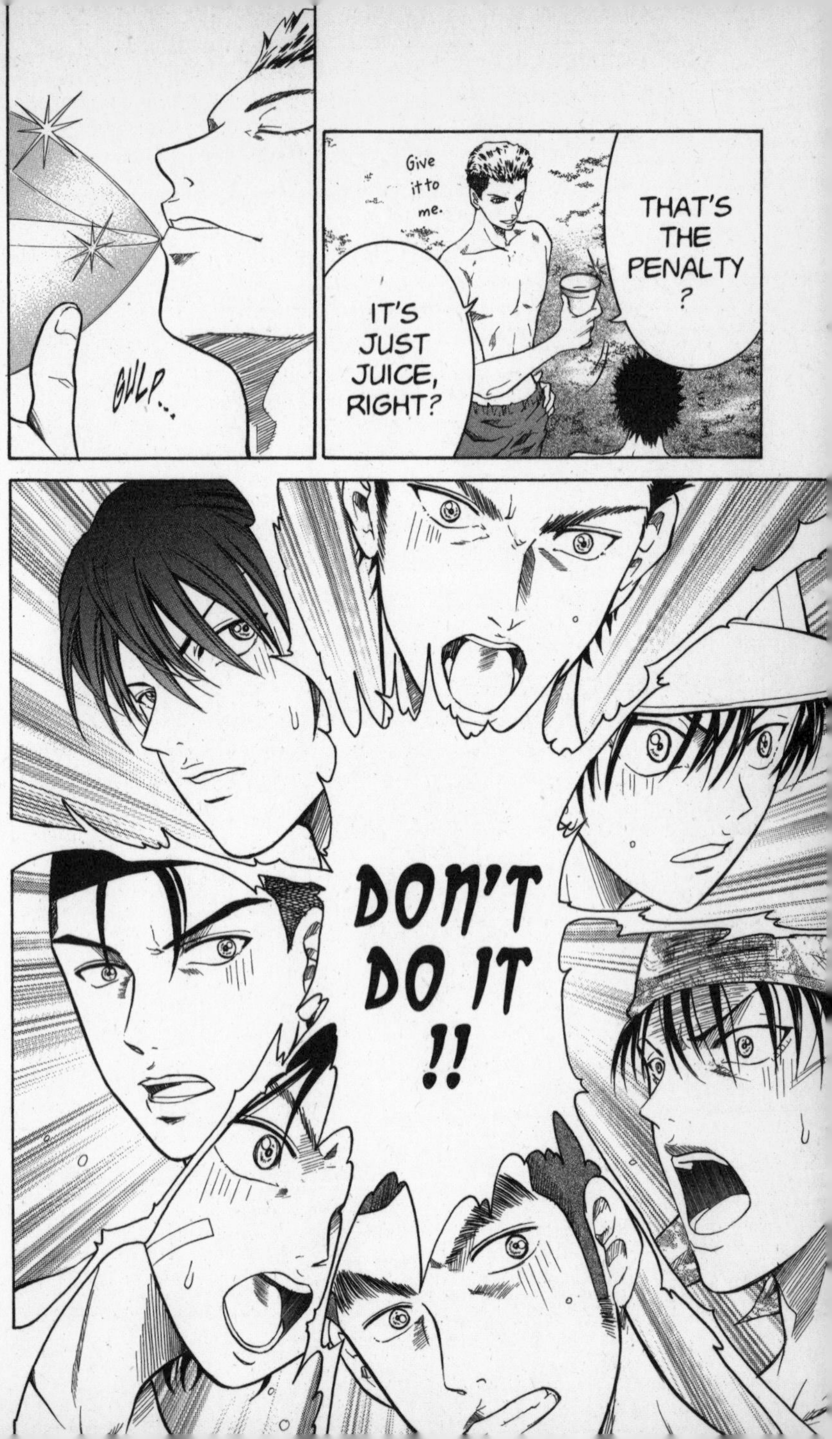
THAT'S THE PENALTY?
Give it to me.
IT'S JUST JUICE, RIGHT?
GULP...
DON'T DO IT!!

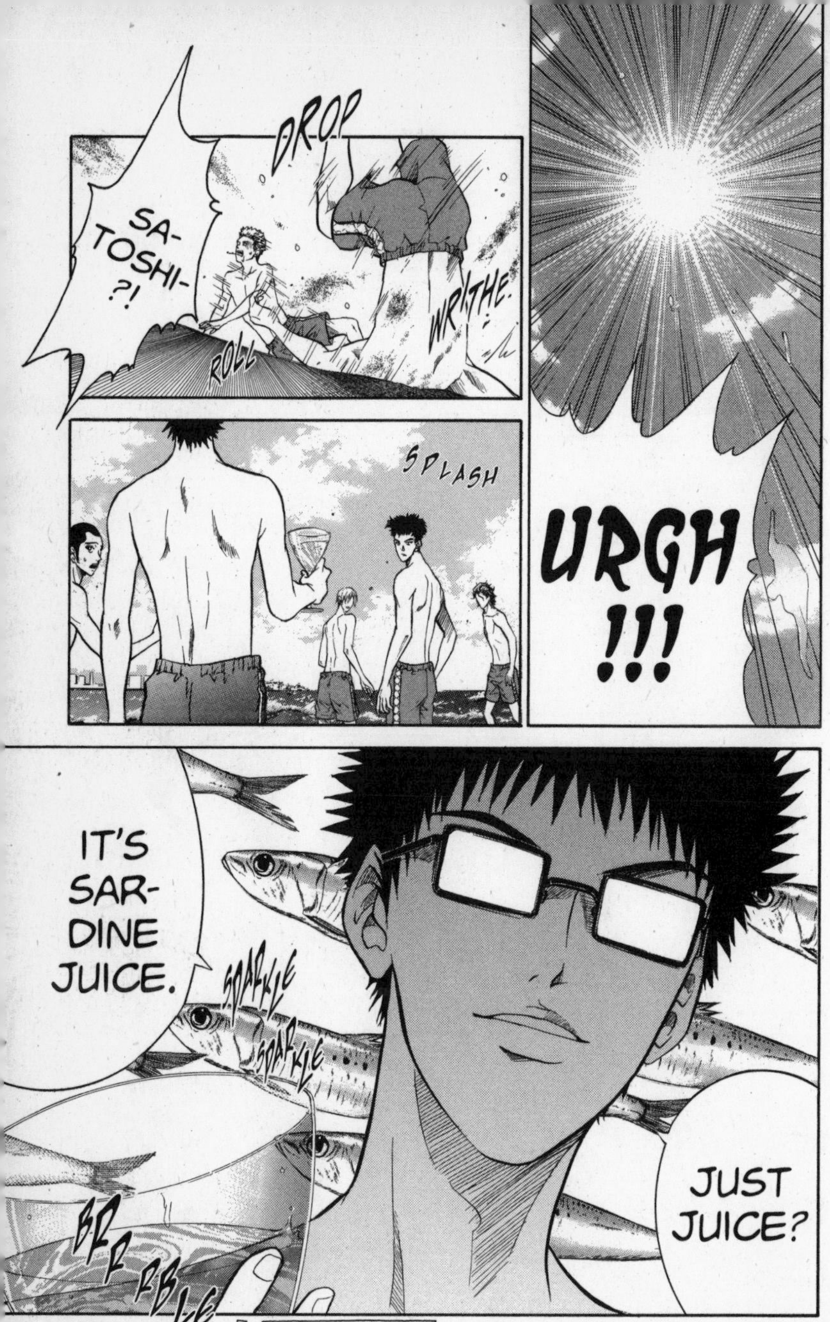
URGH!!!
SA-TOSHI-?!
DROP
WRITHE.
ROLL
SPLASH
IT'S SARDINE JUICE.
SPARKLE
SPARKLE
JUST JUICE?
BRRBBLE

Filled with Sardine DNA.

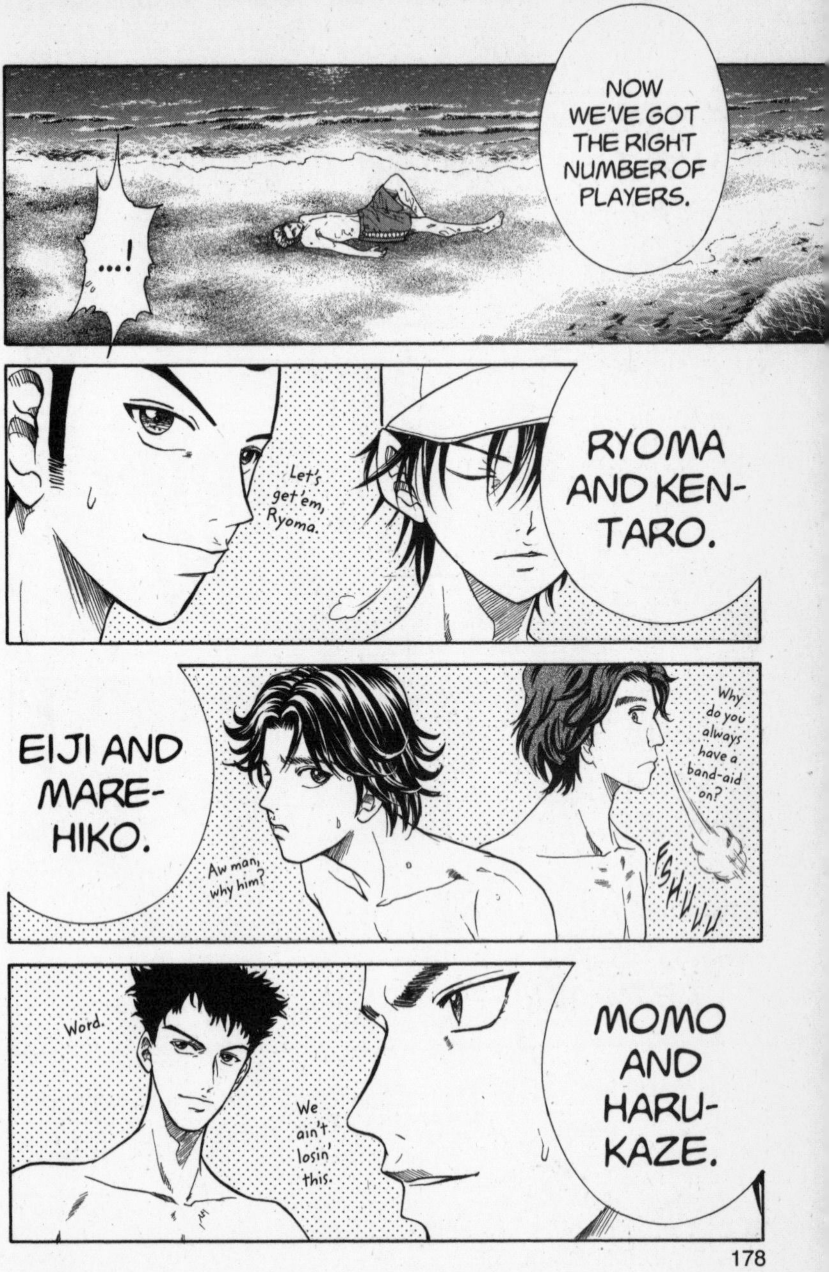
NOW WE'VE GOT THE RIGHT NUMBER OF PLAYERS.
...!
RYOMA AND KEN-TARO.
Let's get 'em, Ryoma.
Why do you always have a band-aid on?
FSHUUU
EIJI AND MARE-HIKO.
Aw man, why him?
MOMO AND HARU-KAZE.
We ain't losin' this.
Word.

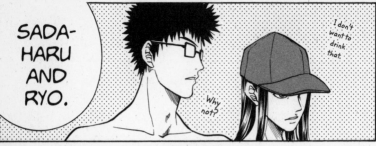

I don't want to drink that.
SADA-HARU AND RYO.
Why not?
SHUSUKE AND KOJIRO.
Heheh...
Heh
TAKA AND HIKARU.
Sardine... That's obscene.
Ha ha...
SHU-ICHIRO AND KAORU.
It's doubles, so we should be fine.
I'd rather die than drink that.

TO BE CONTINUED IN VOL. 28!

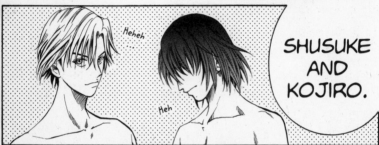

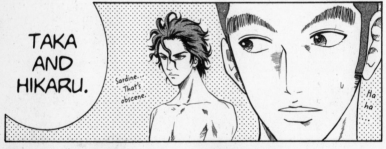

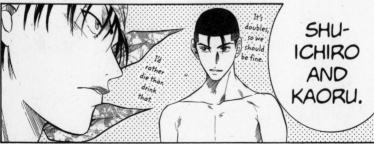

In the Next Volume...

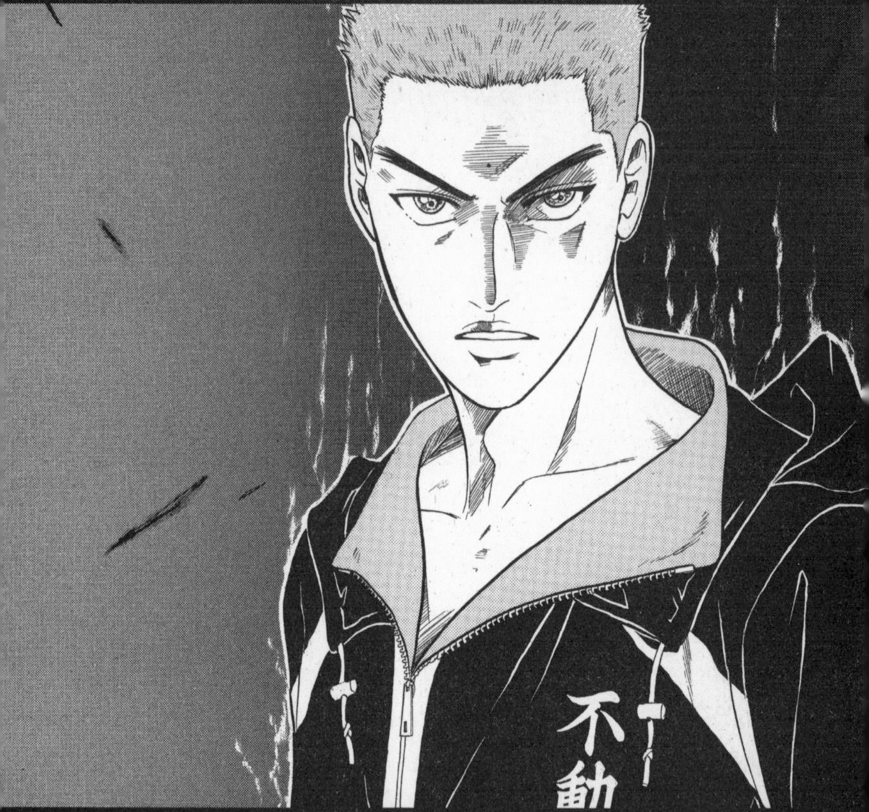

不動

Hyotei Rhapsody

Hyotei gets a shot at redemption when they're granted an invitational berth at the Nationals. With the tournament only days away, Shusuke challenges Fudomine's Kippei in order to test his own skills. But Kippei's game is as aggressive as Akaya's, and Shusuke is only recently recovered from his injury. Is he placing himself in danger? And just what is he trying to discover?

Available November 2008!

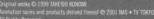

Tell us what you think about SHONEN JUMP manga!

Our survey is now available online.
Go to: ***www.SHONENJUMP.com/mangasurvey***

Help us make our product offering better!

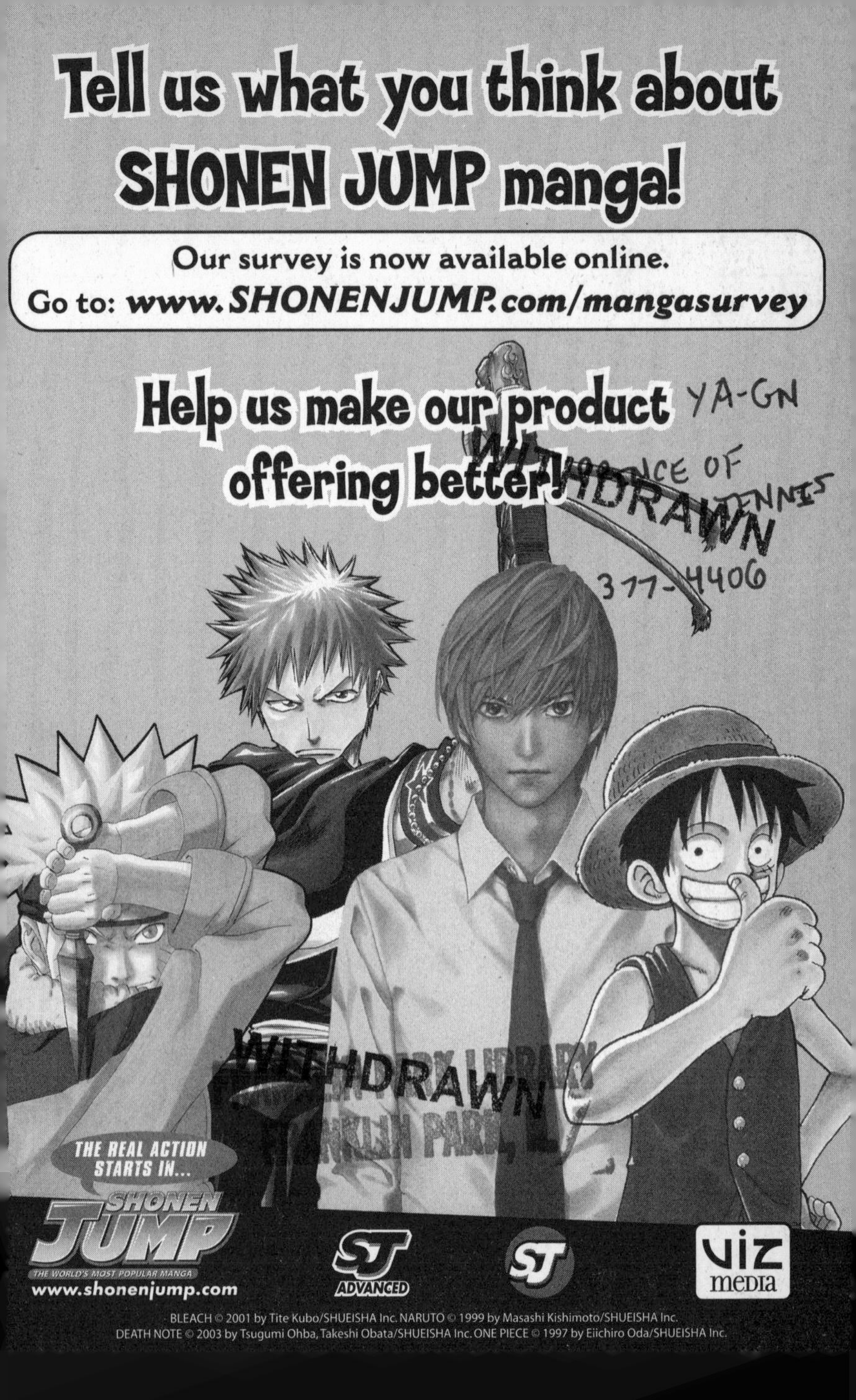
WITHDRAWN

Each
conta
avail
news
card

YE
subsc
to **SHC**
SUBSC

WITHDRAWN

NAME

ADDRE

CITY

E-MA

GNC1

M

CRED

ACCO

SIGN